Psychotherapy in the Third Millennium - Cross-Cutting Themes and Proposals for Reflection

Edited by Federico Durbano, Floriana Irtelli and Barbara Marchesi

Published in London, United Kingdom

Psychotherapy in the Third Millennium - Cross-Cutting Themes and Proposals for Reflection
http://dx.doi.org/10.5772/intechopen.1004487
Edited by Federico Durbano, Floriana Irtelli and Barbara Marchesi

Contributors
Abdullah AlKhathami, Andre Marseille, Barbara Marchesi, Benedict Akimana, Carol Nakanyike, Charlotte Hawkins, Chen Wu, Daphna Ginio Dollberg, Davis Musinguzi, Dorit Noy-Sharav, Ed Mills, Edmund G. Howe III, Eliana Mea, Etheldreda Nakimuli-Mpungu, Fatema Ahmed, Federico Durbano, Felix Egara, Floriana Irtelli, Francis D. Baudry, Jane Iya, Jean B. Nachega, Jeremiah Mutinye Kwesiga, John Mark Bwanika, Joyce Sserunjoji Nalugya, Juliana Lewis, Justine Diana Namuli, Kefang Wang, Kizito Wamala, Li Li, Moeketsi Mosia, Musisi Seggane, Owen Lewis, Paola Clemente, Patricia Cavazos, Qingyuan Ye, Ramona Ardelean, Sabrina Bakeera Kitaka, Waleed Ksebe, Zubair Lukyamuzi

First published in London, United Kingdom, 2025 by IntechOpen
IntechOpen is the global imprint of INTECHOPEN LIMITED, registered in England and Wales, registration number: 11086078, 167-169 Great Portland Street, London, W1W 5PF, United Kingdom

For EU product safety concerns: IN TECH d.o.o., Prolaz Marije Krucifikse Kozulić 3, 51000 Rijeka, Croatia, info@intechopen.com or visit our website at intechopen.com.

British Library Cataloguing-in-Publication Data
A catalogue record for this book is available from the British Library

Psychotherapy in the Third Millennium - Cross-Cutting Themes and Proposals for Reflection
Edited by Federico Durbano, Floriana Irtelli and Barbara Marchesi
p. cm.
Print ISBN 978-0-85466-959-2
Online ISBN 978-0-85466-958-5
eBook (PDF) ISBN 978-0-85466-960-8

Meet the editors

Dr. Federico Durbano is a Doctor of Medicine (MD) with a specialization in Psychiatry. He has worked at various hospitals, including Milan's Ospedale Maggiore Policlinico, Treviglio, Melegnano, and Fatebenefratelli, where he achieved significant career milestones. He is currently the director of the Mental Health and Addictions Department at ASST Melegnano e della Martesana, Milan, Italy. Dr. Durbano has had teaching assignments at the University of Milan (Nursing School). He has attended more than 100 local and national congresses and courses as an invited speaker and published over 180 papers and books. He is also a technical advisor to the court in forensic psychiatry.

Dr. Floriana Irtelli is a psychoanalyst/psychotherapist and member of the International Association for Relational Psychoanalysis and Psychotherapy (IARPP) who has been lecturing for several years at the Catholic University of the Sacred Heart, Milan, Italy. She has worked at Fatebenefratelli Hospital in Milan, engaging in both research and clinical activities. She is among the authors of several books, including *A Fresh Look at Anxiety Disorders and Psychopathy - New Updates on an Old Phenomenon*, and has published articles for the *Journal of Affective Disorders, Research in Psychotherapy*, and the *Journal for Psychiatric and Mental Health Nursing*. She has participated in numerous conferences, seminars, and congresses. She is the author of the books *Illuminarsi di Ben-essere, Familiar-mente*, and *Contemporary Perspectives on Relational Wellness*.

Dr. Barbara Marchesi has worked since 2018 as a psychologist and psychotherapist in the Mental Health and Addictions Department at ASST Melegnano e della Martesana (Milan, Italy). She received her degree in Psychology from the Cattolica University of Milan in 1999. Then, she completed a specialty course in Adolescent and Adult Psychodynamic Psychotherapy. She worked as a private practitioner for almost twenty years and as a psychological consultant at Fatebenefratelli Hospital of Milan, where she completed a master's degree in Psychodiagnostics. She also worked for six years at Papa Giovanni XXIII Hospital in Bergamo, completing the training in Neuropsychology.

Contents

Preface IX

Section 1
General Issues 1

Chapter 1 3
Assisted Psychedelic Psychotherapy: Rethinking the Paradigms of Psychiatric Care?
by Eliana Mea and Paola Clemente

Chapter 2 17
Parent-Child Psychotherapy: Core Elements and Mechanisms of Change
by Daphna Ginio Dollberg

Chapter 3 35
Perspective Chapter: Online Imago Relationship Therapy – Characteristics and Unexpected Advantages
by Dorit Noy-Sharav

Chapter 4 45
Perspective Chapter: Presuppositions Psychiatrists Must Make to Do Most Effective Psychotherapy
by Edmund G. Howe III

Chapter 5 57
Perspective Chapter: Psychological Capacity – A Key Factor in Mental Health Disorders
by Abdullah AlKhathami

Chapter 6 85
Perspective Chapter: Subject-Object Intercorrelation – From Quantum Theory to the New Forms and Applications in Psychotherapy
by Ramona Ardelean

Chapter 7 101
Positive Psychotherapy: A Transcultural Approach to Psychotherapy for the Twenty-First Century
by Andre Marseille

Chapter 8 121
Understanding the Process of Change in Psychotherapy
by Francis D. Baudry

Chapter 9 131
Perspective Chapter: The Overwhelm is the Way – Contextual Relational Mindfulness as the Key to Integrated Executive Functioning
by Juliana Lewis and Owen Lewis

Section 2
Practictal Issues 149

Chapter 10 151
EMDR for Eating Disorders and Body Schema Disorders: An Update
by Federico Durbano, Barbara Marchesi and Floriana Irtelli

Chapter 11 159
Psychological Approaches for Eating Disorders: The Role of Body Image, Self-Esteem, and Quality of Life
by Fatema Ahmed, Chen Wu, Li Li, Qingyuan Ye, Waleed Ksebe and Kefang Wang

Chapter 12 197
Developing and Testing Tele-Support Psychotherapy through Mobile Phones for Youth (15–30 Years) with Depression in Uganda
by Etheldreda Nakimuli-Mpungu, Jeremiah Mutinye Kwesiga, John Mark Bwanika, Davis Musinguzi, Carol Nakanyike, Jane Iya, Benedict Akimana, Charlotte Hawkins, Patricia Cavazos, Jean B. Nachega, Ed Mills, Sabrina Bakeera Kitaka and Musisi Seggane

Chapter 13 225
Developing and Testing Group Support Psychotherapy for Children and Adolescents Living with HIV in Uganda
by Etheldreda Nakimuli-Mpungu, Kizito Wamala, Carol Nakanyike, Jane Iya, Zubair Lukyamuzi, Justine Diana Namuli, Joyce Sserunjoji Nalugya, Benedict Akimana, Sabrina Bakeera Kitaka, Jean B. Nachega, Ed Mills and Musisi Seggane

Chapter 14 253
Alleviating Mathematics Anxiety and Enhancing Achievement through Systematic Desensitization: A Cognitive-Behavioural Approach for Secondary School Learners
by Felix Egara and Moeketsi Mosia

Preface

Psychotherapy is a topic of great interest, and it is also linked to the number of schools that have developed and proposed over the years on the scenario of relational treatments. A recent estimate counts more than 250 schools of psychotherapy active in the world (Allen DM, Psychology Today, https://www.psychologytoday.com/intl/blog/matter-personality/202009/different-schools-psychotherapy).

Each school can be traced back to one of the macro models available:

- Cognitive psychology
- Gestalt psychology
- Psychoanalysis
- Humanism
- Structuralism
- Functionalism
- Behaviorism

The different approaches of each macro model are linked to slight variations, due either to the intuitions of individual therapists who develop their own peculiar model or to the need to identify individual paths for specific problems to be addressed, then generalizing the model developed in a specific school or training path. Not forgetting that many approaches adopt an "eclectic" model, made necessary to resolve inevitable aporias linked to overly rigid, manualized approaches. This element adds further levels of complexity, increasingly shifting the psychotherapeutic approach towards a convenience approach rather than a strong heuristic and, therefore, clinical model. The danger is the excessive subjectivization of individual psychotherapeutic activities without any possibility of objectively and honestly comparing efficacy data (and, therefore, outcome).

What is really missing in the world of "psychotherapies" is, in fact, an approach based on scientific evidence, we would say, on experimental evidence. Since it is clear that the psychotherapeutic approach is a relational approach and, therefore, related to the human sciences, it is equally clear that the scientific method of evaluating individual models cannot be that of the summer sciences. However, it is equally important to develop some form of evaluation to assess the validity of the model, analyze the study outcomes, and determine its effectiveness.

We are fully aware that an editorial proposal that addresses the scientific validation of different psychotherapies is an almost impossible challenge and can generate situations that can be classified as potential unsolvable ideological wars. Our proposal, therefore, was to select specific contributions that can address issues common to the different approaches, with a transversal analysis of shared themes. On the operational level, we selected some operational contributions linked to new trends (i.e. problems posed by "clients"), such as eating disorders or access to a psychological response dedicated to large segments of the population exposed to traumatic factors.

This book, therefore, presents two main sections, one of a general nature concerning some transversal issues on which we believe it is appropriate to encourage some reflections: for example, the new psychedelic approaches, the relational aspects common to the different psychotherapies, the mental models of the clients as factors influencing psychotherapy. The second section focuses on two specific topics, one typical of our Western society (eating disorders and body image) and one typical of complex organizational situations, represented by two intervention models in Uganda.

In this book, we chose not to adopt a verificationist approach but instead aimed to present the practical experiences of many colleagues across different application areas of psychotherapy. We leave it to the readers to take on the challenging task of evaluating the effectiveness of the various proposed operational models.

Federico Durbano
Director,
Department of Mental Health and Addictions,
ASST Melegnano e della Martesana,
Gorgonzola, Italy

Lecturer,
University of Milan,
Milan, Italy

Floriana Irtelli
Catholic University of the Sacred Heart,
Milan, Italy

International Association for Relational Psychoanalysis and Psychotherapy,
New York, USA

Centre for Evolutionary Intersubjective Psychology (CEPEI),
Italy

Barbara Marchesi
Psychologist,
Department of Mental Health and Addictions,
ASST Melegnano e della Martesana
Gorgonzola, Italy

Section 1

General Issues

Chapter 1

Assisted Psychedelic Psychotherapy: Rethinking the Paradigms of Psychiatric Care?

Eliana Mea and Paola Clemente

Abstract

Can psychedelic-assisted psychotherapy (PAT) serve as a paradigm for describing and navigating a profound transformative experience of the self? This model of therapy has ignited an intense debate in recent years that seems aimed at calling into question, more than the various currents of psychotherapy, the model of psychiatric care that has lost over time the real capacity to address the psychological distress of people and to interpret the psychological phenomena observed, too often reducing itself to an aseptic prescription of drugs in which the therapeutic relationship has progressively become emptied of meaning. In this work, we will examine the current schools of thought that animate the debate on PAT and the psychodynamic aspects that allow us to better understand the functioning of this specific psychotherapeutic approach. According to the psycholytic paradigm, psychedelic substances are capable of inducing regression to states of consciousness different from its ordinary state. In such states, fundamental conflicts may emerge in the early years of life that have led to the development of an ego that has realized the adaptive functions to the external environment with various more or less functional configurations. Is it possible through this type of therapeutic approach to access states of temporary psychic deintegration and then arrive at new integrative modalities that broaden the subject's self-awareness?

Keywords: psychedelic-assisted psychotherapy, states of consciousness, unconscious, contraindications, care protocols

1. Introduction

There are several testimonies that highlight how, since prehistoric times, there has been the custom of treating both physical and mental disorders with the administration of psychotropic substances [1].

In the history of human beings, from Homo sapiens onward, there have been behavioral constants, without distinction of races or peoples, which can be defined as trans-cultural behaviors.

Among these is the tendency of man to try, through the most disparate methods, to modify his state of ordinary consciousness, for the purpose of living psycho-physical experiences in other mental states. Such mental states, by their nature, are possible and natural in the same way in which we consider natural the state of consciousness in which we ordinarily conduct our daily existence [2].

The modification of the state of consciousness, in addition to presenting itself in cases perhaps not precisely defined as "spontaneous", can be induced through a wide spectrum of techniques, which man has gradually discovered and developed over the course of history.

The practices that have been used throughout history to induce states of altered consciousness are numerous and range from sensory deprivation and physical mortification, to meditative and ascetic practices, to those that use dance and the sound of certain musical instruments; finally (certainly not in order of importance) there are practices that involve the use of plants with psychoactive effects, mostly of a hallucinogenic type. The latter represents one of the oldest techniques of modification of consciousness and almost certainly originates from the Stone Age.

As anthropological research has shown, this almost exclusive, but not entirely, capacity of the human species to be able to extend the dream experience to the waking state has certainly contributed to the development of the imaginative and artistic faculties of primitive man, with applications that are still testified today by the innumerable figurative schemes and models, that the civilizations of peoples without writing have managed to visualize and transmit from generation to generation through the decoration first of their own body, and subsequently of weapons, tools, caves, dwellings, ceramics and fabrics [2].

In the modern Western world, the first substance to be studied systematically was mescaline. Among these early works in which the administration was carried out on healthy subjects without therapeutic purposes, the phenomenological description offered by the psychiatrist Kurt Beringer in 1927 was particularly interesting [3].

In 1935, a report by Morselli E., during the Second Italian National Neurological Congress, had as its theme the psychic disturbances induced by mescaline which he himself had taken and which became a cornerstone of the first psychiatric studies on the subject [4].

In 1943, with the discovery of the psychoactive effect of lysergic acid diethylamide (LSD) by Albert Hofmann, a new era of research on consciousness began. This raised the hope of being able to delve deeper into the genesis of psychotic phenomena using a model of psychosis induced by this substance.

In Italy, between the 1930s and 1967, various psychedelic substances (mescaline, LSD and LSA-LISERGAMIDE) were used in numerous psychiatric clinics, as demonstrated by approximately 60 published clinical studies [5].

In the mid-1940s, the work of Werner A. Stoll [6] at the University Psychiatric Hospital in Zurich initiated clinical research into the systematic treatment of the mentally ill with psychedelics.

In 1955, during the Second Conference on Neuropharmacology held in Princeton (New Jersey), Ralph W. Gerard proposed to call these drugs psychotomimetics, that is, drugs "that mimic a psychotic state".

In the context of psychotherapy supported by these substances, in the 1960s, the term psycholytics became widespread, referring to substances capable, through a break (lysis), of releasing unconscious material to facilitate its exploration. This term is associated with "psycholytic therapy", one of the main TP techniques in vogue in Europe in the 1950s and 1960s.

According to some authors, it would be possible to identify different phases within the various publications made over the years: the phase of the psychotomimetic paradigm (1905–1957) was dominated by the belief that psychedelic substances could induce states similar to psychosis [5].

The phase of the psychotomimetic paradigm (1905–1957) was characterized by the perception of psychedelic substances as inducing psychotic or similar states [5].

This phase was then followed by the psycholytic phase, which developed in Europe between the 1950s and the 1970s, and developed starting from the psychoanalytic approach in which low to moderate doses of LSD (30–200 mcg) were administered during the various sessions. The aim was to facilitate access to the unconscious and therefore to facilitate the psychoanalytic process [7].

From here, we see the development of an approach that has been defined by some authors as the psychotherapeutic paradigm (1957–1972) in which ample space was given, albeit often with rather different methodologies, to the use of LSD, psilocybin and LSA, as aids in psychotherapy. The main purpose was to facilitate the emergence of unconscious material which would then be reworked during psychotherapy sessions [7].

In the same period in the United States, a psychedelic approach was experimented in which, after some preparatory sessions, the psychedelic substance was prescribed in high doses (>250 mcg of LSD) in a single administration or in several repeated administrations, with the aim of inducing in the patient a particularly intense and transcendent experience which could then lead to the resolution of the psychic symptoms.

The possibility of experiencing new states of consciousness was also considered an opportunity for the therapist to better understand the patient's psychic functioning and therefore support and accompany him in the healing process [7].

The phase of the psychotomimetic paradigm (1905–1957) was characterized by the perception of psychedelic substances as inducing psychotic or similar states [6].

The phase of the neurophenomenological approach (from 2000 to today) finally concerns current psychedelic therapies [5].

Psychedelic-assisted therapy (PAT) is still in the early stages of clinical validation and there are no internationally validated guidelines yet.

In fact, there is an ongoing debate on many aspects of this type of therapy, with positions often very distant from each other. What emerges from the debate is the absence of a common methodology as well as the absence of international guidelines that researchers can turn to [8].

Johnson et al. [9] made a proposal in 2008 for safety guidelines for conducting studies with psychedelic substances; recently, in 2023, also the U.S. The Food & Drug Administration (FDA) addressed the topic by publishing draft guidelines for conducting clinical trials with psychedelic substances [10].

To implement clinical research, in different contexts both in the United States and in Europe, numerous expert groups for PAT have been formed, so to develop effective consensus guidelines for PAT and allow the future development of new more homogeneous studies [11].

Some of the aspects that are still being debated are:

- Should PAT be considered a specific psychotherapeutic approach in which psychedelics are used as catalysts to deepen the experience [12–15], or should it be considered a pharmacotherapy that requires specific supervision by the staff for reasons of safety of use [16]?

- Is PAT really the optimal therapeutic protocol for the administration of psychedelics or does it make sense to continue developing new experimental designs that incorporate little or no psychotherapeutic intervention? The goal of these studies was to evaluate the efficacy of administering the psychedelic drug only with safety support [8].

- Does the sharing of the subjective experience induced by psychedelics experienced by the patient and its subsequent integration into the therapeutic path constitute an important part of PAT [17, 18] or is it useless if not even potentially harmful? [19]

- Is personal experience with the effects of psychedelics a necessary part of the training of a PAT therapist, similar to what is required by many schools of psychotherapy that require a personal analysis process before practicing the profession [20, 21], or is this requirement to be considered not advisable in order to maintain the therapist's neutrality?

Within the therapeutic setting, is physical contact (e.g. holding hands) between therapist and patient a useful or even necessary intervention in some PAT situations [22] or is physical contact only permitted for specific types of therapists, i.e. those with a more bioenergetic-oriented training? [8].

These are just some of the controversial points currently crossing the debate on PAT; other themes instead concern the theories of the mind that would explain the mode of action carried out by psychedelics, beyond the individual pharmacological differences.

2. Toward psychedelic maturity, the resumption of psychedelic research

Until the 1970s, the strict regulation imposed on psychedelics (LSD, psilocybin, DMT, mescaline, etc.), which in some parts of the world were completely banned, prevented the continuation of the initial research begun in the 1940s.

Psychedelic research was actually revitalized in the mid-1990s with the investigation of the neurobiological mechanisms of action of psilocybin [23]. Later, Griffiths and colleagues in Baltimore began studying the psychological effects induced by psychedelics in healthy subjects [24]. This was followed by research on the effects of psilocybin on anxiety symptoms in cancer patients in a randomized, double-blind study [25].

This study, like others that followed, used a hybrid approach of both psycholytic and psychedelic therapy [25]. The same has occurred in recent studies on methylenedioxymethamphetamine (MDMA) in post-traumatic stress disorder (PTSD) [26, 27].

In 2007, a Swiss project [28] studied LSD in a clinical research project for the first time, after a hiatus of more than 35 years.

In December 2019, the European Medicines Agency (EMA) approved intranasal esketamine in combination with an selective serotonin reuptake inhibitors (SSRI) or an serotonin–norepinephrine reuptake inhibitors (SNRI) for the treatment of adults suffering from treatment-resistant depression (TRD) [29], following the previous approval by the Food and US Drug Administration [30].

Although other interesting studies have been carried out for the application of psychedelic substances for PTDS and anxiety, at present, the FDA has not yet given approval for their administration in clinical practice [31, 32].

3. Psychedelic states, dreams and hypnagogic states

The essence of psychodynamic therapy consists first of all in exploring those aspects of the Self that are not fully known or deciphered by the subject and that tend to manifest themselves in the form of psychic or physical symptoms. The centrality of this therapeutic approach is in the therapist-patient relationship and in particular in the transference that is established. The reworking of the past is part of a broader path of transformation and evolution of the subject who, in the therapeutic relationship, will be helped to progressively bring to light aspects of himself denied and not recognized until that moment, in a progressive path of integration of aspects of the personality that until that moment were separated from the conscious part due to the intervention of more or less evolved defense mechanisms.

Recent research suggests that psychedelic substances, taken in the context of psychotherapy, may allow the development of a deeper understanding of oneself and one's life experience [33], the development of a greater ability to relate to others [34] and in general a greater self-acceptance [35], thanks to the collapse of ideational-behavioral patterns that dominate daily life.

In this context, the use of a psychotropic substance within the therapeutic setting can be considered as a sort of "enzyme" that accelerates this process of progressive integration of parts of the personality, acting with transitory episodes of psychic deintegration, which would have the function of leading to a subsequent psychic reorganization more evolved than the starting one.

The psychedelic-assisted psychotherapy (PAT) currently most used in recently published studies usually involves three sessions with different functions: a patient preparation session, one during the drug administration and one at the end of the pharmacological cycle [36].

The number of sessions foreseen for each session, however, is subject to some variability, also in relation to the type of therapeutic approach used.

Whatever the type of psychotherapy used, it appears essential that the therapist's attitude is not excessively controlling and that a strong therapeutic alliance is established with the patient.

In light of the studies carried out so far, it is possible to hypothesize that the therapeutic effect obtained from the administration of the substance is the result of the simultaneous interaction between a series of equally important factors: on the one hand, there is the molecular action of the psychedelic substance used, on the other hand, the patient's "mindset" and last but not least the relationship established with the therapist. These three factors, when adequately valued and protected, would make a negative outcome less likely if difficult or painful experiences were to emerge during the administration sessions.

This event represents, in fact, one of the main reasons of resistance on the part of the patient to the use of psychedelic substances, while adequate preparation and trust in the therapist would allow the former to welcome and work through the painful experience that has emerged, allowing the transformation of past painful occurrences [36].

A neurophenomenological similarity between dreaming and the psychedelic state has been described in the past [37–39] and supported more recently by other authors [40].

In one of his studies, Carhart-Harris [38] analyzed the similarities between the psychedelic state, rapid eye movement (REM) sleep, the onset phase of psychosis and the dream state of temporal lobe epilepsy. These clinical situations would constitute valid examples of an altered state of consciousness with more "primitive" characteristics compared to that of the waking state usually experienced during the daytime phase by healthy adult subjects.

This state of consciousness has been defined as "primary consciousness" and the episodes in which this state of consciousness emerges have been referred to as "primary states".

To access a primary state from normal waking consciousness, it has been hypothesized that the brain must go through what physicists call a "phase transition" [41, 42], i.e. a change of state between different operating modes.

In light of these considerations, we can deduce that the two modes of consciousness coexist within our psyche and alternate constantly throughout the day.

Freud was a great expert on Darwin's work, so much so that it is possible to find numerous references to his work in his writings [43]. In fact, Freud considered his hypotheses as deductions that emerged from the study of evolutionary theory.

In particular, he had observed that dreams and psychosis are both characterized by a primitive style of thought which is predominant during childhood, and which constituted the main way of knowing and processing reality of the primitive human, before the development of the Ego of the modern adult human.

The development of the Ego characterizes what Freud defined as a "secondary state" in which rational thought prevails over more primitive states of consciousness [38, 44, 45].

In the subsequent elaboration of the Freudian topic, primitive states fell within the definition of the unconscious.

Beyond childhood, a resurgence of primitive thinking can be observed in response to severe stress, while taking a psychedelic or certain drugs, and during REM sleep.

The dominant cognitive style in normal waking consciousness has therefore been indicated as secondary consciousness and the (pre-ego) style of cognition that is associated with primitive states has been defined as primary consciousness.

Consistent with Karl Friston's free energy principle [46], it is possible to hypothesize that the mind has progressively evolved to favor the processing of information relating to the surrounding environment in the most reliable and coherent way possible, in order to minimize unforeseen events and uncertainty (i.e. entropy).

This process depends on the brain's ability to organize itself into coherent and hierarchically structured systems [46, 47], in a critical balance between order and disorder [48, 49].

On the contrary, in primary states, the way of knowing external reality is easily influenced by intense emotions, such as desires and fears.

The progressive hierarchical organization of the brain from an evolutionary point of view has allowed the amount of entropy to be progressively reduced, favoring the development of secondary consciousness which inevitably ended up exercising a limiting and restrictive action on the entire psyche.

Freud outlined these ideas in his writings on the "reality principle" [50].

"Magical thinking" [51–54] is an eloquent example of primary consciousness. It has been the subject of numerous studies in the psychological and anthropological fields and can be defined as a form of interpretation of external and internal stimuli that does not respect the cause-effect logic.

Magical thinking is closely linked to an omnipotent nucleus that, in situations of high uncertainty, satisfies the subject in a narcissistic way by providing immediate explanations even in the absence of evidence [46], thus alleviating the sense of anguish.

This modality responds to what Freud called the "pleasure principle" [50].

An example of magical thinking is paranoia; in this case, an individual jumps to negative conclusions about a situation, trying to minimize the resulting uncertainty.

4. Therapeutic indications, absolute and relative contraindications

There are several studies to date that have evaluated the risk factors associated with the therapeutic use of psychedelic substances and their safety, taking into consideration both physical and psychological symptoms.

As regards psychiatric symptoms, only studies in which the administration of psychedelic drugs occurred in the context of a psychotherapy course were taken into consideration, excluding other trials in which only pharmacological administration took place.

A recent systematic review [55] confirmed that ketamine is able to perform an antidepressant action, although it is not possible to establish the efficacy among patients in a standardized fashion, due to the extreme variability among them. Furthermore, a recent study by Gałuszko-Węgielnik et al. [56] highlighted that ketamine can be considered an effective additional treatment in patients with treatment-resistant depression even if they present psychotic symptoms.

In cases of intravenous administration of ketamine, no cases of exacerbation of psychotic symptoms, either short or long term, were recorded, while a stable remission of depressive symptoms and rapid clinical efficacy in reducing suicidal ideation were noted.

It cannot be overlooked, however, that we are witnessing a significant increase in the diffusion of ketamine for recreational purposes and consequent phenomena of dependence on the substance:

when evaluating the eligibility of a patient with TRD, the anamnesis must exclude previous use of ketamine given the sharing of the same neuronal circuits and receptors [57].

With regard to MDMA, cases of amnesia have been observed only with high doses of the drug [58].

In colloquial language, it is often said that "bad trips" can occur after the use of psychostimulant substances. These are intense psychomimetic reactions with serious perceptual alterations which can be associated with intense feelings of anxiety, panic, physical pain or fear [59, 60].

Another possible side effect after the use of psychedelic substances is hallucinogen persistent perception disorder (HPPD) defined as a mental disorder in which a sober, non-intoxicated individual re-experiences the perceptual disturbances experienced during hallucinogen intoxication [61, 62].

According to the DSM-5, typical symptoms of HPPD are characterized, for example, by "geometric hallucinations, false perceptions of movement in peripheral visual fields, flashes of color, intensified colors, image trails of moving objects, positive afterimages, halos around objects, macropsia and micropsia". The estimated prevalence is 4.2%, and the prognosis is variable since it can last for months or years [63].

Good standard clinical practice requires that safety issues and possible adverse events are discussed during informed consent procedures before starting any treatment. This also includes addressing in detail the definition of the clinical context and the goals of treatment, and possibly discussing with the patient the existing evidence regarding the treatment.

In the context of PAT, we find ourselves in a hybrid situation in which the psychotherapist himself carries out both a prescriptive and treatment-supporting function, but what further complicates the setting is that during the intake of the substance, the patient is in an altered state of consciousness and therefore unable to make decisions on the matter.

Therefore, in the context of PAT, it appears particularly important to dedicate time in the preliminary sessions before taking the drug, to discuss with the patient all aspects related to possible behavioral and emotional alterations linked to taking the drug [36].

It is difficult to fully prepare the patient for the psychedelic experience and the clinical difficulties associated with the impossibility of interrupting the session once the substance has been ingested.

Therefore, it is necessary to make it clear in preliminary sessions with patients that once they begin to experience psychedelic effects, their psychic structure may change significantly, which could lead to both conditions in which the patient could withdraw consent to the treatment already underway, and conditions in which it may be necessary to resort to emergency drugs, such as antipsychotics, if the psychomotor agitation could be potentially dangerous.

5. Conclusions

What emerged from the examined studies is that the administration of psychedelic substances in controlled clinical contexts presents low short-term and long-term risks for the subjects. The adequate setting and the possibility for the patient to rely on a relationship of trust with the therapist who will follow the sessions are confirmed as protective factors for the risk of adverse events [36].

It is clear that, at present, research must be implemented according to protocols shared at an international level in order to make future studies more homogeneous, less anecdotal, in order to allow the development of sufficient guidelines to guarantee the applicability of the substances in clinical practice as it has already happened for esketamine [64].

Undoubtedly, further research is needed to better understand the mechanisms and safety profile of psychedelics in and outside of clinical settings.

At present, there is no data that allow us to establish whether one therapeutic approach is more appropriate than another in the context of PAT.

In conclusion, future studies should address the limitations and challenges unique to this research, such as small sample size, difficulty in conducting double-blind studies, sample selection criteria, safety monitoring, protocol variability and variability of effects.

The studies published so far have highlighted how we are still far from having reached a complete and definitive understanding of the real mechanisms of action of psychedelic substances. Precisely for this reason, it seems extremely important that therapists can create and maintain a space for active discussion and debate on the topic in which it is possible to formulate clear indications on the therapeutic setting and on the method of support and processing of the psychedelic experience.

The risk of transforming this therapeutic possibility into an extemporaneous experience for subjects looking for something new and unusual is very high, just as it can represent for the therapist an extemporaneous attempt to alleviate some symptoms in patients in whom psychotherapy has had limited effects.

It also appears essential that the therapist has an in-depth knowledge of the active ingredients and can propose their administration in a safe and coherent context.

Acknowledgements

We thank Doctor Antonio Chimenti, Doctor Mauro D'Alonzo and Doctor Gabriele Ramonda of SIMEPSI (Italian Society of Psychedelic Medicine) for their precious advice and collaboration in the drafting of this chapter.

Author details

Eliana Mea* and Paola Clemente
Mental Health Department, Local Health Authority, Bari, Puglia, Italy

*Address all correspondence to: eliana.mea@asl.bari.it

References

[1] George DR, Hanson R, Wilkinson D, Garcia-Romeu A. Ancient roots of today's emerging renaissance in psychedelic medicine. Culture, Medicine, and Psychiatry (Springer). 2021;**4**:890-903. DOI: 10.1007/s11013-021-09749-y

[2] Samorini G. Hallucinogens in myth. Stories on the Origin of Psychoactive Plants, Nautilus, Turin. 1995;**172**:1-10

[3] Beringer K. Die Versuche an der Heidelberger Klinik. In: Beringer K, editor. Der Meskalinrausch: Seine Geschichte und Erscheinungsweise. Berlin Heidelberg: Springer; 1927. pp. 31-118. DOI: 10.1007/978-3-662-11451-3_5

[4] Morselli EG. Contribution to the study of mescaline disorders. In: AAVV, editor. 1962 Experimental Psychosis. Milan: Feltrinelli; 1935. pp. 35-59

[5] D'Arienzo A, Samorini G. Psychedelic therapies. In: From the Psychotomimetic Paradigm to the Neurophenomenological Approach. Vol. 1. 2019. General and Historical Aspects, Foreword by Torsten Passie, Shake Edizioni

[6] Stoll WA. Lysegsaure-diathylamid, a Phantastikum aus der Mutterkorngruppe. 60.ni, Milan; 1947. ISBN: 978-88-97109-79-2

[7] Garcia-Romeu A, Richards WA. Current perspectives on psychedelic therapy: Use of serotonergic hallucinogens in clinical interventions. International Review of Psychiatry. 2018;**30**:291-316

[8] Aicher HD, Gasser P. Treatment Recommendations for Psychedelic-Assisted Therapy. Swiss Archives of Neurology. Psychiatry and Psychotherapy. 2024. Available from: https://sanp.swisshealthweb.ch/fileadmin/user_upload/SANP/1488043038-en-Raccomandazioni_di_trattamento_PAT.pdf

[9] Johnson MW, Richards WA, Griffiths RR. Human hallucinogen research: Guidelines for safety. Journal of Psychopharmacology (Oxford, England). 2008;**22**(6):603. DOI: 10.1177/0269881108093587

[10] FDA. FDA Issues First Draft Guidance on Clinical Trials with Psychedelic Drugs – Agency Recommendations Aim to Inform Psychedelic Drug Development. 2023. Available from: https://www.fda.gov/news-events/press-announcements/fda-issues-first-draft-guidance-clinical-trials-psychedelic-drugs

[11] APPA. Professional Practice Guidelines for Psychedelic-Assisted Therapy. American Psychedelic Practitioners Association and Brain Futures; 2023

[12] Grinspoon L, Doblin R. Psychedelics as catalysts of insight-oriented psychotherapy. Social Research. 2001;**68**(3):676-695

[13] Grof S. LSD Psychotherapy. 1st ed. Pomona, California Hunter House: United States Publisher; 1980

[14] Grof S, Hofmann A, Weil A. LSD Psychotherapy: The Healing Potential of Psychedelic Medicine. MAPS; 2001. Available from: https://maps.org/images/grof_vaclav-havel/_Grofpgs1-10.pdf

[15] Gründer G, Brand M, Mertens LJ, Jungaberle H, Kärtner L, Scharf DJ, et al. Treatment with psychedelics is

psychotherapy: Beyond reductionism. The Lancet Psychiatry. Dec 2023;**S2215036623003632**:231-236. DOI: 10.1016/S2215-0366(23)00363-2

[16] Goodwin GM, Malievskaia E, Fonzo GA, Nemeroff CB. Must psilocybin always "assist psychotherapy"? American Journal of Psychiatry. 1 Jan 2024;**181**(1):20-25. DOI: 10.1176/appi.ajp.20221043

[17] Mithoefer MC, Grob CS, Brewerton TD. Novel Psychopharmacological Therapies for Psychiatric Disorders: Psilocybin and MDMA2016. DOI: 10.1016/S2215-0366(15)00576-3

[18] Yaden DB, Griffiths RR. The subjective effects of psychedelics are necessary for their enduring therapeutic effects. ACS Pharmacology and Translational Science. 2021;**4**(2):568-572. DOI: 10.1021/acsptsci.0c00194

[19] Olson DE. The Subjective Effects of Psychedelics May Not Be Necessary for their Enduring Therapeutic Effects. American Chemical Society; 2021. DOI: 10.1021/acsptsci.0c00192

[20] Mueller F. The Role of Personal Experience for the Therapeutic Attitude in the Context of Substance-Assisted Therapy Training (TherPsySE). 2022. Available from: https://clinicaltrials.gov/study/NCT05570708

[21] Nielson EM, Guss J. The influence of therapists' first-hand experience with psychedelics on psychedelic-assisted psychotherapy research and therapist training. Journal of Psychedelic Studies. 2018;**2**(2):64-73. DOI: 10.1556/2054.2018.009

[22] Calder A, Hasler G. Extrapharmacological safety topics in psychedelic-assisted psychotherapy. JAMA Psychiatry. 2023;**80**(8):761. DOI: 10.1001/jamapsychiatry.2023.1031

[23] Vollenweider FX, Leenders KL, Scharfetter C, Maguire P, Stadelmann O, Angst J. Positron emission tomography and fluorodeoxyglucose studies of metabolic hyperfrontality and psychopathology in the psilocybin model of psychosis. Neuropsychopharmacology. 1997;**16**(5):357-372. DOI: 10.1016/s0893-133x(96)00246-1

[24] Griffiths RR, Richards WA, McCann U, Jesse R. Psilocybin can occasion mystical-type experiences having substantial and sustained personal meaning and spiritual significance. Psychopharmacology. 2006;**187**(3):268-283. DOI: 10.1007/s00213-006-0457-5

[25] Griffiths RR, Johnson MW, Carducci MA, Umbricht A, Richards WA, Richards BD, et al. Psilocybin produces substantial and sustained decreases in depression and anxiety in patients with life-threatening cancer: A randomized double-blind trial. Journal of Psychopharmacology. 2016;**30**(12). DOI: 10.1177/0269881116675513

[26] Gu J, Baer RA, et al. MDMA-assisted therapy for severe PTSD: A randomized, double-blind, placebo-controlled phase 3 study. Journal of Psychopharmacology. 2021;**9**(1):1-13. DOI: 10.1038/s41591-021-01336-3

[27] Oehen P, Traber R, Widmer V, Schnyder U. A randomized, controlled pilot study of MDMA (±3,4-Methylenedioxymethamphetamine)-assisted psychotherapy for treatment of resistant, chronic post-traumatic stress disorder (PTSD). Journal of Psychopharmacology. 2013. DOI: 10.1177/0269881112464827

[28] Gasser P, Holstein D, Michel Y, Doblin R, Yazar-Klosinski B, Passie T, et al. Safety and efficacy of lysergic acid diethylamide-assisted psychotherapy for anxiety associated with life-threatening diseases. The Journal of Nervous and Mental Disease. 2014;**202**(7):513-520. DOI: 10.1097/NMD.0000000000000113

[29] European Medicine Agency. Available from: https://www.ema.europa.eu/en/medicines/human/EPAR/spravato

[30] Food and Drug Administration. 2019. Available from: https://www.fda.gov/news-events/press-announcements/fda-approves-new-nasal-spray-medicationtreatment-resistant-depression-available-only-certified

[31] Holze F, Gasser P, Müller F, Dolder PC, Liechti ME. Lysergic acid diethylamide–assisted therapy in patients with anxiety with and without a life-threatening illness: A randomized, double-blind, placebo-controlled phase II study. Biological Psychiatry. 2023;**93**(3):215-223. DOI: 10.1016/j.biopsych.2022.08.025

[32] Mitchell JM, Bogenschutz M, Lilienstein A, Harrison C, Kleiman S, Parker-Guilbert K, et al. MDMA-assisted therapy for severe PTSD: A randomized, double-blind, placebo-controlled phase 3 study. Nature Medicine. 2021;**27**(6):1025-1033. DOI: 10.1038/s41591-021-01336-3

[33] Hartogsohn I. The meaning-enhancing properties of psychedelics and their mediator role in psychedelic therapy, spirituality, and creativity. Frontiers in Neuroscience. 2018;**12**. Available from: https://www.frontiersin.org/journals/neuroscience/articles/10.3389/fnins.2018.00129

[34] Carhart-Harris RL. The entropic brain—Revisited. Neuropharmacology. 2018;**142**:167-178. ISSN: 0028-3908

[35] Watts R, Day C, Krzanowski J, Nutt D, Carhart-Harris R. Patients' accounts of increased "connectedness" and "acceptance" after psilocybin for treatment-resistant depression. Journal of Humanistic Psychology. 2017;**57**:520-564. DOI: 10.1177/0022167817709585

[36] Reiff C et al. Psychedelics and psychedelic-assisted psychotherapy. American Journal of Psychiatry. 2020;**177**(5):391-410

[37] Fischman LG. Dreams, hallucinogenic drug states, and schizophrenia: A psychological and biological comparison. Schizophrenia Bulletin. 1983;**9**:73-94. DOI: 10.1093/schbul/9.1.73

[38] Carhart-Harris RL, Robert L, Hellyer Peter J, Murray S, Amanda F, Enzo T, et al. The entropic brain: A theory of conscious states informed by neuroimaging research with psychedelic drugs. Frontiers in Human Neuroscience. 2014. Available from: https://www.frontiersin.org/journals/human-neuroscience/articles/10.3389/fnhum.2014.00020

[39] Jacobs B. Dreams and hallucinations: A common neurochemical mechanism mediating their phenomenological similarities. Neuroscience and Biobehavioral Reviews. 1978;**2**:59-69. DOI: 10.1016/0149-7634(78)90007-6

[40] Kraehenmann R, Pokorny D, Aicher H, Preller KH, Pokorny T, Bosch OG, et al. LSD increases primary process thinking via serotonin 2A receptor activation. Frontiers in Pharmacology. 2017;**8**:814. DOI: 10.3389/fphar.2017.00814

[41] Zeeman EC. Catastrophe theory in brain modelling. The International Journal of Neuroscience. 1973;**6**:39-41. DOI: 10.3109/00207457309147186

[42] Waddington CH. A catastrophe theory of evolution. Annals of the New York Academy of Sciences. 1974;**231**:32-42. DOI: 10.1111/j.1749-6632.1974.tb20551.x

[43] Freud S. The interpretation of dreams (second part). In: Strachey J, Freud A, editors. The Standard Edition of the Complete Psychological Works of Sigmund Freud (1900-1901). London: Hogarth Press; 1900/1953. pp. 533-549

[44] Shimamura AP. Toward a cognitive neuroscience of metacognition. Consciousness and Cognition. 2000;**9**:313-323. Discussion: 324-326. DOI: 10.1006/ccog.2000.0450

[45] Fleming SM, Weil RS, Nagy Z, Dolan RJ, Rés G. Relating introspective accuracy to individual differences in brain structure. Science. 2010;**329**:1541-1543. DOI: 10.1126/science.1191883

[46] Friston K. The free-energy principle: A unified brain theory? Nature Reviews. Neuroscience. 2010;**11**:127-138. DOI: 10.1038/nrn2787

[47] Bassett DS, Bullmore E, Verchinski BA, Mattay VS, Weinberger DR, Meyer-Lindenberg A. Hierarchical organization human cortical networks in health and schizophrenia. The Journal of Neuroscience. 2008;**28**:9239-9248. DOI: 10.1523/JNEUROSCI.1929-08.2008

[48] Friston K, Breakspear M, Deco G. Perception and self-organized instability. Frontiers in Computational Neuroscience. 2012b;**6**:44. DOI: 10.3389/fncom.2012.00044

[49] Schwartenbeck P, Fitzgerald T, Dolan RJ, Friston K. Exploration, novelty, surprise, and free energy minimization. Frontiers in Psychology. 2013;**4**:710. DOI: 10.3389/fpsyg.2013.00710

[50] Freud S. The Ego and the ID. London: L. and Virginia Woolf at the Hogarthpress, The Institute of psycho-analysis; 1927

[51] Frazer JG. The Golden Bough: A Study in Magic and Religion. London; New York: Macmillan and Co. The Macmillan Company; 1900

[52] Subbotskii EV. Magic and the Mind: Mechanisms, Functions, and Development Magical Thinking and Behavior. New York, NY: Oxford University Press; 2010. DOI: 10.1093/acprof:oso/9780195393873.001.0001

[53] Hutson M. The Laws of Magical Thinking: How Irrational Beliefs Keep us Happy, Healthy, and Sane. New York, NY: Hudson Street Press; 2012

[54] Carbonaro TM, Bradstreet MP, Barrett FS, MacLean KA, Jesse R, Johnson MW, et al. Survey study of challenging experiences after ingesting psilocybin mushrooms: Acute and enduring positive and negative consequences. Journal of Psychopharmacology. 2016;**30**(12):1268-1278. DOI: 10.1177/02698 81116 662634

[55] Alnefeesi Y, Chen-Li D, Krane E, Jawad MY, Rodrigues NB, Ceban F, et al. Real-world effectiveness of ketamine in treatment-resistant depression: A systematic review and metaanalysis. Journal of Psychiatric Research. 2022;**151**:693-709. DOI: 10.1016/j.jpsychires.2022.04.037

[56] Gałuszko-Węgielnik M, Chmielewska Z, Jakuszkowiak-Wojten K, Wiglusz MS, Cubała WJ. Ketamine as add-on treatment in psychotic treatment-resistant depression. Brain Sciences. 2023;**13**:142. DOI: 10.3390/brainsci13010142

[57] Kokane SS, Armant RJ, Bolaños-Guzmán CA, Perrotti LI. Overlap in

the neural circuitry and molecular mechanisms underlying ketamine abuse and its use as an antidepressant. Behavioural Brain Research. 2020;**384**:112548. DOI: 10.1016/j.bbr.2020.112548

[58] Pantoni MM, Kim JL, Van Alstyne KR, Anagnostaras SG. MDMA and memory, addiction, and depression: Dose-effect analysis. Psychopharmacology. 2022;**239**:935-949. DOI: 10.1007/s00213-022-06086-9

[59] Carbonaro TM, Bradstreet MP, Barrett FS, MacLean KA, Jesse R, Johnson MW, et al. Survey study of challenging experiences after ingesting psilocybin mushrooms: Acute and enduring positive and negative consequences. Journal of Psychopharmacology. 2016;**30**(12):1268-1278

[60] Barrett FS, Bradstreet MP, Leoutsakos JMS, Johnson MW, Griffiths RR. The challenging experience questionnaire: Characterization of challengingexperiences with psilocybin mushrooms. Journal of Psychopharmacology. 2016;**30**(12):1279-1295

[61] Halpern JH, Lerner AG, Passie T. A review of hallucinogen persisting perception disorder (HPPD) and an exploratory study of subjects claiming symptoms of HPPD. In: Halberstadt AL, Vol-lenweider FX, Nichols DE, editors. Behavioral Neurobiology of Psychedelic Drugs. Curr Top Behav Neurosci. Vol. 36. Berlin: Springer; 2018. pp. 333-360. DOI: 10.1007/7854_2016_457

[62] Vis Pieter J, Goudriaan Anneke E, ter Meulen BC, Dirk BJ. On perception and consciousness in HPPD: A systematic review. Frontiers in Neuroscience. 2021;**15**. Available from: https://www.frontiersin.org/journals/neuroscience/articles/10.3389/fnins.2021.675768. DOI10.3389/fnins.2021.675768

[63] Diagnostic and Statistical Manual of Mental Disorders. 5th ed. Washington, DC: American Psychiatric Association. DOI: 10.1176/appi.books.9780890425596

[64] McNamee S, Devenot N, Buisson M. Studying harms is key to improving psychedelic-assisted therapy-participants call for changes to research landscape. JAMA Psychiatry. 2023;**80**(5):411-412. DOI: 10.1001/jamapsychi atry. 2023.0099

Chapter 2

Parent-Child Psychotherapy: Core Elements and Mechanisms of Change

Daphna Ginio Dollberg

Abstract

Parent-child psychotherapy, also known as dyadic or triadic psychotherapy, is gaining recognition in child psychotherapy. It is used as a treatment intervention for infants, toddlers, and preschoolers (ages 0–6) who display behavioral and emotional difficulties, as well as a preventive intervention for young children at risk. This chapter explores the key features of this approach, presents empirical evidence of its effectiveness, and reviews the common settings and techniques used. It also outlines mechanisms of change, such as repairing ruptures in parent-child interactions, enhancing parental mentalization and reflective functioning, confronting "ghosts and angels" from the parent's attachment history, and addressing maladaptive implicit relational patterns between parents and children. The chapter further discusses the challenges of engaging both child and parent in play therapy, creating epistemic trust and relevance, and dealing with transference and countertransference. Case material is included to demonstrate the practical application of parent-child psychotherapy.

Keywords: parent-child psychotherapy, dyadic/triadic psychotherapy, parental mentalization, parental reflective functioning, implicit relational knowing, relational disorder

1. Introduction

1.1 Definition and scope of parent-child psychotherapy

Parent-child dyadic or triadic psychotherapy is a collaborative intervention involving the child and parent(s) interacting with a therapist during a therapeutic session. This intervention is designed for infants, toddlers, and preschoolers (0–6 years old) and aims to reduce young children's socioemotional symptoms and improve their mental health and adjustment by enhancing parent-child relations. Research shows that experiences shared between parent and child and the parent-child relationship in the early years of life significantly impact the child's psychological and social development.

1.2 Overview of chapter content

The chapter opens with a review of parent-child psychotherapy's theoretical and historical underpinnings, emphasizing dynamically oriented approaches. It explores the social, emotional, and developmental challenges these therapies address and identifies the target age groups. The chapter also outlines the empirical evidence supporting the efficacy of parent-child psychotherapy, delves into its mechanisms of change, and discusses its distinctiveness compared to other child therapy modalities. Additionally, it addresses potential contraindications and the challenges and barriers to implementation. To exemplify the practical application, a fictional case study is included, demonstrating the formulation of the parent-child relationship, establishing treatment goals, and applying interventions. The chapter concludes by advocating for parent-child psychotherapy as the preferred treatment option, except in cases where specific contraindications exist.

2. Rationale behind parent-child psychotherapy

2.1 Theoretical foundations

Parent-child psychotherapy aims to enhance a child's mental health by focusing on their relationships with attachment figures [1–3]. This therapeutic approach addresses early social, emotional, and behavioral challenges by improving the parent-child relationship quality [4–8]. It provides both the parent and child with psychological tools to cultivate a relationship devoid of emotionally damaging perceptions and interactions [1], aligns parental behaviors with the child's developmental needs and emotional stages [4], and promotes culturally appropriate affect regulation [9].

Rooted in the insights of pioneers like Fraiberg, Bowlby, Bick, and Winnicott, parent-child psychotherapy is predicated on the notion that difficulties in parent-infant relationships and the child's symptomatic behaviors often originate from the parent's projection of unresolved issues onto the child [10]. Initially, the therapy aimed to assist parents in resolving their own traumas, thereby enhancing their capacity to understand and respond to their child's developmental needs [11]. Over the years, the scope of parent-infant psychotherapy has broadened to include toddlers, preschoolers, older children, and other family members such as fathers, non-biological parents, and grandparents [1, 12–15]. Informed by developmental models that account for both biological and social factors, this therapy interprets a child's difficulties as stemming from negative bidirectional interactions within their environment, yet it maintains a hopeful outlook toward recovery and positive adaptation [7].

Parent-child psychotherapy has been adapted for use as a primary, secondary, and tertiary intervention across diverse populations and settings [16]. Central to the therapeutic process is the active participation of both parent and child, with a particular emphasis on strengthening their relationship.

2.2 Importance for infants, toddlers, and preschoolers

Research indicates that young children flourish in supportive and nurturing environments where parenting is sensitive and mindful [17]. However, they are also susceptible to challenges such as regulatory difficulties [18] and environmental stressors, including poverty, parental psychopathology, and trauma [19]. The human brain experiences rapid development during infancy and early childhood, undergoing critical processes such as synaptogenesis, pruning, and myelination [3]. This developmental phase is pivotal for forming self-regulation, a coherent sense of self, and psychological resilience [2]. Many psychological disorders have their roots in these early stages, highlighting the critical need for early intervention to modify developmental pathways and diminish the risk of future mental health problems [3].

2.3 Behavioral and emotional difficulties addressed

The increasing focus on enhancing parent-child relationships has led to a proliferation of treatment options. These range from general interventions aimed at addressing nonspecific relational issues between parents and infants to specialized treatments designed for specific conditions such as child trauma, maltreatment, developmental disorders, and particular symptoms like eating and sleeping disturbances. Some interventions are preventive, targeting at-risk parent-child pairs, while others are therapeutic, intended for children already exhibiting symptoms.

Since young children cannot often articulate distress, their relational difficulties frequently manifest as behavioral issues. These can include developmental regression, toileting problems, excessive crying, defiance, tantrums, aggression, withdrawal, flattened affect, dissociation, somatization, and fearfulness. These challenges are typically perceived as either stemming from relational problems within the parent-child system or as inherent to the child, thereby placing strain on the system.

Referrals for these interventions usually come from parents or professionals such as pediatricians, nurses, social welfare services, and childcare providers who notice behavioral, emotional, or developmental issues in the child or observe relational difficulties between the child and caregivers. Specific referrals may concern a child's sleeping habits, eating patterns, mood, behavioral difficulties, or developmental delays. Referrals may also be linked to parental psychopathology, including depression, anxiety, and post-trauma symptoms. In some instances, parents may seek treatment due to difficulties in bonding with the child, experiencing intense negative emotions toward the child, or feeling a lack of parental competence.

3. Empirical evidence of effectiveness

A robust body of research increasingly supports advances in parent-infant interventions. A recent systematic review and meta-analysis by Sleed and colleagues [19] demonstrated that parent-child interventions significantly enhance parental reflective functioning, reduce parental depression, and improve infant socioemotional and behavioral well-being and attachment. Similarly, Barlow and her team [18] found that psychoanalytically oriented parent-infant psychotherapy increased infant security in high-risk populations. Earlier meta-analyses have also affirmed the overall effectiveness of these interventions, particularly in improving maternal sensitivity and interactive patterns [20–22].

Among the most researched and supported therapies is Lieberman and Van-Horn's trauma-focused intervention, Child-Parent Psychotherapy (CPP). Longitudinal studies have underscored its enduring benefits. A six-month follow-up of a randomized controlled trial (RCT) comparing CPP with community case management showed sustained improvements in children's behavioral issues and mothers' distress [23]. A six-year follow-up involving children of depressed mothers who underwent

CPP revealed increased secure attachment, which correlated with greater maternal warmth and reduced child anger and problem behavior at age nine [24]. This study emphasized the mother-child attachment relationship as a pivotal change mechanism [25]. Recent research by Sullivan and colleagues [26] also indicated long-term effects on reducing pediatric epigenetic age acceleration following CPP intervention.

In a naturalistic, pretest-posttest study conducted by the author and colleagues at a psychiatric, community-based infant mental health clinic, significant improvements were observed in maternal sensitivity, child engagement, and maternal narratives about the parent-infant relationship after dyadic psychotherapy. This therapy integrated video-assisted interaction guidance and addressed parents' relational difficulties [27]. A follow-up 6–8 years later revealed that treated children exhibited socioemotional and psychiatric functioning comparable to peers who had not received treatment, suggesting that early intervention may have aligned their developmental outcomes [28].

4. Common settings and techniques employed and the role of the therapist

A hallmark of parent-child psychotherapy is the involvement of both the child and at least one parent in therapy sessions. While some interventions offer flexibility in attendance, ensuring that the child participates in at least some sessions, others employ structured cycles. These cycles might involve parents alternating between attending dyadic sessions with the child and joint sessions as a parental pair. In some cases, both parents may participate in triadic sessions with the child, followed by parent-only sessions.

Rooted in attachment theory, parent-child psychotherapy centers on strengthening the parent-child bond. It emphasizes repairing disruptions in this relationship by bolstering the child's attachment security and enhancing the parent's caregiving responses [29]. The therapy's primary aim is to equip parents to meet their children's attachment needs better and foster positive interactions between them by promoting attuned and sensitive parental responses [30].

The overarching goal of these interventions is to improve communication between parent and child, aiding parents in understanding and responding to their child's emotional needs, often communicated through body language, actions, and behaviors. For parents who may struggle to interpret their child's needs due to their own unresolved childhood trauma or inadequate parenting experiences, therapy provides a space to observe and reassess these interactions. By linking current misunderstandings to past experiences, the therapy seeks to alleviate the child from the impact of the parent's unresolved issues [11].

For older children who can verbally express themselves, therapy focuses on recognizing the differences between their needs and the parent's responsibilities. The therapist contextualizes the child's behavior and symptoms in relation to their life experiences, particularly exposure to trauma [9]. This process enhances communication between the caregiver and child, fostering understanding and the potential for repairing the relationship.

Parent-child interventions can be categorized based on therapeutic goals and strategies, drawing on Daniel Stern's concept of the "port of entry" [8, 31]. Some interventions focus on observing parent-child interactions in real-time or through video to increase parental awareness of their behaviors and their impact on the child. Others concentrate on exploring the parent's thoughts, beliefs, and emotional experiences with the child to uncover the parent's unconscious conflicts and relational trauma. Despite their varied approaches, all interventions agree that parental representations and behavior changes are crucial for improving children's emotional well-being [8, 31].

Interventions may follow a structured protocol and often last between 6 and 12 months, or they may be more flexible, open-ended, and tailored to individual needs [19]. In these sessions, caregivers and children often use play and developmentally appropriate toys and games as therapeutic communication. This interaction allows the parent to observe and understand the child's inner experiences [1, 32], particularly when play reflects traumatic experiences [9]. Engaging in mutual play within a safe therapeutic environment fosters shared pleasure for both child and parent, potentially mitigating risks associated with parental psychopathology [33].

Reflective dialog and the caregiver's capacity to mentalize—understand their child's internal experiences and emotions—are pivotal in parent-child psychotherapy. These processes enhance the parent's understanding of the child's emotions and contribute to the child's socioemotional and behavioral development [34–36]. The therapist facilitates shared interactions, encouraging the parent to observe, wonder, and follow the child's lead during play [1, 36, 37]. The therapist also supports the parent in articulating the child's feelings, normalizing and contextualizing them to bolster the parent's mentalizing capacity—their ability to understand and make sense of their child's internal experiences and foster empathic regulation of the child's emotions [38].

Additionally, parents have sessions with the therapist to discuss their interactions with the child. Away from the child's often challenging behavior, they reflect jointly on the occurrences, further enhancing and expanding the parents' mentalization and reflective functioning. These sessions also improve co-parenting, which is critical for the child's well-being [39].

4.1 Role of the therapist

Establishing a robust alliance between the therapist and parents is crucial for achieving positive outcomes in all forms of child psychotherapy [40–42]. Recent studies indicate that a positive parent-therapist alliance in structured parent-child focal play therapy significantly enhances emotional availability between the parent and child [43]. The parent's active involvement in therapy introduces a unique dynamic among the parent, child, and therapist, necessitating a distinct role for the therapist.

The therapist typically remains in the background in this setting, emphasizing the parent as the child's primary attachment figure. This approach focuses on fostering the child's attachment behaviors toward the parent and enhancing the parent's caregiving responses. Moreover, the therapist avoids adopting the role of an expert who "knows better." Instead, they cultivate a collaborative relationship, acknowledging the parent's sincere intentions to support their child's development.

The therapist adopts a stance of 'not knowing,' which involves demonstrating curiosity about the parent's perspectives and assisting them in deepening their understanding of both their own and their child's thoughts and behaviors [44]. This approach helps to balance engagement with the parents while encouraging them to meet their child's needs [11, 36].

Furthermore, the therapist's role extends beyond identifying disruptions in the parent's past and present experiences. They also highlight positive "angles"—benevolent childhood experiences that can facilitate effective parenting and help counteract the negative influence of childhood "ghosts in the nursery" [45, 46]. This dual focus addresses challenges and reinforces strengths within the family dynamic, contributing to a more holistic therapeutic process.

5. Mechanisms of change in parent-child psychotherapy

The efficacy of dynamically oriented parent-child psychotherapy is rooted in various mechanisms of change. This therapeutic approach promotes reflective dialog, models sensitive caregiving through the therapist's behavior, offers structured and unstructured developmental guidance, and enables parents to practice sensitivity, responsiveness, appropriate stimulation, interactional synchrony, warmth, involvement, and mutually responsive interactions. Collectively, these elements foster a more fulfilling parent-child relationship, enhance the likelihood of corrective attachment experiences for both parent and child [4], and aid in mending past negative attachment experiences [25]. Additionally, the therapeutic environment provides a safe and temporarily isolated space that supports shared pleasurable interactions between parent and child, helping to mitigate daily stress and challenges [47], thereby boosting the well-being of both.

Moreover, with the therapist's support, parent-child psychotherapy allows parents to observe their parenting styles and their child's reactions while identifying communication misunderstandings. Within the secure confines of the therapeutic relationship, these observations can lead to changes in parenting practices. Learning new interaction methods may also assist parents in addressing their own issues, especially those related to emotional dysregulation, as they start to understand its impact on their child [9]. This process can modify rigid attachment defenses related to parenting [48] and other aspects of the parent's life.

The active involvement of both parent and child in therapy sessions, along with the therapist's observation and facilitation of their interactions and discussions about "ghosts in the nursery" [46], enhances the parent's mentalizing and reflective capacities [19]. As the parent's ability to mentalize improves, non-mentalizing cycles can be spontaneously repaired, with the therapist aiding by clarifying misunderstandings, offering alternative perspectives, and emphasizing positive intentions. This helps deepen the understanding of each other's internal experiences for both parent and child [44].

Parent-child psychotherapy also addresses "implicit relational knowing"—the procedural knowledge used by parents and children in their interactions [49]. This knowledge, which forms the basis of internal object relations and influences parenting behaviors, originates early in the parent-infant relationship through non-verbal, embodied, and automatic processes that are often outside conscious awareness [50]. By focusing on moment-to-moment relational patterns, the therapy highlights these embodied experiences and facilitates real-time changes in implicit relational knowing. Through new experiences of mutual regulation, recognition, and shared emotions, relational patterns and intersubjectivity between parent and child evolve [1, 11, 51].

Lastly, parent-child psychotherapy underscores the critical role of parents in fostering change and supporting their child's well-being. It views the parent as an ally and partner, collaborating with the therapist to enhance the child's well-being. By involving parents in sessions and actively engaging them in interactions with their child, the therapist reinforces their capabilities and potential to learn and alter old relationship patterns. The treatment focuses on the parent's challenges and strengths, normalizing and validating parenting difficulties while emphasizing the parent's responsibility to be a nurturing and responsive caregiver. This approach aims to improve parental competence, self-confidence, and well-being, all of which contribute to a healthier parent-child relationship and the child's overall well-being [52–54].

6. Challenges in parent-child psychotherapy

Parent-child psychotherapy can be beneficial for young children and their parents, but it also presents some challenges that need to be addressed before the intervention.

6.1 Building trust and safety within the therapeutic environment

Establishing trust and safety for both the parent and the child within the therapeutic setting is crucial for effective therapy, particularly when both parties are involved in ongoing relational conflicts. The therapist plays a pivotal role in creating a welcoming and non-judgmental space where both parent and child feel secure. The therapist encourages open communication about the parent's and child's conflicts and concerns while adopting an empathetic, supportive, and balanced approach and viewing situations from both parties' perspectives. This approach involves highlighting and advocating for benevolent intentions, preventing any perception of taking sides. Additionally, the therapist works to normalize the behaviors of both parent and child by considering their developmental stages, roles, and life circumstances. The therapist also recognizes instances where the child appears distressed and encourages the parent to soothe and regulate the child as needed while also providing regulation and soothing to the parent. This dual approach ensures a secure and supportive atmosphere throughout the sessions, even when discussing complex and painful issues [9]. Finally, parent sessions allow deeper discussions and resolutions of more complicated family dynamics, which can later be discussed in the parent-child sessions without being too overwhelming for the parent or the child.

6.2 Finding a shared "language" to engage the parent and the child

A key challenge in parent-child psychotherapy is identifying the right approach, pace, and language that resonates with both the parent and the child. Often, it is the parent who must adjust—following the child's pace, communicating in a way the child understands, delaying discussions of pressing issues that concern the parent but the child is not yet ready to address (such as behavioral problems or fears), and participating in the child's play rather than focusing primarily on a conversation. An initial phase with the parents is typically recommended to address this, during which the treatment plan, methods, and expectations are discussed and agreed upon [55]. Together, the therapist and parents create a developmentally appropriate and emotionally supportive explanation for the child about the reasons for attending therapy and the process ahead, emphasizing joint play, safety, and hope for change. However, parents who are unwilling or unable to engage in play due to cognitive or emotional barriers may struggle to be effective partners in parent-child psychotherapy [1].

6.3 Managing resistance and ambivalence and establishing epistemic trust

Resistance or ambivalence from parents toward the therapy process can pose a significant challenge. Some parents may feel skeptical about the benefits of therapy, or they may feel judged or threatened by the prospect of discussing and changing their parenting practices. To overcome this, therapists need to employ strategies such as motivational interviewing to explore and resolve ambivalence, providing psychoeducation about the benefits of therapy, and emphasizing the collaborative nature of the therapeutic process. It is also crucial for therapists to acknowledge and validate the parent's feelings and experiences, building an alliance based on empathy and understanding [55].

Epistemic trust in treatment refers to the patient's perception of the treatment as relevant and aligned with their goals and needs, which is critical for treatment adherence and effectiveness [56]. This trust is especially important when working with parents to improve their child's well-being and address maladaptive parenting patterns [57]. Establishing epistemic trust in parent-child psychotherapy can be challenging due to a potential mismatch between the referral, which often focuses on the child's behavior and functioning, and the treatment's emphasis on the parent-child relationship. To bridge this gap and foster epistemic trust, presenting and discussing a case formulation with the parents before starting the intervention is essential. The formulation should clearly outline the bidirectional influence between the child's issues and the parent-child relationship, emphasizing the relevance of the chosen treatment approach [58]. Additionally, the therapist should be attuned to both explicit and implicit signs of epistemic vigilance in the parents and remain open to addressing any concerns or questions as they arise [56].

6.4 Transference and countertransference

When conducting parent-child psychotherapy, therapists encounter specific challenges related to transference and countertransference. Unlike many psychodynamic therapies that primarily focus on analyzing the patient's transference toward the therapist, parent-child psychotherapy concentrates on the child's transference toward the parent and the parent's transference toward both the child and the therapist. The therapist's goal is to foster positive transference within the parent-child relationship and between the relationship and the therapist, often referred to as "good-grandmother transference" [31]. This involves positioning themselves as a supportive figure for the parent-child pair. However, negative transference may also emerge due to past relational difficulties and should be addressed openly [1, 8, 11].

Countertransference presents an equally significant challenge, as the therapist may be inclined to identify with one member of the pair, typically the child, which can undermine the goal of creating a safe space for both the parent and child. The therapist might experience rescue fantasies toward the child or feelings of criticism toward the parent. Balancing the needs of both parent and child—especially when cultural or contextual differences are present—can lead to countertransference reactions such as criticism, misunderstanding, or failure to address critical issues [9, 36].

Reflective supervision is recommended to help therapists navigate and manage the complexities of transference and countertransference. This supervision provides a space for therapists to explore their feelings, reactions, and biases that arise during therapy sessions, ensuring they maintain a balanced and effective therapeutic stance. It also aids in identifying any blind spots or areas where the therapist may be inadvertently aligning with one party over the other [1, 11, 36, 55]. This reflective practice is crucial for maintaining the integrity of the therapeutic process and ensuring that both the parent and child receive the support they need to foster a healthier relationship.

7. Comparison with other therapeutic approaches and contraindications

Parent-child psychotherapy primarily focuses on the parent-child relationship, distinguishing it from other therapeutic approaches such as parent guidance, parenting groups, family therapy, and individual therapy for the child. The key distinction lies in the direct involvement of both the parent and the child in the therapeutic process.

Unlike parent guidance or parenting groups where the therapist interacts only with the parents, parent-child psychotherapy allows the therapist to observe and engage with the interactions between the parent and child. This firsthand observation enables the therapist to accurately assess the relationship's strengths and challenges rather than relying solely on the parent's reports. The therapist's ability to witness and intervene in real-time when disruptions occur provides immediate feedback and support, which can be crucial for effective therapy. The therapist also supports the child, offering comfort, reassurance, positive reinforcement, and modeling appropriate behaviors. This not only aids the child but also serves as a live demonstration for the parent on how to effectively respond to the child's needs and manage moments of dysregulation.

In contrast, individual play therapy primarily addresses the child's relational issues through transference with the therapist [59], without the direct involvement of the parent in the sessions. While this can be beneficial, parent-child psychotherapy has the advantage of focusing directly on improving the parent-child relationship, which can lead to quicker progress in therapy and better generalization of therapeutic gains to the home environment.

However, parent-child psychotherapy may not be feasible or appropriate in all situations. Some contraindications to administering parent-child psychotherapy are critical. It is not suitable when the parent is absent, unstable, or poses a risk to the child's safety. It is also contraindicated in cases where the parent is actively psychotic or behaves in ways that could overwhelm the child. In such scenarios, individual therapy for the child might be more appropriate. Additionally, if the therapist determines that the child cannot freely express their emotions in the presence of their parent, individual psychotherapy may be recommended.

While there are similarities between family therapy and parent-child psychotherapy, the latter targets explicitly the unique parent-child relational patterns that contribute to the child's emotional health and symptoms, making it a distinct and valuable approach for addressing specific relational dynamics within the family.

8. A case presentation

To demonstrate the use of parent-child psychotherapy in clinical settings, I present a fictional case based on multiple real cases, with details altered for privacy. This overview illustrates parent-child intervention and explores mechanisms of change.

8.1 Background and relationship formulation

Eli, a 4-year-old, was referred to therapy by his parents due to social avoidance in various situations, separation anxiety, bedtime struggles, and severe tantrums. Being an only child, his mother, a teacher, initiated the referral. His father, an accountant, viewed therapy with skepticism, emphasizing the need for Eli to "behave his age." Eli's developmental history revealed high vigilance, fearfulness, and intense negative reactions to new experiences. At home, he was controlling and intense, while at school, he was passive and avoidant and struggled with separations from his parents, particularly his mother.

The mother, who had been a cautious child herself, grew up with protective but controlling parents. She was very close to her parents, who passed away before Eli's birth, and felt compelled to emulate their complete devotion and protection of their children, despite a vague sense that this devotion restricted the children's freedom. She admitted to avoiding setting limits for Eli due to fear of his reactions. His father, raised in a strict, achievement-focused family, believed that his harsh upbringing helped him become self-disciplined and self-reliant and hoped the same for his son. He struggled to connect with Eli, believing his wife's "pampering" reinforced Eli's delicate nature.

To fully understand Eli's dynamics and implicit relational patterns with each of the parents, joint sessions were arranged where their interactions could be observed, and insights regarding the family dynamics could be gained. The observations took place in a therapy playroom equipped with age-appropriate toys, games, and art supplies. The parents were encouraged to engage in free play while the therapist observed.

During the first session, Eli, a well-groomed boy who seemed to be his stated age, attended with both of his parents. He appeared anxious and withdrawn, sticking close to his mother and avoiding interaction. When his father tried to engage him with toys, it made him more anxious, causing him to retreat and seek comfort in his mother's lap. The therapist acknowledged Eli's discomfort and encouraged his parents to support him at his own pace. It was noted that although Eli remained cautious, with his parents' guidance, he gradually started to explore.

The therapist also observed that the parents sometimes gave conflicting messages but were willing to follow her guidance and actively engage Eli. During dyadic sessions, distinct patterns in Eli's relationships with each parent emerged, reflecting his individual attachment dynamics with each of them. With his father, who tended to challenge and exert control, Eli maintained composure and stayed focused on his goals even when appearing frustrated or upset. Conversely, with his mother, Eli displayed more regressive and passive behavior, often experiencing anxiety and having tantrums when she placed demands on him.

The therapist summarized her observations by noting that the parents struggled to effectively balance and coordinate soothing Eli's anxiety while supporting his exploration, often either over-challenging or under-challenging him. She also observed the parents' positive reaction to her remark about Eli's discomfort and their eventual capacity to channel their energies towards easing his tension and encouraging his exploration.

8.2 Developmental relational formulation

Eli's symptoms, as reported by his parents and teachers, suggest a diagnosis of Generalized Anxiety Disorder (GAD, [60]). His inhibited temperament [61], combined with his parents' responses, likely contributed to his anxiety [62]. Additionally, his oppositional behavior with his parents, which causes significant distress to both Eli and his parents and interferes with his developmental potential, is consistent with a relationship-specific disorder of infancy/early childhood [60].

A developmental relational formulation of Eli's symptoms suggests that his temperamental anxiety was reinforced by his parents' responses, which were shaped by their own childhood experiences and intergenerational patterns of parenting. Both parents were deeply committed to supporting Eli's development. However, Eli's mother, who experienced anxiety during her own childhood, became overprotective, reflecting her identification with her deceased parents and unresolved ambivalence about their controlling parenting. This overprotection stifled Eli's independence, potentially contributing to his temper tantrums and aggression. In contrast, Eli's father, raised in a family that emphasized independence, feared reinforcing Eli's dependency and anxiety, leading him to impose demands that created emotional distance. The parents' opposing parental practices interfered with Eli's ability to build a coherent sense of self and to develop age-appropriate self-regulation skills to manage his anxiety.

Despite these challenges, both parents demonstrated potential for more attuned parenting, and consequently Eli showed signs of more mature coping, indicating potential for growth and change. This highlights the importance of therapeutic intervention that focuses on enhancing the parents' understanding of their parenting styles, and improving their ability to respond to Eli's needs in a balanced and supportive manner.

8.3 Treatment planning and process

The therapist held a feedback session with Eli's parents to discuss his symptoms, relational dynamics, and to establish a treatment plan. Both parents expressed concern about Eli's anxiety and avoidance behaviors, which the therapist confirmed were consistent with a psychiatric disorder. She then presented a relational formulation of his symptoms, outlining the risk and protective factors that contributed to his development and difficulties. The therapist explained how the parents' well-intentioned responses to Eli's inhibited and fearful responses may have inadvertently reinforced his anxiety. This formulation resonated with the parents, leading the therapist to explain how parent-child psychotherapy could help them recognize and change maladaptive patterns that perpetuated and worsened Eli's symptoms.

The parents also raised concerns about how shared play could address the daily challenges of Eli's tantrums and avoidance. In response, the therapist explained that the dyadic sessions would provide an opportunity to identify the antecedents of Eli's behavior and explore new parental responses and also strengthen positive aspects of the relationship. The parents agreed to the treatment plan, and parent-child psychotherapy commenced. The year-long treatment involved weekly parent-child play sessions (alternating between mother and father) and bi-weekly meetings with both parents.

In the early sessions, Eli was hesitant to participate, but with the support of his parents, he gradually became more involved. The therapist acted as a mediator during the sessions, identifying misunderstandings between Eli and his parents and working to mend their relationship. For example, during a session with his father, Eli refused to engage in a book-reading activity chosen by his father. In response, his father expressed frustration, saying he was tired of playing with "babyish" toys. The therapist intervened, suggesting that Eli might be interested but worried that the book reading would be too challenging. She recommended that the father adjust the story to Eli's level and that Eli could ask to stop if he felt uncomfortable. Following the therapist's intervention, the father made adjustments, and they ended up having a pleasant reading experience together.

During a later therapy session with his mother, Eli asked her to read the same book, but she suggested a different, easier book, which frustrated him. The therapist intervened, acknowledging Eli's frustration and confusion, given the different attitudes of the parents. She also acknowledged the mother's wish not to challenge Eli with an advanced book as a protective action. After the therapist's intervention, the mother and son read the book together, which, despite the initial rupture, was a positive experience for both.

As the treatment progressed, Eli started to show more disobedience, testing his parents' limits. This change was discussed in the parents' sessions. It was framed as an opportunity for the parents to respond appropriately to his desire for independence and set age-appropriate demands for self-control. In light of the parents' improved mentalizing skills, this guidance was carried out with empathy and thought on the parents' part and proved effective. The treatment also involved guidance for Eli's school staff on how to handle his anxiety and rigid rituals.

The treatment concluded when Eli's anxious symptoms, temper tantrums, and regressive behavior at home and school improved. His parents became more confident, attentive, and patient supporters of his gradual adjustment.

8.4 Discussion

This case exemplifies how parent-child psychotherapy can fortify the parent-child relationship and ameliorate a young child's symptoms. The treatment commenced with an assessment of the parent-child relationship through intake interviews and observations. This was followed by a developmental relational formulation that linked the child's symptoms to the relational histories and patterns of both the child and each parent. This formulation was presented to the parents, and the relevance of parent-child psychotherapy in addressing the child's symptoms and the parents' concerns was discussed.

The treatment involved joint parent-child sessions as well as separate sessions for the parents. The safe and positive atmosphere created by shared play and the therapist's supportive presence facilitated the exploration of both positive and negative parent-child interactive patterns. The therapist observed these interactions and enhanced understanding within the family by reflecting on, mediating, and expanding discussions around emotional needs, motivations, and parenting responsibilities. Interventions were employed to address relational conflicts and misunderstandings that interfered with the family's functioning. Deeper intrapsychic conflicts affecting parenting—such as the mother's unresolved ambivalence toward her parents and the father's oedipal rivalry with his son—were addressed in the parents' sessions, taking into account their childhood experiences.

The treatment focused on enhancing parental mentalizing and fostering mutual understanding between the parents and the child, thereby creating space for fresh experiences of intersubjectivity [1]. The parents became aware of the child's need for a balance between nurturing and age-appropriate challenges, improving their reflective functioning regarding how their practices impacted him. As a result, their parenting became more attuned, leading the child to seek their assistance in a more age-appropriate manner and better regulate his emotions.

The therapist's observations of each dyad's interactive patterns, along with in-the-moment interventions, contributed to corrective emotional experiences [4] and changes in the family's implicit relational knowing [50]. These changes ultimately contributed to a reduction in the child's symptoms, illustrating the effectiveness of parent-child psychotherapy in addressing complex family dynamics and promoting healthier relationships and emotional well-being.

9. Conclusion

Parent-child psychotherapy is highly recommended for young children experiencing difficulties in their relationships with their parents. Given the rapid brain and developmental changes during early childhood, coupled with the strong attachment relationships children form with their caregivers, early intervention is crucial when socioemotional disturbances arise. Young children often struggle to engage in individual therapy, and parent guidance alone may be insufficient, as parents may lack awareness of their own and their child's implicit relational patterns, often holding rigid, defensive, or distorted views that are resistant to change.

In parent-child psychotherapy, both the parent and the child participate, enabling the therapist to observe, reflect on, and mediate misinterpretations or disruptions in their interactions. This process can lead to corrective attachment experiences, enhanced parental mentalizing, improved emotional communication, and ultimately, better well-being and reduced symptoms in the child.

Parent-child psychotherapy is the treatment of choice for young children and parents who exhibit relational difficulties, unless there are contraindications as previously discussed. This approach not only addresses the symptoms but also strengthens the foundational parent-child relationship, which is essential for the child's overall development and emotional health.

Acknowledgements

The author wishes to express gratitude to Prof Judith Harel, Ph.D., and Prof Miri Keren, M.D. for their valuable review and comments on this chapter.

Conflict of interest

The author declares no conflict of interest.

Author details

Daphna Ginio Dollberg
Academic College of Tel-Aviv-Yaffo, Tel-Aviv, Israel

*Address all correspondence to: daphna@mta.ac.il

References

[1] Harel J et al. The child's active role in mother–child, father–child psychotherapy: A psychodynamic approach to the treatment of relational disturbances. Psychology and Psychotherapy: Theory, Research and Practice. 2006;**79**(1):23-36

[2] Opie J et al. Including the infant in family therapy and systemic practice: Charting a new frontier. Australian and New Zealand Journal of Family Therapy. 2023;**44**(4):554-564

[3] Shafi R et al. Evidence based dyadic therapies for 0-to 5-year-old children with emotional and behavioral difficulties. Frontiers in Psychiatry. 2019;**10**:677

[4] Lieberman AF. Infant-parent psychotherapy: Core concepts and current approaches. Handbook of Infant Mental Health. 2000;**2**:472-484

[5] Paris R, Spielman E, Bolton RE. Mother–infant psychotherapy: Examining the therapeutic process of change. Infant Mental Health Journal: Official Publication of The World Association for Infant Mental Health. 2009;**30**(3):301-319

[6] Rosenblum KL. Defining infant mental health. In: Sameroff AJ, McDonough SC, Rosenblum KL, editors. Treating Parent-Infant Relationship Problems. Guilford Press; 2004. pp. 43-75

[7] Sameroff AJ. Ports of entry and the dynamics of mother-infant interventions. In: Sameroff AJ, McDonough SC, Rosenblum KL, editors. Treating Parent-Infant Relationship Problems. Guilford Press; 2004. pp. 3-28

[8] Stern DN. The motherhood constellation: Therapeutic approaches to early relational problems. In: Sameroff AJ, McDonough SC, Rosenblum KL, editors. Treating Parent-Infant Relationship Problems. Guilford Press; 2004. pp. 29-42

[9] Lieberman AF, Van Horn P. Psychotherapy with Infants and Young Children: Repairing the Effects of Stress and Trauma on Early Attachment. New York, NY: Guilford Press; 2008

[10] Woodhead J. Trauma in the crucible of the parent–infant relationship: The baby's experience. In: Baradon T, editor. Relational Trauma in Infancy. New York, NY: Routledge; 2009. pp. 68-81

[11] Baradon T, Campbell C. Psychoanalytic Parent-Infant Psychotherapy and Mentalization: A Dialogue in Theory and Practice. New York, NY: Routledge; 2022

[12] Barrows P. The importance of the parental couple in parent–infant psychotherapy. In: Barlow J, Svanberg PO, editors. Keeping the Baby in Mind. New York, NY: Routledge; 2009. pp. 95-104

[13] Dugmore N. The Grandmaternal transference in parent–infant/child psychotherapy. Journal of Child Psychotherapy. 2013;**39**(1):59-75

[14] Fivaz-Depeursinge E, Philipp D. The Baby and the Couple: Understanding and Treating Young Families. Stroud: Routledge; 2014

[15] Hughes D, Golding KS, Hudson J. Dyadic developmental psychotherapy (DDP): The development of the theory, practice and research base. Adoption and Fostering. 2015;**39**(4):356-365

[16] Barlow J, Svanberg PO. Keeping the Baby in Mind. New York, NY: Routledge; 2009. pp. 1-14

[17] Belsky J, Jaffee SR. The multiple determinants of parenting. Developmental Psychopathology: Risk, Disorder, and Adaptation. 2015;**3**:38-85

[18] Barlow J et al. Parent–infant psychotherapy: A systematic review of the evidence for improving parental and infant mental health. Journal of Reproductive and Infant Psychology. 2016;**34**(5):464-482

[19] Sleed M et al. The Evidence-Base for psychodynamic interventions with children under 5 years of age and their caregivers: A systematic review and meta-analysis. Journal of Infant, Child & Adolescent Psychotherapy. 2023;**22**(3):179-214

[20] Barlow J et al. Health-led interventions in the early years to enhance infant and maternal mental health: A review of reviews. Child and Adolescent Mental Health. 2010;**15**(4):178-185

[21] Bakermans-Kranenburg MJ, Van Ijzendoorn MH, Juffer F. Less is more: Meta-analyses of sensitivity and attachment interventions in early childhood. Psychological Bulletin. 2003;**129**(2):195

[22] Bakermans-Kranenburg MJ, Van IJzendoorn MH, Juffer F. Disorganized infant attachment and preventive interventions: A review and meta-analysis. Infant Mental Health Journal: Official Publication of the World Association for Infant Mental Health. 2005;**26**(3):191-216

[23] Lieberman AF, Ippen CG, Van Horn P. Child-parent psychotherapy: 6-month follow-up of a randomized controlled trial. Journal of the American Academy of Child and Adolescent Psychiatry. 2006;**45**(8):913-918

[24] Guild DJ et al. Attachment and affect between mothers with depression and their children: Longitudinal outcomes of child parent psychotherapy. Research on Child and Adolescent Psychopathology. 2021;**49**:563-577

[25] Alto ME et al. Longitudinal outcomes of child parent psychotherapy: Response to commentaries. Research on Child and Adolescent Psychopathology. 2021;**49**:595-601

[26] Sullivan AD et al. Intervening after trauma: Child–parent psychotherapy treatment is associated with lower pediatric epigenetic age acceleration. Psychological Science. 2024;**35**(9):1062-1073

[27] Dollberg D et al. Maternal representations and mother-infant relational behavior following parent-infant psychotherapy. Journal of Infant, Child, and Adolescent Psychotherapy. 2013;**12**(3):190-206

[28] Dollberg DG, Keren M. Factors contributing to continuity and discontinuity in child psychopathology from infancy to childhood: An explorative study. Clinical Child Psychology and Psychiatry. 2020;**25**(4):891-908

[29] Flynn J, Falkenstien B. Healing attachment ruptures with safety and connection through play. In: Polyvagal Power in the Playroom. New York, NY: Routledge; 2024. pp. 59-70

[30] Hoffman KT et al. Changing toddlers' and preschoolers' attachment classifications: The circle of security intervention. Journal of Consulting and Clinical Psychology. 2006;**74**(6):1017

[31] Stern DN. The Motherhood Constellation: A Unified View of Parent-Infant Psychotherapy. New York, NY: International Universities Press; 1995

[32] Cohen N et al. Six-month follow-up of two mother-infant psychotherapies: Convergence of therapeutic outcomes. Infant Mental Health Journal. 2002;**23**(4):361-380

[33] Mäntymaa M et al. Shared pleasure in early mother–infant interaction: Predicting lower levels of emotional and behavioral problems in the child and protecting against the influence of parental psychopathology. Infant Mental Health Journal. 2015;**36**(2):223-237

[34] Camoirano A. Mentalizing makes parenting work: A review about parental reflective functioning and clinical interventions to improve it. Frontiers in Psychology. 2017;**8**:14

[35] Koren-Karie N, Oppenheim D. Parental insightfulness: Retrospect and prospect. Attachment & Human Development. 2018;**20**(3):223-236

[36] Slade A. Enhancing Attachment and Reflective Parenting in Clinical Practice: A Minding the Baby Approach. New York, NY: The Guilford Press; 2023

[37] Lojkasek M, Muir E, Cohen NJ. Watch, wait, and wonder: Infants as agents of change in a play-based approach to mother-infant psychotherapy. Play Therapy for Very Young Children. 2008;**2**:279-305

[38] Luyten P et al. Parental reflective functioning: Theory, research, and clinical applications. The Psychoanalytic Study of the Child. 2017;**70**(1):174-199

[39] McHale JP, Sirotkin YS. Coparenting in diverse family systems. In: Handbook of Parenting. New York, NY: Routledge; 2019. pp. 137-166

[40] de Greef M et al. Parent-professional alliance and outcomes of child, parent, and family treatment: A systematic review. Journal of Child and Family Studies. 2017;**26**:961-976

[41] Dowell KA, Ogles BM. The effects of parent participation on child psychotherapy outcome: A meta-analytic review. Journal of Child and Adolescence Psychology. 2010;**39**:151-162

[42] Haine-Schlagel R, Walsh NE. A review of parent participation engagement in child and family mental health treatment. Clinical Child and Family Psychology Review. 2015;**18**(5):133-150

[43] Chirico I et al. The focal play therapy: An empirical study on the parent–therapist alliance, parent-child interactions and parenting stress in a clinical sample of children and their parents. International Journal of Environmental Research and Public Health. 2020;**17**(22):8379

[44] Midgley N et al. Mentalization-Based Treatment for Children: A Time-Limited Approach. Washington, DC: American Psychological Association; 2017. pp. 163-183

[45] Lieberman AF, Van Horn P, Ippen CG. Toward evidence-based treatment: Child-parent psychotherapy with preschoolers exposed to marital violence. Journal of the American Academy of Child and Adolescent Psychiatry. 2005;**44**(12):1241-1248

[46] Fraiberg S. Clinical Studies in Infant Mental Health: The First Year of Life. London, UK: Tavistok Publishing; 1980

[47] Lachman A et al. Maternal shared pleasure, infant withdrawal, and developmental outcomes in a high risk setting in South Africa. Frontiers in Psychiatry. 2021;**12**:668009

[48] Powell B, Cooper G, Hoffman K, Marvin R. The circle of security project.

In: Oppenheim D, Goldsmith D, editors. Attachment Theory in Clinical Work with Children: Bridging the Gap between Research and Practice. New York, NY: Guilford Press; 2007. pp. 172-202

[49] Lyons-Ruth K et al. Implicit relational knowing: Its role in development and psychoanalytic treatment. Infant Mental Health Journal: Official Publication of The World Association for Infant Mental Health. 1998;**19**(3):282-289

[50] Boston Change Process Study Group. Change Process in Psychotherapy: Toward a New Paradigm. New York, NY: WW Norton and Company; 2010

[51] Avdi E et al. Studying the process of psychoanalytic parent–infant psychotherapy: Embodied and discursive aspects. Infant Mental Health Journal. 2020;**41**(5):589-602

[52] Coyne J, Powell B, Hoffman K, Cooper G. The circle of security. In: Zeanah C, editor. Handbook of Infant Mental Health. New York: Guilford Press; 2019. pp. 500-513

[53] Armstrong E et al. Parenting interventions for incarcerated parents to improve parenting knowledge and skills, parent well-being, and quality of the parent-child relationship: A systematic review and meta-analysis. Journal of Experimental Criminology. 2018;**14**:279-317

[54] Jones TL, Prinz RJ. Potential roles of parental self-efficacy in parent and child adjustment: A review. Clinical Psychology Review. 2005;**25**(3):341-363

[55] Ghosh Ippen C, Lieberman AF. Child–parent psychotherapy: Acknowledging ruptures in safety and rebuilding the protective shield. In: Osofsky JD et al., editors. WAIMH Handbook of Infant and Early Childhood Mental Health: Cultural Context, Prevention, Intervention, and Treatment. Vol. 2. Cham, Switzerland: Springer International Publishing; 2024. pp. 293-312

[56] Fonagy P, Allison E. The role of mentalizing and epistemic trust in the therapeutic relationship. Psychotherapy. 2014;**51**(3):372

[57] Sharp C et al. Learning to mentalize: A mediational approach for caregivers and therapists. Clinical Psychology: Science and Practice. 2020;**27**(3):50

[58] Dollberg DG, Behrendt H, Shorer M, Bamberger E. Integrative parent psychotherapy: Using the cyclical psychodynamics approach. Journal of Psychotherapy Integration. 2023;**33**:1-16

[59] Rosenbluth D. Transference in child psychotherapy. In: Key Papers from the Journal of Child Psychotherapy. New York, NY: Routledge; 2004. pp. 43-62

[60] ZERO TO THREE. DC:0-5: Diagnostic Classification of Mental Health and Developmental Disorders of Infancy and Early Childhood. Washington, DC: ZERO TO THREE Press; 2016

[61] Kagan J, Reznick JS, Clarke C, Snidman N, Garcia-Coll C. Behavioral inhibition to the unfamiliar. Child Development. 1984;**22**:2212-2225

[62] Fox NA et al. Annual research review: Developmental pathways linking early behavioral inhibition to later anxiety. Journal of Child Psychology and Psychiatry. 2023;**64**(4):537-561

Chapter 3

Perspective Chapter: Online Imago Relationship Therapy – Characteristics and Unexpected Advantages

Dorit Noy-Sharav

Abstract

The onset of COVID-19 compelled couple therapists to reassess their long-established methods of communicating with clients. Online therapy became the new available option and has maintained its popularity to this day. The technical difficulties and limitations of online psychotherapy and of couple therapy in particular, have been discussed at length in the literature. In this chapter, I will share my experience with three couples. Their specific stressful situations, addressed through Imago Relationship Therapy (IRT) via Zoom, enabled a deepening and acceleration of beneficial relationship processes, resulting in a flourishing phase in their relationships. The essential principles of IRT, which focus on "the space between," will be described. Issues such as the interplay between distance and unexpected intimacy, the benefit of transferring the secure setting from the clinic to the home and even the bedroom, and the opportunity to work with couples situated in different locations will be explored.

Keywords: online couple therapy, Imago Relational Therapy (IRT), couple relationship, intimacy versus distance in relationships, psychotherapy during COVID-19

1. Introduction

In the recent past, I was convinced that effective couple therapy, using Imago Relationship Therapy (IRT) can only reach its goals face-to-face in the familiar, holding setting of the clinic. With the onset of COVID-19, I first tried to continue meetings by extending the distance between clients and myself, keeping doors and windows open, etc. However, I soon had to realize that the pandemic and its dangers forced me to plunge into unfamiliar waters and adopt new technology. COVID-19 compelled all of us to be confined, either in solitude or in unusually long proximity to family members, which had become a source of stress and anxiety. This situation was bound to aggravate relationship problems in couples who were not accustomed to spend so much time in uninvited nearness. Many also faced the added stress of caring for children isolated from their usual social environment and struggling with remote learning [1, 2]. So, the need for available therapy was even higher than usual.

The first online meetings were upsetting—technicalities such as achieving continuous contact, sudden disconnections, freezing of the picture on screen, etc. I was also uncomfortable facing my own, not so flattering, reflection on the screen. All these required additional effort, and affected my attentiveness and my self-confidence as a therapist. I suspected that my clients, who were all much younger than me, are more proficient using this computer media than myself. However, as I decided to exit my comfort zone and open myself to new experiences, I discovered some surprising advantages that I wish to share hereafter.

2. Literature review

The special conditions that online therapy enforces on both therapists and clients have been much discussed in the literature. I will mention some that are specifically relevant to couple therapy. Rolnick et al. [3] mention the difficulty of noticing bodily reactions, and of keeping eye contact with each couple member when facing the screen. They also call attention to the fact that there is always conflict in the background when a couple or family turns to therapy, so the therapist has the role of minimizing hostility. This may be more difficult online, when the physiological reactions associated with arousal of anger are not easily detected. However, they also point out some advantages, such as the ability to keep therapy going when couple members cannot be in the same room, for objective reasons or because of marital conflicts that have led to temporary separation. Online couple therapy also offers the possibility of recording sessions and then replaying them so they become an opportunity for couple discussion and for practicing new skills [4].

Machluf et al. [5] surveyed a group of Israeli couple therapists' attitude and experience with online couple therapy. They reported an overall positive attitude toward online work with couples after experimenting with it during COVID-19. However, at that early point in time (2021), they predicted that using couple therapy online would diminish once the crisis was over, a prediction that was not confirmed to this day.

Kysley et al. [6], using cognitive educational therapy, have shown in their comparative study that there was no significant difference between couples randomly allocated to video conferencing or face-to-face meetings, on all therapy outcome measures, as well as on therapeutic alliance. Helps and Le Coyte Grinney [7], in their review of 31 papers, also concluded that online technologies for couple and family psychotherapy were found to be feasible, effective, and satisfying for users, similar to in-person psychotherapies. Another advantage that Rolnick et al. ([3], p. 200) mention, is what they refer to as "expanding the concept of home visits." This feature was also related to Ben-Ari as "a blurring of the boundaries between home and therapy setting" ([8], p. 244). I will later go deeper into this exciting new way of expanding intimacy when discussing my own cases. But first, some introduction of Imago Relationship Therapy (IRT), that I use in treating couples, as readers may not be familiar with it.

3. Imago Relationships Therapy (IRT)

Born from personal struggle and professional insight, Imago Relationship Therapy emerged as Harville Hendrix's brainchild. This American psychologist, once a Christian spiritual counselor, crafted IRT in response to his own marital failure and the challenges he witnessed in couple's therapy. Hendrix's primary goal was to help couples trapped in the disillusionment that follows when the intoxicating haze of romantic love dissipates. Joined by his second wife, LaKelly Hunt and Hendrix crystallized their shared wisdom in a trilogy of influential works: "Getting the Love You Want" [9], "Keeping the Love You Find" [10], and "Receiving Love" [11].

IRT is a tapestry woven from diverse threads of thought: developmental psychology, attachment theory, object relations, Martin Buber's philosophical insights, behavioral modification techniques, and neuropsychological research. At its core lies a profound truth: we are relational beings from birth, inevitably scarred by the imperfect nurturing of our caregivers. Yet, paradoxically, it is within the crucible of a loving relationship that we find our path to healing.

Central to IRT is the concept of the Imago—an unconscious blueprint of love formed in childhood. This internal image, Hendrix argues, is a complex fusion of our caregivers' positive and negative traits [9]. While we might believe we choose partners based on conscious criteria like attractiveness, status, or shared interests, a deeper force is at play. We were unconsciously drawn to those who resonate with our Imago, seeking that ineffable "click" of recognition.

This selection is not merely about recreating the familiar. It is a subconscious quest to mend childhood wounds and reclaim lost aspects of ourselves that were suppressed by socialization. As Winnicott poetically expressed, we yearn for a spouse who can "merge with the dream" [12]. Yet this very longing sets the stage for conflict, as each partner's expectations collide with the other's injured and sensitive areas.

IRT, however, reframes conflict as an opportunity—a catalyst for growth and deeper connection. In therapy sessions, couples face each other, symbolically occupying the "space within" their relationship. The therapist, more coach than traditional analyst, facilitates a structured dialog. Partners learn to truly listen, reflect, validate, and empathize, transforming accusatory deadlocks into voyages of mutual discovery.

This structured interaction, as Hendrix and his colleagues have shown [13, 14], guides couples from futile power struggles to a place of understanding and growing trust. IRT posits that the journey itself becomes a corrective emotional experience, a chance to rewrite old scripts and forge new patterns of connection [15].

Ultimately, IRT offers a vision of caring relationships as a crucible for mutual growth. Nurturing security within the relationship paves the way for healing, personal expansion, and the rekindling of joy—proving that our deepest wounds and greatest happiness often spring from the same source: our connections with others.

4. Case studies

4.1 Couple No. 1

Ella and Ron are a young couple in their late twenties, religious, married for 2 years. They sought therapy a few months earlier as their marriage reached a crisis point because of hardships in communicating and in the ability to respond to each other's emotional needs. The spouses came from very different family backgrounds. This divergence led to challenges in their married life as they attempted to reconcile their contrasting approaches to everyday activities. They struggled to find common ground in their preferred forms of recreation, ways of spending time together, and styles of hosting family members and friends. There were also serious difficulties in intimate relationships. During the first 2 months of therapy, we had already done some work, and a basic therapeutic relationship was established. The couple learned to use intentional dialog and listen to each other in a less judgmental way. Compared to other couples, Ella and Ron were less restricted by the COVID-19 curfew, since the husband worked in a required hospital job, and the wife continued her academic studies online. We decided to try and keep the therapy going by meeting online, and a meeting by Zoom was scheduled.

This was the first couple that I met online. The first meeting was a real shock for me—instead of the traditional setting of the couple in my clinic, sitting in armchairs face-to-face, and myself, close by, facing the space between them, I found myself facing the couple huddled under a blanket on their sofa, very close to each other. I experienced an unexpected intrusion into their intimacy that made me wonder about the implied message transmitted here. One could argue that their physical closeness was simply due to sharing one computer screen. In addition, when the therapy session takes place at the end of a long working day, what is more natural than huddling together on the living room sofa? Nevertheless, I sensed there was a message here, unconscious perhaps, of a readiness to enter a new stage in the process of moving closer, emotionally and sexually. This was confirmed as therapy reached a new depth, and we experienced real progress in the couple's relationship. An interesting indication occurred in a meeting that took place following the Jewish Passover Seder. This holiday typically involves a deeply entrenched tradition of family gatherings. I knew that being religiously orthodox, this couple would not have considered using computers for online family contact, on a High Holiday. In the following meeting, I asked how it was for them celebrating the Passover Seder without the traditional family reunion. I expected reactions of sadness and frustration, as was very common among friends and families and shared in the media. However, to my surprise, they reported a wonderful experience—just the two of them, without the oppressive family, without the usual negotiations about where and with whom to celebrate. They felt an exalting freedom and immense enjoyment. It seems that this forced isolation offered them an unexpected, guilt-free opportunity, to shed the family pressures, and to start developing some schedules of their own as a new family. This actually contributed to grounding the couple unit.

In the final session, 4 months later, Ella says that Ron's developing ability to see her and give her space, enables her to open-up to him. Ron expresses much love and compassion for Ella, and says how important it is for him that she feels held and secure, even if he does not always get what he needs. Ella speaks about the therapy as a lifeline thrown to them when they were struggling in turbulent waters.

4.2 Couple No. 2

Hanan and Amira, both divorced, are living together in Amira's house, along with her teenage children from a former marriage. Both come from an ultra-Orthodox background but have become secular and now lead free and even somewhat adventurous lives. They are veterans of couple therapy, as we have gone together through periods of crisis, loss of trust in the wake of Hanan's one-time infidelity, Amira's extreme mood swings and post-traumatic stress symptoms, and very challenging struggles with various financial and legal difficulties. The relationship with children from each spouse's previous marriages also required dealing with great complexities. The therapeutic relationship is strong, and they persevere in treatment despite the numerous upheavals they go through. The COVID-19 pandemic found them after another crisis that has caused emotional and physical distance between them.

With them, too, I found myself in the first Zoom meeting suddenly transported into their bedroom, as, according to them, it is the only room where they can close the door and talk privately. After I recaptured my balance, we continued the couple's work, which surprisingly progressed more easily than before.

Contrary to expectations, Amira's anxiety was not aggravated by the blocking of her efforts to find work due to COVID-19. In fact, she reported a feeling of calm and release, as there is nothing to rush for or try; everything is closed, and you can sleep and wake up whenever it is convenient. As unemployed due to COVID-19, she also became eligible for help from various organizations. Interestingly, contrary to what happens in many families, I did not hear complaints about dealing with her teenage children. Both of them reported that the children are enjoying the "vacation" and keeping themselves occupied.

Recently, Hanan had been working night shifts at a home for the elderly. The current situation unexpectedly provided more opportunities for Amira to spend time with him. He says that now when he returns from work in the morning—everyone is more available, and they also sleep part of the day, so opportunities for conversations and spending time together without pressure are created.

Through Imago work in couple sessions via Zoom, new possibilities opened up, and significant insights emerged—regarding the meaning of friendly and emotional closeness versus sexual closeness and regarding the barriers that block their ability to enjoy either tender or erotic touch.

With them too, I felt that the invitation to the bedroom constitutes, perhaps unconsciously, an invitation to in-depth work in these areas. In fact, a breakthrough occurred that allowed them to experience an enjoyable and more varied sexuality. More trust was created, and a new place opened for emotional closeness and the possibility of sharing experiences. The emotional connection among us also warmed up, and I felt that despite our being physically in different locations, there was more closeness in the meetings. For example, although they expressed that I missed the face-to-face meetings, they were concerned about my safety, as, due to my age, I was in a high-risk group. Amira says—I tell my friends, who are much younger, that I have to protect my couple therapist's safety, so we will continue online meetings until COVID-19 passes.

The experience with both couples raises some questions for which I do not have a well-grounded answer. What in this situation enabled this enhanced openness? True, in both cases we were not talking about couples enclosed in isolation or full lockdown, as at least one of the partners continues their usual work habits. Couple No. 2 was also not very strict about social distancing, in line with their permissive lifestyle in many areas, so they also did not reach "cabin fever," the feeling of suffocation from the forced enclosure.

Is this then a stage in treatment that was bound to happen even without the special conditions of online therapy? Or did the change in setting—the special form of distance/closeness between the therapist and patients—enable or accelerate the change? Did my flexibility as a therapist willingness to experiment with new forms of contact, serve as a model for the couple to experiment with novel practices and try out new skills?

In the last Zoom session with couple No. 2, which took place at a stage where there was already the beginning of the opening up of the curfew and a gradual return to regular everyday frameworks, Amira gave an interesting answer to this question. She says, and Hanan nods his agreement—"These were the best months in our life in recent years. The bonus we experienced is like we took this safe place that was your room, and we brought the treatment home and even to bed, which is a bit stressful for me but it is our place, and that's a very big plus."

4.3 Couple No. 3

In presenting this couple, who started online therapy while being many miles apart, I will also go into some principles of IRT that are based on Neuropsychological studies.

Alon and Melissa started Imago couple therapy when they were situated in two different countries. Melissa had returned to her country of origin and to her parental family after a serious crisis in their relationship. Alon and Melissa are a couple in their thirties, married several years ago, and had been planning to undergo fertility treatments in Israel. However, Alon suddenly got cold feet and requested to halt the process. Melissa was deeply hurt and decided to leave the country and their relationship. Alon did not stop her. However, he started individual psychotherapy, and several months later, having reached some insights into his own motivations and defenses, he initiated couple therapy online, and Melissa agreed. The sessions were carried out in the English language, although this is not the mother tongue for either the therapist or clients, and it is the only common language for all. Despite these challenges, a secure setting was gradually created for both spouses. They were asked to use time in the session to recover cherished memories from the beginning of their romantic relationship. Additionally, it was suggested that this crisis could serve as a welcome opportunity for positive change and growth.

In the dialog Melissa expressed her frustration about Alon's overdependence upon his family of origin, by which she felt rejected—"We are in the backseat of our marriage, we are not the driver." In ensuing dialogs, Alon worked on his growing need to become more independent, and shed the role of being the youngest child, pampered but also managed and directed by his elders.

Two months into therapy Alon, decided to join Melissa in her own country, and since, then the meetings continued in their apartment, with both sharing the same computer screen. They usually sat close to each other on a sofa in their living room, and as is my practice with all couples, they were instructed to face one another and not the therapist on the screen, looking into each other's eyes. Eye contact was shown by recent advances in neuroscience to activate mirror neurons [16]. These neurons form part of a larger circuit that enables a person to resonate with another person's feelings through the process of interoception [17, 18]. This resonance enables two persons to "feel felt" by each other, though each retains a sense of differentiation [19]. As they were sitting not too close to the camera, I could also see more of their bodies and their apartment background, and sometimes, their cat joined our session, curling up close to Melissa.

As they began establishing their new life together as a couple, Alon started to voice his anxiety about the impending IVF treatments. During their time in Israel, Alon had grappled with confusion and anger, questioning why they could not conceive naturally. He directed his frustration at nature, God, and fate. Alon was apprehensive about the responsibilities ahead, particularly about providing emotional support to Melissa throughout the complex and unpredictable IVF process.

At that time, he felt overwhelmed but was not accustomed to sharing his feelings, so he had to escape. Now Melissa's listening and validating him with true empathy encouraged him in his personal development. Alon says "Even now there are fears, all these stressing procedures we have to undergo, can I really become a father? but now I want to cope, not to avoid dealing with all these challenges."

As they became more proficient in the dialog and the relationship between them warmed up, Melissa began expressing the pain she had experienced about Alon's sudden change of heart. As Alon, on his part, listened, reflected, and validated her feelings with deepening empathy, she could open up more, and we could relate her disappointment in the marriage and her dramatic act of leaving the relationship and the country to early wounding in her childhood and adolescence relationship with her mother. Her separation anxiety, her questioning of her own worth, and her well-entrenched defensive strategies of avoiding close relations all were now re-experienced *in vivo* in the couple's relationship. These were topics that she had been working on in individual therapy on and off for years before. However, working together with Alon by means of IRT offered a new experience, a recurrent corrective emotional experience [15, 20, 21]. In spite of the rigidity characteristic of painful memories, brain research literature shows that the brain has a surprising degree of neuroplasticity, and the retelling and re-experiencing of painful memories in a different, secure, loving atmosphere has the potential of reshaping memory traces, so the biochemical synaptic signature in the brain is rewritten [22–24]. New neural connections in the brain stabilize and thicken, so that perception of self and other changes, and novel behavior patterns are established [15].

To help transform their fears into positive expectations, the therapist employed another technique, of providing sentence stems for Melissa to complete. Therapist says—"I can imagine myself holding my baby." Melissa repeats and continues—"he is warm, soft, smells good, I sense Alon sitting with me, holding us both, I feel happy, secure"... and so on. Appropriate sentence stems were also used with Alon to help him visualize himself as a caring, responsible, and well-appreciated father.

When they decided to take a break from therapy, Alon and Melissa were more grounded in their relationship and more secure in each other's love and support. They have started IVF procedures and have been able to accept help from their families, while concomitantly making their own decisions and plans.

5. Conclusion

The author's experiences with these three couples illustrate the efficacy and potential of online Imago Relationship Therapy (IRT) in treating couples.

Despite technical challenges, these cases demonstrate that a productive therapeutic relationship can develop online. Moreover, key IRT principles—such as focusing on the "space between" and facilitating appreciative, empathetic dialog—can be effectively actualized in a virtual setting.

Another significant advantage is the ability to provide such therapy to couples who are geographically separated.

An unanticipated benefit emerged: the transfer of the safe, empathic communication space from the therapist's office to the couple's home environment. This shift in setting facilitated surprisingly deep explorations of intimacy and trust issues within the couple relationships.

Nevertheless, many therapists and couples feel that online therapy lacks what Resnick and Resnick [25] aptly term the "animal presence," inherent in sharing a physical space. Therefore, I recommend that, wherever possible, at least the first meeting, and occasional subsequent meetings be conducted offline, in the usual setting. This could balance the benefits of online therapy with the advantages of face-to-face interactions.

Author details

Dorit Noy-Sharav
Private Practitioner in Clinical Psychology, Jerusalem, Israel

*Address all correspondence to: noysharavdo@gmail.com

References

[1] Crawford P, Crawford JO. Cabin Fever: Surviving Lockdown in the Coronavirus Pandemic. Bingley: Emerald Group Publishing; 2021

[2] Arenas-Arroyo E, Fernandez-Kranz D, Nollenberger N. Intimate partner violence under forced cohabitation and economic stress: Evidence from the COVID-19 pandemic. Journal of Public Economics. 2021;**194**:104350. DOI: 10.1016/j.jpubeco.2020.104350

[3] Rolnick A, Leighton A, Weinberg H. An introduction to online couple and family therapy. In: Weinberg H, Rolnick A, Leighton A, editors. Advances in Online Therapy. New York: Routledge; 2023. pp. 199-240. DOI: 10.4324/9781003205029-24

[4] Hellman S, Cole D, Rolnick A. Gottman method: Assessment and treatment in the age of online therapy. In: Weinberg H, Rolnick A, Leighton A, editors. Advances in Online Therapy: Emergence of a New Paradigm. London and New York: Routledge; 2023. pp. 230-239. DOI: 10.4324/9781003205029

[5] Machluf R, Abba Daleski M, Shahar B, Kula O, Bar-Kalifa E. Couples therapists' attitudes toward online therapy during the COVID-19 crisis. Family Process. 2021;**61**(1):146-154. DOI: 10.1111/famp.12647

[6] Kysely A, Bishop B, Kane R, Cheng M, De Palma M, Rooney R. Expectations and experiences of couples receiving therapy through videoconferencing: A qualitative study. Frontiers in Psychology. 2020;**10**:2992. DOI: 10.3389/fpsyg.2019.02992

[7] Helps S, Le Coyte Grinney M. Synchronous digital couple and family psychotherapy: A meta-narrative review. Journal of Family Therapy. 2021;**43**(2):183-214. DOI: 10.1111/1467-6427.12333

[8] Ben-Ari K. Healing through the screen: Using Imago relationship therapy online. In: Weinberg H, Rolnick A, Leighton A, editors. Advances in Online Therapy: Emergence of a New Paradigm. London and New York: Routledge; 2023. pp. 240-248. DOI: 10.4324/9781003205029

[9] Hendrix H, LaKelly Hunt H. Getting the Love You Want. revised ed. St. New York: Martin Griffin; 2018

[10] Hendrix H. Keeping the Love You Find. A Guide for Singles. New York: Pocket Books; 1992

[11] Hendrix H, Lakelly HH. Receiving Love. New York: Atria Books; 2004

[12] Winnicott DH. Marion Milner: Critical notice of "on not being able to paint". In: Winnicott C, Shepherd R, Davis M, editors. Psycho-Analytic Explorations. Cambridge, Massachusetts: Harvard University Press; 1989. pp. 390-392

[13] Hendrix H, LaKelly Hunt H, Luquet W, Carlson J. Using the Imago dialogue to deepen couples therapy. The Journal of Individual Psychology. 2015;**71**(3):253-272. DOI: 10.1353/jip.2015.0029

[14] Hunt LH, Hendrix H. The practice of wonder towards psychological well-being. Voices, the Art and Science of Psychotherapy. 2016;**52**(2):61-67

[15] Noy-Sharav D. Corrective emotional experience in couple therapy: An integration between Imago approach and psychoanalytic concepts in

light of neuropsychological studies. Journal of Couple & Relationship Therapy. 2021;**20**(4):319-339. DOI: 10.1080/15332691.2020.1860178

[16] Rizzolatti G, Fadiga L, Fogassi L, Gallese V. Premotor cortex and the recognition of motor actions. Brain Research. Cognitive Brain Research. 1996;**3**(2):131-141. DOI: 10.1016/0926-6410(95)00038-0

[17] Laurie Carr MI, Marie-Charlotte D, Gian LL. Neural mechanisms of empathy in humans: A relay from neural systems for imitation to limbic areas. Biological Sciences. 2003;**100**(9):5497-5502. DOI: 10.1073/pnas.0935845100

[18] Critchley HD, Garfinkel SN. Interoception and emotion. Current Opinion in Psychology. 2017;**17**:7-14. DOI: 10.1016/j.copsyc.2017.04.020

[19] Siegel DJ. Pocket Guide to Interpersonal Neurobiology: An Integrative Handbook of the Mind. New York: W.W. Norton & Company; 2012

[20] Alexander FG, French TM. Psychoanalytic Therapy: Principles and Applications. Lincoln and London: Ronald; 1946

[21] Winnicott DW. The Child and the Family, and the Child and the Outside World. Massachusetts: Tavistock Publications; 1957

[22] Kandel E. A new intellectual framework for psychiatry. The American Journal of Psychiatry. 1998;**155**(4):457-469. DOI: 10.1176/ajp.155.4.457

[23] Lane R, Ryan L, Nadel L, Grinberg L. Memory reconsolidation, emotional arousal and the process of change in psychotherapy: New insights from brain science. The Behavioral and Brain Sciences. 2015;**38**:1-64. DOI: 10.1017/S0140525X14000041

[24] Mehuron K. Memory reconsolidation: Hope for a terminal analysis? Journal of Cognition and Neuroethics. 2019;**6**(1):57-73

[25] Resnick RF, Resnick RW. Online contemporary couples gestalt therapy "two become one"—And then there are none! From a Fusion model to a connection model of relationships. In: Weinberg H, Rolnick A, Leighton A, editors. Advances in Online Therapy. New York: Routledge; 2023. p. 255

Chapter 4

Perspective Chapter: Presuppositions Psychiatrists Must Make to Do Most Effective Psychotherapy

Edmund G. Howe III

Abstract

I explore here several presuppositions that therapists may make when they conduct psychotherapy. These presuppositions often guide the interventions they pursue. Yet, some presuppositions provide greater guidance than others, and some do not always apply. Therapists must decide in these cases when to make critical exceptions. Therapists pre-considering the presuppositions they are making and which should allow exceptions may enable them to provide their patients with better treatment. This piece presents eleven critical presuppositions that therapists should pre-consider when treating their patients. Nine apply to their helping patients make changes within themselves. Two apply to interactions that patients may have with others. After presenting each presupposition, I shall provide a real case example illustrating its application. Finally, following each case example, I shall provide a succinct summary of how therapists might best apply the presupposition in their clinical practice. This focus here is on presuppositions often not specifically identified. Therapists recognizing these presuppositions explicitly and then more deeply considering them should, it is hoped, increase therapists' success with their patients.

Keywords: presuppositions, psychotherapy, humor, validation, vulnerability, ambiguity

1. Introduction

Effective psychotherapy requires above all a safe, warm, and trusting patient/therapist relationship [1]. Only then can patients maximally understand the deeper meanings of their therapists' interventions and respond maximally to them. When this relationship is optimal, several different kinds of therapeutic endeavors may then be most successful. Therapists usually, naturally, have the interpersonal strengths to establish this necessary, more intimate bonding. Their desire to achieve and experience this exceptional closeness with others is likely, of course, what moves many to enter this field. There are, however, notwithstanding this likelihood, numerous subtle, less self-evident ways in which therapists may particularly most enhance their having an optimal underlying relationship with their patients and conversely, there are several ways, less obvious, in which they inadvertently may impair it, sometimes even stripping their therapy of its efficacy in no more than an ill-advised moment. Just one sentence that therapists speak, intended to help, may affect some patients adversely. This especially may occur of course with more fragile patients; however, this characteristic, "fragile", is taken to apply. These patients may exceptionally need their therapists to exercise forethought regarding their presuppositions and as a result of these prior reflections have a greater sensitivity to these patients' more hidden emotional vulnerabilities. Therapists identifying these risks better as a result of examining beforehand the presuppositions underlying their practice may enable them to better avoid these unintended mishaps.

In this chapter, therefore, I will present multiple presuppositions that may help prevent this risk. I will do this in two main sections. The first section will involve presuppositions that therapists should consider when they seek to help patients make changes within themselves. The second will involve presuppositions regarding interactions their patients have with others.

After I present each presupposition and discuss how it in general applies, I will follow this with a real case illustrating how in practice this presupposition might apply. I will then prior to going on to discuss the next presupposition put in a few sentences in summary form the core of its essential clinical use, wording this summary as a "take-home" key instruction. In instances in which a presupposition often already made in clinical practice may be likely to be faulty and thus cause therapy to go awry, I will suggest an alternative presupposition that therapists might use to replace this suboptimal presupposition.

2. Presuppositions that involve patients changing themselves

2.1 There is some validity to every patient view

Many patients seeking psychotherapy fear being judged by their therapist. Their having this fear is exceptionally plausible because they know that they may disclose in their therapy past behaviors they regard still with shame. They may also not disclose this fear, in part because they regard their having this fear as an additional ground on which they should feel shame. It may be critical therefore for therapists to make clear to their patients that they can expect them to fully respect both them and their views. One way in which they can do this is to convey that they see and share their patients' conviction that they have some valid basis for every view they have, illogical though these patients' view may be in its entirety when they first view it. Therapists should convey this validity early on and ideally from the start of their interactions. Therapists can point out this validity when they first hear it, and they can also then go beyond this and note how they see this valid ground as both an insight and, more broadly, a strength. Even if the therapist ca not see the validity of a patient's view initially, they should seek to discern this. *Some* valid aspects are always there. Their seeking to discern this will itself convey to the patient their respect, thus increasing their trust.

An example illustrating this practice is how a therapist might approach parents whose presenting problem is stress due to their having mentally and physically disowned a teenage child after he informed them that he is gay. The optimal therapeutic goal here may be for both these parents and this adolescent to be able to resume a

DOI: http://dx.doi.org/10.5772/intechopen.1006961

mutually fulfilling and caring relationship with each other enjoyed prior to their child sharing this.

The therapist's initial goal is to gain these parents' trust. This is particularly important in this case because these parents may be anticipating that the therapist will negatively judge them for disowning their son. An optimal way in which therapists may approach overcoming their fear and gaining their trust is paradoxical. The therapist may state initially that the therapist imagines that these parents responded as strongly and adamantly as they have due to their exceptionally great love for their child.

This may seem on its face problematic. Some may believe that therapists making this statement will support and reinforce these parents responding as they have. The therapist's ultimate goal is, however, the opposite—to restore, if possible, this mutually caring relationship *by first indicating to the parents that the therapist values them*. The therapist's doing this and forming an initial alliance in this way by perceiving or inferring a positive quality within them and then relating this to them may make the difference in whether or not in the end therapists succeed in achieving this goal.

Take-home presupposition: Patients *always* have *some* valid rationale underlying what they think or feel, regardless of what this is. The therapist's task is to identify this validity and then communicate this. If therapists cannot see this validity, their coming to see it is the first thing they should try to do. It may be only then that their patients can see them as working together as if side by side and in a joint alliance.

2.2 Every weakness is at the same time a strength

Patients inevitably reveal in time some aspect of themselves that they regard as a weakness that limits them. Often these patients compare themselves to others and then find themselves lacking, relative to these others. An example here is their seeing themselves as overly sensitive to slights because after they see themselves as having been slighted, they hurt for an especially long time thereafter. They may recall this slight painfully and obsess about it so much that this destroys the quality of their lives.

A presupposition that therapists might adopt generally and especially apply in these cases is that every quality that the patient sees as a weakness—about which they may be right—is at this same time also in some way a strength. This may be the case, even if throughout the patient's whole life, they have never seen this quality in this positive way. It, to them, may always have remained hidden.

An example here is the tendency noted above, they are having a heightened sensitivity to real and perceived slights. Their exceptional sensitivity is at this same time, likely, a profound, perhaps innate gift and asset. It may allow them, more than most other people to pick up on when others feel hurt, even just slightly, and for only an instant, when others lack the capacity they have to perceive this. This exceptional sensitivity to their own and others' emotions could then enable these patients to be remarkably effective therapists, especially, perhaps, to patients who especially need therapists who can recognize when they are hurting and do not voice this themselves. Such manifestations of more subtle signs of hurting may be no more, for instance, than their casting their eyes downward for no more than a fraction of a second. Therapists can point then how what this patient has always seen as only a liability is also a strength, thus reframing this liability in a different way such that now such patient can view their exceptional sensitivity not with shame but with pride.

Take-home presupposition: Every weakness is at the same time a strength. Therapists can and should always imagine and share this with their patients.

Therapists can even add that they believe these qualities are innate and thus that they regard them and other people who like them have this asset as lucky to have been born with this strength.

2.3 Encourage patients to cherish their vulnerabilities

We are all in many ways far from perfect. We tend then often to seek to hide what we see as our vulnerabilities from others. We also may unintentionally tend to hide these limitations from ourselves by consciously or unconsciously denying them. Both endeavors may require quite an effort. We, as our patients, may even make up falsehoods to hide from others our vulnerabilities. We may particularly do this with loved ones because we care most about how they regard us. Therapists may then again go the opposite way and encourage patients to accept their vulnerabilities and indeed even cherish them as part of who and how they uniquely are.

I think here of a patient most vulnerable to panic attacks that could come on at any time but especially when he was in crowded places. His son then went away to college and this patient, his father, shortly afterward drove alone for the first time to visit his son there. His son asked him to join him and some friends to have dinner in a restaurant. This father was afraid, however, that in this setting he would have a panic attack and thus told his son that he was too tired to go from his long drive. He wanted his son, he said, to see him only as a strong father in every way.

We in therapy discussed as an alternative his being open with his son about this vulnerability and, as well, his accepting this about himself and accepting himself just as he is. We all, we discussed, have facets of ourselves that we see as suboptimal. These qualities may make us feel more vulnerable. We still can accept and cherish, though, that this is how we are. Thus, by acknowledging that he had panic attacks to his son, he could also model for him how he, too, could accept and even cherish himself just as he is. We hope and strive to love our children unconditionally, we agreed. We can thus strive, too, to love ourselves in this way. This includes our accepting our vulnerabilities as who we uniquely are.

Take-home presupposition: Our vulnerabilities are part of who are. We need not seek to hide them from others. Rather, we can acknowledge them openly even to those whom we love most.

2.4 Do not understate how patients hurt

Patients often experience discomfort that to them is nothing short of profound pain. Often the extent of their pain cannot be easily imagined. A question often difficult for therapists is what words to use when referring to patients' pain. Some may believe that patients' pain in some cases is, likely, less than it is and thus that the patient is exaggerating it when they report it. This may be the case. Some patients embellish. They may have a flair for the dramatic and, sadly, then also, lose credibility with others because they overstate their troubles. This is then an issue that therapists should sometimes address, and how they do this may be most challenging because even just raising this possibility may to these patients question how they see themselves and are.

Therapists may fear that their using the word "pain" may reinforce patients' pain. If, then, therapists not only underestimate patients' pain but also refer to it as "discomfort", not pain, they may, due to their doing this, lose patients' trust. This is an example of how just one wrong word can undo therapists' credibility, a possibility I alluded to previously.

They alternatively, however, may speak of patients' pain as "pain", despite their fear, to retain patients' trust. More generally, of course, for this same reason, there is much to be said for therapists using the same words patients use when describing their symptoms. This does not risk their patients feeling trivialized, talked down to, or disrespected.

Take-home presupposition: Patients may have what they experience or take to be severe pain. When therapists are in doubt and think this pain is more likely to be just discomfort, they should use the word "pain", not "discomfort", regardless. They may fear that their doing this will reinforce these patients' pain, but therapists' not risking losing their patients' trust is more important.

2.5 Anticipate ambiguity

Much of what we say has ambiguity. This is the nature of words. The possibilities of patients hearing what we *do not* mean lie far beyond what we can within ourselves, in advance, always imagine [2]. This possibility is illustrated by a therapist who said simply, "What can I do for you," a not uncommon, introductory comment. The patient, misinterpreting this therapist's intent in his own, idiosyncratic way, responded with hostility. "How should I know?" he retorted. "You're the therapist!" That is, even everyday comments may have other plausible, adverse interpretations. Every statement conveying that a glass is half full, using this as a generic example, also conveys that the glass is half empty, a possible absence that, metaphorically speaking, a patient may not want to hear.

Therapists can avoid or limit this risk of patients seeing latent criticism or disapproval in what therapists say by seeking to anticipate this risk and if identifying such a second meaning, sharing this with patients beforehand and clarifying what the therapist *does not* mean prior to saying it. A tragic example of how one therapist's not doing this may have caused profound harm is the following: This therapist had just attended a session on medical ethics that emphasized the importance of providers fully informing patients so that they can then best exercise their autonomy. He feared that a patient who had to remain always in a hospital to survive due to her illness might not know that she could refuse further life-maintaining treatment. He told her therefore that she could free her family from coming to see her so that they could then go on with their lives by refusing life-prolonging interventions if she wanted to. His intent was, though, not to suggest this. It was just to be sure that she knew this.

She and all her family had been happy with their lives, all said emphatically, prior to this time. She declined further treatment the next day and died.

Take-home presupposition: Seek to identify in advance all statements one will make that could have toxic ambiguity. When this is the case, share this awareness with the patient and clarify the meaning one intends and the meaning one does not. If patients hear a toxic ambiguity that the therapist has not pre-recognized, seek to recognize any signs of the patient feeling hurt, inquire as to why, and once understanding this, apologize. Say here *not* "I am sorry you felt hurt," but "I am sorry *I* hurt *you*." The former fails to recognize yourself as the "hurter". The latter recognizes and owns up to the fact that it was you who caused the hurt even though you did not mean to. By doing this, you avoid presenting a second possible ambiguity—that the patient's feeling hurt was *another* product of the patient's emotional illness.

2.6 Spot and note for patients whenever they make excuses

Patients often set up for themselves standards that are impossible to meet. They may reveal this by regularly adding mitigating excuses when they report with guilt things they have done or did not do that they believe they should not have or should have done. "I did this and it was wrong. But I was depressed at the time," they might, for example, say—all in an attempt to reduce their shame and self-blame. Therapists might best remain alert to this at all times, because each time patients make for themselves an excuse and this goes unchallenged, the presupposition that underlies their doing this is strengthened, reinforced, and harder for them, thereafter, even with the help of their therapist, to reverse. Their erroneous presupposition is that they should not make mistakes, as opposed to their noting and again accepting that they will always do things they later regret because we are imperfect humans.

Therapists optimally may tell them then that their goal for themselves rather than making repeated excuses should be to accept in advance that they will always make mistakes and not at these times make excuses for themselves. Rather, they do what they can to make amends and, if appropriate, apologize.

Take-home presupposition: Interrupt patients on the spot whenever they self-excuse. Note why you are interrupting, namely, to catch the patient's excuse-making while this is hot and they can recall it. Apologize for the connotative hurt of interrupting, but state that to help the patient, they believe that they have no other choice. Share with these patients that their continuing to make up excuses for not living up to standards they cannot meet will only increase their ongoing practice of heaping onto themselves unwarranted guilt. Rather, they can say as they recognize their doing this that they are only human, and thus need not make excuses for what they have done and will continue to do.

2.7 Tell stories

There are of course many ways to do therapy, but for patients more fragile, again, howsoever defined, therapists telling stories that have therapeutic insights embedded within them may be particularly beneficial. Patients may see within these stories what they need to know whereas if the therapist says this directly, the patient's emotional defenses may block them from understanding and then "getting" what they most need to know [3]. A paradigmatic message they may not be able to get from straightforward explanations, for example, is that they have, already within themselves, the capacity to transcend their present difficulties. If the therapist says this directly, the patient may merely dismiss this as their therapist's just saying this when the therapist does not know how truly impaired, they are. They, in addition to inferring this, may then also lose some trust in their therapist.

I learned this story-telling approach firsthand from Milton Erickson in his house in Phoenix long ago. He pioneered the use of conversational suggestion and indirect hypnosis [4]. As a result, there is now still an annual convention at which therapists present each year new therapeutic approaches some therapists among them have developed that are built on his early work. In addition to learning from him with a group, I saw him once individually in his living room in my twenties. He believed, I believe, that the best use of this time for me would be for him to tell me a story. Thus, he told me about a young man, my age, who had gotten in all sorts of trouble with the law until he fell in love with a woman. Then, over time, bit by bit, he did better, eventually becoming a respected mayor in his small city. Erickson did not know much about me then, but he imagined, I suspect, that this story would unconsciously benefit me by conveying to me through this story how I, too, could succeed regardless of where I was then when I saw him.

I have adopted this same practice of telling a story when one occurs to me and this seems possibly optimal. I feel secure enough in doing this that when medical students shadow me doing therapy, I may even then ask them if they know a story involving themselves or someone else that relates to the patient's circumstances—like that of a person being able to prevail at least somewhat and go on after having a life-shattering experience. One student shared a story involving her mother. Her mother had had breast cancer and then had a bilateral mastectomy. She said thereafter, her daughter reported, that this was not so bad because she "had little there to begin with," laughing with her daughter as she said this. This story, I believe, based on the later report of the patient she was shadowing, inspired him. It moved him, he said, to imagine that he, too, could cope better with the harm he had undergone.

Take-home presupposition: Share stories regarding oneself or others. Say in advance why you are doing this so the patient does not misconstrue your presuppositions. In the above example of the medical student shadowing, for example, you do not intend to imply that the patient can and thus should do better. You are offering it merely because the patient *may* get something out of it though you can not know in advance what this might be. You can not predict this.

2.8 Risk using humor

Humor is risky. All humor may of course rest on some underlying reality that poses some kind of amusing irony or rests upon some laugh-inducing inconsistency. This is what makes humor funny. This irony and/or another factor that tends to evoke laughter may however at this same time pose risks. The patient is for example hurting. Thus, the therapist's using humor at this time may to the patient be insensitive. Yet, humor can provide also both a different and greater perspective on what the patient is experiencing. This new insight may provide greater meaning to patients regarding both their symptoms and their lives [5, 6]. Victor Frankel pointed this out after he had lost several people he most loved and had been himself in a concentration camp. He later developed a new approach to psychotherapy called logotherapy. This therapy focuses on the meaning patients find in their lives. He emphasized here the singular gains also of using humor [7].

Therapists can most safely use humor by laughing at themselves. Here, a risk exists also. Therapists may risk their patients, due to their therapists' poking fun at themselves seeing them as being less competent and possibly insufficiently competent than to be able to successfully treat them. Patients may also see their therapist using humor as insensitive as stated above. Here, though, therapists may reduce this risk by asking patients before using humor whether this would be something these patients would welcome and want.

This use may too deepen the patient/therapist relationship. I recall as an example a time I laughed at myself telling a patient that though I had just called him over the phone I had misplaced his number during our conversation. I asked him then whether he could give it to me again. He then responded as if giving me a gift by asking me if I knew how to best hammer in a nail. I said I did not know this. He then told me that you tap it in just slightly at first and only then hammer it fully in.

The best end result of using humor I believe is patients becoming willing to poke fun at their therapists. This outcome implies, of course, a prerequisite degree of shared, felt equality, which is I would propose an inherit goal that should underly all therapy. This goal is for all patients and therapists to always be aware that while they are interacting in a mutually agreed upon role at the time, once outside that role they are both equal human beings, facing, for example, together, upcoming death.

I with one patient for example had at an earlier time helped him obtain an appointment with another medical provider because he was exceptionally suffering and needed this. I should note here before proceeding that what I did here, using my professional identity to seek exceptional care for this patient some would find ethically problematic. I in any case asked this same patient again at a subsequent time whether he would like me to do this for the same reason. Again. He said, "No thanks, I'll keep trying myself for a bit, but if I do not succeed, I'll *sic* you on him again!" He laughed as he said this, fully aware that he was then poking fun at me.

Take-home presupposition: Consider using humor when this possibility arises. Consider then also, if thinking of using humor, of also asking these patients beforehand if this would or would not be something they would want. Appreciate that humor may be among the most healing of interventions and this may, too, enhance therapists' relationships with patients.

2.9 Discuss religion if and when patients want this

We as a profession are sometimes cautioned and counseled to not discuss religion with patients, but rather, to refer patients wanting to discuss religion to clergypersons. They, after all, have expertise in their religion's views, and they, too, have special training in how best to discuss this. I have found, however, contrary to this advice, as have some others, that my discussing patients' religious concerns with them when they raise these during psychotherapy may benefit them and, again, the relationship immensely [8]. Explicitly or implicitly in some way rejecting these discussions risks, I believe, on the other hand, patients perceiving this as an emotional rejection. They may view their religious beliefs as what makes them who they are.

I discovered this for the first time when I was teaching a patient a meditation technique. I asked her to envision her being at a place like a beach on which she could feel relaxed. To my surprise, she closed her eyes, relaxed for a bit and then told me that she had imagined the Virgin Mary holding and comforting her. I afterward suggested she enhance her experience using all her senses. She then imagined Mary whispering caring thoughts and even giving her peppermint life savers to taste and swallow.

This patient thereafter repeatedly shared her fears as of being beset by the devil, what had triggered these fears and how they left her even thinking of ending her life to escape them. Our discussing this openly helped her, I believe, to no longer have these fears to at least this extent over time. I have come too to discuss her religious beliefs with her for positive gains. She is exceptionally, for example, altruistic. I have said at times that I believe her caring for others is what Jesus would want. I also introduced her belief in Jesus when she feels wronged by others due to no fault of her own. She would obsess and painfully feel this thereafter. I would suggest after we looked at this together to see if there was any way she too was at fault that Jesus had been so wronged too. This enabled her it seemed to find the pain of others' wronging her more bearable and made it persist for a much shorter time.

Take-home presupposition: Do not invariably shy away from discussing religion. Again, therapists may ask, "Would you like us to discuss the religious concerns you just noted or would you prefer discussing this with a clergy person?" Even just asking

DOI: http://dx.doi.org/10.5772/intechopen.1006961

patients this question could, of course, to a degree place them in a bind. They might find it hard to say, "No, I'd prefer to discuss this with a clergyperson." Therapists might therefore add, "Either is just fine with me. Patients differ." This may make it easier for patients to decline.

3. Presuppositions regarding patients interacting with others

3.1 Instruct patients not to say "you should..."

The word "should" in any context is likely to cause and evoke an oppositional response. Patients may use this word in regard to themselves, on one hand, to capture and expressing their personal aspirations and, on the other, more ominously to blame themselves after they have done or not done something that they believe they should have. This self-blaming outcome from looking back is always plausible. It thus can be most self-destructive. This source of shame is ever present because retrospectively we can always see past options we could have taken but did not or did not see at the time. A heart-breaking example of this can always occur after a loved one has committed suicide. We could have called, could have called earlier or could have taken innumerable steps that could have possibly altered this outcome.

Similarly, if we say "should" to others, this may be destructive as well. Others may feel berated. If referring to the past, the range of negative judgments is again limitless. Saying others should have always places them on guard. Some reflexively judge. They may think and say, for example, routinely after another speaks, "It is good that you did that." The obverse implication of this, this other may not miss. The person who just made this judgment of good would next time be that they did something bad. People who judge may do this compulsively.

If then one's patient does judge others reflexively, this compulsive proclivity may result in others self-protectively distancing themselves from these patients. They may do this regardless of how they appear. These patients may never know or even imagine this. Their therapists must, then, alert them to this. If they do not, perhaps no one will.

Take-home presupposition: Presume that all expressions and even shielded references to a should are toxic whether patients use this word against themselves or to judge others. Patients may not know that this offends others or that their doing this keeps others at a distance and in this way decreases the quality of their lives.

Some people speak a native foreign language that has endings that convey an imperative. Translating their native language, they may too tell others what they should do. Therapists seeing such patients may want them too to inquire about this.

3.2 Give priority to others' emotions over ethics

People find sacred their personal moral views. They may see these as part of who they are. Thus, when ethical issues arise that affect patients, therapists then may want to support them by supporting their ethics. This may, though, be a mistake. People imposing on others their own ethics may result in these others again severing their relationships with them. These others may be the most precious to them. Therapists should therefore forewarn their patients of this risk, ideally, prior to their patients conveying their moral views when they have not been asked and as a result, losing these others' love irreversibly. Also.

Their criticizing family members whom they most love may, for example, have these disastrous endings. I think here of grandparents visiting their adult children, now also parents themselves, and telling these parents that with their grandchildren they are too strict or lax. Their criticisms may range most widely. They may include, for example, that these parents, their own children, are not inculcating their children with religion enough. Grandparents doing this whenever they visit may find to their dismay, even horror that they are no longer invited as much.

Therapists should forewarn these patients therefore that when they critique their children's ways of raising their grandchildren, they might prioritize not offending their adult children emotionally over telling them what they believe for their grandchildren is right. Therapists may extend this advice then to all persons. Others too may feel in response hurt and anger, but not share this but withdraw from the relationship. Patients should know this and why. They should know that our emotions tend to respond more quickly and strongly and thus are likely to most often prevail.

Take-home presupposition: Alert patients to the reality that people do not take advice nor criticism easily—at least unless they have asked for it. In this sense, therapy is misleading, People want help, then their therapists help. They want them to tell them, hopefully, most gently, what they are doing wrong.

This is the opposite of how everyday relationships work. Grandparents could risk saying, as gently as they can, "Would you want me to share with you a thought I have regarding how you might parent better?" Grandparents sharing just this may, however, be much too much. This may be a tough pill for grandparents to swallow. The challenge in these cases, they should also know, is to do what is least bad as opposed to what they see as being best.

4. Conclusion

When therapists conduct therapy, they are often guided by multiple presuppositions. Some of these they may be aware of. Others, they may not. Some of these presuppositions may also be more helpful than others. Some may though also in exceptional cases do harm.

This chapter highlights key, sometimes unrecognized presuppositions that therapists may or may not tend to follow. Therapists knowing and reflecting on all these presuppositions ideally before they apply them may hopefully enhance their success. The presuppositions here recognized and discussed are generally those less self-evident but take-home synopses are provided nonetheless to assist therapists in applying them.

Conflicts of interest

The author declares no conflict of interest.

Disclaimer

The opinions and assertions expressed herein are those of the author(s) and do not reflect the official policy or position of the Uniformed Services University of the Health Sciences or the Department of Defense." Neither I nor my family members have a financial interest in any commercial product, service, or organization providing financial support for this research. References to non-Federal entities or products do not constitute or imply a Department of Defense or Uniformed Services University of the Health Sciences endorsement. This work was prepared by a military or civilian employee of the US Government as part of the individual's official duties and therefore is in the public domain and does not possess copyright protection (public domain information may be freely distributed and copied; however, as a courtesy it is requested that the Uniformed Services University and the author be given an appropriate acknowledgement).

Author details

Edmund G. Howe III
Center for the Study of Traumatic Stress, Uniformed Services University, Walter Reed National Military Medical Center, Bethesda, Maryland, USA

*Address all correspondence to: edmund.howe@usuhs.edu

References

[1] Podolan M, Gelo OCG. The functions of safety in psychotherapy: An integrative theoretical perspective across therapeutic schools. Clinical Neuropsychiatry. 2023;**20**(3):193-204. DOI: 10.36131/cnfioritieditore20230304

[2] Everaert J. Interpretation of ambiguity in depression. Current Opinion in Psychology. 2021;**41**:9-14. DOI: 10.1016/j.copsyc.2021.01.003

[3] Kabrel M, Tulver K, Aru J. The journey within: Mental navigation as a novel framework for understanding psychotherapeutic transformation. BMC Psychiatry. 2024;**24**(1):91. DOI: 10.1186/s12888-024-05522-8

[4] Fabre RC. Ericksonian family constellation work with metaphoric objects: Discussion and illustration. The International Journal of Clinical and Experimental Hypnosis. 2020;**68**(4):483-492. DOI: 10.1080/00207144.2020.1802734

[5] Sarink FSM, García-Montes JM. Humor interventions in psychotherapy and their effect on levels of depression and anxiety in adult clients, a systematic review. Frontiers in Psychiatry. 2023;**13**:1049476. DOI: 10.3389/fpsyt.2022.1049476

[6] Berger P, Bitsch F, Falkenberg I. Humor in psychiatry: Lessons from neuroscience, psychopathology, and treatment research. Frontiers in Psychiatry. 2021;**12**:681903. DOI: 10.3389/fpsyt.2021.681903

[7] Bushkin H, van Niekerk R, Stroud L. Searching for meaning in chaos: Viktor Frankl's story. Europe's Journal of Psychology. 2021;**17**(3):233-242. Published 2021 Aug 31. DOI: 10.5964/ejop.5439

[8] Captari LE, Hook JN, Hoyt W, Davis DE, McElroy-Heltzel SE, Worthington Jr EL. Integrating clients' religion and spirituality within psychotherapy: A comprehensive meta-analysis. Journal of Clinical Psychology. Nov 2018;**74**(11):1938-1951

Chapter 5

Perspective Chapter: Psychological Capacity – A Key Factor in Mental Health Disorders

Abdullah AlKhathami

Abstract

Psychological capacity encompasses cognitive, emotional, behavioral, social, motivational, and coping abilities crucial for effective functioning and well-being. These capacities play a pivotal role in mental health, influencing resilience, self-efficacy, and overall psychological stability. Theoretical frameworks like cognitive processing, emotional intelligence, and resilience theory explain how individuals harness these capacities to manage stress and adapt to challenges. Psychological capacity is influenced by biological, environmental, and social factors, and its compression can lead to increased vulnerability to mental health disorders, such as depression and anxiety. Enhancing psychological capacity through targeted interventions—ranging from cognitive-behavioral therapy to lifestyle adjustments—can improve resilience and mental health outcomes. Recognizing early warning signs of psychological capacity compression and understanding its interaction with mental health disturbances are critical for timely intervention. Integrating pharmacological and non-pharmacological strategies, alongside regular medical consultations, can provide comprehensive management of psychological stress and enhance overall well-being. The Root and Branches Theory underscores the importance of addressing the root causes of psychological capacity compression to alleviate symptoms of mental distress, promoting a holistic approach to mental health care.

Keywords: psychological capacity, mental health, stress management, root and branches theory, well-being

1. Introduction

Psychological capacity, a multifaceted concept, encompasses an individual's cognitive, emotional, behavioral, social, motivational, and coping abilities. These capacities are fundamental to adaptive functioning and overall well-being, enabling individuals to perform cognitive tasks, regulate emotions, and manage interpersonal interactions effectively [1]. Cognitive functions, such as memory, attention, problem-solving, and decision-making, are crucial components of psychological capacity, influencing how individuals learn and reason [2]. Emotional intelligence, including self-awareness, empathy, and emotional regulation, plays a significant role in managing social interactions and personal well-being [3].

The importance of psychological capacity extends to behavioral aspects like self-control, adaptability, and resilience, which help individuals navigate stress and adversity. Social capacities, including interpersonal and communication skills, are essential for building supportive relationships and resolving conflicts. Motivational capacities, such as goal setting, intrinsic motivation, and self-efficacy, drive personal and professional achievements. Coping capacities, involving stress management and problem-solving skills, are vital for maintaining mental health.

Understanding the theoretical frameworks that explain psychological capacity is crucial for developing effective interventions. These frameworks include cognitive theories, emotional intelligence theory, resilience theory, social cognitive theory, and self-determination theory, among others. Each provides insights into how individuals harness their capacities to manage stress and enhance well-being.

Psychological capacity is influenced by a range of factors, including biological, environmental, and social elements. These factors can either enhance or compress psychological capacity, affecting an individual's ability to cope with stress and maintain mental health. Chronic stress, adverse childhood experiences, lack of social support, and physical health problems are among the factors that can compress psychological capacity, leading to increased vulnerability to mental health disorders, such as depression and anxiety.

Enhancing psychological capacity through targeted interventions can improve resilience and mental health outcomes. These interventions include cognitive-behavioral therapy, mindfulness-based stress reduction, lifestyle adjustments, and building social support. Recognizing early warning signs of psychological capacity compression and understanding its interaction with mental health disturbances are critical for timely intervention [4–6].

The Root and Branches Theory offers a holistic approach to addressing psychological capacity compression, emphasizing the need to focus on root causes rather than merely managing symptoms. By enhancing overall psychological resilience and balance, individuals can achieve better mental health and well-being. This manuscript explores the components, influences, and interventions related to psychological capacity, providing a comprehensive understanding of its critical role in mental health.

2. Understanding psychological capacity

2.1 Introduction

Psychological capacity refers to an individual's mental abilities to perform cognitive tasks, regulate emotions, and manage social interactions. It includes cognitive functions like memory, attention, problem-solving, and decision-making, as well as emotional and social intelligence. This capacity is crucial for coping with stress, adaptive functioning, and personal well-being. It also supports intellectual functioning, including learning, reasoning, and problem-solving. Mental health, in contrast, is a state of well-being where individuals realize their potential, manage life stresses, work productively, and contribute to society [2].

2.2 Psychological capacity components

2.2.1 Psychological capacity has six components

Cognitive capacity: Cognitive capacity includes attention, memory, executive functioning, and perception. Attention enables focus on tasks, while memory involves storing and recalling information. Executive functioning refers to higher-level processes like planning and decision-making. Perception helps interpret sensory information [6, 7].

Emotional capacity: Emotional capacity includes emotional regulation, self-awareness, and empathy. Emotional regulation allows healthy management of emotions, self-awareness involves understanding one's own feelings and traits, and empathy is the ability to understand and share others' emotions [4–8].

Behavioral capacity: This text covers self-control, adaptability, and resilience. Self-control involves regulating behavior and impulses, adaptability is the ability to adjust to changes, and resilience is the capacity to recover from stress and setbacks [9].

Social capacity: Social capacity comprises interpersonal skills, communication skills, and conflict resolution. Interpersonal skills facilitate effective interaction with others, communication skills ensure clear expression of thoughts and needs, and conflict resolution involves managing disputes constructively [10].

Motivational capacity: Motivational capacity includes goal setting, intrinsic motivation, and self-efficacy. Goal setting involves pursuing personal and professional goals, intrinsic motivation refers to engaging in activities for personal satisfaction, and self-efficacy is the belief in one's ability to succeed [11].

Coping components: Coping components include stress management, problem-solving skills, and support seeking. Stress management involves strategies to handle stress, problem-solving skills help resolve complex issues, and support seeking refers to reaching out for help when needed. These components are shown in **Table 1**.

2.3 Link between psychological capacity and well-being

Psychological capacity, which includes resilience, self-efficacy, coping mechanisms, and emotional regulation, is crucial for well-being. Resilience helps individuals recover from adversity, while self-efficacy boosts confidence and promotes better mental health. Effective coping strategies reduce stress, and emotional regulation ensures emotional stability, all of which enhance well-being. Additionally, psychological capacity significantly impacts resilience, enabling individuals to adapt to stress

Component	Description
Cognitive Capacity	Attention, memory, executive functioning, and perception
Emotional Capacity	Emotional regulation, self-awareness, and empathy
Behavioral Capacity	Self-control, adaptability, and resilience
Social Capacity	Interpersonal skills, communication skills, and conflict resolution
Motivational Capacity	Goal setting, intrinsic motivation, and self-efficacy
Coping Capacity	Stress management, problem-solving skills, and support seeking

Table 1.
Psychological capacity components.

and challenges. Strengthening psychological capacity through interventions that promote self-efficacy, optimism, and hope can improve resilience, highlighting the importance of psychological resources in maintaining well-being.

3. Psychological capacity compression

3.1 Causes of psychological capacity compression

Psychological capacity compression refers to the diminishing ability of individuals to manage psychological stressors and maintain mental well-being. Various factors contribute to this phenomenon, often intersecting and compounding the effects, as shown in **Table 2**.

3.2 Psychological capacity compression impacts

Psychological capacity compression can negatively impact various competencies. Here's how each of the competencies might be affected:

3.2.1 Cognitive functioning

- *Memory*: Compressed psychological capacity can lead to difficulties in retaining and recalling information, which can affect both short-term and long-term memory.

- *Attention*: Sustained attention and the ability to focus on tasks may be impaired, leading to distractibility and reduced productivity.

- *Problem-solving*: The ability to think clearly and solve problems logically can be hindered, resulting in slower processing speed and ineffective decision-making.

Cause	Description
Chronic Stress	Prolonged exposure to stressors, leading to diminished psychological resilience and coping capacity [12].
Socioeconomic Factors	Lower socioeconomic status associated with increased stressors, such as financial instability, lack of access to health care, and educational disadvantages, which can compress psychological capacity [13].
Environmental Factors	Exposure to adverse environmental conditions, such as noise pollution, overcrowding, and poor living conditions, can contribute to stress and cognitive disruption affect psychological capacity negatively [14].
Trauma and Adverse Childhood Experiences	Early exposure to trauma resulting in long-term mental health issues and reduced resilience [15].
Lack of Social Support	Social support is a critical buffer against stress. The absence of a supportive social network can lead to exacerbating stress and reducing mental resilience, feelings of isolation and helplessness [16].
Physical Health Problems	Chronic physical health issues increasing psychological stress and decreasing coping ability [17].

Table 2.
Causes of psychological capacity compression.

- *Decision-making*: Under stress, decision-making may become more impulsive or indecisive, with a tendency to avoid complex choices or rely on less optimal solutions.

3.2.2 Emotional regulation

The ability to manage and respond to emotional experiences may be compromised, leading to increased vulnerability to emotional outbursts, mood swings, or emotional numbness. This can result in heightened sensitivity to stress, anxiety, or depression.

3.2.3 Behavioral control

Compressed psychological capacity can impair self-control, making it difficult to manage impulses and resist harmful behaviors. This may lead to increased risk-taking, trouble maintaining routines, and reliance on unhealthy coping strategies like substance use.

3.2.4 Social skills

The ability to interact and communicate effectively with others may decline, leading to social withdrawal, misunderstandings, or conflicts in relationships. It contributes to isolation or loneliness, further exacerbating psychological stress.

3.3 Protective vs. risk factors for psychological capacity stress (compression)

Psychological capacity, comprising cognitive, emotional, and social resources, is essential for handling challenges. It can be strengthened by protective factors like social support and positive coping, or compressed by risk factors like stress and trauma. Recognizing these influences is key to developing interventions that boost capacity and improve mental well-being [18], as shown in **Table 3**.

Factor type	Protective factors	Risk factors
Biological Factors	Genetic resilience, brain plasticity	Family history of mental health disorders, neurotransmitter imbalances
Psychological Factors	Emotional regulation, cognitive flexibility	Difficulty in managing emotions, negative thinking patterns
Behavioral Factors	Healthy coping mechanisms, regular exercise	Maladaptive behaviors, substance abuse
Social Factors	Strong social support, effective communication	Social isolation, poor communication skills
Environmental Factors	Stable environment, access to resources	Exposure to violence, lack of access to resources

Table 3.
Protective vs. risk factors for psychological capacity.

4. Early warning signs and symptoms of psychological capacity compression

Recognizing early signs of psychological capacity compression is key to identifying stress and mental health struggles. Early intervention can prevent worsening and improve outcomes, as shown in **Table 4**.

Recognizing these signs early is vital for intervention and support. If someone is exhibiting these symptoms, it is important to seek help from a mental health professional to address these issues promptly and effectively.

5. Psychological capacity compression is the root of depression and anxiety types "the root and branches theory"

5.1 Psychological capacity stress (compression)

When psychological capacity is compressed, it can lead to dysregulation in the body's hormonal balance, particularly involving adrenaline, cortisol, and happiness hormones like serotonin, dopamine, and endorphins [19]. This is illustrated in **Figure 1**.

5.2 Link psychological capacity compression and hormonal changes

1. *Hypothalamic-pituitary-adrenal (HPA) axis*: Chronic stress activates the hypothalamic-pituitary-adrenal axis, causing prolonged cortisol release, which disrupts the balance of adrenaline and happiness hormones [20].

2. *Neuroplasticity*: Stress impairs brain plasticity, affecting mood-regulating areas like the prefrontal cortex, which hampers the production of happiness hormones [21].

3. *Inflammation*: Chronic stress induces inflammation, reducing serotonin and dopamine levels, contributing to mood disorders [22].

4. *Behavioral changes*: Psychological capacity compression often leads to unhealthy behaviors (poor diet, lack of exercise, and substance abuse), further disrupting hormonal balance and worsening stress effects [23].

5.3 "Root and branches theory" (new theory by AlKhathami Abdullah, 2024)

5.3.1 Empirical evidence

The "Root and Branches Theory" suggests that psychological stress is a core underlying cause of various mental health disorders. By addressing this stress, symptoms can be alleviated, and recurrence can be prevented. Empirical research supports this theory, demonstrating that managing chronic stress through therapeutic interventions significantly reduces symptoms of anxiety, depression, and other related disorders.

Category	Symptoms
Emotional Symptoms	*Increased Irritability and Anger:* Frequent or intense episodes of irritability and anger, often disproportionate to the situation.
	Persistent Sadness or Anxiety: Continuous feelings of sadness, anxiety without a clear cause.
	Mood Swings: Rapid and unexplained shifts in mood, from high energy to feeling down.
Cognitive Symptoms	*Difficulty Concentrating:* Trouble focusing on tasks, making decisions, or remembering information.
	Negative Thought Patterns: Increased prevalence of pessimistic thoughts, self-doubt, or feelings of hopelessness.
	Indecisiveness: Difficulty in making even simple decisions.
Behavioral Symptoms	*Withdrawal from Social Activities:* Avoidance of social interactions, hobbies, or activities that were previously enjoyable.
	Changes in Eating or Sleeping Patterns: Significant changes in appetite or sleep, such as eating too much or too little, or experiencing insomnia or oversleeping.
	Decreased Performance: Noticeable drop in performance at work or school, often accompanied by a lack of motivation.
Physical Symptoms	*Chronic Fatigue:* Persistent feelings of exhaustion not alleviated by rest.
	Unexplained Aches and Pains: Physical symptoms, such as headaches, muscle tension, or stomach problems, without a clear medical cause.
	Frequent Illness: Weakened immune system, leading to more frequent colds or other illnesses.
Social Symptoms	*Isolation:* Increased tendency to isolate oneself from friends, family, and colleagues.
	Conflict in Relationships: More frequent conflicts or tension in personal and professional relationships.
	Dependence on Substances: Increased use of alcohol, drugs, or other substances as a coping mechanism.
Psychological Symptoms	*Feeling Overwhelmed:* Persistent feelings of being overwhelmed by everyday tasks and responsibilities.
	Loss of Interest: Reduced interest in activities and hobbies that were once enjoyed.
	Emotional Numbness: Feeling emotionally detached or numb, struggling to experience a full range of emotions.
Warning Signs of Severe Distress	*Suicidal Thoughts or Behavior:* Expressions of wanting to harm oneself or others, or actual attempts to do so, are critical warning signs that require immediate attention.
	Panic Attacks: Sudden episodes of intense fear or discomfort, often accompanied by physical symptoms like heart palpitations, shortness of breath, or dizziness.

Table 4.
Early warning signs and symptoms of psychological capacity stress.

- *Psychological stress and depression*: Chronic stress is a key predictor of depression, overwhelming an individual's psychological capacity and leading to mood dysregulation [22].

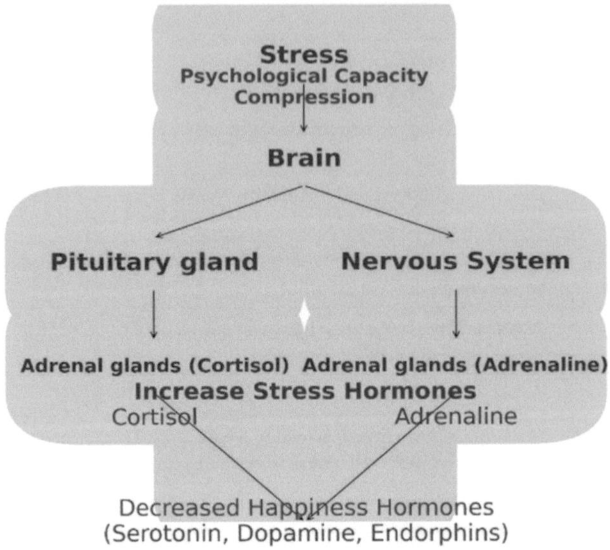

Figure 1.
Psychological capacity compression impacts.

- *Stress and anxiety disorders*: Chronic stress is closely linked to anxiety disorders like generalized anxiety disorder (GAD), panic disorder, and phobias. Stress alters neurochemical pathways, particularly in the HPA axis, contributing to anxiety [20].

- *Obsessive-compulsive disorder (OCD) and stress*: Stress exacerbates OCD symptoms by intensifying anxiety and compulsions. Effective stress management techniques, such as exposure and response prevention, are crucial [24].

- *Panic attacks and phobias*: Chronic stress often triggers or worsens panic attacks and phobias by causing hyperarousal of the autonomic nervous system [25].

- *Hormonal imbalance due to stress*: Chronic stress disrupts the HPA axis, leading to elevated cortisol and adrenaline levels, which negatively impact mood regulation [20].

- *Neuroplasticity and chronic stress*: Chronic stress can lead to hippocampal atrophy, impairing cognitive function and increasing vulnerability to mood disorders [20].

Overall, addressing stress as a root cause is essential for alleviating symptoms and preventing the recurrence of these disorders.

5.4 Visual representation of the root and branches theory

Psychological capacity compression, caused by reduced happiness hormones and increased stress hormones like adrenaline and cortisol, is visualized as the root of a tree. The symptoms—such as depression, anxiety disorders, OCD, phobias, and panic attacks—are depicted as branches, as illustrated in **Figure 2**. These symptoms vary among individuals, with some experiencing one or multiple issues. The "root and

Figure 2.
Visual representation of the "Root and Branches Theory" represents psychological capacity compression.

branches" theory highlights the importance of holistic mental health treatment that focuses on addressing the root cause—hormonal balance—rather than just treating individual symptoms, as supported by the common use of antidepressants.

5.5 Cultural considerations in psychological capacity compression

The expression of psychological distress varies across cultures. For instance, in collectivist cultures, stress may be managed through community and family support, which can buffer against psychological capacity compression [26]. Conversely, in cultures emphasizing individualism, people may feel pressured to manage stress alone, potentially increasing psychological burden. Additionally, some cultures may express psychological distress through physical symptoms, a phenomenon known as somatization [27].

Therefore, Clinicians must be culturally competent, understanding how cultural beliefs affect mental health and treatment preferences. This may involve collaborating with cultural mediators or integrating traditional practices into treatment plans to ensure they are culturally appropriate and effective.

5.6 Assessing psychological capacity compression in clinical settings

Psychological capacity compression has traditionally been assessed in clinical settings using a range of methods. These include clinical interviews, self-report questionnaires, such as the Perceived Stress Scale (PSS) [28] and the Connor-Davidson Resilience Scale (CD-RISC) [29], as well as psychological assessments like the Beck Depression Inventory (BDI) [30] and measures of Heart Rate Variability (HRV) [31]. Additionally, observational methods have been utilized.

Recently, the assessment of psychological capacity compression has become more practical and effective with the implementation of the "Stress Assessment Screening Step" within the AlKhathami Approach (Step 2). This method has shown high validity and reliability, surpassing the performance of expert psychiatrists and well-established tools like the PHQ-9 (Patient Health Questionnaire-9) and GAD-7 (Generalized Anxiety Disorder-7) questionnaires [32].

5.7 Influences on psychological capacity compression and mental health outcomes

Psychological capacity compression refers to the diminished ability of individuals to manage stress, emotions, and cognitive demands due to internal or external pressures. This phenomenon has significant implications for mental health outcomes, as it impacts resilience, coping mechanisms, and overall psychological well-being.

Psychological capacity compression and mental health outcomes are influenced by genetics, personality traits, and life experiences:

- *Genetics and psychological capacity compression*: Genetic factors, such as variations in serotonin transporter genes, can increase susceptibility to stress, heightening the risk of psychological capacity compression [33].

- *Personality traits and stress resilience*: Personality traits like neuroticism increase vulnerability to anxiety and depression, while traits like resilience and optimism protect psychological capacity [34].

- *Life experiences impact on stress and mental health*: Adverse childhood experiences can lead to long-term changes in the brain's stress response, increasing vulnerability to psychological capacity compression [15]. Positive life experiences can enhance psychological resilience [35].

5.8 Indicators and signs of psychological compression

Psychological compression refers to the state where an individual's mental capacity to manage stress, emotions, and cognitive demands is overwhelmed. Recognizing its indicators and signs is crucial for early intervention and effective support.

When stress hormones like adrenaline and cortisol rise, and the levels of happiness hormones decrease due to psychological capacity compression, there are three key signs and three indicators of these changes in the body:

5.8.1 Indicators of psychological stress

Consider psychological stress as a contributing factor in a patient's condition, if they exhibit any of the following:

- Persistent physical symptoms or an uncontrolled chronic illness, such as diabetes, hypertension, irritable bowel syndrome, headache, low back pain … ..etc.

- Frequent visits to healthcare providers

- Difficulty with sleep

If any of these indicators is present, psychological stress may play a significant role in the patient's overall health.

5.8.2 Signs of psychological stress

i. Sleep disturbances: Difficulty in falling asleep, staying asleep, or experiencing restless sleep, interrupted sleep [36].

ii. Decline in performance and concentration: Reduced ability to focus, decreased productivity, and impaired cognitive functions [5].

iii. Impact on social relationships: Increased irritability, easy anger, and a tendency to withdraw and prefer isolation [37].

These indicators reflect the body's response to heightened stress and the subsequent imbalance in hormone levels, affecting overall well-being and daily functioning.

Practical point: Assessing psychological capacity

When you meet a patient or a person, assess their psychological capacity by asking the following questions:

1. Sleep:
   - *Are you experiencing any difficulties with sleep?*
2. Performance and Concentration:
   - *Have you noticed any decline in your performance or concentration?*
3. Relationship:
   - *Is there easy anger or do you prefer isolation?*

If the answer to any of these questions is "yes," it indicates that the person might be suffering from psychological stress.

6. Integrated mental healthcare management

6.1 Combining therapy approach

A comprehensive approach to mental health care involves combining interventions that target various domains, including biological, psychological, behavioral, social, and environmental factors. These interventions are categorized into four key domains: pharmacological, non-pharmacological, nutritional, and routine visits. When used together, these strategies offer a holistic and effective way to manage a wide range of health conditions, often resulting in superior health outcomes compared to a single-treatment approach [38].

Pharmacological treatments provide immediate relief from symptoms, while non-pharmacological and nutritional strategies contribute to long-term benefits and help prevent recurrence [39]. This combined approach is particularly beneficial for patients with multiple health conditions, as it can enhance overall health and well-being [40]. Additionally, it serves as a preventive measure, reducing the likelihood of developing chronic diseases and potentially leading to a reduction or cessation of medication [41].

To optimize mental health outcomes, it is essential to balance pharmacological and non-pharmacological treatments while addressing individual patient needs and potential barriers. Integrated treatment strategies frequently result in improved health outcomes and a higher quality of life [42]. Lifestyle interventions, such as regular physical activity and a balanced diet, play a crucial role in mitigating the negative effects of stress on hormonal balance, thereby enhancing mental health outcomes [43], look at **Figure 3**, and are demonstrated in **Table 5**.

6.2 Psychological capacity compression: "A container analogy"

The process of psychological capacity compression can be represented by a container filled with water that is being externally compressed, with stones inside it taking up

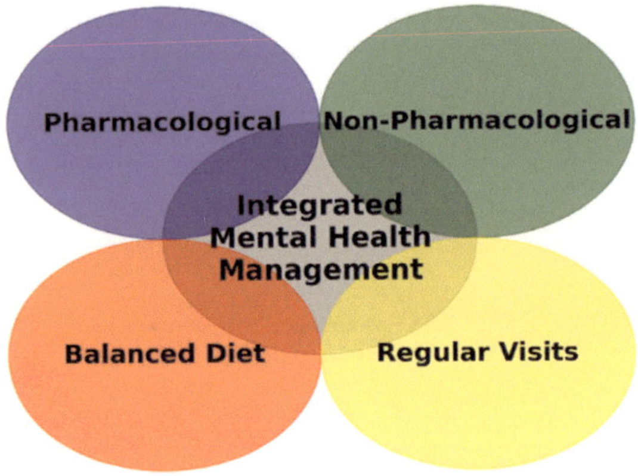

Figure 3.
A balanced integrated management approach.

Intervention	Description
Medication Management	Antidepressant usage.
Enhancing Happiness Hormone Production	Lifestyle adjustments, such as promoting regular physical activity like daily walking.
Preventing Breakdown of Happiness Hormones	Avoiding harmful arguments, and self-blame by focusing on positive ownership of things.
Balanced Nutrition	A healthy diet that includes magnesium and vitamins B1, B6, B12, and D.
Regular Doctor Visits	Administer for 2 to 3 weeks until remission is achieved, then continue to complete a total of 9 months since remission. After that, gradually reduce the dosage until discontinuation.

Table 5.
Enhancing psychological capacity: Interventions and strategies.

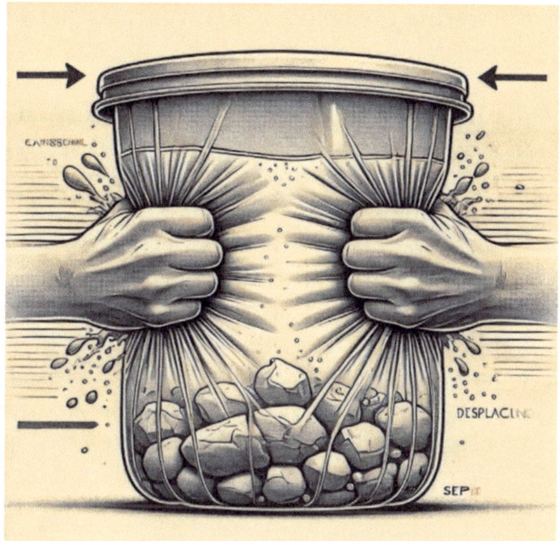

Figure 4.
Psychological capacity compression: "A Container Analogy."

space within the container. This analogy illustrates that the effective capacity of the container decreases due to the principle of buoyancy (Archimedes' law). As the external pressure on the container increases (representing life stressors), and the volume of the submerged stones inside it grows (symbolizing the decrease in happiness hormones and the increase in stress hormones), more water is displaced from the container. This displaced water represents the symptoms that the person experiences, as illustrated in **Figure 4**.

6.3 Restoring psychological capacity: "A factory approach to mental well-being"

The process of addressing psychological capacity compression can be represented by restoring the compressed container to its natural capacity. This can be illustrated as the operation of a factory:

1. Producing happiness hormones: Achieved through regular walking.

2. Maintaining happiness hormones: By avoiding provocative discussions and not self-blaming; instead, focusing on existing blessings, such as the ability to hear, see, and care for oneself without relying on others.

3. Reducing stress hormones: Through relaxation techniques like deep breathing.

4. Providing raw materials for happiness hormone production: By ensuring a healthy diet and essential minerals, such as magnesium and vitamins B1, B6, B12, and D.

5. Preventing the breakdown of happiness hormones: Using antidepressants, when necessary, in moderate to severe cases.

6. Supporting and monitoring the body's needs: With regular follow-ups with a therapist.

This approach emphasizes the holistic management of mental well-being, likening it to the continuous and systematic operations within a factory.

6.4 Pharmacological management

Goal: To prevent the breakdown of happiness hormones.

Antidepressants, such as SSRIs (selective serotonin reuptake inhibitors) and SNRIs (serotonin and norepinephrine reuptake inhibitors), are first-line treatments for depression and anxiety, and commonly prescribed. They are used to manage emotional dysregulation, improve mood, motivation, and treat trauma-related disorders [44]. However, pharmacological treatments like SSRIs are effective but may cause side effects such as sexual dysfunction and weight gain should be considered. Atypical antidepressants like bupropion are alternatives for patients who do not tolerate SSRIs or SNRIs.

6.5 Non-pharmacological management

Goal: To increase happiness hormones and lower stress hormones.

- *Enhancing happiness hormone production*: Promoting the production of happiness hormones can be achieved through regular activities like walking and encouraging hobbies and interests, which help improve mood. However, patient compliance is essential, as severe depression or anxiety may impede adherence to these lifestyle interventions [45].

- *Preventing breakdown of happiness hormones*: To maintain happiness hormones, it's important to avoid harmful arguments and self-blame. Instead, focus on taking positive and constructive ownership of situations [46].

- *Lowering stress hormones*: Reducing stress hormones can be achieved by incorporating relaxation techniques, such as deep breathing exercises [47].

- *Improving conflict resolution and problem-solving abilities*: Techniques such as narrative therapy can be effective in resolving interpersonal conflicts, which in turn helps reduce the likelihood of stress development [48].

6.6 Healthy diet for supporting happiness hormones

Goal: To promote the production of happiness hormones and overall mental well-being.

6.6.1 Natural diet recommendations for optimal health

- Use of natural oils: It is recommended to incorporate natural oils, such as olive oil and natural animal fats, while avoiding hydrogenated oils. Research indicates that olive oil, a key component of the Mediterranean diet, is associated with a reduced risk of cardiovascular disease and improved mental health. Conversely, hydrogenated oils, which contain trans fats, are linked to an increased risk of heart disease and have a negative impact on mental health [49, 50].

- Full-fat products vs. low-fat products: It is preferable to avoid low-fat products and instead opt for full-fat natural products. Studies suggest that full-fat dairy consumption may be associated with a lower risk of obesity and metabolic disease, along with benefits for mental health [51].

- Natural sweeteners: Reducing the intake of sweets and processed sugars is advised, replacing them with natural sweeteners like dates and natural honey, which can also support mental health [52].

- Avoiding soft drinks: It is advisable to avoid soft drinks, as their consumption has been associated with negative cardiometabolic outcomes and adverse effects on mental health [53]. Relying more on natural food sources is generally healthier and more beneficial.

6.6.2 Supporting brain health

- Fruits, vegetables, and essential nutrients: Consuming a diet rich in fruits, vegetables, healthy fats, vitamins B1, B6, B12, and vitamin D (1,000–2000 IU (international units) daily, especially for those with low sunlight exposure), folic acid, and magnesium (200–400 mg/day) supports brain health and reduces anxiety [54].

- Omega-3 fatty acids: Taking 1000–2000 mg of omega-3 fatty acids daily can reduce inflammation and improve mood [55].

6.7 Regular doctor visits contribute to

- *Consistent case monitoring*: Ensuring conditions are monitored and managed effectively to reduce the risk of complications.

- *Medication management*: Adjusting medications based on the patient's current health status and response to treatment for optimal therapeutic outcomes.

- *Lifestyle recommendations*: Providing tailored advice on diet, exercise, and other lifestyle factors that contribute to overall well-being, helping patients make informed decisions about their health.

- *Mental health support*: Offering opportunities for patients to discuss mental health concerns, receive support, and get referrals to mental health specialists, if needed.

- *Building a doctor-patient relationship*: Regular visits help build a trusting relationship between the patient and the doctor, facilitating open communication and a better understanding of the patient's health needs.

6.8 Collaboration with mental health specialists

Mental health professionals may collaborate to provide holistic care, particularly in cases where mental health and social factors intersect.

6.8.1 Psychiatrist

If a patient were suspected to have a psychotic ement, suicidal thoughts, drug abuse, postpartum depression, child psychotic disorder, or show resistant behavior, then it should involve a psychiatrist in the diagnosis and management plan (AlKhathami Approach, Step 3) [32].

6.8.2 Psychologist

Psychologist primarily focuses on assessing, diagnosing, and treating mental health issues through therapeutic interventions, such as psychotherapy, cognitive-behavioral therapy, and counseling. They often work with individuals to understand their thoughts, emotions, and behaviors, providing strategies to manage mental health challenges and improve overall well-being. Thus, the Family doctor should collaborate with the psychologist to provide specific psychological therapy as needed for the patient.

6.8.3 Social worker

A social worker focuses on helping individuals, families, and communities improve their well-being by addressing social, economic, and environmental factors that impact their lives. They provide support, advocacy, and resources to help the person navigate challenges, such as poverty, addiction, domestic violence, and mental health issues. Social workers often connect the person with community resources and work to improve social systems and policies.

6.9 Regular follow-up visits' schedule

- *First visit*: Apply Step 5 of the AlKhathami Approach [32]. Initiate management, which may include pharmacological interventions, non-pharmacological treatments, and nutritional supplements, such as magnesium, vitamins B1, B6, B12, and vitamin D (as needed).

- *Second visit (after 2 weeks)*: Assess the improvement in the patient's usual symptoms. Conduct a reassessment and provide supportive therapy. Introduce narrative therapy to enhance problem-solving skills. Continue with the established management plan.

- *Third visit (after 3 weeks)*: Significant improvement or remission is typically observed, although conditions like panic disorder or social phobia may require more time and higher doses. Adjust the dosage, if there is no remission.

- *Follow-up visits*: Schedule follow-up appointments every 3–4 weeks, until remission is achieved. Once remission is stable, extend the interval between visits to every 2 months, continuing this schedule for 9 months. After maintaining remission, gradually taper the medication dosage over time, until it can be safely discontinued.

DOI: http://dx.doi.org/10.5772/intechopen.1008151

6.10 Management prognosis

Typically, based on experience, when a patient fully adheres to the treatment plan—taking prescribed medication, engaging in non-pharmacological therapies, following the recommended diet and supplements, and attending regular follow-up visits—improvements are often observed within 1 to 2 weeks. By 6 to 8 weeks, symptoms of generalized anxiety, depression, and related physical issues usually subside. However, conditions like panic disorder, phobias, and obsessive-compulsive disorder often require additional follow-up, an increase in medication dosage, or even the introduction of new medications to manage the condition effectively.

During follow-ups, it's important for the healthcare provider to monitor which symptoms are improving, which are not, and any side effects from the medication. Decisions about dosage and medication choice should be based on this information. Since each patient responds differently to treatment, understanding the patient's unique needs and adjusting the plan accordingly are essential.

6.11 Comorbidities management

Managing patients with coexisting mental health issues, such as depression or anxiety, alongside chronic physical illnesses like diabetes or cardiovascular disease, requires a customized, integrated approach that addresses the complexities of both mental and physical health. Pharmacological treatments must be carefully chosen to manage both the mental health disorder and the chronic physical condition, with attention to avoiding adverse interactions.

In patients with chronic physical diseases, effective stress management that reduces stress hormones often leads to significant improvements in controlling the physical condition. Therefore, it is essential to regularly review and adjust the treatment plan for the physical disease, including medication dosages, as needed. Collaborative care models, which involve a multidisciplinary team including primary care providers and specialists, are particularly effective in managing these dual conditions.

Personalized lifestyle changes are crucial for managing both mental health and chronic physical illnesses. For example, a tailored exercise program for a patient with depression and cardiovascular disease can improve both mood and cardiovascular health [56]. Nutritional counseling, such as adopting a Mediterranean diet, can support both mental health and chronic illness management [57].

Regular follow-up is essential to monitor progress and adjust treatment plans. This includes assessing mental health outcomes and physical health metrics, ensuring that any emerging issues are addressed promptly. Educating patients about the interconnectedness of mental and physical health empowers them to manage their conditions actively.

7. Modern narrative therapy: An approach to problem externalization and solution finding

7.1 Rational

Modern Narrative Therapy helps individuals separate their emotions from their problems to find more effective solutions. When people address their own issues, emotions can cloud their judgment and lead to overthinking. By projecting the problem onto a "friend," individuals can analyze it more objectively, using their own knowledge and reasoning without emotional interference. This approach empowers them to develop practical, effective solutions, leading to better problem-solving and personal growth.

7.2 Objective

The goal of Modern Narrative Therapy is to help individuals address their problems, make appropriate decisions independently, and interact with others in a manner that best suits their abilities.

7.3 Modern narrative therapy steps

1. *Externalization*: This technique involves separating the person from the problem. By externalizing and defining the issue, it becomes easier to manage and address.

2. *Identifying a "friend"*: The individual is encouraged to project the problem onto a "friend," whether imaginary or real. This projection allows the patient to step out of the problem and view it as a therapist would, rather than as someone directly affected by it.

3. *Ensuring separation from the problem*: The therapist ensures that the patient successfully detaches himself or herself from the problem and perceives it as an issue affecting the friend only. The patient then takes on the role of an advisor, providing guidance and support to solve the friend's problem.

4. *Offering solutions and advice*: The patient offers appropriate advice and solutions to help the friend resolve their issue. The therapist ensures that these solutions do not involve escaping from the problem. If such a solution is proposed, the therapist asks the patient to consider the potential consequences if the friend were to act on advice based on avoidance. The aim is for the patient to realize that this solution is not suitable and to rethink a more appropriate solution.

5. *Application request*: Once the therapist is confident that the patient has successfully distanced himself or herself from the problem and proposed suitable solutions from their perspective, the therapist asks the patient to apply the advice they offered to the friend to their own situation, thus addressing their problem.

7.4 Example of modern narrative therapy in practice

Let us imagine a scenario where a person, Sarah, is struggling with feelings of anxiety related to her performance at work. She often feels overwhelmed and fears that she might not meet her employer's expectations.

1. *Externalization*: The therapist begins by helping Sarah to externalize her anxiety. Instead of saying, "I am anxious," Sarah is encouraged to view the anxiety as something separate from herself. The therapist might say, "Let us imagine that this anxiety is not part of you but rather something outside of you, like a cloud that sometimes follows you around."

2. *Identifying a "friend"*: The therapist then asks Sarah to imagine that a close friend, Emma, is dealing with the same anxiety about work. The problem is now externalized onto Emma, making it easier for Sarah to think about the issue objectively.

3. *Ensuring separation from the problem*: The therapist checks in with Sarah to ensure she has fully separated herself from the anxiety, seeing it as Emma's problem and not her own. Sarah now takes on the role of a supportive friend who wants to help Emma navigate this issue.

4. *Offering solutions and advice*: Sarah is then asked what advice she would give to Emma. Sarah might suggest that Emma could break down her work tasks into smaller, more manageable steps, or that Emma could speak to her supervisor to clarify expectations. The therapist ensures that these solutions are proactive and not about avoiding the problem. For example, if Sarah suggests that Emma should just ignore her anxiety, the therapist would ask, "What might happen if Emma ignores this anxiety? Could it grow worse?"

5. *Application request*: After Sarah has provided thoughtful advice for Emma, the therapist asks her to consider applying this advice to herself. Sarah is encouraged to use the strategies she recommended, such as breaking tasks into smaller steps or discussing her concerns with her supervisor, to manage her own anxiety.

Outcome: By externalizing the problem and viewing it as something that her "friend" is dealing with, Sarah can see her situation from a new perspective. This allows her to identify practical solutions without being overwhelmed by the emotional burden of anxiety. By the end of the session, Sarah feels more empowered and equipped to handle her work-related anxiety using the strategies she developed for Emma.

This example illustrates how Modern Narrative Therapy helps individuals to detach from their problems, think critically about them, and apply effective solutions in their own lives.

7.5 Scenario-1: Managing work-related stress through modern narrative therapy

Background: Mosa is a 35-year-old marketing manager who has been feeling extremely stressed at work. He worries constantly about meeting deadlines, managing his team, and delivering successful campaigns. His stress is affecting his sleep, relationships, and overall well-being.

Therapy session:

1. *Externalization*: The therapist starts by helping Mosa separate himself from his stress. Instead of saying, "I am stressed," the therapist asks Mosa to think of the stress as something outside of him. The therapist might say, "Let us think of your stress as a heavy backpack that you are carrying around. It's not a part of you, but something that you are carrying."

2. *Identifying a "friend":* Next, the therapist introduces the idea of a friend. "Imagine you have a close friend, Ali, who is also a marketing manager and is dealing with the same stress you are. He's carrying this heavy backpack of stress just like you."

3. *Ensuring separation from the problem*: The therapist checks to make sure Mosa is able to fully visualize the stress as Ali's problem and not his own. "Now that you are thinking about Ali, how do you feel about the stress he's experiencing? What would you say to him?"

Mosa begins to feel a bit of distance from his own stress and starts to think more clearly. "I would tell Ali that he's doing the best he can and that he should try to delegate some of his tasks to his team."

4. *Offering solutions and advice*: The therapist encourages Mosa to offer more advice to Ali. "What else could Ali do to manage this stress better?"

Mosa suggests, "Maybe Ali could set more realistic deadlines for himself and communicate more openly with his boss about what's feasible. He could also take short breaks during the day to clear his mind."

The therapist listens and then probes further. "Those are great suggestions. What if Mosa just tried to ignore the stress? What could happen?"

Mosa thinks and responds, "If Ali ignores the stress, it might build up even more and affect his performance at work and his health."

5. *Application request*: The therapist then asks Mosa to apply these solutions to his own life. "What if you tried some of these strategies that you suggested for Ali? How could you start delegating tasks, setting realistic deadlines, and communicating with your boss?"

Mosa starts to see how the advice he gave Ali could also benefit him. He commits to talking to his boss about his workload, delegating more tasks to his team, and taking regular breaks during the day.

Outcome: By the end of the session, Mosa feels more in control of his stress. He's able to view his situation from a new perspective, making it easier to implement practical solutions. The act of separating himself from the stress and advising "Ali" helped Mosa gain clarity and develop a plan to manage his own stress effectively.

This scenario demonstrates how Modern Narrative Therapy can help individuals like Mosa step back from their problems, see them from a different angle, and find constructive ways to address them.

7.6 Scenario-2

Patient: (Basim).

Therapist: (Dr. Ibrahim).

Dr. Ibrahim: Hi Basim, it's great to see you again. Last time, you mentioned feeling overwhelmed with work, especially with managing your deadlines and team. How have things been since our last session?

Basim: It's been tough, honestly. The stress just keeps piling up. I feel like I'm carrying this huge weight all the time, and I'm not sure how much longer I can handle it.

Dr. Ibrahim: It sounds like that stress is really weighing you down. I'd like to try something different today to help you think about this stress in a new way. Are you open to that?

Basim: Sure, I'm willing to try anything at this point.

Dr. Ibrahim: Great. Let us start by imagining that this stress you are feeling is not a part of you, but something you are carrying, like a heavy backpack. How does that image feel to you?

Basim: Yeah, that makes sense. It's definitely like a heavy backpack, one that I cannot take off.

Dr. Ibrahim: Now, let us take it a step further. I want you to imagine that your friend, Mosa, is the one carrying this heavy backpack of stress. He's in a similar position as you—a marketing manager dealing with a lot of pressure. Can you picture that?

Basim: Yeah, I can see that. Mosa's a hard worker too, so I can imagine him feeling the same way.

Dr. Ibrahim: So, if Mosa came to you and told you about how he's struggling with this stress, what advice would you give him? What could he do to manage this heavy load?

Mosa: Hmm… I'd probably tell him that he does not have to do everything on his own. He has a team, so he should delegate more tasks. Maybe he could also set more realistic deadlines instead of trying to be a superhero.

Dr. Ibrahim: That's great advice. How do you think Mosa would feel if he started delegating more and setting those realistic deadlines?

Basim: I think he'd feel a bit of relief, like the weight is not all on his shoulders anymore. He'd probably feel more in control.

Dr. Ibrahim: What if Mike just tried to ignore the stress? What do you think would happen then?

Basim: Ignoring it would just make things worse. The stress would keep building up until he could not handle it anymore, and that could lead to burnout.

Dr. Ibrahim: Exactly. Now, let us bring this back to you. You've offered some really insightful advice to Mosa. How might you apply this same advice to your own situation?

Basim: I guess I could start delegating more to my team. I've been trying to do everything myself because I want it done right, but I see now that it's too much. I could also talk to my boss about what's realistic with the deadlines we have.

Dr. Ibrahim: That sounds like a solid plan. What small steps could you take this week to start making those changes?

Basim: I could start by having a meeting with my team tomorrow to go over the tasks we have and see what I can delegate. And I'll set up a meeting with my boss to discuss the project timelines.

Dr. Ibrahim: That's a great approach, Basim. You've identified some very practical steps that can help lighten that heavy backpack of stress. How do you feel about trying this out?

Basim: I feel more hopeful. I think if I follow through, I can start managing the stress better.

Dr. Ibrahim: I'm confident you can. Let us check in next week to see how things are going and if there are any adjustments we need to make. Does that sound good?

Basim: Yeah, that sounds good. Thanks, Dr. Ibrahim.

Dr. Ibrahim: You're welcome, Basim. You're doing great work, and I'm here to support you every step of the way.

This method helps individuals gain perspective, reduce emotional interference, and apply practical solutions to their problems.

8. Conclusion

8.1 Root and branches theory

The Root and Branches Theory suggests that psychological capacity compression, driven by a reduction in happiness hormones and an increase in stress hormones, plays a central role in the development of mental health disorders, such as depression, anxiety, OCD, and panic attacks. The metaphor of a tree is used to explain this concept: psychological stress acts as the "roots," which feed into the system and cause various symptoms that emerge as "branches." These symptoms manifest as emotional, behavioral, and cognitive disruptions, indicating a strained psychological state. Rather than focusing solely on alleviating these symptoms, the theory advocates for addressing the root cause—psychological stress itself. This is achieved through increasing happiness hormones like serotonin and reducing stress hormones like cortisol through interventions, such as mindfulness, exercise, and positive social interactions.

In addition to focusing on stress management, the Root and Branches Theory also acknowledges the complex role of genetics, personality, and life experiences in shaping an individual's mental health. These factors determine how susceptible a person is to psychological capacity compression and how they respond to various stressors. Furthermore, the theory emphasizes the importance of culturally sensitive approaches to mental health care, recognizing that cultural factors significantly influence how people experience and express psychological distress. The AlKhathami Approach, validated for early detection and intervention in primary care settings, aligns with this theory, offering a structured, holistic method for addressing mental health issues at their core.

8.2 Modern narrative therapy

Modern Narrative Therapy is a therapeutic approach that encourages individuals to externalize their problems, separating themselves from their issues. By treating the problem as an external entity, people can analyze it from a more objective and detached perspective. This separation allows individuals to view their challenges with greater clarity, reducing the emotional burden associated with internalizing issues. By personifying the problem—sometimes treating it metaphorically as a "friend"—they can apply their own experiences and knowledge to tackle the issue, promoting a sense of empowerment and control over their circumstances.

This approach builds emotional resilience by fostering confidence and helping individuals see that they are not defined by their problems. Modern Narrative Therapy also encourages the development of practical, actionable solutions, as people can engage with their challenges from a place of emotional detachment. It is particularly effective in diverse cultural contexts, where externalizing issues may resonate with cultural narratives or symbolic forms of expression. This culturally adaptable approach allows individuals to work through their mental health struggles in a way that respects personal and cultural values, promoting mental well-being and long-term recovery.

Acknowledgements

The authors acknowledge the use of ChatGPT for language polishing and the figure creation in the manuscript.

Author details

Abdullah AlKhathami
Eastern Health Cluster, Dammam, Saudi Arabia

*Address all correspondence to: mabna@yahoo.com

References

[1] Smith EE, Kosslyn SM. Cognitive Psychology: Mind and Brain. Upper Saddle River: Pearson Prentice Hall; 2007

[2] Sternberg RJ. Handbook of Intelligence. 2nd ed. Cambridge: Cambridge University Press; 2000

[3] Mayer JD, Salovey P. What is emotional intelligence? In: Salovey P, Sluyter D, editors. Emotional Development and Emotional Intelligence: Educational Implications. New York: Basic Books; 1997. pp. 3-31

[4] Gross JJ. Emotion regulation: Affective, cognitive, and social consequences. Psychophysiology. 2002; **39**(3):281-291

[5] Jones L. Decline in performance and concentration. Journal of Cognitive Neuroscience. 2019;**33**(1):45-60

[6] Anderson V. Attention deficit hyperactivity disorder. In: Lyon JR, Fletcher JM, editors. Learning Disabilities: From Identification to Intervention. New York: Wiley; 2003. pp. 280-295

[7] Diamond A. Executive functions. Annual Review of Psychology. 2013;**64**: 135-168

[8] Goleman D. Emotional Intelligence: Why it Can Matter More than IQ. New York: Bantam Books; 1995

[9] Masten AS. Ordinary magic: Resilience processes in development. The American Psychologist. 2001;**56**(3): 227-238

[10] Burleson BR. The experience and effects of emotional support: What the study of cultural and gender differences can tell us about close relationships, emotion, and interpersonal communication. Personal Relationships. 2003;**10**(1):1-23

[11] Deci EL, Ryan RM. The "what" and "why" of goal pursuits: Human needs and the self-determination of behavior. Psychological Inquiry. 2000;**11**(4): 227-268

[12] McEwen BS. Protection and damage from acute and chronic stress: Allostasis and allostatic load reconsidered. Neuropsychopharmacology. 2004;**29**(5): 2-10

[13] Evans GW, Kim P. Childhood poverty and health: Cumulative risk exposure and stress dysregulation. Psychological Science. 2007;**18**(11): 953-957

[14] Stansfeld SA, Matheson MP. Noise pollution: Non-auditory effects on health. British Medical Bulletin. 2003; **68**(1):243-257

[15] Felitti VJ, Anda RF, Nordenberg D, Williamson DF, Spitz AM, Edwards V, et al. Relationship of childhood abuse and household dysfunction to many of the leading causes of death in adults: The adverse childhood experiences (ACE) study. American Journal of Preventive Medicine. 1998;**14**(4):245-258

[16] Cohen S, Wills TA. Stress, social support, and the buffering hypothesis. Psychological Bulletin. 1985;**98**(2): 310-357

[17] Katon W. Clinical and health services relationships between major depression, depressive symptoms, and general medical illness. Biological Psychiatry. 2003;**54**(3):216-226

[18] Smith JA, Brown LM. Psychological capacity and resilience: The role of protective and risk factors. In: Psychological Resources and Well-Being. Oxford, UK: Oxford University Press; 2023. pp. 45-67

[19] Sher L. The impact of psychological stress on the body: Hormonal regulation and mental health implications. Frontiers in Public Health. 2023;**11**: 1122334. DOI: 10.3389/fpubh.2023.1122334

[20] Stalder T, Kirschbaum C. Chronic stress and the hypothalamus pituitary-adrenal (HPA) axis: A conceptual and empirical synthesis of recent developments. Current Opinion in Psychology. 2022;**45**:101294. DOI: 10.1016/j.copsyc.2022.101294

[21] Slavich GM, Irwin MR. From stress to inflammation and major depressive disorder: A social signal transduction theory of depression. Psychological Bulletin. 2014;**140**(3):774-815. DOI: 10.1037/a0035302

[22] Felger JC, Haroon E. Chronic inflammation and proinflammatory cytokines in depression: Neurobiological mechanisms and therapeutic implications. Neuropsychopharmacology. 2023;**48**(1): 223-242. DOI: 10.1038/s41386-022-01367-3

[23] Lazarus RS, Folkman S. Stress, Appraisal, and Coping. New York: Springer; 1984

[24] Abramowitz JS, Taylor S, McKay D. Obsessive-compulsive disorder. Lancet. 2009;**374**(9688):491-499

[25] Barlow DH. Anxiety and its Disorders: The Nature and Treatment of Anxiety and Panic. 2nd ed. New York: Guilford Press; 2002

[26] Kirmayer LJ, Ryder AG. Culture and psychopathology. Current Opinion in Psychology. 2016;**8**:143-148. DOI: 10.1016/j.copsyc.2015.10.020

[27] Tsai JL, Chentsova-Dutton Y, Wong Y. Why and how we should study cultural influences on emotion: The example of somatization. Social Science & Medicine. 2002;**55**(11):1795-1805. DOI: 10.1016/S0277-9536(01)00395-1

[28] Cohen S, Kamarck T, Mermelstein R. A global measure of perceived stress. Journal of Health and Social Behavior. 1983;**24**(4):385-396. DOI: 10.2307/2136404

[29] Connor KM, Davidson JR. Development of a new resilience scale: The Connor-Davidson resilience scale (CD-RISC). Depression and Anxiety. 2003;**18**(2):76-82. DOI: 10.1002/da.10113

[30] Beck AT, Steer RA, Brown GK. Manual for the Beck Depression Inventory-II. San Antonio: Psychological Corporation; 1996

[31] Thayer JF, Åhs F, Fredrikson M, Sollers JJ, Wager TD. A meta-analysis of heart rate variability and neuroimaging studies: Implications for heart rate variability as a marker of stress and health. Neuroscience and Biobehavioral Reviews. 2012;**36**(2):747-756. DOI: 10.1016/j.neubiorev.2011.11.009

[32] AlKhathami AD. An innovative 5-step patient interview approach for integrating mental healthcare into primary care Centre services: A validation study. General Psychiatry. 2022;**35**:35. DOI: 10.1136/gpsych-2021-100693

[33] Caspi A, Sugden K, Moffitt TE, Taylor A, Craig IW, Harrington H, et al. Influence of life stress on depression:

Moderation by a polymorphism in the 5-HTT gene. Science. 2003;**301**(5631): 386-389

[34] Smith BW, Yang L. Stress resilience: Personality traits and the genetic factors underlying individual differences. Current Opinion in Psychiatry. 2017; **30**(3):153-158

[35] Masten AS, Reed MGJ. Resilience in development. In: Snyder CR, Lopez SJ, editors. Handbook of Positive Psychology. Oxford, UK: Oxford University Press; 2002. pp. 74-88

[36] Vgontzas AN, Chrousos GP. Sleep, the hypothalamic-pituitary-adrenal axis, and stress. Sleep Medicine Clinics. 2017; **12**(2):271-278. DOI: 10.1016/j.jsmc.2017.03.011

[37] Slavich GM. Life stress and health: A review of conceptual issues and recent findings. Teaching of Psychology. 2016; **43**(4):346-355. DOI: 10.1177/0098628316662768

[38] Brandt J, Epstein RM, Saint S. Comprehensive management strategies. Journal of Integrated Care. 2010;**18**(4): 24-31

[39] Muth C, Blom J, Mallen CD. The combined effect of pharmacological and non-pharmacological interventions in patients with multimorbidity. BMC Health Services Research. 2014;**14**:515

[40] Boyd CM, Boult C, Shadmi E, et al. Guided care for multimorbid patients. Annals of Internal Medicine. 2005; **143**(8):545-554

[41] Yarnall KS, Pollak KI, Ostbye T, et al. Primary care: Is there enough time for prevention? American Journal of Public Health. 2003;**93**(4):635-641

[42] Martinsen EW. Physical activity in the prevention and treatment of anxiety and depression. Nordic Journal of Psychiatry. 2008;**62**(S47):25-29

[43] Van der Kolk BA. The Body Keeps the Score: Brain, Mind, and Body in the Healing of Trauma. New York: Viking; 2014

[44] Cipriani A, Furukawa TA, Salanti G, Chaimani A, Atkinson LZ, Ogawa Y, et al. Comparative efficacy and acceptability of 21 antidepressant drugs for the acute treatment of adults with major depressive disorder: A systematic review and network meta-analysis. Lancet. 2018;**391**(10128):1357-1366. DOI: 10.1016/S0140-6736(17)32802-7

[45] Tugade MM, Fredrickson BL. Positive emotions and the regulation of negative emotions. Annual Review of Psychology. 2022;**73**(1):397-423. DOI: 10.1146/annurev-psych-021220-121423

[46] Fredrickson BL. The role of positive emotions in positive psychology: The broaden-and-build theory of positive emotions. The American Psychologist. 2001;**56**(3):218-226. DOI: 10.1037/0003-066X.56.3.218

[47] Pascoe MC, Thompson DR, Jenkins ZM, Ski CF. Mindfulness mediates the physiological markers of stress: Systematic review and meta-analysis. Journal of Psychiatric Research. 2017;**95**:156-178. DOI: 10.1016/j.jpsychires.2017.08.004

[48] White M. Narrative therapy in practice: The archaeology of hope. Journal of Family Therapy. 2020;**42**(1): 22-39. DOI: 10.1111/1467-6427.12345

[49] Estruch R, Ros E, Salas-Salvadó J, Covas MI, Corella D, Arós F, et al. Primary prevention of cardiovascular

disease with a Mediterranean diet. The New England Journal of Medicine. 2013; **368**(14):1279-1290. DOI: 10.1056/NEJMoa1200303

[50] Mozaffarian D, Rimm EB, Willett WC. Fish intake, contaminants, and human health: Evaluating the risks and the benefits. Journal of the American Medical Association. 2006;**296**(15): 1885-1899. DOI: 10.1001/jama.296.15.1885

[51] Gupta R, Binns CW. Full-fat dairy consumption and health outcomes: A review of evidence. Advances in Nutrition. 2023;**14**(4):785-798. DOI: 10.1093/advances/nmac095

[52] Pourfarzi S, Keshavarz M. Natural sweeteners and their impact on human health: A comprehensive review. Nutrients. 2022;**14**(11):2234. DOI: 10.3390/nu14112234

[53] Hu FB, Malik VS. Sugar-sweetened beverages and risk of obesity and type 2 diabetes: Epidemiologic evidence. Nature Reviews. Endocrinology. 2023; **19**(3):169-182. DOI: 10.1038/s41574-022-00710-3

[54] Boyle NB, Lawton C, Dye L. The effects of polyunsaturated fatty acids on cognitive performance and mood in healthy adults: A systematic review of randomized controlled trials. Nutrition Reviews. 2017;**75**(6):504-513

[55] Grosso G, Micek A, Godos J, Sciacca S, Pajak A, Martínez-González MA, et al. Dietary n-3 PUFA, fish consumption and depression: A systematic review and meta-analysis of observational studies. Journal of Affective Disorders. 2014;**156**:118-126. DOI: 10.1016/j.jad.2013.12.013

[56] Blumenthal JA, Babyak MA, Doraiswamy PM, Watkins L, Hoffman BM, Barbour KA, et al. Exercise and pharmacotherapy in the treatment of major depressive disorder. Psychosomatic Medicine. 2012;**74**(1): 29-37. DOI: 10.1097/PSY.0b013e31823a3c27

[57] Jacka FN, O'Neil A, Opie R, Itsiopoulos C, Cotton S, Mohebbi M, et al. A randomised controlled trial of dietary improvement for adults with major depression (the "SMILES" trial). BMC Medicine. 2017;**15**(1):23. DOI: 10.1186/s12916-017-0791-y

Chapter 6

Perspective Chapter: Subject-Object Intercorrelation – From Quantum Theory to the New Forms and Applications in Psychotherapy

Ramona Ardelean

Abstract

If the paradigm of classical epistemology follows the logic of the part, being tributary to the principle of subject-object separability, in which the subject, that is, the part, is considered separate from the object, that is, the whole, then the new paradigm of the quantum theory has replaced the principle of separability, specific to the logic of the part, with the principle of subject-object nonseparability or global intercorrelation, specific to the logic of the whole. Starting from this principle of quantum nonseparability, I will show that it can be explored and applied in new forms of psychotherapy. I mean here the art of meditation, as the art of the whole, that is, the art of perceiving the world and ourselves in a nondualistic nonanalytical, and nonfragmentary way, in which the subject and the object, the observer and the observed, the part and the whole, are not separated, but interconnected.

Keywords: paradigm of separability, paradigm of nonseparability, quantum theory, analytical-nonanalytical way of thinking, psychological model of human consciousness nonseparability, subject-object, observer-observed, meditation, nonduality

1. Introduction

If from a scientific point of view, the great theories of physics give us the most general image and conception of the world and the universe, then these theories of physics can be seen as reference systems or *epistemological paradigms*, respectively the theories of knowledge that produce a major impact at the level of all disciplines in the entire field of knowledge (not only in science and technology but also in art, philosophy, psychology or psychotherapy), the reason for why they must be reviewed into the light of the new vision or principle.

Thus, the great "revolutions" in physics can be considered emergent or fundamental creations, consisting in the discovery of a new principle, which revolutionizes not only the local level, specific to a field but also the *global* level, specific to the entire field of knowledge, becoming therefore epistemological paradigms, respectively reference systems to which all fields of knowledge must be related. It is enough to mention here the atomist-Newtonian theory, the theory of relativity, or, more recently, the quantum theory, to give some notorious examples of scientific and epistemological paradigms.

The present chapter, extremely significant from the perspective of scientific and epistemological *actuality*, is an attempt to legitimize a *psychological/psychotherapeutic model* of human consciousness nonseparability, respectively the *subject-object nonseparability* starting from the scientific/epistemological paradigm of quantum theoretical nonseparability. It has a double stake. (1) *Scientific/epistemological* stake, given by the "cognitive revolution" of quantum theory, which consisted of replacing the classical principle of separability with the principle of *nonseparability* or *global intercorrelation*. (2) *Psychological/psychotherapeutic* stake, given by the profoundly psychological implications of the principle of quantum nonseparability upon human consciousness, a fact which raises the question whether the human consciousness could suffer, on the basis of nonseparability or global intercorrelation of reality, a profound "psychological revolution," analog to the quantum revolution in physics, which would put an end to the classic paradigm of human consciousness separability in subject and object, part and whole, observer and observed, revealing the profound understanding of a nondualistic and nonfragmentary way, in which these distinctions no longer appear as separate, but interconnected. This nondualistic perception, specific to the art of meditations, as the art of the whole, could therefore constitute the premise or condition of possibility for new, nonfragmentary, forms and perspectives in psychotherapy.

For a better understanding of the relevance of the quantum paradigm of nonseparability and the epistemological implications of the principle of quantum nonseparability, I will first refer to the classical paradigm of separability and the epistemological implications of the principle of separability in classical physics.

2. The paradigm of consciousness separability or subject-object separability in classic physics

Newton's famous precept, "physics, beware of metaphysics," which led to the autonomy and the separation between all sciences and disciplines of knowledge, can be considered tributary to the classical epistemological paradigm of *analyzing the world in separate and independent parts*, respectively the principle of separability in subject and object, part and whole or observer and observed. David Bohm, one of the most remarkable representatives of quantum theory, considers that this kind of thought is specific to the *classical model of analysis*, according to which the *subject*, the one who thinks is considered completely separate and independent from the *object*/reality upon which the subject thinks [1], this separation is equivalent to the classical distinctions between subject-object, consciousness-matter, part-whole or observer-observed.

This principle of classical separability is based on the following presuppositions from which its main implications derive: (1) *The belief in an objective/external reality*, separated from the subjective/internal reality, in which our thought is seen in reflective correspondence with objective reality, like a mirror that reflects and describes reality "as it is" [1]. Given that our thought operates with differences, distinctions, and divisions, then our habit of using them will make us see these *mental distinctions* as real so that the world will appear to be in reality made up of separate parts or fragments [1]. I mean here the confusion between the *mental image and reality*, through which the mental image tends to substitute reality. This belief results in (2) *the status of the objective, neutral and impartial observer*, which excludes the subjective factor, as well as (3) the classic *distinctions*: subject-object, conscience-matter, part-whole, (4) circumscribed to *the logic of parts*, in which the part is considered to precede the whole, and is therefore primordial, thus involving (5) *the substantial conception* of the fundamental constituents, from which results (6) *determinism*—the interpreting of causality through mechanisms which are strictly *local*, that is, localizable or determinable in space-time [2], as well as (7) the separation between different specialized fields of knowledge (art, science, technology), all specialties being considered to be separate in essence from the others [1].

3. The paradigm of consciousness nonseparability or subject-object nonseparability in quantum physics

The new "cognitive revolution" of quantum physics in the twentieth century fundamentally changed this separatist-fragmentary view of the world, affirming that the world is a coherent and indivisible whole that cannot be analyzed in terms of separable reality, as claimed by classical atomist-Newtonian physics. On the contrary, the world emerges as a network or dynamic "weave" of events in permanent interaction, in which *each part is connected globally and instantaneously to the whole universe*, any action upon the parts reflecting outwards on the whole and vice versa, the part undergoing influences from all events in the whole. This fundamental presupposition of quantum mechanics, which led to a paradigm shift, that is, a revolution in the way of thinking reality, is called the principle of *nonseparability or global intercorrelation* [3].

Considering that the part cannot be separated from the whole, the fundament of the world cannot therefore be the part, which is to say the isolated and separate entities, but the *whole*, considered logically and ontologically prior to the part. Physicist Fritjof Capra states in this sense that in classical physics the properties of the parts determine the whole, in quantum physics, on the contrary, *the whole determines the properties of the parts* [3]. It follows that the fundament of the world is no longer the part, but the whole, considered logically and ontologically prior to the part. Thus, as David Bohm claims, the idea of the classical analysis of the world in separate and elementary parts is rejected and replaced by the idea of the "inseparable quantum interconnectedness" of the entire universe, seen as the fundamental reality [4]. The principle of quantum nonseparability, therefore, negates the separability of the world in favor of its unity or nonseparability, Heisenberg affirming in this sense that the world appears as a complex and organic tissue of interconnected events, who's global intercorrelation determines the texture, the structure or the fundament of the whole [5].

The transition from separability to nonseparability has occurred since it has been determined that by probing into matter at a deeper atomic and subatomic level, the principle of separability loses its validity moving from macrophysical level to a microphysical or quantic level of reality. Since at this level, there are no material objects with mass and weight, those having lost their substantial character while dissolving into probabilistic structures of events, particles cease to appear as *objects* and emerge as *processes*, or "probabilities of interconnection materialisation," which describe nonseparability or global intercorrelation.

The notion of global intercorrelation, initially brought forward by Niels Bohr and Werner Heisenberg, representatives of the Copenhagen school, at the end of the third decade of the twentieth century, represents beyond divergent interpretations, the element of convergence or quantum theory quintessence, in which "the behaviour of the part is always determined by its global connexions," by its connections with the whole [3]. This connection or universal interconnectivity negates any fundamental constituent, any elementary particle or an isolated and separate entity, considered abstractions or idealisations without correspondents in reality. Niels Bohr demonstrates in this sense that material isolated particles are nothing more than abstractions, one only being able to observe the properties of these particles through their interactions with other particles or systems, or more precisely with the whole of which they pertain [6]. This signifies that contrary to classical physics, in which predictions regarding hidden/unknown variables depend on a *local* mechanism, the probability of producing events is determined by a local system, in which the properties and behavior of parts determine the behavior of the whole, in quantum physics, conversely, the hidden variable is attributed to a *global, nonlocal* mechanism, in which the whole "determins" (in the indeterminist sense of Heisenberg's uncertainty) the behavior of the part, the probability of event production being determined by the dynamic of a global/nonlocal system, in which every part has *a spontaneous and instantaneous* (nonlocal or noncausal) *connection* with the entire universe, based on *mutual global intercorrelation* [3].

Probing the subatomic world has thusly revealed that all phenomena in the universe are *interconnected*, being parts that have spontaneous and global connections with the whole, quantum theory thus abolishing at the subatomic/microphysical level the classical distinctions of the subject-object, observer-observed object, conscience-matter, part-whole type and replacing the principle of separability with the principle of nonseparability or global intercorrelation.

The notion of quantum intercorrelation, according to which the universe cannot be reduced to entities, particles or elementary fields, has led, starting with the 1960s, to the idea that the universe could manifest an ever more subtle intercorrelation, that of self-consistency, through which "all its components being consistent both with one another and with themselves" [3].

This idea of self-consistency, formulated by the physicist Geoffrey Chew within the bootstrap theory, embraces the conception "much older than particle physics, that nature is as it is because this is the only possible nature consistent with itself" [7]. By permanently dismissing the traditional, atomist-Newtonian view, based on elementary entities or particles, the criterium of self-consistency, suggested by Chew, states that the universe is a dynamic, indivisible and coherent whole, in which the properties of the part are connected with the properties of the whole, *none of which being fundamental*—since the properties of the parts are not independent/separate, but result from their mutual interconnection, which determines the structure, respectively the self-consistency of the whole [4]. This approach was very suggestively called *nuclear democracy* [7]. Chew probably refers here to an attitude of epistemological fair-play, specific to the bootstrap, which rejects as unfunded, at a subatomic level, the traditional point of view of the elementary particles, this attitude is considered one of "aristocratic," respectively hierarchic type [7].

Summarizing now all that has been stated regarding the paradigm of quantum nonseparability, we can say that the principle of quantum nonseparability is based on the following assumptions from which its major implications derive: (1) The belief in a *nonseparable* reality, by including the *consciousness of the observer in the observed* object [5], whereby the observer, depending on his targets, hypothesis or measuring instruments, changes the reality he observes, (2) the observer thus losing his status as an objective, neutral and impartial observer, (3) This led to the restoration of the classical distinctions in the sense of nonseparability between subject-object, observer-observed, consciousness-matter and part-whole, the principle of classical separability being replaced by the principle of nonseparability or global intercorrelation. From this principle of nonseparability also derives, (4) the *nonsubstantial* character, since at the quantum/subatomic level we can no longer speak of objects with mass and weight, these being dissolved into probabilistic structures of events and interactions, in which each part has a global and instantaneous connection with the whole. Thus, if in the principle of separability in classical physics the foundation of the world is considered to be the *part*, in the new principle of nonseparability in quantum physics (5) the foundation of the world is, on the contrary, the *whole*, considered logically and ontologically prior to the part. From here also follows (6) the *indeterminism*, that is, the interpretation of causality, not through local mechanisms, but through nonlocal/global mechanisms, nonlocalizable or indeterminable in space-time. Finally, in contrast to the separatist-fragmentary view of the world, which generated, as a final consequence, the separation between sciences/disciplines, the nonseparatist view of the world, specific to quantum physics, can lead (7) to the re-establishment of *all separations between fields* (art, science, technology).

Although the implications of this nonfragmentary view of quantum physics have enormous significance, closely related to the complete re-evaluation of all relationships between human-human, human-nature, human-society and human-universe, the current society has invested a little energy, creativity and disponibility in this sense, our mentality still remained tributary to the analytical, fragmentary and mechanistic paradigm of thinking. Therefore, I consider it is of vital importance for us to understand and be aware of the crucial significance of this unitary, organic and nonfragmentary way of thinking, which could put an end to the *analytical-fragmentary* way of thinking, which generates endless crises and conflicts in the intra and intersubjective space.

4. The negative implications of the classic paradigm of separability due to the analytical way of thinking: David Bohm's perspective

Since this paradigm of subject-object separability is based on a dualistic and fragmentary way of perceiving and thinking about reality, specific to the *classical model of analyzing in separate parts*, David Bohm highlights that this analytical way of thinking led to a fragmentary view of reality, this fragmentary view standing, according to him, at the origin of a series of psychological, social, economic, ecological and cultural crises. Bohm thus draws attention to the destructive consequences that this fragmentary way of thinking implies, causing a series of conflicts or crises in the intra and intersubjective space.

In his well-known book, *Wholeness and the Implicate Order*, David Bohm raises the worrying problem of fragmentation, so widespread at the psychological and social level, showing that our fragmentary way of thinking, feeling and acting is so universal, that fragmentation seems to be, paradoxically, "the one thing in our life which is universal" [1]. Bohm illustrates this fact by describing the general picture of fragmentation, which includes: (1) human society—fragmented into separate nations, into economic, political, religious, racial groups, (2) the human individual—fragmented into distinct and conflicting compartments (the most significant split is, for example, between rationality and affectivity or between the left and right hemisphere of the brain, which are in opposition and conflict), (3) the natural environment—fragmented into parts that are exploited by different interest groups, (4) human activity—split into specialties considered independent, autonomous and unrelated to each other [1].

The idea that all these fragments are separate is, according to Bohm, an illusion, which generated all psychological, social, political, economic, ecological and cultural disorders. Analogously, the physicist Fritjof Capra shows that this analytical-fragmentary way of thinking is at the origin of all crises, conflicts, imbalances and injustices, thus making our lives physically, mentally and socially unhealthy [3].

Investigating the major source of fragmentation, David Bohm states that fragmentation has its origin in that way of thinking reality, in which *the subject*, the one who thinks, considers him/her self completely *separate* from *the object*, respectively the reality upon which he/she thinks, this conception being tributary, as I have shown, to the classical model of analysis the world in separate parts or fragments. Thus, as long as each subject is considered to be a *separate part* from the object, respectively from the rest of humanity, as a *whole*, he/she will tend to defend the interests of his/her own "I" against the interests of another "I." Analogously, as long as the *subject* identifies with a *partial object*—a group, a nation, a race, a religion, an ideology, he/she will tend to defend the interests of these "parts" or partial objects in a similar manner, which will inevitably lead to the perpetuation of fragmentation and conflict, causing people's energies to be wasted in opposing and contradictory actions, thus preventing them from thinking of humanity as a "whole" or as the fundamental reality, whose claims are primordial [1].

It is interesting to notice that this logic of the "parts," specific to the epistemological paradigm of subject-object separability becomes, from a psychological and social point of view, the separatist-conflictual paradigm of the "I" that is, of fragmented consciousness in subject and object. This fragmented consciousness, which is the "I," by virtue of it being fragmented and separated from the whole, will be the basis of *psychological* fragmentation, as well as the basis of *social* fragmentation [2], the social/external fragmentation being nothing but the expression or mirroring of the psychological/internal fragmentation.

The inner fragmentation of the subject, says physicist Fritjof Capra, mirrors his view of the world "outside" which is seen as a multitude of separate objects and events. This fragmented view is further extended to society [3]. It is considered, for instance, that the fragmentation of nations, religions, social, political or economic systems, as well as the competition, conflicts, wars or violence represents the reality itself or a description of the world "as it is," our thinking being seen in reflective correspondence with the reality, respectively as a mirror of reality. Since, as Bohm showed, *our thinking operates with distinctions and divisions*, *the habit of using them will make us consider these distinctions as real*, so that the world will be seen as actually being made up of fragments.

Given that our *analytical way of thinking generates the fragmentation* of reality, which then seems to have an objective and independent existence of our thinking, it follows, according to Bohm, that the fragmentation resides first of all in the ignorance of the way we thinking, the *ignorance through which we separate the content of thought from the process of thinking that produces that content*, which seems to have an objective/independent existence of the process [8]. In other words, we focus only on the content, that is, on the *object* of thought, and ignore the process, that is, the "I" or the subject of thinking.

Since this separation of the process from its content is similar to the separation between subject and object, part and whole or observer and observed, we will have to *clarify* first of all *who is the subject of thinking that produces the object, respectively the content of thought.* We will have to clarify, therefore, both the subject and the object of knowledge, both the observer and the observed, in short, both the process of thinking and the content of thought.

Referring to this aspect, David Bohm considers that one of the most difficult and subtle points is to clarify the relationship between the content of thought and the process of thinking that produces this content [1]. This is because our way of thinking is tributary to the classic model of analysis of the world in separate parts, being deeply rooted in our Western tradition the presupposition that the process of thinking is separated from and independent of its content, which creates the illusion that our thinking can be split or detached from its content in order to properly judge this content as correct or incorrect, rational or irrational, fragmentary or whole. But the fragmentation resides not only at the level of the *object*, that is of the *content of thought*, but primarily at the level of the *subject*, that is of the *process of thinking*, the reason why fragmentary content of thought/*object* and fragmentary process of thinking/*subject* have to come to an end *together* [1].

This is why, to put an end to the analytical model of fragmentation, specific to the classic paradigm of separability, we will have to solve, according to Bohm, the unity of the relationship between the thinking process and its content, analogous to the unity of the relationship between subject and object, part and whole or observer and observed.

I will approach this matter of the unity or nonseparability between the subject-object, observer-observed, part-whole, process of thinking-content of thought from the perspective of the oriental thinker and mystic Jiddu Krishnamurti, one of the most authentic spiritual messengers of the contemporary world. Since his view is very similar to that of the physicist David Bohm, both emphasizing that fragmentation resides in the ignorance of the thinking process, the *ignorance by which we separate, within the analytical process, the content of thought from the thinking process that produces this content*, it must be specified that this similarity is not accidental at all. David Bohm mentions in this regard that he wanted to meet Krishnamurti in order to discuss with him the unity/nonseparability of the observer and the observed which the new paradigm of quantum physics required, Krishnamurti offers Bohm a series of important insights into this sense.

5. Jiddu Krishnamurti or a new psychological/psychotherapeutic perspective of a nonanalytical and nondualistic way of perception, thinking and acting

If the greatness of a thinker resides in revolutionizing a way of thinking, then Jiddu Krishnamurti can be considered "one of the most revolutionary thinkers of the 20th century," as the Dalai Lama called him, while the great physicist David Bohm considered him among the few thinkers able to combine spirituality with science. Called philosopher, spiritual master or mystic, Krishnamurti attracted attention for his unusual lucidity with which he systematically rejected any doctrine, any current of thought, any academic philosophical system and any traditional mysticism. However, his deeply revolutionary message, expressed in a series of conferences held all over the world, had a very strong impact not only on the general audience but also on the Western and Eastern cultural and scientific elites. It should not be overlooked the enormous appreciation that David Bohm had for Krishnamurti's thought, especially his profoundly revolutionary insights regarding the unity of the relationship between the observer and the observed, Bohm confessed that this difficult problem constituted the core of his concerns in *quantum theory—the one that introduced for the first time in the history of physics the nonseparability of the two concepts*.

The topic constantly developed by Krishnamurti is the fragmentation of human consciousness, given by the self-division of consciousness into subject and object or observer and observed. Considering that all our problems, as well as the inability to solve them, have their origin in the fact that we perceive ourselves as separate beings from the rest of humanity, Krishnamurti states that our fragmented consciousness is nothing more than the result of thousands of years of "programming" to consider ourselves individuals, respectively, separate beings [9].

Wondering what is the factor that generates fragmentation, Krishnamurti points out that this factor is our thinking. Since each subject/each "I" thinks according to his prejudices, experiences, ideas, ideals, beliefs, education, religion, culture or tradition, it is evident, says Krishnamurti, that the subject's identification with these images, symbols or partial objects will generate fragmentation and conflict between subjects, thus making each subject/"I" to be in opposition, struggle, competition or rivalry with another subject/"I" [9]. This is why Krishnamurti compares the fragmentation of our mind to the "programming" of a computer, each human thinking according to his "program," each being caught in the network of his own thinking, all these producing fragmentation and conflict [9].

Used to giving extraordinary importance to our thinking and considering that it can solve all our problems, we have never investigated whether *our thinking itself is the source of fragmentation*. Krishnamurti considers in this sense that, full of limits, our thinking creates all kinds of problems and divisions (psychological, social, political, economic, cultural, religious), and then the same thinking aims to solve them, the functioning mechanism of thinking being, therefore, a dualistic and contradictory one.

This brings us to what David Bohm considers to be Krishnamurti's most important discovery, namely that the main cause of fragmentation comes from the fact that we are completely ignorant of the *process of thinking*, focusing our attention only on the *content of thought*, that is, on the ideas, images, notions and symbols that, objectifying, materializing, end up being extracted from the thinking process and considered a separate and independent reality. In this regard, Krishnamurti criticizes the classical model of analysis, in which the thinker considers himself separate from the reality upon he thinks or in which the observer considers himself separate from the observed, a separation by which we make the distinction between subject and object, observer and observed or, analogously, between the process of thinking and the content of thought.

5.1 The analytical "trick" of self-dividing thinking into observer (subject) and observed (object)

Closely related to the functioning mechanism of our thinking, Krishnamurti claims that one of the oldest analytical "tricks" used by it consists in the separation between subject and object, emphasizing that our entire way of thinking, looking and acting is conditioned by the analytical process in which there is a *subject that analyzes and an analyzed object*. There is, therefore, a *duality*, the subject, the one who thinks, considering himself separate from the object of his thought and, implicitly, a conflict, a struggle, an effort to correct, censor or modify what is thought.

Because of this separation, we have looked at everything: people, nature, things, ideas, or various psychic contents, such as suffering, fear, anger, greed, pleasure, etc., as observers observing a thing. We have looked at everything through a screen or images made up of knowledge, memories, prejudices and previous experiences—all of which being time, the past, so that we have never had direct contact with the present, with "what it is" [10]. There is, according to Krishnamurti, a separation, *an interval between the observer (the subject)*, which is the sum of past experiences, *and the observed (the object)*, which is the present moment, this *separation between the observer (the subject), which is the past, and the observed (the object), which is the present moment*, being considered the fundamental cause of the analytical-fragmentary way of thinking [11].

Our thinking process produces the content of our thought, but then the same thinking tends to regard this content as existing independently of it, which, in fact, it does not. *The analytical "trick" of our thinking is that it divides itself into subject and object, observer and observed, analyzer and analyzed, thinking and thought*, all these distinctions being, according to Krishnamurti, nothing more than an illusion [12]. Our thinking projects a separate entity—the thinker, the subject, the "I"—placed outside the content of thought, which would have the possibility to think more clearly and rationally about the content, thus being able to modify it, to change it. But, in reality, there is no thinking entity separate from the content of thought, so that the *subject who thinks, observes or analyzes the content* of thought *is the content/the object itself*. The "container" (the subject) and the "content" (the object) form, therefore, a single movement, being one and the same thing and not two separate things [11].

Thus, to avoid the analytical trick and the division of thinking, says Krishnamurti, it is essential to *understand the entire process of thinking*, because it generates contradiction and fragmentation, and this understanding is possible only through a full awareness of the phenomenon. *An awareness without dissociation or discrimination between the observer (the subject) and the observed (the object)*—an extremely difficult point! Only then can the analytical-fragmentary way of thinking disappear [13].

The inner fragmentation can therefore disappear only through intense awareness of the present, a very difficult thing for our *mind*, *which is not used to facing a thing directly*, without deluding itself, that is, *without trying to analyze it, change it, modify it, project it or intervene on it*. However, in order to avoid this analytical-fragmentary way when we are confronted with a fact, we must be aware of the present, without any prior preference or discrimination, complete understanding not being possible as long as the mind operates on itself, trying, unconsciously, to analyze, change, modify or intervene [13].

This is why Krishnamurti believes it is so important to first understand *the thinking process, how we think, before we understand what we are thinking*, that is the content of our thoughts. It is essential to first understand the observer, the thinker or the subject, that is, the one who thinks, analyzes, searches, projects, fights, hopes, desires, chooses or rejects. *Is* the observer, the thinker or *the subject* separate *from the object* of his thoughts, analyses, searches, projections, struggles, hopes, desires, choices or rejections?

This is the reason why it is necessary to clarify the relationship between the observer and the observed from the perspective of its unity—analogous to the unity of the relationship between the content of thought and the process of thinking that produces this content.

5.2 The observer (the subject) and the observed (the object)

The content of our thought, says Krishnamurti, consists of an enormous succession of images made up by our thinking process and centered on the observer (the subject). But who is the observer (the subject)? The observer (the subject) is the thinker, the experimenter, the evaluator, the judge, the censor, that is, the central image—the "I"-, created over time by the totality of images, as a result of experiences, memories, tradition, nationality, religion, education, family, culture, etc. all these making up the past, the background of the observer (the subject). *Is the observer (the subject) different from these images, respectively from the object*? Isn't the observer (the subject) just another image? [10]. The observer himself is an image, says Krishnamurti, the central image—the "I," the subject—which was created by all the other images in the course of time, only that the observer (the subject) has separated from the other images (from the object), and believes that there is a separation, a space-time interval within which the observer (the subject) could analyze, modify, compare, measure, judge, repress or even destroy the observed objects [10].

Krishnamurti considers that as long as there is a center from which the observer or the thinker looks, *this center creates a space-time interval between the subject and the observed object*, which disappears only when there is no longer any center. It is said, for instance, that in ancient China before an artist began to paint a tree, he would sit down in front of it until *he became the tree* [10]. In that state of fusion or unity with the tree, there was no space-time interval between the painter and the painted tree, that is between the subject and the object or the observer and the observed so that the painter (the subject) became the tree (the object painted).

Rejecting the classical analytical process, on the grounds that, by examining step by step each thought, feeling or intention, this approach introduces a division or a *space-time interval which distorts the direct vision*, Krishnamurti believes that the only way to truly know is that in the present, i.e., out of time. Since the only truth that can be total, immediate, spontaneous or outside of time, is the *present*, Krishnamurti distinguishes between *having knowledge about myself*, which always involves the past, time and *knowing directly myself*, which does not involve time, because knowing in my own psychological field is always something related to the present, that is the field of perception, attention, observation and action, as a unitary whole. Therefore, if we observe with our *whole attention*, with our whole being, with everything that is in us, with our eyes, with our ears, with our nerves and if we abandon ourselves to our own presence, *we will become one with it*, there being no more a space-time interval between the observer (the subject) and the observed (the object).

Let us give an example and see what actually means this direct, nonanalytical, nondualistic and nonfragmentary perception in which *the observer (the subject) becomes the observed (the object)*. Let us take, for instance, one of the fundamental states of our consciousness, which is *suffering*. There are a variety of forms of suffering, but the main element of suffering is the structure of that central image which is the "I," the subject or the observer, so that this central image, which is the observer (the subject), comes to suffer [9]. Is it possible, ask Krishnamurti, a direct perception of the fact itself? Is it possible for the observer to look directly at suffering, without the intention of overcoming it, of running away from it, of wanting a way out and *without the intention of analyzing it*—all these being based on time, on the thought of becoming from "what it is" to "what should be"—but simply "living" with it, being aware of it and carefully observing all its movements? When the thought—which is the past—does not intervene, does not invade the suffering trying to escape it, what happens? *Is the observer different from suffering or is the observer, the subject itself that object of suffering?* The observer (the subject) is the suffering (the object), he is not something different from the suffering, so there is no fragmentation, but only total attention and awareness. Before, the observer separated from his suffering precisely because he was trying to escape from it, but now, *when the observer realizes that the suffering is himself*, without any separation, any intervention becomes useless, because there is no longer the center to suffer. Thus, a *radical transformation* took place, in the sense that the suffering (the object), no longer separated from the observer (the subject), disappeared completely, without the intervention of the thought, will or choice [10]. Advising us, therefore, to remain in suffering without trying, through thought, to run away, escape or separate from it, Krishnamurti shows that suffering disappears when we approach it in its entirety, without trying to avoid it.

5.3 The observer (the subject) is the observed (the object)

Any other movement of the observer, who has not become aware of the fact that he is the observed thing, creates a series of mechanisms of thoughts and images that chain him even more in a vicious circle. Therefore, Krishnamurti believes that in the case of any psychological problem, it is very important to solve it immediately, in order not to catch "roots" in the soil of our mind, which will distort our perception. Thus, putting an immediate end to fear, suffering, attachment, jealousy, violence, anger, lying or other destructive states is, according to Krishnamurti, the only total and liberating action, because any action that is not immediate introduces the notion of time and the thought of becoming, which leads to the endless postponement of our problems [14]. Therefore, *any psychological problem must be approached with that sense of urgency*, that is "now," immediately, *in the present*, because otherwise we will be "caught" in the very source of the problem—a vicious circle from which it will be difficult to escape.

So, can we—as observers—to look directly, without any distortion of the thought of becoming, the entire content of our consciousness? Regarding the question of consciousness and its content, it is very important to discover whether we—as observers—observe or whether consciousness becomes lucid by itself. This is, according to Krishnamurti, an essential difference. If we, as observers, observe the movement of our consciousness (desires, fears, sufferings, ambitions, hopes, attachments, beliefs and all other contents of consciousness) as if *we were looking at them from the outside*, *as a separate entity* that intervenes saying: "this is good/this is bad," then we find ourselves "caught" in the same web of thought, perpetuating the same old pattern of fragmentation or separation [9].

But there is another approach, a *nonanalytical or nonfragmentary/nondualistic* one, *when consciousness becomes lucid by itself*, that is, when our thinking realizes that it only observes itself, that is, it observes everything it has created, namely the content of our consciousness. Only in this pure observation, in which there is no movement of thought, does the observer realize that he and what he observes are one and the same, in the sense that all the content of consciousness—fear, suffering, desire, beliefs, anger, jealousy, etc.—are not separate from the observer, but he is all these.

When the observer (the subject) realizes that he is the observed object and that *the content of his consciousness is his very consciousness* [11], *then any movement of the observer stops.* He no longer intervenes at all, because he realizes that the object on which he was acting was nothing but "himself"—as an observer [10]. When he was separated, he tried to change, modify and correct, but now, when he realizes that any action is, in fact, returning to him, any action or intervention ceases. What can the observer do "with that something which is itself?" He can neither fight against it, nor run away from it, nor even accept it. That something is "there." Then, any action that is the result of the reaction to pleasant or unpleasant ends and a lucidity appears that has become extremely alive and that no longer depends on the analytical activity of a center. From the intensity of this awareness is born an attention of such a special quality, "that the mind—which is this awareness—has become extraordinarily sensitive and highly intelligent" [10].

This *total attention* is, according to Krishnamurti, the true *meditation* by which the movement of thought comes to an end, thereby taking place a total action that has put an end to the analytical-fragmentary way of perception, thinking and acting.

5.4 Meditation: The model of a nondualistic, nonanalytical and nonfragmentary way of perception, thinking and acting

The meaning that Krishnamurti gives to meditation is completely different. To meditate is not to follow a certain technique, a certain result or a certain target. Meditating does not mean analyzing, controlling our thoughts or disciplining our emotions and feelings. All these are based on concentration, on that operation of thought that tries to modify, compare, correct or measure something according to a "program" or pattern, so that concentration brings with it conformity, obedience, authority, mechanism, automaticity and control.

Based on exclusion, division, censorship and effort, concentration is itself a source of fragmentation, preventing the brain from functioning at its full capacity and energy. On the contrary, *meditation, which is attention, means the understanding of the totality of life in which any form of (analytical) fragmentation has ceased*. In other words, meditation is the capacity of the brain, to free itself from its own conditioning, functions not partially, but totally [9]. This is possible when the structure of thought is understood, that is, the process of thinking and its content, this understanding being equivalent, according to Krishnamurti, to his own discipline. To meditate means to investigate every moment of what is happening within ourselves, to be aware of every thought, of every feeling, without analyzing or condemning, but only observing that inner phenomenon, just letting it "blossom" and reveal its content. This is the meaning that Krishnamurti gives to meditation, considering that only meditation can bring order to the thinking process without the intervention of thought, will, desire or choice.

Thus, meditation becomes a nondualistic, nonanalytical and nonfragmentary model of perception, thinking and acting, based on the direct vision of the present, of "what it is". It is about the art of being in a state of passive or nondiscriminating receptivity, which allows things to blossom from themselves and reveal their content, their interiority. In this pure observation, which is a spontaneous act of awareness of what exists, *there is no more a space-time interval between the observer (the subject) and the observed (the object)*, there is only total attention, i.e., total meditation. Only this total and nondiscriminating attention/meditation, similar to the spontaneous, nondualistic or nonanalytical perception, thinking and acting could put an end, according to Krishnamurti to the analytical-fragmentary vision and illusion.

6. Conclusion: From the quantum revolution to the psychological/psychotherapeutic revolution

Because this nondualistic, nonanalytical and nonfragmentary model of perception, thinking and acting suggested by Bohm and Krishnamurti, is in perfect harmony, coherence, resonance and correspondence with the principle of nonseparability from the new paradigm of quantum physics, then this *nondualistic way of perception, thinking and acting* could therefore constitute *the new reference system for any new psychology and psychotherapy*, especially since this nondualistic and nonfragmentary way of perception and thinking is legitimized by the new epistemological paradigm of quantum physics.

Since the assumption that led to the quantum revolution is that the world cannot be analyzed in terms of separable entities, but in terms of nonseparable entities of an entire cosmic, inseparable and indivisible, whose fundamental property is the nonseparability or global intercorrelation, I consider that from this principle of quantum theory derives the most significant psychological implications for human consciousness, which could legitimate a new *psychological or psychotherapeutic model of subject-object nonseparability*.

As a result, the attempt to legitimize a *psychological/psychotherapeutic model of human consciousness nonseparability or subject-object nonseparability*, based on another way of perceiving and thinking reality, a *nonfragmentary* one, which could put an end to the classic paradigm of subject-object separability, becomes all the more actual and vital for the future of humanity, as this way of thinking is legitimized by the new scientific paradigm of quantum theory.

This is why, the psychological/psychotherapeutic stake targets, on the basis of the law of symmetry and nonseparability between microcosmos and macrocosmos, subject and object, observer and observed, part and whole, consciousness and matter, individual and society, which is to say on the basis of the self-consistency of the whole, moving from the paradigm of quantum nonseparability to the paradigm of psychological/psychotherapeutic subject-object nonseparability. Overall, it is about the awareness of the profound psychological/psychotherapeutic implications of quantum nonseparability upon human consciousness, a fact which raises the question if it is possible that human consciousness to suffer, given the nonseparability or global intercorrelation of reality, a profound "*psychological revolution*," analog to the quantum revolution in physics, which would put an end to the classic analytical-fragmentary model, that is, the subject-object separability.

I consider that the most challenging implication of quantum nonseparability is of psychological nature, it targets the human consciousness, respectively the fact that the individual (*the subject*) can no longer be perceived as a separate consciousness from *the object*, that is from the world's consciousness, the human consciousness being seen in the sense of the nonseparability between individual and society, subject and object or part and whole. The principle of nonseparability can thus become *the principle of the new psychological model of subject-object nonseparability*, based on the profoundly psychological understanding that the *individual (the subject) fundamentally represents the entire humanity (the object)*, being responsible for its future or destiny.

This model of human consciousness nonseparability or subject-object nonseparability, legitimized by the new paradigm of quantum physics, could therefore constitute a basis for new, nonfragmentary, nondualistic and nonanalytical forms, perspectives or applications in psychotherapy.

Conflict of interest

The authors declare no conflict of interest.

Author details

Ramona Ardelean
National University of Science and Technology POLITEHNICA Bucharest, Romania

*Address all correspondence to: ramona.ardelean.m@gmail.com

References

[1] Bohm D. Wholness and the Implicate Order. London and New York: Routledge Classics; 2002. pp. Xİ-Xİİİ, 1-23

[2] Ardelean R. Bootstrap's monadology. Symmetry and mirroring connections between Chew's bootstrap monadology and Leibniz's monadology. Balkan Journal of Philosophy. 2022;**14**(2):173-182

[3] Capra F. The Tao of Physics. An Exploration of the Parallels between Modern Physics and Eastern Mysticism. Boston, Massachusetts: Shambhala Publications; 1991. p. 23, 286-310

[4] Bohm D, Hiley BJ. On the intuitive understanding of non-locality as implied by quantum theory. Foundations of Physics. 1975;**5**:93-105

[5] Heinsenberg W. Physics and Philosophy. London: Allen & Unwin; 1963. pp. 75-96

[6] Bohr N. Atomic Physics and the Description of Nature. London: Cambridge University Press; 1934. p. 57

[7] Chew GF. Bootstrap: A scientific idea? Science. 1968;**161**:762-764

[8] Bohm D. Thought as a System, Seminars. Routledge, London and New York; 1994. p. 6

[9] Krishnamurti J. The Network of Thought. London: Krishnamurti Foundation Trust Ltd.; 1982. pp. 12-80

[10] Krishnamurti J. Freedom from the Known. Krishnamurti Foundation India: Vasanta Vihar; 1999. pp. 130-135

[11] Krishnamurti J. The Awakening of Intelligence. England: Krishnamurti Foundation Trust Ltd.; 1973. pp. 57-125

[12] Krishnamurti J, Bohm D, Shainberg D. The Wholeness of Life: Seven Dialogues. Krishnamurti Foundation India: Vasanta Vihar; 1997. p. 204

[13] Krishnamurti J. The First and Last Freedom, with a Foreword by Aldous Huxley. Krishnamurti Foundation India: Vasanta Vihar; 2001. pp. 52-101

[14] Krishnamurti J, Bohm D. The Ending of Time: Thirtheen Dialogues. Krishnamurti Foundation India: Vasanta Vihar; 2000. pp. 30-95

Chapter 7

Positive Psychotherapy: A Transcultural Approach to Psychotherapy for the Twenty-First Century

Andre Marseille

Abstract

In the context of globalization's transformative effects on culture, which often engender heightened anxiety and fear, therapists must delve deeply into their clients' cultural backgrounds. This exploration must extend beyond surface-level discussions of multicultural issues such as race, ethnicity, gender, gender identity, sexual orientation, age, anxiety, and religion. Instead, therapists should investigate how the intersectionality of these factors shapes their clients' identities and influences the values and meanings they derive from their experiences. Given the frequent media coverage of existential crises in our rapidly evolving world, an existential cross-cultural approach to therapy is increasingly relevant. This book chapter introduces Positive Psychotherapy as a new, innovative therapy approach for transcultural use. Positive Psychotherapy, introduced by Peseschkian in 1977 and translated into English in 1987, emphasizes concrete human experiences by focusing on "positive" or "positivus" principles, distinguishing it from other therapeutic approaches. This article explores the rationale for adopting Positive Psychotherapy to address the complexities of modern therapeutic needs.

Keywords: globalization, culture, psychotherapy, multiculturalism, mental health

1. Introduction

In an era defined by globalization, therapists have an important and ethical responsibility to understand and address the cultural dynamics that shape their clients' identities, world views, and perceived problems in living. As technological and engineering innovations bring nations closer, cultural exchanges among diverse peoples become more frequent and intense. Many view this as an example of Cultural globalization [1], which explains the spread of ideas, meanings, and values across the globe that amplify social relations and expand our collective consciousness. Martin Luther King Jr., Paulo Freire, Thich Nhat Hanh, the Dalai Lama, Antonio Gramsci, Aung San Suu Kyi, Barack Obama, James Baldwin, and others have long illuminated a fundamental truth, that our humanity, liberation, and future are inextricably bound. It appears that globalization is undoubtedly making that case.

As such, globalization not only represents a robust exchange of ideas, values, and relations but also amplifies cultural anxiety—emotional suffering from cultural collisions and the disorienting pace of cultural change. In such moments, the members of a society or particular culture feel this anxiety, but the marginalized and powerless often bear more significant emotional, psychological, financial, and even spiritual burdens. From an existential view, the marginalized and their struggles diminish the collective human spirit. This is a view of humanity embraces the inevitability of globalization. Though a bit existential, in a singular context, namely, counseling, understanding cultural anxiety mandates not just a surface-level exploration of patients' backgrounds but a proactive and genuine comprehension of the intricate ways culture and multiculturalism shape their identities, including beliefs, values, and patterns of behaviors.

Remaining in the existential space, to help deepen our comprehension of culture and multiculturalism, the impacts of globalization, one must grapple with what it means to be human; that is, in what ways do we engage meaningfully with culture and its philosophical and practical terms? Through this lens, we begin to appreciate a crucial, often overlooked aspect of multiculturalism: culture is not an external construct separate from the person but the very context in which human existence unfolds. Hence, any discussion about humanity is, at its core, a conversation about culture, for every human is born into and shaped by culture, and culture can be anything that is not nature. Culture is the fuel that helps construct our social maps, or Weltanschauungs', as the German philosophers termed it. It helps us interpret the world and subtly guides our reactions, values, perceptions, and behaviors. In this way, culture does not merely define our collective humanity; it forms the foundation of our experience and existence. It is not merely an external influence but a collected consciousness embedded deeply into one's humanness, unconsciously shaping our core beings [2].

While multiculturalism highlights the diverse ways in which different groups navigate life, it is equally crucial to recognize the shared human experience that underlies these differences. Culture helps define the existential nature of our collective humanity. It helps us distinguish between nature and nurture, the meaningful and the meaningless, and that humanity has much more in common than simply otherwise [3]. So, despite the rich tapestry of cultural variations, all humans start from a common origin. The shared aspects of our existence are evident in that, as a species, the human genome is, on average, ~99.6% identical and ~ 0.4% different [4]. Hence, the variations found in humankind are superficial at best, reflecting our adaptability to nature, geography, and climate.

Perhaps a universal maxim, across the globe, in both urban and rural settings, individuals often seek ways to address their mental health concerns. For example, in Argentina, Puerto Rico, and Ecuador, many turn to curanderos or shamans to address emotional and psychological concerns. Similar practices are evident in Kyrgyzstan, Nigeria, and rural South Africa. In Iceland, people may consult fortune-tellers, while in India, some seek the guidance of astrologers for psychological support. In Pakistan, Islamic teachings heavily influence the frameworks of counseling. Malaysia sees the integration of Buddhist, Hindu, and Islamic principles into its counseling paradigms, while Singapore incorporates Buddhist ideologies. Japan's cultural context has given rise to distinctive counseling approaches, such as Morita therapy and Naikan therapy, which emphasize acceptance and understanding of one's own and others' feelings and perspectives. Hence, culture profoundly influences how we interpret the past and history, shaping our understanding of the present and our approach to the future.

As globalization continues to augment our interconnectedness, culture will remain a powerful force, guiding how we define ourselves and navigate the complexities of an interconnected world.

I would be remiss not to denote the existential issue of climate change and its inevitable impact on culture and mental health. In a world facing the profound challenges climate change will bring in the next 30–50 years, the field of mental health care must evolve to view climate change as an issue that is not separate from culture but thoroughly intertwined with it. As the manifestations of climate change, such as eco-anxiety, grief over environmental losses, and the stress of adaptation, become increasingly entwined with cultural and social realities, the role of mental health care will become ever more critical [5]. The universality of the climate crisis and the existential threat to humanity it presents also provides mental health professionals with a unique opportunity to transcend traditional boundaries, views, and perspectives on culture and foster more inclusive, holistic approaches to mental health care.

Enter Positive Psychotherapy (PPT). PPT views culture not as a mere backdrop to human experience but as a dynamic, ever-present force interwoven into the fabric of people's existence. PPT is a form of psychotherapy that offers a systematic but flexible framework that meets the transcultural needs of a globalizing world because it emphasizes integrating cultural understanding and diverse healing practices into its therapeutic interventions. PPT recognizes that culture and contexts shape not only the way people know but also influence the types of stressors clients face, the clinical assessments conducted, and the interventions employed. PPT's transcultural approach in its theory and application is sensitive to patients needs as they navigate the complex interplay of personal, cultural, and global challenges to their well-being and mental health, often requires a deeper exploration of how factors like race, ethnicity, and gender, sexual orientation, class, social and economic capital, intersectionality, and religion intersect to shape an individual's identity and worldview [6].

2. Positive psychotherapy—An introduction

"All men have been created to carry forward an ever-advancing civilization."
Ref. [7].

Founded by the late Dr. Nossrat Peseschkian—an influential psychotherapist, psychiatrist, and neurologist in 1960s Germany—Positive Psychotherapy (PPT) emerged from his own transcultural experience as an Iranian-born man living in Europe in the mid-1950s. This transition heightened his awareness of the cultural differences in behavior, customs, and attitudes between Europe and the Middle East, which profoundly shaped his thinking. These observations became the foundation for his innovative and evolving form of psychotherapy deeply anchored in transcultural principles and a positive conception of humanity.

PPT integrates elements from various psychological schools, including psychodynamic, humanistic, medical, behavioral, and cognitive approaches, offering a transcultural model for understanding mental health and well-being. In this approach, culture and religion are not peripheral but central themes, similar to their application in Viktor Frankl's logotherapy and Irvin Yalom's existential psychotherapy, both of which influenced Peseschkian's thinking.

Moreover, PPT draws heavily on philosophical insights from both religion and existentialism, with the Bahá'í Faith serving as a cornerstone of Peseschkian's belief in the spiritual dimension of human existence. This spiritual perspective underscores the inherent potential within each individual, allowing for a holistic approach to therapy that transcends cultural and existential boundaries, promoting personal growth and well-being through an integrated understanding of human nature.

At the heart of PPT is a fundamentally positive view of humanity, positing that each individual possesses inherent physical, mental, and spiritual capacities that can be nurtured and developed. These capacities, when harnessed, lead to personal growth and fulfillment. This optimistic perspective emphasizes human potential rather than pathology, guiding individuals toward realizing their innate strengths [8]. By focusing on possibilities for growth and transformation, PPT seeks to foster a sense of empowerment and self-awareness, helping individuals navigate life's challenges while maintaining a connection to their cultural and spiritual identities.

In developing his form of therapy, Dr. Peseschkian, an active and respected figure in the psychological and psychiatric community, collaborated with prominent mental health professionals like Heinrich Meng in Basel, Raymond Battegay, Jacob Levy Moreno, and Gaetano Benedetti throughout the 1960s and 1970s. During this period, he delivered lectures on his evolving theory and approach to psychotherapy, articulating the principles that would later define PPT. His ideas culminated in the publication of several books, with his first major work, *Positive Psychotherapy*, serving to introduce and name this innovative approach formally. By 1979, PPT had gained further recognition by establishing structured training programs and founding key institutions, including the Psychotherapeutic Group of Wiesbaden, the German Association for Positive Psychotherapy, and the launch of the Journal of Positive Psychotherapy. These developments solidified PPT's role as a transformative and transculturally oriented therapeutic model that continues to influence the landscape of psychotherapy today.

A number of perspectives underpin PPT, including Humanistic/Existential, Psychodynamic, Cognitive-Behavioral, and Spiritual. The Humanistic perspective of Positive Psychotherapy emphasizes the individual's capacity for rational decision-making and personal growth. This approach is rooted in the principles of humanistic psychology, which highlight the importance of self-awareness and the potential to confront and navigate fundamental existential concerns such as loneliness, the search for meaning, the experience of freedom, and the inevitability of death. In this context, PPT aligns closely with humanistic philosophy, which values individuals' innate dignity and potential.

The Psychodynamic perspective of PPT focuses on uncovering the unconscious meanings and motivations that underlie problematic behaviors, feelings, and thoughts. Central to this approach is the concept of conflict analysis, where PPT views conflicts as clashes of values and interests, often stemming from the disparity between expectations and reality. These values are deeply embedded in cultural contexts, serving as primary motivators for behavior and thought. By examining these culturally conditioned values—referred to as Actual Capacity—PPT allows for a nuanced understanding of how cultural factors shape individual experiences and conflicts.

Positive Psychotherapy draws on the principles of Cognitive Behavioral Therapy (CBT), which emphasizes the role of learning in shaping both adaptive and maladaptive behaviors. This dimension of PPT is action-oriented, focusing on identifying and altering dysfunctional thought patterns that lead to emotional or behavioral distress. The premise here is that by changing one's thoughts, it is possible to change one's emotional responses and actions, thereby improving overall well-being.

The Spiritual perspective of PPT is perhaps the most distinct, drawing inspiration from the teachings of the Bahá'í Faith. Influenced by the comprehensive theory of knowledge presented by 'Abdu'l-Bahá (1844–1921), PPT incorporates four methods of knowing: sensation, reason, tradition, and inspiration. It is also the foundation of the Balance Model. Historically, different fields of inquiry have prioritized one or two of these methods—philosophers leaning on reason, empiricists on sensation, and religious scholars on tradition. Peseschkian adapted these methods to psychology, proposing that both conscious and unconscious experiences fundamentally shape the capacity to know and that this capacity is deeply intertwined with spiritual understanding.

Positive Psychotherapy embraces a holistic and integrative approach that honors the intricate tapestry of human experience. It recognizes the delicate interplay between life's physical, mental, and spiritual dimensions, all within a culturally attuned framework. By doing so, PPT addresses the immediate symptoms of distress and fosters the emergence of a deeper, more resilient sense of self. This approach reflects the transcultural principle that, despite the diversity of human experiences, a shared potential for growth and healing exists that transcends cultural and existential boundaries. In the subsequent sections of this chapter, we will delve into the foundational aspects of Positive Psychotherapy, exploring its core principles and concepts, including basic and actual capacities, life energy and balance, and the PPT counseling process.

3. Three core principles of positive psychotherapy

Positive Psychotherapy has three central tenets: the Principle of Hope, the Principle of Balance, and the Principle of Consultation that must be conveyed in therapy to achieve a positive outcome for patients [9]:

3.1 The principle of hope

Hope emphasizes a positive conception of humanity. Rather than focusing solely on eliminating disruptions, individuals are encouraged to examine them thoroughly to decipher their positive or actual (given) qualities. The therapist helps individuals understand the true purpose of these disruptions and see them from a new perspective. For instance, a sleep disturbance might be reinterpreted as the ability to function with little sleep, and a low mood might be seen as the capacity to respond to internal or external conflicts. Symptoms are viewed as signals indicating the need to bring life qualities back into balance.

3.2 The principle of balance

This principle addresses the dynamic nature of conflict and its contents. According to Peseschkian's balance model, individuals cope with conflict in four areas of life: body/sense, achievement/activities, contact/environment, and fantasy/future. These areas are innate to each person, but cultural tendencies influence their emphasis. People often focus more on body-oriented and achievement-oriented coping in the Western Hemisphere, whereas relationship-oriented and future-oriented coping mechanisms are more prevalent in the Eastern Hemisphere. When these coping mechanisms are out of balance, illness and negative symptoms may arise.

3.3 The principle of consultation

The principle of consultation emphasizes the humanistic part of PPT. It defers to the patient as the expert in their own lives. The therapist, through consultation, works with the patient through five phases of therapy. They include:

- Observation: Identifying and understanding the problem.
- Inventory: Collecting detailed information about the individual's life and issues.
- Situational Encouragement: Providing support and motivation.
- Verbalization: Expressing and articulating thoughts and feelings.
- Goal Expansion: Developing and striving toward new, positive objectives.

PPT employs a semi-structured approach, ensuring therapy is accessible, relatable, and effective for diverse populations. This fosters a deeper understanding and connection between therapist and client. While most psychotherapeutic approaches focus on treating disturbances and illnesses, Peseschkian and his school prioritize human capacities as the core and indispensable focus of therapy. Swiss psychoanalyst Raymond Battegay [10] characterizes Positive Psychotherapy (PPT) as a method of depth psychology that engages the individual and collective unconscious through transcultural comparison. According to Battegay, PPT goes beyond the scope of manualized cognitive behavioral therapy and process-oriented analytical psychotherapy, offering a more integrative approach by drawing on the transcultural aspects of human experience and exploring the deep-seated influences of culture and shared human heritage on the individual psyche [10]. This perspective underscores PPT's unique ability to bridge individual psychological processes with broader cultural and collective dimensions.

4. Two basic capacities

Existentialists assert that human existence is fundamentally 'basic', meaning it cannot be fully understood or explained through external observation alone. Instead, it must be studied from within the individual's own experience. This perspective emphasizes the subjective nature of existence, where personal perceptions, emotions, and consciousness shape meaning and reality [11]. Like Existentialists, Positive Psychotherapy (PPT) asserts that all individuals, regardless of gender, age, ethnicity, status, or psychological state, are endowed with two basic capacities that cannot be fully understood by external observation alone: the capacity to love and the capacity to know. These basic capacities (BC) form the foundation of a person's Actual Capacities (AC), which will be explored in more detail in the following section.

The capacity to love encompasses the ability to form attachments and encapsulates the inherent need for warmth and security within relationships. It is an inborn aspect of our emotional sphere and is foundational in shaping how we connect with others and navigate interpersonal relationships. From infancy, we develop our understanding of love and attachment through interactions with caregivers who nurture us. These early nurturing experiences influence our rapidly developing primary capacities, namely trust, contact, and love, that will serve as a baseline for future relationships with others and the broader social world. As we grow, the love we receive and give becomes a cornerstone for developing other relational abilities (primary capacities), shaping our emotional responses and how people engage in the world.

The capacity to know involves the ability to investigate oneself and the world using reason and logic. It fosters interaction, adaptation, and transformation, enabling us to explore and understand our environment and ourselves. This capacity not only shapes our sense of individuality but also drives our quest for knowledge, leading to the development of actual capacities through education and life experiences. As individuals engage with the world, they form secondary capacities, such as punctuality, orderliness, and reliability, which are acquired through learning and shaped by cultural influences. These capacities are integral to how we function in society, affecting our daily interactions and relationships.

In Positive Psychotherapy (PPT), the two basic capacities—love and knowing—serve as the foundation for personal growth and change. The capacity to love enables individuals to form meaningful connections, express emotions, and foster relationships, while the capacity to know equips them to understand and navigate the world around them. Together, these capacities underpin the development of actual capacities, which are further shaped by cultural exchanges and social influences. As individuals engage with their culture and environment, they cultivate these actual capacities, which coalesce into what Sullivan [3] described as a person's Orientation in Living or Personality. This concept reflects "the relatively enduring pattern of recurrent interpersonal situations which characterize a human life" ([3, 12], p. 10). It provides a framework for how individuals navigate life, guiding their interactions, choices, and self-concept.

Nossrat Peseschkian emphasized that these basic capacities are both theoretical and practical, influencing thoughts, behaviors, and emotional responses in all aspects of human life. The capacity to love and know is fundamental to making sense of one's existence, shaping how individuals relate to themselves, others, and the broader world. Through these capacities, individuals uncover their potential for growth and healing, transcending cultural, psychological, and existential boundaries. In this way, the development of love and knowing forms the bedrock for personal transformation, allowing people to navigate the complexities of life and relationships with greater awareness and resilience.

5. Actual capacities: The primary and secondary capacities

Peseschkian identified two fundamental capacities in every person: the capacity to love and the capacity to know. The capacity to love, representing emotionality, provides the groundwork for primary Actual Capacities (ACs), which are developed through relational experiences and observation. This basic capacity fosters the ability to form attachments, seek warmth, and build security within relationships. The capacity to know, representing cognition and learning, involves exploring oneself and the world with reason, facilitating interaction, adaptation, and transformation. The capacity to love manifests in primary actual capacities, such as patience, trust, and emotional connection. The capacity to know is expressed in secondary actual capacities, like orderliness, thrift, and cleanliness, which align more with culture, social norms, and intellectual understanding [13]. Conflicts arise when these capacities are misaligned with the individual's current life situation or when the coping strategies associated with these capacities fail (**Table 1**) [14].

In developing his theory of PPT, Peseschkian researched over twenty-five cultures and engaged with countless notable psychologists and medical doctors, which led him to conclude, "There is hardly a book on psychotherapy, psychosomatic medicine, social psychology, psychiatry, or pedagogy that does not refer, implicitly or explicitly, and in one way or another, to the actual capacities". Peseschkian observed that regardless of cultural background, these basic capacities evolve into dynamic patterns of psychosocial behavior.

In his writings, Peseschkian underscored the crucial role of actual capacities in shaping human interactions and relationships. Although often unspoken and unconscious, these capacities significantly influence how individuals perceive and engage with one another. Problems arise when certain capacities are either overdeveloped or underdeveloped, often leading to neurosis and interpersonal conflict [13]. These capacities frequently operate beneath the surface, acting as hidden sources of tension that manifest in various ways. Peseschkian explains that these capacities function as both "weapons" and "shields," depending on how they are applied within relationships and social interactions. These capacities are continuously tested in the social milieu, where individuals negotiate their existence. Misused or improperly applied, they can trigger immediate emotional responses like fear, insecurity, sadness, anger, hopelessness, and powerlessness. Over time, such misuse can lead to deeper psychological issues, including anxiety disorders, depression, and even psychosomatic conditions [15]. Conversely, when nurtured and employed appropriately, these capacities foster resilience, contributing to emotional stability and a sense of security—both vital for maintaining mental health [16, 17].

For therapists, basic and actual capacities are not viewed as fixed traits but rather as potentials for further development. Positive Psychotherapy recognizes these capacities as resources to be activated and harnessed in therapeutic practice, aiming not just to resolve conflicts but to promote personal growth. While cultural

Secondary capacities	Primary capacities
Punctuality	Love/acceptance
Orderliness	Model/example
Cleanliness	Patience
Obedience	Time
Politeness	Sexuality/tenderness
Honesty	Contact
Faithfulness	Trust
Justice	Hope
Thrift	Faith
Reliability	Doubt
Accuracy	Confidence
Diligence	Unity/integrity

Table 1.
Primary and secondary capacities.

and environmental influences shape these capacities, they are also unconsciously driven and evolve with the changing world, particularly as globalization reshapes human interactions. The central focus of Positive Psychotherapy is on unlocking human potential. It offers tools and strategies that provide a straightforward analysis of conflict dynamics, encouraging a deeper understanding of one's innate capacities. These capacities are seen not as static but as evolving potentials that can be developed to meet life's challenges. By activating these human resources, Positive Psychotherapy seeks to solve problems in a way that is both accessible and meaningful, fostering an approach that embraces the possibility of transformation and growth in every individual.

6. Life energy

The concept of a vital life force that permeates the universe and all living beings is deeply embedded in various cultural traditions [18]. From *qi* in China to *prana* in India, *pneuma* in Ancient Greece, *spiritus* in Latin, and *ruach* in Hebrew, these beliefs share a common understanding of an animating energy that sustains life. In the Western tradition, this idea is captured by "vitalism," the belief that living organisms possess a life-giving force that differentiates them from non-living matter. English physicist Oliver Joseph Lodge echoed this in his theory of the "G-field," which suggests that matter is a concentrated form of this vital life force, aligning with the notion that energy is the underlying substance of the physical world [19].

This holistic perspective aligns closely with Harry Stack Sullivan's conception of personality as an energy system, where energy manifests as tension (the potential for action) or as energy transformations (actions themselves). Sullivan saw personality as a dynamic interplay of needs, anxieties, and the potential for positive and negative outcomes, all rooted in this underlying energy. Sullivan also emphasized the dynamic nature of interpersonal relationships, where energy is continuously exchanged between individuals, shaping their psychological environment. These energy exchanges, or dynamisms, are patterns of energy transformation that characterize behavior and influence our interactions.

The larger point is that across different cultures and psychological theories, the concept of life energy serves as a unifying factor, highlighting the universal human experience of a vital force that animates and sustains us. This shared understanding of life energy transcends cultural and disciplinary boundaries, offering a common thread in exploring what it means to be human [18, 20]. The concept of life energy resonates with Nossrat Peseschkian's Positive Psychotherapy, which views life energy as evenly distributed across four key domains: body/sensation, achievement/activities, contact/environment, and fantasy/future in order to acquire and sustain optimum mental and physical health.

7. Life balance

Inspired by a concept from the Bahá'í Writings called "The Four Criteria of Comprehension" [21]. Nossrat Peseschkian developed the Balance Model, a central component of his psychotherapeutic method. This model offers a holistic framework for understanding how life energy is distributed across four essential domains of human existence. Rather than proceeding from a pathogenesis perspective, which focuses on disease and dysfunction, the Balance Model aligns with concepts of salutogenesis, emphasizing health, well-being, and personal growth.

At its core, the Balance Model asserts that human beings live and function within four interconnected areas of life, each influencing a person's overall satisfaction, self-worth, and ability to manage conflicts and challenges. These domains serve as the hallmarks of one's personality and capacity for adaptation in the present moment. The Balance Model describes the interaction between the biological–physical, rational–intellectual, socio-emotional, and imaginative–spiritual spheres of existence. These four domains form the foundation of daily life, reflecting the multidimensional nature of human experience. Each sphere is interdependent, influencing how individuals navigate relationships, health, personal growth, and existential concerns. For example, the biological–physical domain addresses bodily health and physical well-being, while the achievement–intellectual domain focuses on cognitive processes, efficacy, and the pursuit of knowledge. The socio-relational domain speaks to the quality of interpersonal relationships and emotional expression, and the imaginative–spiritual domain encompasses creativity, aspirations, inner meaning, and spiritual connection [22].

In everyday life, these domains are not isolated. Instead, they intertwine, shaping how individuals perceive the world and respond to its challenges. The Balance Model encourages therapists and clients alike to explore how these four dimensions manifest in one's life and to seek harmony between them. By recognizing and nurturing each domain, the model promotes a *comprehensive approach* to personal well-being, addressing not only the mind, but also the body, emotions, and spirit. Peseschkian's Balance Model offers a *health-oriented approach* that invites a deeper understanding of how individuals live in balance with themselves and the world. It reminds us that mental health is not simply the absence of pathology but the result of harmony across all aspects of life. [23]. These domains comprise:

1. *Body/Health*: This encompasses physical activities and perceptions, including eating, drinking, tenderness, sexuality, sleep, relaxation, sports, appearance, and clothing. It reflects how we care for and experience our physical selves.

2. *Work/Achievement*: This domain involves professional achievements and capabilities, including work, household duties, gardening, education, and money management. It represents how we engage with tasks, responsibilities, and our sense of accomplishment.

3. *Relationships/Social contact*: This area covers our interactions with partners, family, friends, acquaintances, and participation in social engagements. It captures the essence of our social connections and the support systems we build.

4. *Future/Fantasy/Meaning*: This domain includes our future plans, religious or spiritual practices, meditation, reflection, and the development of vision or imagination. It speaks to finding meaning, purpose, and direction in life.

The Life Balance Model posits that our well-being depends on the dynamic energy distribution across these domains. In therapeutic practice, the goal is to help individuals recognize and harness their resources to maintain equilibrium among these areas. Balance does not imply equal time allocation but rather the appropriate attention and energy to each domain, ensuring no area is neglected. Prolonged imbalance—where

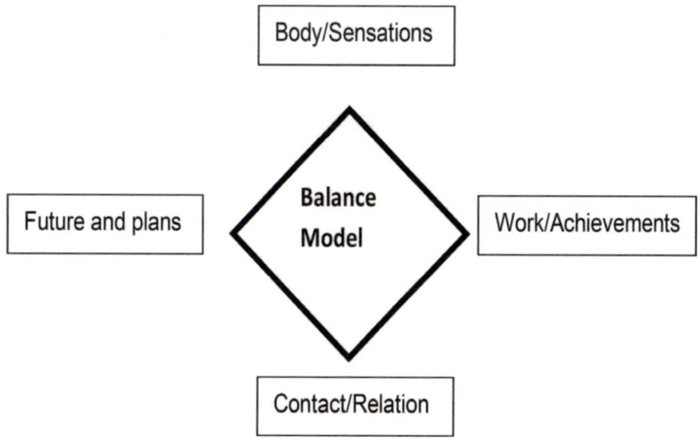

Figure 1.
The life balance model.

one or more domains are overlooked—can lead to internal conflicts and physical or psychological illnesses.

Peseschkian's model encourages us to view life as a complex interplay of physical, mental, social, and spiritual energies. Individuals foster resilience, well-being, and a more integrated sense of self by achieving balance among these domains.

The Life Balance Model is a practical framework for understanding how life energy is allocated across these domains. It offers insights into maintaining well-being and effectively addressing conflicts (**Figure 1**).

Life energy in Positive Psychotherapy is a concept that transcends cultural and disciplinary boundaries, emphasizing its universal significance in human experience. The partial goal of therapy is to restore equilibrium among the four domains by ensuring that each area receives an appropriate share of life energy. This balance is not about equal time but dynamic and proportional attention to each domain, recognizing that prolonged neglect or overemphasis in any area can lead to conflicts and illness.

In **Figure 2**, for example, we can see that the patient is allocating a significant amount of life energy to the work and achievement domains. From this view, the

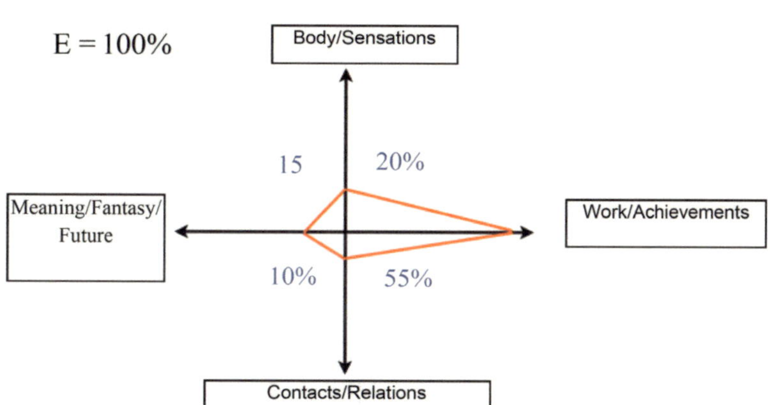

Figure 2.
Balance model and life energy distribution.

therapist can surmise that the patient may be neglecting significant aspects of his social life and not attending to his well-being. The model helps clarify the connections between conflicts and the resulting behaviors and attitudes by analyzing how individuals distribute their energy across these areas. In this way, Positive Psychotherapy offers a comprehensive approach to managing life's challenges, rooted in the balanced flow of life energy across all aspects of existence.

8. Conflicts

> *"According to the concept of Positive Psychotherapy, a healthy person is not one who has no conflicts, but rather one who has learned to deal adequately with these conflicts. Here "adequately" means not to neglect any of the four areas of life, but to distribute one's energy (not necessarily time!) approximately evenly into the four areas of life" ([24], p. 99).*

Positive Psychotherapy (PPT) offers a distinct and comprehensive approach to understanding and resolving conflicts by recognizing the complex interplay between external and internal struggles. PPT's conflict model is valuable for its ability to dissect the layers of conflict, showing how unresolved issues from the past intertwine with present struggles, and how these conflicts manifest both mentally and physically. The term "conflict," rooted in the Latin *confligere*, meaning to clash or fight, encapsulates the essence of this tension—whether it arises from incompatible inner values or external forces. PPT's psychodynamic view of conflict provides a nuanced framework for exploring how: conflicts manifest within the psyche, delineating the layers of conflict and their cumulative impact on the individual.

In this model, three primary types of conflicts are identified: the actual conflict, the basic conflict, and the inner conflict. Each represents a different dimension of how conflict operates within the human experience, contributing to both psychological and physical symptoms [14]. An actual conflict refers to a current life situation that creates emotional stress due to a mismatch between expectations and reality. This conflict is immediate, arising from day-to-day challenges such as a divorce, job loss, or other significant life events. These conflicts often test the individual's internal values, and though rooted in the present, they frequently trigger unresolved emotional issues from the past. For instance, the emotional pain of a divorce may reopen old wounds from an earlier experience, such as the loss of a parent, amplifying the intensity of the current situation [25].

The basic conflict is deeper and more unconscious, rooted in past experiences and long-held beliefs, values, and expectations—many of which were internalized during childhood. It represents a clash between primary and secondary capacities; hence, though an actual conflict may trigger it, it operates on a different level. The basic conflict often emerges when an individual's long-standing values or ideals are challenged by current events, causing an intense emotional reaction. For example, a person's strong belief in loyalty, formed in early childhood, may create a deep sense of inner turmoil when faced with the prospect of ending a toxic relationship.

Finally, inner conflicts are unconscious struggles between opposing desires or ideals. These conflicts often involve a clash between one's primary capacities, such as the deep need for love and connection, and secondary capacities, such as moral beliefs or societal expectations. Inner conflicts are experienced as a state of emotional tension, manifesting as indecision, ambivalence, or repetitive, dysfunctional behavior. For example, an individual may want to leave an unhappy marriage (an actual conflict) but be paralyzed by an ingrained moral belief against divorce (a basic conflict). This internal ambivalence often leads to cycles of emotional distress, anxiety, or depression as the person grapples with conflicting desires and values.

Conflicts arise from a clash of capacities, where emotions, affective states, and physical reactions signal a deeper inner conflict. These signals indicate a disturbance in the distribution of actual capacities—those values and virtues that shape how we navigate our lives. The extent that capacities are over or underdeveloped will influence how individuals perceive and react to conflicts in everyday life [15]. Culture will dictate the varying interpretations of concepts like love, justice, punctuality, and trust one has that can lead to psychological distress when mismatches occur.

Further, conflict reactions in PPT inspire the use of defense mechanisms or security operations to cope with the conflict. When the conflict or source of the conflict begins to cause notable emotional suffering, individuals might retreat into illness or somatization, where the body becomes the vehicle for unresolved psychological distress. For some, this manifests in excessive body-building, reflecting an overcompensation for perceived vulnerabilities or insecurities within the physical realm. This extreme focus on the body is a means of regaining control over what feels uncertain, yet it only highlights the deeper, unresolved conflicts within. In the work/achievement- sphere, people might overemphasize activity and achievement, rationalizing their distress through productivity. This often leads to feelings of overburdening and maladaptive adaptation—the relentless pursuit of success masks the inner turmoil, yet the individual finds themselves disconnected from true fulfillment, merely achieving for achievement's sake.

In the socio-relational domain, responses to conflict can manifest as refusal to perform, as withdrawal into loneliness, or an opposite extreme—excessive gregariousness. Both extremes are often accompanied by idealization or deprecation of relationships, leading to affective disturbances that erode social bonds. This results in changes in social behavior, where emotional intimacy is either avoided or idealized, leading to deep feelings of isolation or shallow interactions that fail to meet the individual's emotional needs. Finally, in the future/fantasy meaning domain, individuals may retreat into fantasy or become trapped in cycles of denial, resulting in psychological conditions such as anxiety, phobias, panic attacks, or addictive behaviors. The inability to fully engage the imaginative or spiritual aspects of life may lead to a lack of imagination, rendering the individual disconnected from the creative and existential aspects of their being, further perpetuating feelings of anxiety and alienation (**Figure 3**).

In this model, conflicts and imbalances across these four qualities of life highlight the complex interplay between the physical, intellectual, emotional, and spiritual dimensions of existence. Unresolved inner conflicts often lead to neurotic fixation, where individuals become stuck in predetermined patterns of experience and behavior, unable to break free on their own. The energy generated by these internal conflicts can result in symptomatic expressions, serving as temporary solutions to the underlying issues. Each domain, when overextended or neglected, can contribute to psychosomatic disturbances, emotional dysregulation, and distorted perceptions of reality. This underscores the importance of achieving balance, not only to prevent illness but also to foster holistic well-being and personal growth [22]. Finally, Positive Psychotherapy emphasizes the importance of understanding and addressing both actual and inner conflicts, using the balance model to restore harmony across the four domains of life. By differentiating between actual, basic, and inner conflicts,

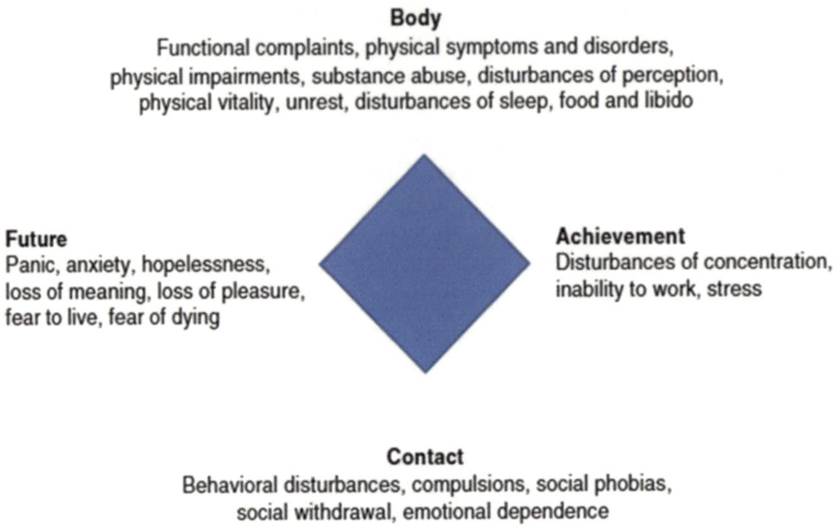

Figure 3.
Conflict reactions model.

recognizing the underlying capacities at play, and the cultural and individual factors that shape them, therapists can guide individuals toward more effective coping strategies and greater psychological resilience. In this therapeutic approach, understanding the content of the conflict is crucial.

9. The counseling process

In Positive Psychotherapy (PPT), culture is not merely an additional factor in understanding the origins of mental health concerns but a central theme within the counseling process. It is viewed as a source of both empowerment and inspiration for clients. Thus, the therapeutic interaction in PPT is designed to be a stage for culturally reflective interventions, where clients are encouraged to consciously reflect on their cultural backgrounds and how these shape their identity, challenges, and growth. This reflective process is then followed by intentional actions that help the client navigate life more effectively. The counseling process in PPT emphasizes the client's active participation in their own healing journey. Therapists draw upon a variety of interventions tailored to the individual's expressions during sessions. This client-centered approach allows the therapy to unfold according to each person's unique needs and experiences, fostering a deeper engagement with the therapeutic process.

One of the distinct components of PPT interventions is the integration of imagination and intuition. These are not just supplementary tools but fundamental aspects of the therapeutic work. For example, storytelling plays a key role in helping individuals articulate their journeys, challenges, and aspirations. Through narrative, clients begin to build a coherent sense of self, embedding their lived experiences into the stories they tell about themselves. This method promotes self-awareness and facilitates emotional expression in a culturally resonant way.

During the counseling process, the therapist may introduce cultural models of problem-solving by drawing on traditional resources, such as proverbs, stories, or wisdom from the client's own cultural background. These culturally grounded interventions help bridge the gap between the client's internal world and their cultural heritage, offering tools for coping that feel authentic and familiar. This approach aligns with Abraham Maslow's concept of positive psychology, which emphasizes the importance of focusing on an individual's positive qualities and inherent potential. By recognizing and nurturing the client's developmental possibilities, PPT helps individuals not only overcome their mental health concerns but also flourish by tapping into their strengths and capacities, promoting a holistic sense of well-being (**Figure 4**).

As discussed in previous sections, in PPT, symptoms and disorders are not seen as isolated problems to be eradicated but rather as responses to underlying conflicts. This perspective allows the therapist to address both the origins of the client's illness and the sources of their joy, strength, and potential. The term "positive" reflects this integrative approach, which balances the understanding of pathogenesis (the development of illness) with salutogenesis (the creation of health and well-being). By engaging both concepts, the therapist helps the client navigate their psychological struggles while also cultivating health.

A key element in PPT is the Principle of Consultation, which introduces a structured approach to therapy involving five stages. These stages integrate therapy with self-help, empowering the client to take an active role in their healing process. The five stages are:

Observation and distancing: This initial stage involves the patient identifying and expressing their desires and problems while maintaining a level of emotional detachment. The therapist aids this process by offering constructive interpretations of symptoms, often using metaphors and symbolic elements to help the patient gain perspective.

Taking inventory: In this stage, the focus shifts to exploring the patient's actual capacities. Using tools like the WIPPF (Wiesbaden Inventory for Positive Psychotherapy and Family Therapy) and the Balance Model, the therapist and patient reflect on significant life events and current circumstances, gaining insight into how these have shaped the patient's experiences.

Situational encouragement: Here, the therapy emphasizes activating the patient's internal resources and strengths. The patient is encouraged to draw on past successes and available capacities to confront and resolve current conflicts, fostering a sense of self-efficacy and resilience.

Verbalization: This stage involves helping the patient articulate and express the underlying conflicts related to the four dimensions of life: body/sensation, achievement/activities, contact/environment, and fantasy/future. The goal is to identify and address the secondary gains that may perpetuate the conflict while balancing openness and responsibility for emotional reactions.

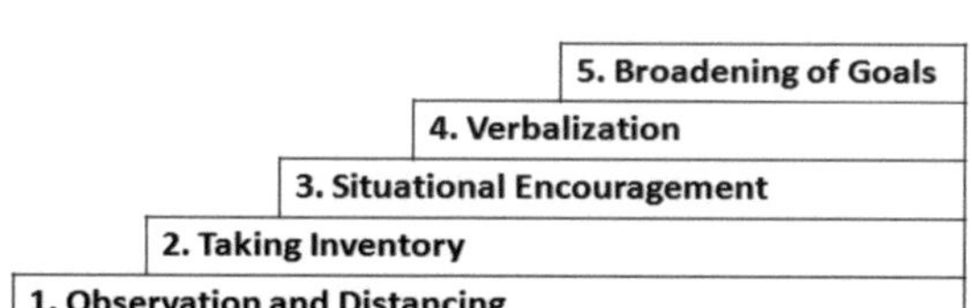

Figure 4.
PPT counseling process.

Expansion of goals: The final stage focuses on looking beyond the resolution of current problems to envision a future free from conflict. The therapist guides the patient in considering their goals and aspirations for the future, encouraging a forward-looking orientation in life. This stage includes reflection on changes in feelings, achievements, significance, and relationships with family and friends.

These five stages provide a comprehensive and flexible therapy system for addressing various aspects of an individual's well-being, promoting personal growth, and fostering future aspirations. By progressing through these stages, patients are guided toward resolving their immediate conflicts and empowered to envision and work toward a more fulfilling and balanced life. Positive Psychotherapy thus offers a holistic approach that integrates the therapeutic process with the patient's capacity for self-help, ultimately aiming to enhance overall well-being and resilience [26].

10. Conclusion

In our increasingly globalized world, where cultural transformations often heighten anxiety and fear, therapists must engage deeply with their clients' cultural backgrounds. This engagement must go beyond superficial discussions of race, ethnicity, gender, sexual orientation, age, and religion. Instead, therapists must explore how the intersection of these factors shapes their clients' identities and influences the values and meanings they derive from their experiences. An existential cross-cultural approach to therapy is becoming more relevant in a world frequently confronting existential crisis.

In Positive Psychotherapy, culture is not merely a backdrop to human experience but a dynamic, ever-present force that intertwines with the very fabric of our existence. While multiculturalism emphasizes the diverse ways different groups navigate life, it is equally crucial to acknowledge the shared human experience that underlies these differences. Culture plays a vital role in defining the existential nature of our collective humanity, guiding us in distinguishing between nature and nurture, the meaningful and the meaningless. It serves as a reminder that, despite our differences, humanity shares much more in common than we often recognize.

Positive Psychotherapy's five stages offer a transcultural therapeutic system for addressing the multiple aspects of an individual's well-being, promoting personal growth, and nurturing future aspirations. As patients progress through these stages, they are not only guided toward resolving their immediate conflicts. However, they are also empowered to envision and work toward a more fulfilling and balanced life. In this sense, positive psychotherapy presents a holistic approach that seamlessly integrates the therapeutic process with the patient's inherent capacity for self-help, ultimately enhancing overall well-being and resilience. Positive Psychotherapy invites us to view culture not as a barrier but as a bridge, connecting the diverse expressions of human life with the universal quest for meaning, balance, and well-being.

DOI: http://dx.doi.org/10.5772/intechopen.1007778

Author details

Andre Marseille
Chicago State University, Chicago, USA

*Address all correspondence to: amarse20@csu.edu

References

[1] James P. Globalism, Nationalism, Tribalism: Bringing Theory Back In. Sage Publications; 2006

[2] Vontress CE, Johnson JA, Epp LR. Cross-Cultural Counseling: A Casebook. American Counseling Association; 1999

[3] Sullivan HS. The Interpersonal Theory of Psychiatry. W.W Norton & Company; 1953

[4] Ahmed Z, Zeeshan S, Xiong R, Liang B. Debutant iOS app and gene-disease complexities in clinical genomics and precision medicine. Clinical and Translational Medicine. 2019;**8**(26). DOI: 10.1186/s40169-019-0242-3

[5] Koger SM, Leslie KE, Hayes ED. Climate change: Psychological solutions and strategies for change. Ecopsychology. 2011;**3**(4):227-235. DOI: 10.1089/eco.2011.0041

[6] Tseng W. Culture and psychotherapy: Asian perspectives. World Cultural Psychiatry Research Review. 2004;**13**(2):151-161. DOI: 10.1080/09638230410001669282

[7] Bahá'u'lláh. Gleanings from the Writings of Bahá'u'lláh. Bahá'í Publishing Trust; 1976

[8] Cohen B. Intervention and supervision in strengths-based social work practice. Social Work Journal. 1999;**80**(5):460-466. DOI: 10.1606/1044-3894.1475

[9] Rashid T. Positive psychotherapy: A strength-based approach. The Journal of Positive Psychology. 2014;**10**(1):25-40. DOI: 10.1080/17439760.2014.920411

[10] Battegay R. Salutogenese und Positive Psychotherapie. In: Jork K, Peseschkian N, editors. Salutogenese und Positive Psychotherapie. Huber; 2006

[11] Encarta. Existentialism. 2003. Available from: http://encarta.msn.com/encnet/refpages/RefArticle.aspx?refid=761555530andpn=1#s [Accessed: October 20, 2003]

[12] Sullivan HS. Conceptions of Modern Psychiatry. Washington D.C.: William A. White Psychiatric Foundation; 1947

[13] Peseschkian N. Positive Psychotherapy: Theory and Practice of a New Method. Springer-Verlag; 1987

[14] Goncharov M. Conflict model of positive psychotherapy. In: Messias E, Peseschkian H, Cagande C, editors. Positive Psychiatry, Psychotherapy and Psychology: Clinical Applications. Switzerland AG: Springer Nature; 2020. pp. 331-348. DOI: 10.1007/978-3-030-33264-8_27

[15] Peseschkian N. Positive psychotherapy in psychosomatic medicine. International Academy for Positive and Trans-cultural Psychotherapy—Professor Peseschkian Foundation. 2013

[16] Sue S, Cheng JKY, Saad CS, Chu J. Asian American mental health: A call to action. American Psychologist. 2012;**67**(7):532-544. DOI: 10.1037/a0028900

[17] Nela A, Parruca E. Impact of social media disinformation and of fake news overexposure on the actual capacities and the psychological wellbeing during the COVID-19 pandemic: A systemic literature review. Global Psychotherapy. 2023;**3**:126-132

[18] Ryan RM, Deci EL. From ego depletion to vitality: Theory and findings concerning the facilitation of energy available to the self. Social and Personality Psychology Compass. 2008;**2**(2):702-717. DOI: 10.1111/j.1751-9004.2008.00098.x

[19] Pranic energy sensations experienced by Indian adolescents: A cross-sectional study. Indian Journal of Traditional Knowledge. 2020;**19**(3). DOI: 10.56042/ijtk.v19i3.41448

[20] Fosha D. A heaven in a wild flower: Self, dissociation, and treatment in the context of the neurobiological core self. Psychoanalytic Inquiry. 2013;**33**(5):496-523. DOI: 10.1080/07351690.2013.815067

[21] Abdu'l-Bahá. The four criteria of comprehension. In: Some Answered Questions. Bahá'í World Centre; 2014. pp. 343-345

[22] Peseschkian H, Remmers A. Positive Psychotherapie. Ernst Reinhardt; 2013

[23] Remmers A. New trends in psychodynamic psychotherapy. In: Keynote Lecture Presented at the 4th World Conference on Positive Psychotherapy. Nikosia, Cyprus; 2007

[24] Jork K, Peseschkian N. Salutogenese Und Positive Psychotherapie. 2nd ed. Hans Huber; 2006

[25] Remmers A. The therapeutic process in positive psychosomatics: "Five fingers" forming a therapeutic relationship in psychosomatic medicine. In: Lecture Presented at the Tianjin Annual Academic Conference on Psychosomatic Diseases. 2021

[26] Schippers MC, Hogenes R. Energy management of people in organizations: A review and research agenda. Journal of Business and Psychology. 2011;**26**(2):193-203. DOI: 10.1007/s10869-011-9217-6

Chapter 8

Understanding the Process of Change in Psychotherapy

Francis D. Baudry

Abstract

This paper first presents the evolution of the theory of change in psychotherapy from Freud onwards. The second part presents my own struggle to foster change by overcoming obstacles. I believe it is important to avoid confronting defenses that foster an adversarial point of view. Instead, it is helpful to approach the understanding of behavior by focusing on the purpose it serves, i.e., the adaptive point of view.

Keywords: change, treatment process, relationship personal and professional, adaptation, supervision

1. Introduction

This chapter will explore the disconnect between the theory of change as it evolved since Freud's discoveries and what actually happens in the clinical situation and how difficult it is to pin down and explain the nature of change, what fosters it, and what impedes it.

My answer after working on the topic of how change actually works in the clinical setting is a disappointing 'I don't really know.' One major reason is that often when positive changes occur we do not try to figure out the complex dynamics with the patient. It can occur suddenly during an hour or some time afterwards quickly, or periodically as a result of some understanding that sinks in after working through. As an example, one of my patients was suffering from some GI symptoms that we assumed were at least in part psychosomatic. During a recent session in which he complained about their recurrence, we were able to deal with some aspects connected with a profound grief coupled with anxiety, which until then had been only partially put into words. For the following 2 days my patient's symptoms all but disappeared. Then they slowly came back. I have no way of ascertaining whether the improvement was coincidental, or whether it was related to beginning to master the sense of loss, or whether just the idea itself that we were hitting pay dirt was sufficient to bring temporary relief to this very insightful individual.

2. Review of literature on methodology

The available literature on methodology is, not surprisingly, disappointing; for reasons to be spelled out in my paper, it is almost impossible to identify what the specific dynamics are that account for change.

The first identified review by A Kazdin [1]: 'Mediators and Mechanisms of Change in Psychotherapy Research' comes up empty handed and concludes that there are no evidence-based explanations about how our best interventions lead to change. Another article by Murphy and Cooper [2] attempting to study mechanisms of change in depression likewise comes up empty handed. A third article by Werbart [3] concludes that the dream of a concerted uniform methodology in psychotherapeutic research must probably be abandoned since the actual situation is characterized by methodologic pluralism.

3. Definition of change

What we mean by change has to be clarified. I will limit myself in this paper to positive change, although one could also explore what leads to negative change. There can be transient change due to external circumstances, for example, a lessening of anxiety after the patient is promoted in his or her job. There can also be a temporary dramatic change, for example when a patient enters treatment with magical expectations of cure related to the emergence of an idealized transference. In this paper, however, I will focus on the process of change that results from increase in effective understanding as a result of lengthy therapeutic work.

The change can lead to lessening of painful moods or affects such as anxiety, depression, or mourning or to a decrease of particular symptoms. The most reluctant and slow aspect of change, if not resistance to change, however, is rooted in the dynamics of a person's character. I have written a number of papers on this particular topic [4, 5]. Our character is part of our personal identity. By nature quite stable and also rigid, it is heavily invested with narcissism and in general it is that part of a person that is most resistant to change particularly in training analysis, which may impose an additional burden on the candidate fearful of raising too many controversial issues. As an example, I remember supervising, many years ago, a rather narcissistic and angry candidate who could not tolerate disagreement and was quite fixed in her views. One day she brought a session in which she identified some changes, which she attributed to her good work. There was very little she would tolerate except my reluctant agreement that her work seemed to be progressing at this time.

An aspect that has changed over time is the nature of what can be defined as a complete interpretation. During my training in the 1960's, I was taught that following Waelder's system an interpretation to be complete and effective required an ego part, a superego part, a drive aspect, and a reference to reality. My supervisors did not seem to adhere to this model as far as I can remember.

4. Freud's views

Freud's initial views were related to the bringing into consciousness deeply repressed unconscious fantasies often based on early trauma. Repeated interpretations with working through would lead to insight, the pathway to change. Defenses and resistances would be brought to consciousness and interpreted. The understanding of dreams as the pathway to the unconscious occupied an important role in the process of cure as dreams occurred during a partially normal state of regression during sleep and thus opened a window into an aspect of the unconscious not previously available. Later in his work, he pointed out the crucial role of transference and the need to interpret it as a key component of treatment.

The superego was seen as an internal object filled with projections of pathological parental objects. In the process of cure the pathologic object will be analyzed. These pathologic objects can be seen sometimes as the only available link with an important sometimes deficient early childhood parent. Hopefully the superego would come under the control of the rational ego. 'Where superego was, ego shall be.' From a related point of view the ego was seen as the precipitate of abandoned object cathexes; if ego syntonic these cathexes contribute to growth, if ego-alien, it leads to conflicts and pathology.

The nature of the process can be described as including a number of steps: first the analyst has to listen to the patient's associations, second he would infer unconscious meaning, third he would share these with him, and finally, (very importantly) he would draw inferences from the patient's responses. Beginning students often fail to follow up and listen to the patient's responses to their interpretations, thinking erroneously that once an interpretation is given the analyst can move on to the next issue. I sometimes use the analogy of a tennis game to describe the back and forth interaction of the analytic process.

The increasing role of transference with new stages in our evolving theory should not be underestimated and it opened a window on the subtle influence of hidden object relationships that govern all human interactions, not just those limited to the treatment setting.

5. Obstacles to change

In my clinical work in supervision I sometimes note that my supervisees are often not connecting with the patient, talking at the wrong level, sometimes because of their inexperience. They are either too intellectual or unable to understand the level at which the patient is functioning at the moment. They may also be caught in an enactment of a pathologic object relationship.

The same thing happened to me a number of years ago. I was treating in an analysis a borderline patient, and to my dismay he was becoming angrier and angrier with me, making me feel very uncomfortable and leading me to suggest he might take some medication. Some time after, he interrupted the treatment. A few years later, he came back and confronted me with the issue of his increasing anger. He told me that I had completely misunderstood him and that I had not realized that his anger was a desperate reaction to his feeling he could not reach me emotionally at the time. I did not realize then that he was repeating with me his pathologic reaction to a distant father. My so-called neutrality was seen as an abandonment.

To avoid this not uncommon pitfall, I try to pay attention in the treatment setting to what unconscious object relationships are being repeated during the session. This may change during the course of an hour and can be initiated by either party. The therapist may be totally unaware of this fact and of his possible role in the pathologic interaction.

To manage these difficulties, the role of countertransference, initially downplayed, becomes central. It has a dual origin both as a projection from the patient of unmanageable issues (more important in borderline or psychotic patients) and second as related to the therapist's own unresolved conflicts. It needs to be explored in some detail. This is a thorny issue from a historical point of view as the approach to this topic dramatically altered during the course of the history of psychoanalysis.

As the rules of proper behavior for the analyst slowly emerged, in the early 1920's some genuine differences of opinion had to be gradually confronted and clarified.

Early in the days of analysis, some Hungarian analysts felt it would make sense for the same person to both treat and supervise the candidate as it was deemed he was the person who knew his supervisee best and therefore could understand his countertransference best. Freud did this with some of his early patients. On the opposite end, some other early analysts felt that this dual role interfered with the proper management of the transference. Even further, some supervisors felt reluctant to address a countertransference issue that they saw as part of the supervisee's analysis.

To complicate matters further, most institutes have no seminar to discuss the management of supervision or its method or structure. They assume that training analysts could be left on their own to decide on their model of supervision. As a result the individual style of each training analyst will influence the manner in which he conducts supervision. One of my more challenging supervisors treated supervision like an analysis. As I came into his office, he would nod his head, give a short grunt, and wait for me to begin. I do remember during my training expressing my dismay at the wide variety of my supervisor's style. 'This can't all be supervision,' I exclaimed to my analyst one day. I must have felt at the time that there must be just one proper way of conducting supervision!

One of my early supervisors, discussing with me a very volatile and impulsive patient I was trying to treat analytically, told me one day, 'The patient has you on the ropes!' Of course I knew this already, but besides making me both anxious and a bit ashamed, this statement was totally unhelpful. Perhaps my supervisor thought I would discuss my issue with my analyst. Neither of us realized at the time that it might have been more helpful to help me figure out the dynamics of the situation that led me to feel quite helpless. Another of my early supervisors used the material I presented as an entry to describe the dynamics of the patient within the system of ego psychology. I learned a great deal from this interaction, but a crucial piece of my relationship with the patient was never discussed. Still another supervisor sitting very far from me in her living room would conduct supervision by imagining or reconstructing (or constructing?) the story and fantasies she derived from my patient's associations, creating deeper and new meaning from the more disorganized material I presented. I felt better after each supervision thinking I had gained new insight into this patient. As this patient was very astute, she usually could tell when I had my supervision as the following hour with her would be richer. I would sometimes anxiously disgorge the understanding I had gained in my recent supervision, not always realizing that the reconstructions we had arrived at applied very nicely to the Friday hour but did not always fit in with the material of the following Monday hour! I do not think that at the time I was aware that the urge to disgorge the supervisor's interpretations had more to do with my anxiety about missing some crucial connections arrived at by my supervisor than with what was happening during the session with my patient. The supervisor did not necessarily ask about my subjective experience, so I was surprised and a bit dismayed when she suddenly told me one day that she thought we could end our supervision as she felt I understood the patient well enough. I remember telling my analyst the next session that I did not share my supervisor's opinion. He urged me to discuss it with my supervisor. I think I was reluctant to challenge her view. I also recall that I found another early supervisor rather empty just mouthing theoretical banalities. In order to deal with this issue I asked another training analyst to periodically discuss the case with him. I was fearful of confronting the supervisor. What a relief it turned out to hear the fresh human views of this other supervisor!

What was missing during all my supervisory experience was the nature of the process during supervision, the nature of my relation to the supervisor, and any attention to my countertransference. I have written a paper to address just those issues [6]. This should not obscure the fact that for the most part I valued the many supervisions I had during my training and learned a great deal from the majority.

Another obstacle to change is the patient's expectations that as long as he is in treatment he can take his time and not rush the boat. Patients can give as reason that after all they cannot control their feelings. I will then point out that indeed what they say is true but they can control their behavior. This is very important with dysfunctional couples where each partner is locked in repeating toxic object relationships often with a sadomasochistic tint or remain withdrawn to avoid being hurt.

6. Process of change

Not all patients are able to change. There are certain basic requirements for change to be possible. This includes three components: (1) being curious about oneself, (2) being able to observe oneself, and (3) being able to communicate mostly verbally, one's inner life. Related to this last issue is the role of trust the patient experiences towards the therapist. Monitoring its change during the course of time and its management in the transference is crucial to progress. The capacity for change also requires the ability to confront guilt and shame.

One of my favorite teachers Rudolph Loewenstein said the following about work and change: There are patients who want to both work and change. A second group wants to change without working, a third group wants to work without changing, and a final group wants neither to work nor to change. In order to find out to which group the patient belongs, it is essential to find out first why the patient came to treatment and second how he imagines it will work. Often one encounters patients who imagine treatment is like bringing your car to the garage to be fixed; you leave it and pick it up once the work is done. The patient has to realize he is the one in charge of change, the therapist only giving him tools to do so.

Somewhat related is the role of masochism as a resistance. There are some patients who seem to derive pleasure in exposing their suffering to the analyst (or parent) as a sadistic attempt to regain power and make the recipient suffer. This can also be an act of revenge against the parent who is unconsciously blamed for some defect bodily or otherwise. For example it was true of Marie Bonaparte who almost consciously blamed her father for depriving her of the masculine organ she so coveted.

Even though I seem to suggest that change is at the bottom of most good therapy, nothing could be further from the truth. There is a difference between how we think we can make a difference analytically and by non-analytic means. The former is generally based on interpretations, the latter by a type of subtle caring and acceptance of the patient as he /she is.

For example, I have had patients whose mate gradually deteriorates due to an irreversible disease. In these cases, it is most helpful for me to validate their feelings of frustration and anger and helplessness mixed with anxiety. Occasionally I may point out some hidden unconscious component, but I feel I am more in the role of a good friend to whom they can reveal all their issues. Such modes of treatment might fit into the 'supportive mode' sometimes with a subtle implication that this is second class therapy. Nothing could be further from the truth. As a result these patients change subtly, become more accepting of a bad reality, and are very gratified they can share their guilty thoughts without reproof. Another option is for the patient to be able to differentiate between guilt and responsibility. The former leads to conflict and symptoms; the latter is a view of reality, which must be accepted. There are also other types of intervention outside what is strictly considered analytic behavior, for example the role of humor, which can lighten the atmosphere, introduce a human element, or even help resolve a situation where the analyst feels stuck.

However, a final note on so-called supportive interventions: one must be aware that on occasions the patient may clamor for support as a way of avoiding more in-depth work that he is very capable of undertaking.

7. Changes in theory

With the emergence of new theories three aspects drew attention, both centered on an object relation previously minimized: first the role of the analyst as a new object, ie, one who does not behave like the pathologic parent, second following the emergence of object relation theories therapists began to focus on the crucial importance of the relationship including the role of love and caring.

Second, different theories paid attention to differing data. For example, the Kleinian theory emphasizes early aggression, Kohut's theory looks for failures in empathy behaviors as damaging to the self. Laplanche looks for projections of unconscious fantasies onto the child by the mother as the cause of problems.

The role of the analyst as a new object has been studied by Loewald [7]. However, it is important to state that this new relationship is not an end in itself but rather the first step in a long road. It is a bit like the softening of a crust to allow some removal or change. It occurs as part of the transference neurosis that remobilizes frozen pathological earlier object relations. As a result of the new relationship it is hoped that the patient can also begin to identify with the analyst and develop more neutral ways of observing himself.

Loewald compares the analytic relationship with that of the parent-child relationship. Because of his experience the parent is not distracted by temporary obstacles but holds in his mind the capacities of the child and his assets and talents leading to growth in the future. This could be seen as an aspect of benevolent caring and love.

The problem of the match between therapist and patient is very crucial and has been the focus of study in recent years. This would also include aspects of the therapist's character that clash with the patient's personality characteristics. For example, a therapist who was brought up by submitting to parental authority and behaving according to rules might have trouble dealing with a narcissistic demanding patient or a patient with anger issues.

7.1 Decreasing focus on defenses

There is another change in my clinical work, which renders the patient-therapist relationship less adversarial. Instead of focusing on defenses I focus on the adaptational approach. For example, I have a patient who needs to be in total control with a wife who is very loving, gentle, and totally devoted to his welfare. With the passage of time and aging my patient has become more vulnerable, and in reaction to his increasing weakness he has become more controlling, leading to some arguments and difficulties in the marriage. In response to his behavioral change I say to my patient: 'Of course I can understand why you need to do this; because during all of your childhood you were faced by a difficult controlling and castrating mother so it makes sense that in spite of differences you cannot take a chance and become vulnerable. You are still struggling with an internal mother and you are afraid your wife could become like her.'

In another case one of my patients dealing with massive anger problems expresses massive rage towards a very critical and controlling sibling and seems to want to justify his behavior but is a bit overwhelmed with his feelings. I say to him, 'We have to differentiate two aspects of your reaction; first your sibling's behavior is unacceptable. There is no problem with this, but can you see that because of the massive anger you are struggling with, you also use this opportunity to discharge some of the anger that has nothing to do with the problem with your sibling.' To my relief the patient agreed with my distinction and our work could proceed.

8. The issue of the relationship

Unfortunately the theoretical role of the relationship is not easy to examine in a neutral fashion as it has occasionally been used by a group of object relations theorists who want to make it the central core of their theoretical edifice instead of seeing it as only one aspect of a very complicated situation.

There are two components that need to be distinguished: first the therapeutic relationship and second the admixture of the real relationship theoretically independent from the therapeutic one. A bit like ivy growing on a tree, the so-called real relationship may silently lead to enactments particularly if either patient or analyst is not aware of its corrosive potential because on the surface it seems so benign and acceptable. Freud himself allowed the personal relationship to intrude on the professional. An extreme example can be found in the 1000-page book of his correspondence with Marie Bonaparte who sought analysis with him. Her wealth allowed her to ply Freud with many gifts from Greece, including rare vases, honey, and later an urn to contain his ashes. Marie also developed a close relationship with Freud's daughter Anna, and Mrs. Freud often brought her strawberries in a basket as she boarded the Orient Express back from Vienna to Paris. Freud also allowed Marie to send her daughter Eugenie to Freud for analysis, and he was willing to have the latter's potential husband come to Vienna so he could judge his appropriateness as mate.

In one of his letters to Marie Bonaparte, Freud commented that he was aware that the so-called real relationship would not have existed apart from the transference and that it could also be used as a resistance but in the end he said that he thought the two could coexist.

8.1 Therapeutic relationship

I will first deal with the problem of the therapeutic relationship. First in order for the treatment to take a hold there must be a combination of hope, optimism including an expectation of gain, and a minimal amount of trust. This often makes it difficult for patients with major trust issues as part of their character, such as paranoid personalities, to develop a workable relationship with their therapist. Even if this develops, the suspicious patient may see it as phony because the relationship is not genuine, it is bought or even further care is given not spontaneously but in response to the patient's pleas, demands, or complaints. What the patient does not realize is that independently of the pure therapeutic part the therapist may genuinely care about his patient.

Recently Celenza [8] put together a very thoughtful book of short essays entitled 'Transference, Love, Being'. Perusing the book I note the great difficulty in exactly stating what we mean when we use the word love, and we sometimes connect it with surrounding sexuality.

The limits of what the therapeutic relationship can include have evolved considerably over the course of history of the theoretical foundations of our field. It has altered from the initial view of the analyst as a reflecting mirror to a slowly growing involvement without clear limits. I do remember during my training analysis that I was completely surprised when one day I entered my analyst's office with a limp having hurt my ankle and my analyst questioned me about what had happened.

In a recent lecture, I heard David Tuckett present various models illustrating different types of possible interactions during the course of an analysis. The first was asymmetric, described as the theater where two people watch a live play where the patient casts the analyst in various unconscious picture roles. The second model was 'cinema' with two people watching a film projected on a screen. The third model (symmetric) was that of immersive theater with audience and players, and both patient and analyst cast each other in a different role. Each model would modify the interaction between patient and analyst.

The role of neutrality can be confusing as the analyst has to have the capacity to observe in a scientific fashion what is going on but also has to experience and allow human interactions with feelings in both directions, which then he needs to observe and utilize as appropriate.

8.2 The real relationship

We do know that as I detailed earlier in this paper, Freud was comfortable in having a real relationship with many of his patients. He gave food to some of them or even gave them money.

This is a very complex topic to address. I will start with the question of self-revelation. As a student, if a patient asked me where I was going on vacation I was taught rather mechanically to say back: 'Why do you ask?' In my view this is a toxic unhelpful response. If I am puzzled and not sure how to respond I might say: 'How would this help if you knew?' With sicker patients, I err on the side of revealing rather than hiding. I am supervising a candidate whose patient cannot hold the image of the analyst in his absence. If such a patient asked me where I was going on vacation, I might offer an interpretation: 'Would it make me more real when we are separated if there were a place you could connect with me?' I would also be more likely to simply say where I was going without needing to interpret the meaning or request the patient to associate. The latter could be seen as intrusive rather than a reasonable demand within the confines of analytic work.

Another aspect of the real relationship is the question of whether and when to accept gifts from a patient. Again there is no clear answer and the therapist must anticipate whether the patient could tolerate a refusal without being badly hurt. In my early days a patient who was about to terminate an analysis (which was only partially satisfactory because of what I thought was the appropriate emotional distance) said she intended to give me a genuine letter signed by Freud, which was quite rare and I assume quite expensive. Reluctantly I thanked her for her care but said I did not think it was right for me to accept such a gift.

With increasing experience, rules that in my early days were to be followed have become principles to guide me but not to force me to adhere to them. As a result my work is much looser, less rigid, and much more spontaneous. I see this as a gain rather than a loss.

Author details

Francis D. Baudry
Independent Researcher, Falmouth, Massachusetts, USA

*Address all correspondence to: fdb176@gmail.com

References

[1] Kazdin A. Mediators and mechanisms of change in psychotherapy research. Annual Review of Clinical Psychology. 2007;**2007**(3):127-164

[2] Murphy R, Cooper Z. Clinical Psychotherapy Review. 2016;**1**:50-95

[3] Werbart A. Psychotherapy research, between process and effect. Acta Psychiatrica Scandinavica. 1989;**79**(6):511-522

[4] Baudry F. Character, character type and character organization. Journal of the American Psychoanalytic Association. 1987;**37**(3):655-686

[5] Baudry F. The relevance of the analyst's character and attitudes to his work. Journal of the American Psychoanalytic Association. 1990;**39**(4):917-938

[6] Baudry F. The personal dimension and management of the supervisory situation. The Psychoanalytic Quarterly. 1993;**LXII**:588-614

[7] Loewald H. Papers on Psychoanalysis: Psychoanalytic Theory and Psychoanalytic Process Chapter 161980. New Haven and London: Yale University Press; pp. 277-302

[8] Celenza A. Transference, Love, Being. London and New York: Routledge; 2022

Chapter 9

Perspective Chapter: The Overwhelm is the Way – Contextual Relational Mindfulness as the Key to Integrated Executive Functioning

Juliana Lewis and Owen Lewis

Abstract

Executive function (EF) skills are crucial in managing adult Attention Deficit Hyperactivity Disorder (ADHD), yet current methods often fail to integrate an individual's emotional connection to the task at hand. Integrative Executive Function (IEF) Coaching introduces a holistic approach to strengthening EF skills in people with ADHD and related attentional disorders. IEF Coaching incorporates emotional and contextual awareness through Contextual Relational Mindfulness—a practice that combines traditional mindfulness with a heightened awareness of the relational dynamics between the client, their environment, and the coaching process. This chapter proposes a new approach to EF coaching; it presents the theoretical foundations, goals, and methodologies of IEF Coaching that emphasize the importance of developing emotional self-awareness and authentic communication in EF training.

Keywords: executive functions, executive function coaching, relational mindfulness, ADHD, authentic relating, mindfulness

1. Introduction

Executive function (EF) skills are crucial in managing adult Attention Deficit Hyperactivity Disorder (ADHD, understood to include a spectrum of attentional disorders, including Attention Deficit Disorder), yet current methods often fail to integrate an individual's emotional connection to the tasks at hand. They are typically taught outside of the relevant context where these skills are most needed, and without an intentional approach to cultivating mindful awareness of one's emotional state. Integrative Executive Function (IEF) Coaching, developed by co-author J. Lewis, is an approach to executive function training that addresses the client's emotional relationship to the tasks at hand by integrating Contextual Relational Mindfulness into coaching sessions. Contextual Relational Mindfulness is a concept that blends traditional mindfulness with a relational orientation to the present moment. It refers to an awareness of the field of relationality that co-exists between client and coach, and also includes the field of relationality that co-exists between the client and their environment and the actions they take in that environment.

The application of Contextual Relational Mindfulness in the IEF coaching setting provides a promising outlet for rewriting the narrative around what overwhelm and stress mean. This happens through developing a curiosity about the present moment, as modeled and guided by the coach, alongside the hands-on practice of EF training.

The goals of IEF Coaching, broadly defined, are to (1) strengthen the client's executive functions, (2) foster a client's Contextual Relational Mindfulness; and (3) inspire a client's self-confidence and intrinsic motivation to take action. These goals, while described distinctly, are interrelated. Each supports and furthers development across goals.

This aim of this chapter is to introduce the practice of IEF Coaching through a discussion its precedents in existing literature on EF and Relational Mindfulness (as distinct from, though interrelated to, the concept of Contextual Relational Mindfulness); outline the core goals and methodologies of IEF, and present clinical vignettes to illustrate core goals and methodologies. In Section 2, "Literature Review," we provide a review of existing research on EF, a summary of existing approaches to EF, and a broad overview of the concept of Relational Mindfulness in therapeutic, mindfulness, personal growth and spiritual contexts. In Section 3, "The keys to Integrative Executive Function Coaching," we outline the goals and associated principles of IEF Coaching. In Section 4, "The Overwhelm is the Way: clinical vignettes illustrating core elements of Integrative Executive Function Coaching," we present clinical vignettes that illustrate the goals and principles discussed in Section 3. In Section 5, "Conclusion," we summarize key threads of continuity between IEF Coaching with existing threads of approaches to EF, and discuss directions for future research.

At the heart of this chapter is the co-authors' deep desire to expand the discussion of EF and the practice of EF coaching beyond the domain of "skills" to include the experiential and emotional domain of the individuals seeking to strengthen their EF. Our wholehearted belief is that mindfulness around the contextual relational field that a person struggling with ADHD (and other conditions which affect EF) resides within and is the key to unlocking their potential to strengthen their EF "muscles." The title of this paper, "The Overwhelm is the Way," points to a belief that the improvement of EF skillsets truly begins with an appreciation, awareness, and acceptance of the emotional experience of how very intense it can sometimes be to find oneself in a sea of overwhelm triggers. This sea seems to be the common denominator of what it's like for people with ADHD to exist in the world. We cannot build a better boat to navigate these seas if we are going to fear the tide; the understanding and curiosity about the waters we are in is where our EF boat building begins.

The collaborative authorship between a coach (J. Lewis) and psychiatrist/therapist (O. Lewis) represents first a belief that all mental health interventions are ideally delivered in a collaborative team approach, and secondly, represents an attempt to bridge the conceptual and language divide between the worlds of coaching and psychotherapy, most broadly defined.

2. Literature review

2.1 Research on executive functions

Executive functions (EF) have been broadly defined as that set of cognitive functions involved with the execution of tasks. Practically these functions include organization, planning, prioritization, and execution. From a psychometric perspective these functions include working memory, inhibitory control, and set-shifting [1]. While difficulties with EF may span neurodiversity broadly, the most common diagnosis contributing to EF compromise is Attention Deficit Disorder (ADHD, also referred to as Attention Deficit Hyperactivity Disorder.) While ADHD has long been considered a childhood disorder, symptoms may persist in 90% of adults [2]. Based on diagnostic interview data from the National Comorbidity Survey Replication [3], overall prevalence of current adult ADHD is 4.4%. Prevalence was higher for males (5.4%) versus females (3.2%).

Among adults, ADHD has a higher association with unemployment, job turnover, and job burnout, and is associated with poor organization, time management, interpersonal relationships, and lower earning power [4]. It has been noted that EF compromise in particular mediates the effects of ADHD on work performance and further contributes to work burnout which in turn leads to job instability [5] ADHD has technically been diagnosed a childhood onset disorder. However, currently under consideration is the notion of subthreshold ADHD considering DSM-5 criteria. In this scenario, additional patients will come to professional attention as adults whose symptoms should not be dismissed because they were not first apparent in childhood [2].

While EF deficits contribute to compromises of school and work performance, effects of EF deficits are not limited to school or workplace settings. Emotional Dysregulation often accompanies EF deficiency [6]. Consider, for example, the higher rates of divorce in individuals with ADHD. According to the last U.S. census, overall divorce rates were 33%, while for individuals with ADHD, 66% [7]. EF has also been implicated in making and keeping friends [8], lower rates of substance abuse [9], and overall lower quality of life [10].

Are work and marital instabilities, for instance, cause or effect? The obvious answer is both. However much EF impairment contributes, work and marital instability contribute to emotional dysregulation, that goes hand in hand with ADHD and EF impairment. While individuals seek referral for multiple reasons, usually focusing on one aspect of the ADHD, EF impairment, or emotional dysregulation complex, any successful intervention must include an approach that addresses EF in this context. Clearly, an intervention that does not include a component of EF skills training will not help the individuals in their core deficiencies. Yet, EF skills training is often delivered as either isolated exercises or in the narrow focus of school work or employment tasks. While the latter is important (i.e., how to cope with this particular work week), skills training often ignores the component of emotional dysregulation and how this affects EF skill acquisition and the implementation of those skills even if successfully "acquired." In addition, stress, sadness, loneliness, sleep deprivation and lack of physical fitness have been shown to affect EF brain function disproportionately [11].

Of the three core EF skills (working memory, inhibitory control, and set shifting), working memory has been persuasively argued to be linked to emotional dysregulation [1], "Working memory abilities uniquely covary with children's emotional regulation skills, and this relationship is driven in party by working memory's influence on ADHD behavioral symptoms, which, in turn, predict emotional regulation skills." This relationship has been noted to hold across the lifespan [12]. If emotional dysregulation and EF are so closely linked, this must, in turn, inform any intervention that addresses either emotional dysregulation or EF.

Furthermore, mind functions corresponding to EF skills have been divided into what has been referred to as "hot" and "cool" components. These describe mind functioning being accessed (or measured) in conditions of emotional challenge or emotional neutrality. These functions reside in different parts of the brain [13–15]. Stable EF constructs emerge in adolescence and persist, including learning accessed in both "hot" and "cool" emotional states [16].

These findings must inform how, where, and when learning EF can occur, and raises the question whether skills learned in a "cool" state can even be accessed by an individual in a "hot" state. While "cool" state EF failures result in chronic lack of productivity, "hot" state EF failures are what acutely lead to aberrant behaviors and life disruption. These are the times when an individual most needs EF scaffolding. The model of EF coaching proposed uniquely addresses both "cool" and "hot" states of EF learning.

2.2 Existing approaches and research on EF coaching - what works and does not work

Approaches to EF coaching include behavioral, educational, time management and organization strategies, individualized education programs (IEP's), mindfulness, relaxation practices, and monitoring. Settings include tutorial, group and computerized approaches. While there is no standardized, evidence-based approach, various approaches can improve EF across the lifespan [17]. However, the question remains how these gains are internalized and generalized. That most efforts to train specific EF skills do not transfer to real-world outcomes [17]. Most EF skills training occurs within a limited context [18] that limits training in a "hot state."

"Near transfer" of skills refers to transfer to cognitive tasks similar to what has been trained for; "far transfer", to tasks involving other cognitive abilities. Results for "far transfer", namely to situations which occur in real life settings, have been inconsistent [19]. Even "near transfer" of skills may be incomplete as noted, "EF skills are associated with outcomes such as school success only to the extent they first contribute to intermediate-level EF-based skills that are more directly instrumental in achieving key outcomes [20]. In other words, skills can be trained in isolation, but they remain isolated skills, not able to be deployed in the domains that cause the most life disruptions. Zelavo et al. [20] further hold that an effective way to bridge the gap between specific EF skills and real-world outcomes is to train specificEF-based life skills which people need to function effectively in society. Diamond and Ling [21], almost ten years earlier, alluded to this same idea, "The most successful approach for improving EF's will also address emotions, social, and physical needs."

Zelazo [21] notes, "It is these intermediate-level configurations of EF and non-EF skills, not component EF skills in isolation, that are invoked and applied across real-world situations and adaptive challenges. He further notes [22] these intermediate-level configurations of EF and non-EF skills are used intentionally, and with effort, to pursue meaningful goals (e.g., to foster social relationships) across a range of situations and problems."

Proposed here is an approach to EF training which intentionally moves from focused training to the intermediate-level problems, an approach which "bridges the gap" to real life situations and addresses the human who operates with whatever executive functions are accessible at any given "hot" moment and as well as planning and training in the "cool".

2.3 What is Relational Mindfulness?

Relational Mindfulness is an emergent term that has been used across therapeutic, mindfulness, personal growth and spiritual contexts that points to the application of mindfulness practices to interpersonal dynamics and relationships. Mindfulness, more generally, is an awareness practice that has roots in Buddhist meditation traditions, though has been further developed by psychology and non-religious wellbeing practices. Broadly defined, mindfulness is a practice of orienting to the present moment of one's experience, either through intentional focus practices like meditation, or in everyday life. Mindfulness practices are intended as a training ground for returning to presence, and often involve points of focus, including the breath, the body, or even a candle. Relational Mindfulness takes this orientation to awareness in the present moment, and expands it to the interpersonal dynamics. So, the point of focused awareness becomes the experience unfolding between two or more individuals.

The practice of Relational Mindfulness varies depending on context, just as the term mindfulness also varies. However, there are some core principles common across all. These include: (1) An orientation to the present moment of connection; (2) self-awareness, whereby an individual learns to pay attention to their inner thoughts, feelings, and sensations; (3) authentic communication, whereby individuals share the unfolding of their present moment awareness to others; (4) active listening, whereby individuals practice placing their full awareness on the person, without interrupting; and (5) cultivating an attitude of acceptance and curiosity over reactivity.

In the field of psychotherapy, it has been defined, for instance, as "the practice and cultivation of mindfulness in an engaged, person-to-person relational context" [23]. So, for example, the application of Relational Mindfulness in a therapeutic setting would involve a therapist bringing their own internal awareness of their feeling state into the therapeutic relationship, in particular, with regard to their empathic relationship to the patient [23]. Relational Mindfulness also has roots in Interpersonal Psychoanalysis and Harry Stack Sullivan's concept of therapist as participant observer [24]. In such approaches, therapy is always a two person interaction in which the patient will affect the therapist just as the therapist attempts to affect the patient. Interpersonal clarity means knowing "Who is doing what to whom" [25]. More contemporary iterations of this idea phrased in the language of classical psychoanalysis appear in the concepts of Inter-subjectivity [26].

Relational Mindfulness also appears as a practice in the field of mindfulness and spirituality practices. For example, the Insight Dialogue Community shares a practice of Insight Dialog, which "extends the cultivation of meditative qualities of mind – mindfulness, tranquility, concentration – into the relational. Meditating together we call each other into this moment in a powerful way" [27]. As an additional example, A.H. Almaas's Diamond Approach sees Relational Meditation as a core practice for exploring one's one relationship with oneself and others. The Diamond Approach is a system for personal development and growth that draws on a range of traditions, such as psychology, Buddhism and Suffism. In this system, Relational Meditation provides a basis for carrying out contemplative inquiry on relationships, while also practicing emotional awareness and self-observation [28].

Finally, Relational Mindfulness is a core component in the interpersonal practices of Authentic Relating Games, Circling, and Relatefulness. Authentic Relating Games are practices that invite groups to deepen their ability to connect in the present moment and practice authentic communication skills. Groups like ART International and Authentic Revolution are designed to maximize Relational Mindfulness through short game-like interactions that encourage authenticity, presence, and deep listening [29–30]. Circling is a related interpersonal practice that creates space for groups to explore the unfolding of connection, alongside relational dynamics and presence [30]. Groups like the Integral Institute, Circling Europe, and The Circling Institute guide groups in facilitated experiences that orient towards the cultivation of Relational Mindfulness. Finally Relatefulness, as created by the Relateful Company in Austin, Texas provides a related model of interpersonal facilitation of Relateful practices. Relatefulness, in their words, is "the unique (and ordinary) practice that emphasizes present-moment relating, construct-awareness, and non-duality. We believe that Relatefulness can help individuals accept what's really going on in any given moment while embracing the creative impulse of the universe that's always moving into more freshness" [31].

In sum, Relational Mindfulness is simply an orientation to the unfolding of interpersonal dynamics in the present moment. Though it's still an emergent concept, developments across the fields of spirituality, psychology, mindfulness and personal development point to its benefit to expanding an individual or group's field of awareness, and potentially contribute to the deepening of connection to oneself and to others.

3. The keys to Integrative Executive Function Coaching

The goals of Integrative Executive Function (IEF) are to (1) strengthen the client's executive functions (EF), (2) foster a client's Contextual Relational Mindfulness; and (3) inspire a client's self-confidence and intrinsic motivation to take action. These goals, while described distinctly, are interrelated. Each supports and furthers development across goals. In this section, we will break down the three goals of IEF and discuss the mechanisms by which these goals are attained through coaching. The basic tenets of Integrative EF Coaching were first developed in the coaching practice of one of the authors (J. Lewis).

As mentioned in the introduction, the collaborative authorship with a psychiatric/therapist (O. Lewis) represents first a belief that all mental health interventions are ideally delivered in a collaborative team approach, and secondly, represents an attempt to bridge the conceptual and language divide between the worlds of coaching and psychotherapy, most broadly defined.

3.1 Improving executive functions

IEF Coaching is designed to help individuals improve their EF including cognitive processes for planning, organizing, attention to detail, and time management. IEF's strategy for improving a client's EF is not a one-size fits all approach, but rather follows a step-by-step process for custom tailoring the approach to an individual client's needs.

The core methods used in service of improving EF are: (1) creating a collaborative atmosphere around goal setting throughout the coaching; (2) introducing task-oriented tools for structuring time; (3) co-creating systems of habit accountability for in-between sessions; and (4) maintaining a strong relationship between the client's context and structural elements introduced in the coaching.

When it comes to improving EF, IEF takes a deeply contextual approach. IEF sees client's current problems (which they identify as goals to be solved) as stemming from a more broadly disordered or chaotic functioning on a cognitive level, a psychological/historical level, or from a lack of developed "know-how" or experience. While these three possible sources of the current problems need to be identified, clarified, and sometimes explored, the process of identification and exploration is not an open-ended goal in itself but a means to make problem-solving more effective.

Clarifying the source of current problems begins with truly getting to know the client and what the client contends with in their day-to-day life, both through written questions, dialog, and supplementary conversations with a client's therapist, psychiatrist or other mental healthcare professional, with the aim of providing complementarity of care, identifying key challenge areas, and bringing awareness to areas of cognitive or mental health risk.

IEF sees learning about the client's life, and rethinking the approach based on new information about their life, as a process. This learning happens through an ongoing co-creative approach to goal setting and accountability in the context of the lived experience of the client. Goals become grounds for addressing areas of challenge with EF, and between-session accountability providing the client with a chance to exercise new "muscles" in their daily reality.

3.2 Fostering Contextual Relational Mindfulness

Contextual Relational Mindfulness is a concept that blends traditional mindfulness with a relational orientation to the present moment. It goes beyond existing working definitions of Relational Mindfulness (as previously discussed), which tend to apply traditional mindfulness practices with interpersonal dynamics. It extends the field of relationality to also include the context in which the present moment is unfolding. It includes the field of relationality that co-exists between client and coach, and also includes the field of relationality that co-exists between the client and their environment and the actions they take in that environment. It attempts to bring conscious awareness to the point of interaction between an individual and others, as well as the field of objects and actions that surrounds them. Oftentimes, the practice of Contextual Relational Mindfulness has the effect of improving a client's resiliency to overwhelm and stress. The goal of practicing Contextual Mindfulness is simply presence and curiosity with what is, though it's interesting to note that a shift in a person's self-narrative overwhelm tends to occur as an after-effect.

A basic assumption of IEF Coaching is that life is lived in relationship and problems exist in relation to others. Thus, the coach-client relationship becomes itself a vehicle for problem-solving. Contextual Relational Mindfulness of those interactions is encouraged and highlighted, ultimately becoming a capacity carried into a mindfulness of interactions with others in all settings.

The core methodology for fostering Contextual Relational Mindfulness in IEF Coaching is facilitated through the coach's orientation to the client. In all interactions, including navigating seemingly practical matters, such as creating a schedule, the coach: (1) models an orientation to the present moment; (2) invites the client to "embrace the overwhelm" (and any other emotions that arise) by feeling what's happening while also inviting curiosity about it; and (3) demonstrates a willingness to (appropriately) self-reveal their experience relating to the client.

This fourth point is particularly important when it comes to co-creative goal setting and accountability, as the approach requires the coach to reveal their authentic experience of what it's like to be with the client. For instance, if a client does not maintain agreements around accountability check-ins in between sessions, the coach is invited to share their experience of the process with the client. Again, the intent of "self-revealing" is primarily for the coach to model self-awareness and communication in the present moment. The "appropriateness" factor should be determined by how directly the instance of self-revealing works to invite the client into their own practice of Contextual Relational Mindfulness. Though authenticity may vary from coach to coach, the principle is practiced in service of the client, rather than as a pure mode of self-expression for the coach.

3.3 Inspiring self-confidence and intrinsic motivation

The fourth goal of IEF Coaching is to inspire self-confidence and intrinsic motivation in the client. The methodologies used to achieve this goal overlap with the goals outlined in Section 3.1, though expand to include elements common to the practice of Life Coaching. These are: (1) grounding all coaching work in a deep understanding of the client's world; (2) taking a collaborative approach to goal setting and accountability structures; (3) inviting inquiry into the client's beliefs about their innate capacity; and, mostly importantly; and (4) taking a strength based approach to coaching.

"Strength based," used in this context, refers to a concrete inclusion of the client's strengths in all coaching sessions. IEF coaching begins sessions with celebrating wins to foster an orientation towards what *is* working. Beginning with an orientation towards the client's strength at the start of a session creates a terrain of possibility for constructive inquiries into moments of overwhelm that are likely to arise later on.

"Inquiry into the client's beliefs systems" is a process that must occur organically when sufficient trust has been built between coach and client. This process can take a variety of forms and formats, though typically involves drawing awareness to the client's articulation of a negative belief about themselves, coupled with an invitation to "try on" a different perspective.

4. The overwhelm is the way: clinical vignettes illustrating core elements of Integrative Executive Function Coaching

In this section, we present vignettes from client sessions as a means of illustrating core elements of Integrative Executive Function (IEF) Coaching, as presented in the Section 3. Each vignette is accompanied with a discussion of what goals and associated methods it illustrated.

The vignettes from client sessions cited below will be phrased in the first-person, both to indicate as previously noted attribution to the practice of one author (J. Lewis), and importantly, to indicate that a personal, self-reflective "I" of the coach or therapist must be present in all clinical encounters. All names and identifying details have been changed to protect client confidentiality.

4.1 Embracing the overwhelm and collaborative goal setting in a coaching session with Aaron

As noted in the previous section, two core methodologies of IEF Coaching are embracing the overwhelm and engaging in a collaborative process of goal setting, which serves to support the goals of fostering Contextual Relational Mindfulness, and inspiring self-confidence and intrinsic motivation. This vignette illustrates a session with a client, Aaron, where these two methodologies came into play.

Aaron is a 45-year old corporate consultant and educator who came to me to work on issues relating to time management. At the start of our fifth coaching session, Aaron shared that he had been missing appointments with his staff, and wanted my help, explaining that he was really concerned for the state of his team at work.

In particular, some of his staff members had complained to the Human Resources department about his forgetfulness around important scheduled appointments.

We began the session by discussing the problem, and then continued into an investigation of what positive behaviors Aaron was looking to establish.

I invited him to share with me about what changes he'd like to make.

"Well, obviously I want to stop missing meetings. I literally don't know how I forget, these are important moments with my staff. I really don't know how I just blank."

"Can you tell me more about what it would feel like to show up in a different way? How is it that you'd like to show up for your meetings?"

"Like I said, I want to be there on time. But it's not just about getting into the right Zoom or the right office at the time we agreed on. I don't want to be scrambling. I really want to feel calm and prepared, like I'm not a complete ball of chaos. I mean, we're just talking about Zoom meeting so you'd think I could do it, but it's easier said than done."

"Is there a name you'd like to give to this state of showing up calm and prepared, and also on time to your scheduled appointments?"

"Yeah, I want to call it the Steady State."

From here, I guided Aaron into a brainstorm of all the things he might require to get himself into the "Steady State." Together we identified four key behavioral goals that were needed to achieve "Steady": (1) checking his automated work calendar at key moments during the day; (2) establishing clear communication around meeting expectations; and (3) blocking time before meetings for remote access set-up. As an intermediate step, we break down each behavior into discrete steps, so that we'd be able to assess how much time would be required to turn each behavioral goal into daily action. Finally, we came up with a daily rhythm for Steady State behaviors, broken down into two 15 minute blocks:

In the a.m., with breakfast (15 minutes total): (1) check calendar for daily meetings; block off time to prepare for the day's meetings; (2) make sure a minimum of 5 minutes has been reserved before each meeting to set up Zoom; and (3) send relevant confirmation emails or communications relating to meetings. In the p.m., at end of the workday (15 minutes total): (1) review the next day's meetings; (2) block off time for relevant travel to meetings for the next day; (3) make sure a minimum of 5 minutes has been reserved prior to each meeting to set up Zoom; and (4) send relevant confirmation emails or communications relating to meetings.

At this point, I paused to check in with Aaron, noticing that his eyebrows were furrowed and he was beginning to look away, out the window.

"I'm noticing you're looking away, out the window, and I have a story that something's concerning you. Would you be up to share what's happening for you?" I asked.

"I'm kind of freaking out and I'm embarrassed that I'm freaking out."

"What's the freak out like?" I inquired.

"My heart's racing. And every time I think about doing this stuff I just get crazy overwhelmed feeling like I'm going to fail."

"Noticing overwhelm is a really important step in getting to the Steady State; is your overwhelm in response to any of the items of the list we came up with?"

"Yes. It's in response to 'block off time to prepare for meetings.' I have no idea what that would even look like. I usually just do things like that in a rush and don't even know how long it takes."

From here, I invited Aaron to see the value of his overwhelm as a prime indicator that he either (1) would benefit from taking a movement/breathing break, or (2) that the task he was feeling overwhelmed about wasn't clear to him. Aaron shared that the second option was true, he did not actually know what was required of him to "show up prepared," and the thought of not knowing how to prepare, combined with the fear of failing, was at the root of his experience of overwhelm.

As this brief example illustrates, IEF flows organically between a focus on practical EF skills and an awareness of how the client is relating to the tasks at hand, with a particular emphasis on naming the emotions and fears that arise in connection to a task. This flow between the relational and practical is carried in a real world context that is directly relevant to a client's goals.

Awareness of the relational and emotional sphere of a client's world provides a window of opportunity to connect to the heart of client's experience, while helping them to expand their capacity for communication and relationship building.

4.2 Accountability, authenticity, and collaborative processes with Erica

As noted in the review of research, effective integration and internalization requires that EF skills become established not just in conscious, deliberate ways, but in an automatic way, and these involve learning that is located in different parts of the brain [19]. This concept recalls an older psychoanalytic concept of the eventual automaticity of ego functions [32]. In much the same way a toddler learns to walk with deliberate concentration and grit to overcome the many and inevitable falls, within months of taking the first steps, a toddler is running with abandon, thinking only where he wants to go, not what his once pedestrian feet are doing. This section's vignette illustrates how the co-creation of a check-in structure, to support practice and accountability in-between sessions, supported improvement across all three of this coaching methodology's goals. Further it demonstrates a micro-instance of "self-revealing" on the part of the coach. By modeling authentic communication, the coach invites the client to do the same, while fostering an atmosphere of non-judgment and collaboration.

Erica is a 24 year old client struggling with disorganization in everyday life who chose to work with me, as a complementary source of care to her work with her psychiatrist. During our first month of coaching together, Erica and I worked on goals relating to her physical environment. At the end of each session, we'd discuss her goals for the week, and she was given an opportunity to decide if and how she wanted to check-in on her goals in between sessions. For the first four weeks, Erica opted for a daily check-in email, where she would let me know how the day's goals went. These goals varied week-to-week, though included things like making her bed, doing laundry, putting away laundry, and organizing papers on her desk. Each week, Erica would send me an optimistic email at the end of the day, detailing how she had met her goals.

During our fifth week of coaching together, Erica's goals shifted from her physical environment to cooking and meal preparation. The complexity of the goals increased, as did the amount of time they required. Erica continued to opt-in to daily accountability emails on her fifth week, though her consistency with the emailing process dropped to two messages per week. After this week of lagging check-ins, I decided to explicitly discuss the process with her, so that we could redesign it together.

"So let's talk about last week's check-ins, if you're up for it," I introduced the topic to Erica. "How was this week for you?"

"Honestly I got overwhelmed and the daily part was too much so I kind of just ignored my tasks and didn't check-in with you," Erica shared.

DOI: http://dx.doi.org/10.5772/intechopen.1006972

"That's great awareness. How was it to not check in?" I asked (inviting greater Contextual Relational Mindfulness around the check-ins.)

"Actually it was more stressful to not check-in and ignore what I had said I would do. The idea of sending an email felt overwhelming and also *not* checking in felt really bad, too."

"My sense of things this week was that the goals started feeling like chores you had to do. Does that sound true?" I revealed an assumption I had about what was happening for her.

"Yeah, that's exactly it. That's what it felt like. It felt like you were the chores assigner."

"Well, my nightmare as a coach is to become the person that gives you chores to do, and ends up being the bad cop," I revealed an aspect of my authentic experience and desires, as her coach, modeling comfort with authenticity and self-awareness about my own internal process.

Erica laughed, "Yeah that doesn't sound fun to me, either. I don't want a cop coach either."

"Would you be up for designing a new check-in process together, that makes it less like chores, and more like something you actually *want* to do?" I asked.

Erica agreed, and we proceeded to brainstorm alternatives to daily email check-ins. Together, we landed on replacing daily check-ins with a single ten minute phone call check-in per week.

Knowing that the check-in process had brought up feelings of "chores" (i.e. tasks that Erica was "supposed" to do, and had been assigned to her) I knew it was time for a mindset check-in as well.

"So you want to cook some healthy meals this week. Why is that important?"

Erica looked at me with a blank stare.

"I can guess why that might be important to other people, but these sessions are about you. Why do you want to make healthy meals?"

"Well, because I just feel really great when I eat good food, and feel bad about myself when I buy unhealthy snacks."

From here, I guided Erica in a series of sentence stem exercises around the topic of food and health. Sentence stems are a tool used in therapeutic, coaching, interpersonal development settings, or even journaling that encourage a client or participant to use the first part of a sentence as a tool for speaking or writing. With Erica, I introduced sentence stems and invited her to "complete the sentence." Here are some examples of sentence stems we worked worked with in our session:

Coach: "When I eat good food, I..." *Client*: "...feel great about myself."

Coach: "When I feel great about myself, I..." *Client*: "...feel motivated to do things."

Coach: "When I feel motivated to do things, I" *Client*: "...know I'm not broken."

Finally, we explored her experience around her feeling of being motivated from within, versus "being forced to do chores." Inviting Erica to notice how she was relating to her experience of the "tasks as chores," along with the sentence stem exercise, are examples of a specific methodologies that support two of IEF Coaching's key goals: (1) fostering Contextual Relational Mindfulness; and (2) inspiring self-confidence and intrinsic motivation.

I chose to include this vignette because it demonstrates how the coach's willingness to offer a moment of appropriate authentic self-revelation in the context of collaborative renegotiation around structure can work to *invite* the client to take greater agency in the process of their own growth and learning. Further, it provides a concrete glimpse at the types of conversations that are involved in taking a co-creative approach to goal-setting and accountability structures.

4.3 Developing contextual relational mindfulness around workplace relationships with Alice

As previously noted, IEF Coaching views human experience through the lens of Contextual Relational Mindfulness. Our experience is always *in relation* to our world, our actions, and other people. Thus far we have primarily focused on vignettes that illustrate Contextual Relational Mindfulness in relation to the client's goals and associated tasks. In this section, we illustrate how Contextual Relational Mindfulness can directly support a client in strengthening their interpretation of social cues, and slowing down impulsivity reactions that could have detrimental effects on their personal and professional aspirations.

Alice is an Associate Regional Manager in her late 30s at a mid-size technology company. Her main focus in our coaching was managing workplace overwhelm, while also working towards specific performance goals to help her secure a promotion. Two months into our coaching together, Alice was tasked with collaborating remotely with a Regional Manager from abroad on coordinated product testing, whom she described as "a difficult and aggressive person who wants to make me look bad." Alice asked me for her help in addressing the overwhelm she felt in "dealing with this guy's emails," so she could focus on the goal of successfully corresponding with him.

Together, we used Contextual Relateful Mindfulness to help Alice prepare for a conversation with him.

"When I see an email from this guy I want to scream. I know it's going to have a list of demands he has of me, that he knows I can't actually do."

"What kind of demands does he make?" I asked.

"I don't know, his language is just demanding," she insisted.

"Would you be up to open and read his latest email together, and unpack next steps from there?" I asked.

Together, we then used his email as an opportunity to get curious about the overwhelm trigger. First, I had Alice read the email out loud, and stop whenever she noticed overwhelm arising. Second, I invited her to get curious about the overwhelm. Finally, once we had moved through the charged moments in the email, we broke down what the email was actually requiring of her, and came up with a clear plan of action for (1) how she would plan to do the tasks requested of her in the email, and (2) how and when she would answer.

As discussed in the Literature Review, IEF Coaching proposes an approach to EF training which intentionally moves from focused training to the intermediate-level problems, an approach which "bridges the gap" to real life situations and addresses the human who operates with whatever EF are accessible at any given "hot" moment and as well as planning and training in the "cool". This interaction with Alice illustrates how IEF's approach addresses a "hot" moment (of charge, anger, overwhelm) in the context of a client's lived experience, while also providing a bridge to a "cool" state, and only introduces the EF tools after the "cooling" has occurred. Further this example illustrates the application of Contextual Relational Mindfulness to Alice's communication with a coworker. In this instance, IEF's approach supported Alice in developing greater interpersonal awareness and providing hands-on guidance for engaging systematically and effectively in an important email exchange.

5. Conclusions and directions for future research

Integrative Executive Function Coaching (IEF) is based on an understanding of when and how executive functions (EF) can be taught, integrated, and utilized. Tutored in isolation of the lived life, they have relatively little impact on improving overall functioning. The conceptual underpinnings of this approach are based on two scientific findings. First, the brain in a "hot" state differs from a "cold" state which impacts learning and accessing what has been learned [13, 14, 22]. Second, it has been shown that "near" transfer of skills differs from "far" transfer of skills [19], meaning that the domain in which EF skills are taught must approximate that in which they will be used. This point has been emphasized in the notion of imparting EF skills in the "intermediate" domain of experience [20].

This chapter describes the approach of Relational Mindfulness to the effective teaching of EF skills, an insight derived from the coaching practice of one of the authors (JL) and her concept of "the overwhelm". By working on EF skills in the intermediate zone, it more fully affects a "far transfer" of skills, that is, a set of skills utilizable in everyday situations. It posits that "the overwhelm" must be identified by a client at its inception, not by looking at its consequences (inadequate school or work performance, interpersonal chaos.) Teaching a client to identify when they are moving towards the overwhelm, that is, the mind moving from a cold towards a hot state, through Contextual Relational Mindfulness, is the first step of subsequent application of newly learned EF skills.

Techniques of Contextual Relational Mindfulness include: (1) creating a collaborative atmosphere around goal setting throughout the coaching; (2) introducing task-oriented tools for structuring time; (3) co-creating systems of habit accountability for in-between sessions; and (4) maintaining a strong relationship between the client's context and structural elements introduced in the coaching.

It is an approach that can be integrated with on-going insight-oriented or behavioral psychotherapies, or can be integrated into the practice of other clinicians.

This chapter describes a conceptual, clinical approach based on the existing research on what works and does not work regarding EF training. It has not been formalized into a "testable" method that has the potential to satisfy the standards of an evidence-based treatment. To date, there are no established evidence-based methods of remediating EF skills that will affect overall school or work performance or life satisfaction.

However, given the ubiquity of EF compromise, it is incumbent on any clinician to assess a client's competence in this regard. To treat as purely psychological the distress of an individual without regard to their potential cognitive compromise is a mistake. However, to attempt to remediate EF compromise outside of the psychological and social life of a client is equally a mistake. One client described above (Erica) in a sequence of applying EF to a real-life situation discovers she is "not broken." She can only discover this in the process of fixing what was broken, not by merely exploring what might be called a self-concept of being broken. To have been taught the necessary EF "fix" outside of her lived-experience of being broken would not have imparted the necessary skills. Her discovery occurs simultaneously as she both "fixes" something in her daily life and her idea of herself. Thus, the "micro-frame" analysis of the self in relation to itself, others, and the demands of life, the owning of the overwhelm, is itself a necessary EF skill that sets the stage for acquiring and integrating skills overwise lacking in a client's life. The pairing of Contextual Relational Mindfulness and the teaching of applied EF skills have been shown to have powerful clinical synergy.

Thanks

Thank you to Judith Brisman, PhD and Robert Abrams, MD for their critical readings of this manuscript.

Author details

Juliana Lewis[1*] and Owen Lewis[2]

1 National Philosophical Counseling Association, USA

2 Columbia University, Vagelos College of Physicians and Surgeons, New York City, USA

*Address all correspondence to: juliana@julianalewiscoaching.com

References

[1] Groves NB, Kofler MJ, Wells EL, Day TN, Chan ES. An examination of relations among working memory, ADHD symptoms, and emotion regulation. Journal of Attention Disorders. 2020;**48**(4):525-537. DOI: 10.1007/s10802-019-00612-8

[2] Rodgers AL. The state of adult ADHD today. In: ADDitude. New York (NY): New Hope Media; 2024. Available from: https://www.additudemag.com/how-is-adult-adhd-diagnosed-guidelines/

[3] Kessler RC, Adler L, Barkley R, Biederman J, Conners CK, Greenhill LL, et al. The prevalence and correlates of adult ADHD. In: Buitelaar JK, Kan C, Asherson P, editors. ADHD in Adults. Cambridge, United Kingdom: Cambridge University Press; 2011. pp. 9-17

[4] Sarkis E. Addressing attention-deficit/hyperactivity disorder in the workplace. Postgraduate Medicine. 2014;**126**(5):25-30. DOI: 10.3810/pgm.2014.09.2797

[5] Turjeman-Levi Y, Itzchakov G, Engel-Yeger B. Executive function deficits mediate the relationship between employees' ADHD and job burnout. AIMS Public Health. 2024;**11**(1):294-314. DOI: 10.3934/publichealth.2024015

[6] Tamm L, Richard L, James P, Ciesielski H. The association of executive functioning with academic, behavioral, and social performance ratings in children with ADHD. Journal of Learning Disabilities. 2021;**54**(2):124-138. DOI: 10.1177/0022219420961338

[7] United States Census Bureau. Press Release: Number, Timing, and Duration of Marriages and Divorces. 2021. Available from: https://www.census.gov/newsroom/press-releases/2021/marriages-and-divorces.html

[8] Bailey CE. Cognitive accuracy and intelligent executive function in the brain and in business. Annals of the New York Academy of Sciences. 2007;**1118**:122-141. DOI: 10.1196/annals.1412.011

[9] Miller HV, Barnes JC, Beaver KM. Self-control and health outcomes in a nationally representative sample. American Journal of Health Behavior. 2011;**35**(1):15-27. DOI: 10.5993/AJHB.35.1.2

[10] Moffitt TE. Childhood Self-Control Predicts Adult Health, Wealth, and Crime. Copenhagen: Multi-Disciplinary Symposium Improving the Well-Being of Children and Youth; 2012

[11] Diamond A. Executive functions. Annual Review of Psychology. 2013;**64**:135-168. DOI: 10.1146/annurev-psych-113011-143750

[12] Charles ST, Carstensen LL. Emotion regulation and aging. In: Gross JJ, editor. Handbook of Emotion Regulation. New York (NY): The Guilford Press; 2007. pp. 307-327

[13] Davis H, Valcan DS, Pino-Pasternak D. The relationship between executive functioning and self-regulated learning in Australian children. British Journal of Developmental Psychology. 2021;**39**:625-652. DOI: 10.1111/bjdp.12391

[14] Brock LL, Rimm-Kaufman SE, Nathanson L, Grimm KJ. The contributions of 'hot' and 'cool' executive function to children's academic achievement, learning-related behaviors,

and engagement in kindergarten. Early Childhood Research Quarterly. 2009;**24**:337-349. DOI: 10.1016/j.ecresq.2009.06.001

[15] Zelazo PD. Executive function and psychopathology: A neurodevelopmental model. Annual Review of Clinical Psychology. 2020;**16**:431-454. DOI: 10.1146/annurev-clinpsy-072319-024242

[16] Miyake A, Friedman NBP, Emerson MJ, Witzki AH, Howerter A, Wager TD. The unity and diversity of executive functions and their contributions to complex "frontal lobe" tasks: A latent variable analysis. Cognitive Psychology. 2000;**41**(1):49-100

[17] Diamond A, Ling DS. Review of the evidence on, and fundamental questions about, efforts to improve executive functions, including working memory. In: Novick JM, Bunting MF, Dougherty MR, Engle RW, editors. Cognitive and Working Memory Training: Perspectives from Psychology, Neuroscience, and Human Development. Oxford (UK): Oxford University Press; 2020. pp. 143-431

[18] Smith SM. Enhancement of recall using multiple environmental contexts during learning. Memory and Cognition. 1982;**10**:405-412. DOI: 10.3758/bf03197642

[19] Karbach J, Kray J. Executive function training. In: Strobach T, Karbach J, editors. Cognitive Training. Cham: Springer; 2021. DOI: 10.1007/978-3-030-39292-5_14

[20] Zelazo PD et al. Fostering executive-function skills and promoting far transfer to real-world outcomes: The importance of life skills and civic science. Current Directions in Psychological Science. 2024;**33**(2):12-127. DOI: 10.1177/0963721424122966

[21] Diamond A, Ling A. Conclusions about interventions, programs, and approaches for improving executive function that appear justified and those that, despite much hype, do not. Developmental Cognitive Neuroscience. 2016;**18**:34-48. DOI: 10.1016/j.dcn.2015.11.005

[22] Zelazo PD, Carlson SM. Reconciling the context-dependency and domain-generality of executive function skills from a developmental systems perspective. Journal of Cognition and Development. 2023;**24**(2):205-222. DOI: 10.1080/15248372.2022.2156515

[23] Surrey JL, Kramer G. Relational mindfulness. In: Germer CK, Siegel RD, Fulton PR, editors. Mindfulness and Psychotherapy. 2nd ed. New York (NY): The Guilford Press; 2013. pp. 94-111

[24] Spiegel R. Development of Sullivan's theory of participant observer. Contemporary Psychoanalysis. 1977;**13**(3):372-376

[25] Thompson C, Mazer M, Wittenberg E. An Outline of Psychoanalysis. New York (NY): Modern Library; 1955

[26] Bohleber W. The concept of intersubjectivity in psychoanalysis: Taking critical stock. International Journal of Psychoanalysis. 2013;**94**:799-823. DOI: 10.1111/1745-8315.12021

[27] Insight Dialogue. (n.d.). Relational Dhamma. Available from: https://insightdialogue.org/relational-practices/relational-dhamma/

[28] Ali H. The Diamond Approach: An Introduction to the Teachings of A.H. Almaas. Berkeley (CA): Diamond Approach Press; 2001

[29] Kestano R. Authentic Relating: A Guide to Rich, Meaningful. Nourishing Relationships: Self-Published; 2022

[30] Beneteau M. Circling and Authentic Relating Practice Guide. 2nd ed. Self-Published; 2022

[31] Relateful Co. (n.d.). Mission. Available from: https://www.relateful.com/mission

[32] Hartmann, H. Ego Psychology and the Problem of Adaptation. (Original work published 1939). Translated by D. Rapaport. International Universities Press, Inc. 1958

Section 2

Practictal Issues

Chapter 10

EMDR for Eating Disorders and Body Schema Disorders: An Update

Federico Durbano, Barbara Marchesi and Floriana Irtelli

Abstract

Eye Movement Desensitisation and Reprocessing (EMDR) is emerging as a complementary therapy for eating disorders (EDs) and body image disorders, which are often interrelated. Initially developed for post-traumatic stress disorder (PTSD), EMDR has shown promising results in addressing trauma and cognitive distortions associated with these disorders. Recent studies suggest that EMDR may reduce symptom severity, improve body acceptance, and decrease anxiety related to body image. For this reason, a narrative case study has been included in this chapter. The EMDR protocol targets traumatic memories and negative beliefs, facilitating an adaptive reframing of distorted experiences. This chapter explains the theoretical basis of EMDR, its role in overcoming trauma, including relational trauma, and its application in treating EDs and body image disorders. Furthermore, research findings, critical limitations, and future applications are discussed. The integration of EMDR with traditional therapies has demonstrated synergistic potential, accelerating recovery and reducing the risk of relapse. Although further research is needed to validate these preliminary findings and the scientific literature remains limited, EMDR appears to be a promising and complementary approach in the treatment of complex and often therapy-resistant conditions.

Keywords: EMDR, anorexia, bulimia nervosa, body image disorder, trauma

1. Introduction

This technique consists of desensitising and reprocessing memories of traumatic experiences through eye movements, it is one of the acquisitions among PTSD treatments, and summarising we can say that it is configured to bring unprocessed information to an adaptive level, through alternating and rhythmic bilateral hemispheric stimulation, stimulating both cerebral hemispheres [1–11]. This procedure was first used in this field by Dr. Francine Shapiro, in 1989; EMDR rather than being the result of a specific theoretical perspective was a discovery, thanks to an accidental observation made by its creator, who recounted how, while walking in a forest, she noticed certain movements of her eyes were associated with a reduction in the perception of disturbing thoughts [7–11]. The theoretical assumptions on which EMDR is based focus on the importance of facilitating the processing of disturbing material; in fact, according to the theories behind EMDR, if this processing does not take place, the information remains enclosed in a neural network in its original state, and is dysfunctionally stimulated by various stimuli that resemble the initial memory, causing flashbacks and unpleasant emotions [7–11]. This is due to the fact that all images, sounds and sensations related to the original moment are stored in the same way as they were experienced, which is why some are constantly re-experienced psychologically [7–11]. This factor becomes generalised over time and can cause symptoms, such as anxiety, depression and post-traumatic stress. In summary, trauma can result in interference with the psychological and biological process that normally promotes the adaptation of events to memory. It must also be specified that traumatic memories are often partly dissociated from the subject's general affective and semantic network, and are represented in a form that leads to distortions in perceptions, feelings and responses [7–11]. Through a number of 'dual attention' exercises, therefore, both cerebral hemispheres are alternately stimulated: the left and the right. This activates an intrinsic self-regulating mechanism in people, which reintegrates traumatic memories into a normalised form in memory: with the eye movements performed during the EMDR procedure, this mechanism is activated. In short, this procedure aims to progressively promote improved cognitive and affective well-being [7–11].

2. The EMDR protocol for the treatment of eating disorders

As various researches have focused on the connection of the onset of eating disorders and a history of traumatic events [4, 12–15], interest in the use of EMDR in the treatment of eating disorders has recently been stimulated in the scientific community [4], we would also point out that the present manuscript has a particular narrative focus specifically on anorexia. We should also point out that the effectiveness of EMDR treatment in eating disorder situations has emerged as early as the 2000s [3–4].

This protocol is based on the original eight-step standard EMDR model proposed by Shapiro [8] and can be adapted specifically for the treatment of eating disorders and body image disorders (which are often interrelated). Traumatic memories are considered to underlie the development of the disorder [4].

In the preparation phase, a secure and trusting therapeutic relationship is established between patient and therapist and the subject is informed about the principles and techniques behind EMDR. The patient's emotional stability and ability to cope with reprocessing are assessed, the person is taught stress management techniques, and finally, treatment goals are discussed and established.

In the assessment phase, a detailed clinical history is collected of the patient, who often has no compassion for himself and is extremely self-critical [4], and in this specific case the specific symptoms of the eating disorder (restriction, binge eating, purging, etc.) are also identified. Traumatic or negative experiences related to body image and eating are explored and comorbidity with states such as anxiety, depression or post-traumatic stress disorder is also assessed, specific memories regarding body image are also precisely focused on [3, 12].

In the assessment phase, priority treatment targets are identified, i.e. in this case traumatic memories related to the body or food, but also negative beliefs about oneself. At this stage, it is also important to identify the specific triggers that provoke dysfunctional behaviour, to identify the Negative Cognition and Positive Cognition for each target, to measure the validity of Positive Cognition and to measure the subjective disturbance the person feels when thinking back on the traumatic material.

During the EMDR protocol, the SUD (Subjective Units of Distress) scale and the VOC (Validity of Cognition) scale are used: the SUD (Subjective Units of Distress) scale and the VOC (Validity of Cognition) scale are essential components of the EMDR protocol. The SUD scale measures the level of distress a client feels on a scale from 0 to 10, where 0 indicates no disturbance and 10 represents the highest level of distress imaginable. The VOC scale, on the other hand, assesses how true a positive belief the client feels on a scale from 1 to 7, where 1 is completely false and 7 is completely true [16].

These scales help therapists gauge the progress of the client during EMDR sessions and adjust the treatment accordingly. The SUD scale is used to monitor the reduction in distress, while the VOC scale measures the increase in the client's belief in positive cognitions [16].

The next phase is called desensitisation and in this phase bilateral eye movements are used to process and reprocess traumatic memories related to the body and food. At this time, the negative emotions associated with the traumatic theme are worked on and any reactions are monitored and managed during the process.

The next phase is called the installation phase [8], during which new positive beliefs about the body and the relationship with food are reinforced, positive cognitions are increased and bilateral stimulation is used to consolidate the new beliefs [4]. Finally, work is done on body acceptance and a healthier relationship with food.

The next phase consists of body scanning, in which the patient is guided through a full body scan in order to identify areas of residual tension or discomfort.

The closing phase then takes place, in which the aim is to stabilise the patient emotionally; restraint and visualisation techniques can also be used. In this phase, it is possible to discuss and plan coping strategies for the week and provide instructions on how to handle any emerging disturbances between sessions.

The last phase is called the re-evaluation phase, in which the patient's progress is assessed at the beginning of each new session, the stability of the results obtained is verified, new targets or residual aspects to be treated are identified and the treatment plan is updated according to emerging needs.

It should also be specified that this protocol can be supplemented with differently oriented therapy pathways for eating disorders, pathways that go beyond the exclusive focus on a single symptom [17], and that it is important to constantly monitor the patient's nutritional and medical status and to include collaboration with a multidisciplinary team (nutritionist, doctor) in the pathway, as this is often necessary. In one study, the frequency of treatment for this type of case study was proposed to last for 6 months twice a week [4], but this standard cannot be generalised for all patients; in fact, we must add that the pace and intensity of treatment must be adapted to the needs of the individual patient.

3. Clinical example, a narrative description of the application of the EMDR protocol

As an example, here is a narrative that follows the EMDR protocol for eating disorders.

Alex is 32 years old and works as a clerk in a company, comes from a wealthy family, is gender fluid and has developed severe anorexic symptoms for many years.

The patient comes to a psychotherapy centre for help in coping with anorexia.

After several anamnestic sessions in which Alex's life history is reconstructed, the therapist establishes a relationship of trust, then, in agreement with the patient, the principles of EMDR are explained and Alex's emotional stability at that stage is assessed.

Further along the way, Alex learns stress management techniques, such as deep breathing and visualisation, and it is explained to the subject that the aim of the treatment is to improve body perception and reduce dysfunctional eating behaviour. The therapist has collected a detailed medical history of Alex, who reports symptoms of severe food restriction and an intense fear of gaining weight, trauma related to school bullying for his gender identity, and intense criticism from his parents for his weight have also emerged in previous sessions, and comorbidities such as anxiety and depression are also assessed.

In the assessment phase, the targets to be addressed with EMDR are identified [18]: traumatic memories of bullying at school, hypercritical parental relationships towards her and dysfunctional cognitions, concerning being horrible. The therapist points out that the symptoms are often stimulated by comments about weight and comparisons with the bodies of others. The patient agrees to undergo EMDR, and the desensitisation phase using bilateral stimulation then takes place, the therapist works with Alex on memories of humiliation and bullying, emotions of shame and fear are processed and Alex begins to feel more detached from these events.

During the course, Alex's emotional reactions are closely monitored and new positive beliefs, such as being a deserving person, are installed and reinforced. Bilateral stimulation helps to consolidate these new beliefs, working on body acceptance and a healthier relationship with food [17, 18].

During the EMDR protocol, body scanning is also explored and the therapist guides Alex through a full body scan to identify areas of tension or discomfort and using alternating bilateral stimulation, any residual negative feelings are processed, promoting a positive connection with his body. At the end of each session, Alex is stabilised emotionally using relaxation techniques, and finally, coping strategies are discussed and planned for the following week, ensuring that Alex knows how to manage any emerging discomfort between sessions. At the beginning of each new session, a re-evaluation of the patient's state takes place and the therapist assesses Alex's progress, the stability of the results obtained is checked and any new targets or residual issues to be treated are identified. The therapeutic plan is updated according to Alex's needs, the EMDR protocol and the general expressive therapeutic pathway, integrated with each other have the aim, as in other studies on this subject, of catalysing the reconnection between body, emotions and cognition, without being overwhelmed by destructive emotions [17, 18]. Alex's psychotherapy using the EMDR protocol likely resulted in improvements in emotional stability, body perception and reduction of dysfunctional eating behaviours.

4. EMDR application for relational trauma

Finally, we have to point out the intricate relationships between eating disorders, trauma and comorbid psychiatric conditions, with a particular emphasis on post-traumatic stress disorder: childhood sexual abuse has been identified as a nonspecific risk factor for eating disorders [19]; the spectrum of trauma includes also various forms of abuse and neglect; trauma is more prevalent in bulimic compared to nonbulimic EDs; and trauma is linked to greater comorbidity, often mediated by PTSD [19].

We have to point out also that EMDR has also been studied specifically for relational traumas exploring the integration of attachment theory with EMDR therapy to address relational trauma [20]. The importance of secure attachment experiences in early childhood for healthy brain development and how EMDR can be adapted to repair attachment wound have been emphasised, and EMDR techniques for attachment trauma have been explored, highlighting the significance of building a strong therapeutic relationship and tailoring EMDR protocols to meet the unique needs of these clients [19, 20].

5. Limitations of EMDR in the treatment of eating disorders

Despite the potential benefits of EMDR in the treatment of eating disorders, it is important to consider and highlight the following limitations: although EMDR is well established for the treatment of PTSD, research on its efficacy specifically for eating disorders is still limited. Further randomised controlled trials are needed to confirm its effectiveness in this area, and the single case study that has been reported in this chapter is only an example and it cannot be taken for granted that others will achieve the exactly same results with the same procedure because the individual variability is significant, and the sample is not statistically significant (this is only one case).

It is also necessary to emphasise the complexity of eating disorders: they are multifactorial conditions involving biological, psychological and social aspects; EMDR, by focusing mainly on traumatic and cognitive aspects, may not adequately address all the factors involved.

It should also be specified that the process of reworking can be emotionally intense and in patients with severe eating disorders or significant psychiatric comorbidities, this may lead to temporary destabilisation, requiring careful clinical management.

It should also be emphasised that the standard EMDR protocol might require significant modifications to adapt to the specific needs of patients with eating and body image disorders, which might influence its effectiveness or standardisation [4].

It can also be observed that while many patients with eating disorders present a history characterised by trauma [17], not all of them present these components, so logically EMDR may be less effective for patients whose eating disorders are not rooted in traumatic experiences.

Of course, in cases of severe malnutrition or high medical risk, it may be necessary to prioritise medical stabilisation before starting EMDR, potentially delaying the start of psychological treatment whose effective application requires specialised training combining expertise in EMDR and eating disorders, which may limit the availability of qualified therapists.

6. Conclusions

In conclusion, it should be noted that while some studies have shown promising short-term results, more research is needed to evaluate the effectiveness of EMDR in maintaining long-term outcomes in eating disorders, and as with many psychological treatments, the effectiveness of EMDR can vary significantly from individual to individual, and identifying reliable predictors of treatment response remains a challenge to date [21].

Author details

Federico Durbano[1*], Barbara Marchesi[2] and Floriana Irtelli[3]

1 State University, Milan, Italy

2 Azienda Ospedaliera Melegnano La Martesana, Milan, Italy

3 Associazione Italiana Psicologi, Milan, Italy

*Address all correspondence to: federico.durbano@asst-melegnano-martesana.it

References

[1] Kazén M, Baumann N, Twenhöfel JF, Kuhl J. When do anorexic patients perceive their body as too fat? Aggravating and ameliorating factors. PLoS One. 2019;**14**(2):e0212612. DOI: 10.1371/journal.pone.0212612

[2] de Jongh A, Amann BL, Hofmann A, Farrell D, Lee CW. The status of EMDR therapy in the treatment of posttraumatic stress disorder 30 years after its introduction. Journal of EMDR Practice and Research. 2019;**13**(4):261-269

[3] Bloomgarden A, Calogero RM. A randomized experimental test of the efficacy of EMDR treatment on negative body image in eating disorder inpatients. Eating Disorders. 2008;**16**:418-427. DOI: 10.1080/10640260802370598

[4] Zaccagnino M, Cussino M, Callerame C, Civilotti C, Fernandez I. Anorexia nervosa and EMDR: A clinical case. Journal of EMDR Practice and Research. 2017;**11**(1):43-53. DOI: 10.1891/1933-3196.11.1.43

[5] Zaccagnino M, Cussino M, Callerame C, Civilotti C, Fernandez I. EMDR for depression: A systematic review of controlled studies. Clinical Neuropsychiatry. 2017;**14**(5):306-312

[6] Balbo M, Zaccagnino M, Cussino M, Civilotti C. Eye movement desensitization and reprocessing (EMDR) and eating disorders: A systematic review. Clinical Neuropsychiatry. 2017;**14**(5):321-329

[7] Shapiro F. Eye movement desensitization: A new treatment for post-traumatic stress disorder. Journal of Behavior Therapy and Experimental Psychiatry. 1989;**20**:211-217

[8] Shapiro F. Eye Movement Desensitization and Reprocessing (EMDR): Basic Principles, Protocols, and Procedures. New York: Guilford Press; 1995

[9] Shapiro F. Eye movement desensitization and reprocessing (EMDR) and the anxiety disorders: Clinical and research implications of an integrated psychotherapy treatment. Journal of Anxiety Disorders. 1999;**13**:35-67

[10] Shapiro F. Eye movement desensitization and reprocessing (EMDR) in the treatment of trauma. Journal of Clinical Psychology. 2001;**57**(8):933-946

[11] Shapiro F. Eye Movement Desensitization and Reprocessing (EMDR) Therapy: Basic Principles, Protocols, and Procedures. 3rd ed. New York, NY: Guilford Press; 2018

[12] Johnson JG, Cohen P, Chen H, Kasen S, Brook JS. Parenting behaviors associated with risk for offspring personality disorder during adulthood. Archives of General Psychiatry. 2006;**63**(5):579-587

[13] Speranza AM, Alberigi E. La relazione tra abuso e disturbi alimentari: Il ruolo della dissociazione [The relationship between abuse and eating disorders: The role of dissociation]. Maltrattamento e Abuso all'Infanzia. 2006;**8**(1):23-47

[14] Steiger H, Zankor L. Sexual traumata among eating-disordered, psychiatric, and normal female groups: Comparison of prevalences and defense styles. Journal of Interpersonal Violence. 1990;**5**:74-86

[15] Welch S, Fairburn C. Sexual abuse and bulimia nervosa: Three integrated case control comparisons. American Journal of Psychiatry. 1994;**151**:402-407

[16] Brooker E. Eye movement desensitisation and reprocessing: Transforming trauma and the emotional mind. In: Brooker E, editor. Transforming Performance Anxiety Treatment Using Cognitive Hypnotherapy and EMDR. Oxford: Routledge; 2019. pp. 22-31

[17] Cooke LJ, Grand C. The neurobiology of eating disorders treatment into the early phases of the EMDR protocol. In: Shapiro R editor. EMDR solutions II: For depression, eating disorders, performance, and more. New York, NY: Norton; 2009. pp. 129-150

[18] Zaccagnino M, Civilotti C, Cussino M, Callerame C, Fernandez I. EMDR in Anorexia Nervosa: From a Theoretical Framework to the Treatment Guidelines. London, UK, London: Intechopen; 2017. DOI: 10.5772/65695

[19] Brewerton TD. Eating disorders, trauma, and comorbidity: Focus on PTSD. Eating Disorders. 2007;**15**(4):285-304

[20] Parnell L. Attachment-Focused EMDR: Healing Relational Trauma. New York, NY: W W Norton and Co.; 2013

[21] Linardon J, Fairburn CG, Fitzsimmons-Craft EE, Wilfley DE, Brennan L. The empirical status of the third-wave behaviour therapies for the treatment of eating disorders: A systematic review. Clinical Psychology Review. 2017;**58**:125-140

Chapter 11

Psychological Approaches for Eating Disorders: The Role of Body Image, Self-Esteem, and Quality of Life

Fatema Ahmed, Chen Wu, Li Li, Qingyuan Ye, Waleed Ksebe and Kefang Wang

Abstract

Eating disorders (EDs), including anorexia nervosa (AN), bulimia nervosa (BN), and binge eating disorder (BED), are severe mental health conditions involving complex psychological, emotional, and physical factors. This chapter explores Cognitive Behavioral Therapy (CBT) as a leading psychological treatment for EDs, focusing on its impact on body image, self-esteem, and quality of life (QoL). It also highlights the importance of personalized and integrated approaches in treating EDs, emphasizing the need for tailored interventions and multidisciplinary care. CBT is highly effective for BN and BED, supported by evidence showing reductions in binge eating, purging, and restrictive behaviors, alongside improvements in psychological well-being and QoL. Core CBT techniques help individuals challenge maladaptive beliefs about body image and self-worth, regain control over eating habits, and enhance social functioning. The chapter reviews empirical evidence supporting CBT's mechanisms of action. However, CBT's effectiveness for AN is limited, particularly in adults, where Family-Based Therapy (FBT) has shown greater promise for adolescents. Challenges in CBT implementation include the importance of the therapeutic alliance, the need for culturally sensitive adaptations, and the underutilization of CBT due to a lack of trained clinicians. The chapter also highlights the global rise in ED prevalence, driven by sociocultural factors like Western media influence, urbanization, and acculturation. It calls for ongoing research and the integration of digital interventions to improve accessibility and long-term outcomes. By addressing these gaps, CBT and other evidence-based treatments can evolve, offering hope for improved recovery and QoL for individuals affected by these debilitating disorders.

Keywords: eating disorders, body image, self-esteem, quality of life, cognitive behavioral therapy

1. Introduction

Eating disorders (EDs) have become a significant global health issue, transcending cultural and geographical boundaries [1]. Historically perceived as conditions primarily affecting Western populations, recent research indicates that EDs are prevalent worldwide, including in non-Western countries such as Zimbabwe, Ghana, Taiwan, and Pakistan [2]. This global spread is attributed to various factors, including the worldwide reach of Western media, and the fashion industry has played a crucial role in spreading the thin body ideal, which is a significant risk factor for EDs [3, 4]. Modernization, urbanization, and changes in family dynamics have also been implicated in the increasing rates of EDs worldwide [1, 5], and immigrants and individuals in multicultural societies are at higher risk of developing EDs due to the stress of acculturation and the clash between traditional and modern body ideals [6, 7]. The prevalence of EDs has increased globally, with notable rises in Asia, the Arab region, and among minority groups in North America [1]. For instance, a study in Saudi Arabia reported a 12-month prevalence of 3.2% for EDs, which is higher than global averages [8]. EDs such as AN, BN, and BEDs are severe mental health conditions. They involve distorted eating behaviors and significant weight changes, which can severely impact a person's QoL and social interactions [9, 10]. Moreover, individuals with EDs may develop severe somatic complications that can cause a higher risk of suicide [11] and increased mortality rates, especially AN [12]. Personalized and integrated treatment approaches are essential for effectively managing EDs [13, 14]. By addressing the unique biopsychosocial factors of each patient and combining various therapeutic modalities, healthcare providers can offer more effective and comprehensive care, ultimately leading to better outcomes for individuals with EDs [15].

AN is an extreme restriction of food intake, intense fear of gaining weight, and a distorted body image [16, 17], which results in a high mortality rate and severe physical complications such as malnutrition, hypotension, bradycardia, and osteoporosis [18]. There are limited effective treatments for adults; family-based therapy shows promise for adolescents [19, 20]. BN is recurrent episodes of binge eating followed by inappropriate compensatory behaviors like vomiting, excessive exercise, or laxative use, which results in electrolyte imbalances, gastrointestinal issues, dental erosion, and psychological distress [17]. CBT and pharmacotherapy are effective [21, 22]. BED is episodes of eating large quantities of food without subsequent purging behaviors, leading to feelings of shame and distress [17], which results in obesity, cardiovascular diseases, and psychological issues [23], and CBT is the gold standard; pharmacotherapy can also be beneficial [19]. This chapter aims to provide an in-depth exploration of CBT as a psychological approach for treating eating disorders, with a specific focus on its impact on body image, self-esteem, and QoL. We will assess the efficacy of CBT in altering dysfunctional thoughts and behaviors related to eating, examine the empirical evidence supporting its positive effects on psychological factors, and discuss the mechanisms and techniques that constitute CBT for eating disorders. Additionally, we will address the challenges and considerations associated with CBT, including its limitations and the need for ongoing research and adaptation to better serve the diverse needs of individuals with eating disorders. The chapter seeks to highlight CBT's role as a cornerstone in treatment and to emphasize the importance of continued development in therapeutic approaches to enhance long-term outcomes for those affected by eating disorders.

2. The prevalence of different EDs in the worldwide population

The prevalence and burden of EDs, including AN, BN, and binge eating disorders, have been rising worldwide. The Global Burden of Disease Study 2017 data indicate a continuous increase in the age-standardized rates (ASRs) of prevalence and disability-adjusted life years (DALYs) for EDs from 1990 to 2017. This growing burden highlights the urgent need for effective treatments, such as CBT, which has been shown to reduce symptoms and improve QoL for individuals with EDs significantly [24], and high-income regions such as Australasia, Western Europe, and North America exhibit the highest burden of EDs. Significant increases in the prevalence of EDs have been observed in East Asia and South Asia, indicating a shift in the geographical distribution of these disorders [1, 25]. EDs are more prevalent in females than males, but the rate of increase in prevalence is higher in males [26, 27]. There is also a spread of EDs beyond Western cultures to diverse global populations, influenced by factors such as media, market economy, and urbanization [1, 5, 28], as we can notice that migrants and individuals from non-European countries show higher prevalence rates of ED symptoms, suggesting the impact of cultural and environmental changes [7]. The rising prevalence of EDs globally underscores the need for enhanced public health strategies, early intervention, and equitable access to treatment. CBT has been widely recognized as an effective treatment for BN and BED [24, 29], with growing evidence supporting its use in AN [30]. CBT addresses the psychological factors that contribute to the development and maintenance of EDs, such as body dissatisfaction, low self-esteem [22, 31, 32], and maladaptive eating behaviors [22, 31, 32]. By targeting these factors, CBT reduces symptoms and improves the overall quality of life (QoL) for individuals with EDs [32–34]. As the global burden of EDs continues to rise, the widespread implementation of CBT and other evidence-based treatments will be crucial for improving outcomes and reducing the long-term impact of these disorders (**Table 1**).

The prevalence of EDs has been rising worldwide. The graph below illustrates the increase in ED cases from 2024 in different regions, highlighting the growing burden of these disorders globally. The **Figure 1** shows the prevalence of EDs in other areas (e.g., North America, Europe, Asia).

Disorder	Lifetime prevalence (women)	Lifetime prevalence (men)	Regional highlights
Anorexia nervosa	0.16–0.8%	0.06–0.3%	Higher in Western countries [26, 35, 36]
Bulimia nervosa	0.5–2.6%	0.1–0.5%	Increasing in Eastern Europe [27, 37]
Binge eating	1.0–6.1%	0.3–2.0%	More prevalent globally [38]

Note: The prevalence and burden of EDs have been rising worldwide, with significant increases observed in both high-income and developing regions. As the global burden of these disorders grows, effective treatment strategies become increasingly important. Among these, CBT is the most effective treatment for BN and BED.

Table 1.
The prevalence of different eating disorders in the worldwide population.

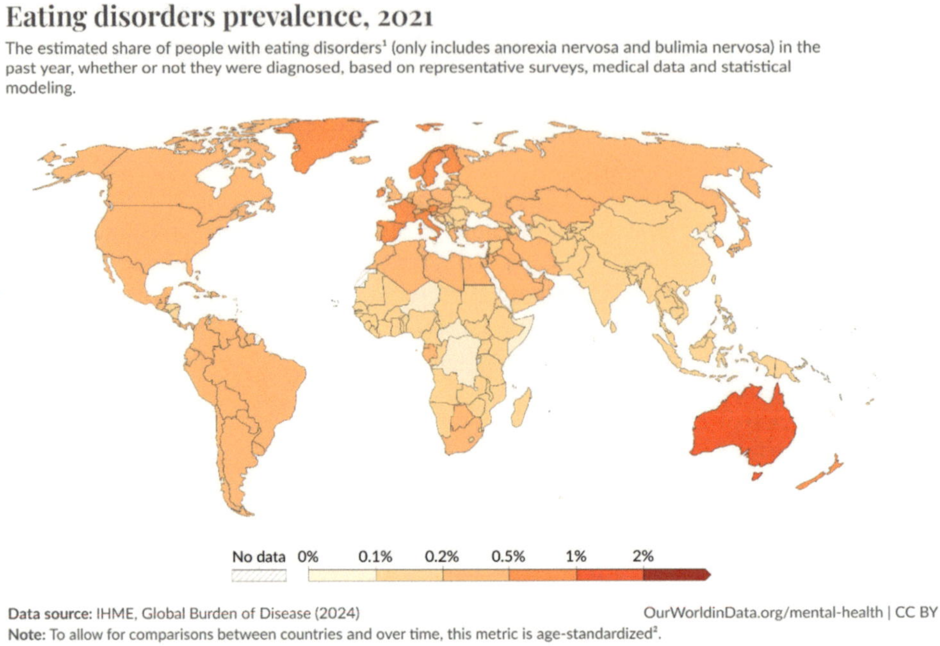

Figure 1.
Estimated prevalence of eating disorders (anorexia nervosa and bulimia nervosa) in the past year, age-standardized, based on representative surveys, medical data, and statistical modeling. Data source: IHME, Global Burden of Disease (2024). Visualization by OurWorldinData.org/mental-health / CC BY.

3. The effectiveness of various treatments for eating disorders

To understand the effectiveness of various treatments for EDs, it is crucial to examine the evidence backing different therapeutic methods. In the case of AN, particularly among adolescents, the evidence for CBT's effectiveness is less robust [29, 30, 39]. CBT adaptation for younger patients includes family involvement, which is vital for children and adolescents [40]. Recent advancements in CBT for EDs (CBT-ED) aim to enhance its efficiency, accessibility, and suitability for younger patients [41–43]. Family-based treatment (FBT) is the most effective and well-supported treatment for adolescent AN, with a strong evidence base and adaptability to various clinical settings. Its focus on family involvement and structured phases of treatment contributes to its success in promoting recovery and normalizing eating behaviors in adolescents with AN [44–47]. It involves empowering parents to aid in their child's recovery [48, 49], especially regarding re-feeding and weight restoration [50, 51]. However, further research is necessary to refine family involvement and identify the conditions that make FBT the most effective [52, 53]. Interpersonal Psychotherapy (IPT) is strongly supported for treating BN and BED, focusing on the social and interpersonal contexts of the disorder [54, 55]. IPT is strongly supported for treating BN and BED, focusing on the social and interpersonal contexts of the disorder [44, 45]. Research indicates that while IPT is a well-supported treatment for BN and BED, its effectiveness for AN remains unclear and requires further investigation [56–58]. When it comes to combining psychological treatments with medications, studies have shown limited additional benefits, with no significant advantage for combined treatments over psychological treatments alone for AN, BN, and BED [59–62]. Self-help interventions, especially for bulimic disorders,

Treatment	Effective for	Notes
Psychological therapies		
Cognitive-behavioral therapy (CBT)	BN, BED, AN (adults)	Most established, first-line treatment for BN and BED [30, 75–77].
Family-Based Therapy (FBT)	AN, BN (adolescents)	Highly effective for adolescents [78, 79].
Interpersonal Therapy (IPT)	BN, BED	Effective alternative to CBT [30, 75].
Dialectical Behavior Therapy (DBT) and other third-wave therapies like Acceptance and Commitment Therapy (ACT) and Mindfulness-Based Interventions (MBI)	Various eating disorders	Promising but need more research [76, 80].
Pharmacotherapy		
Selective Serotonin Reuptake Inhibitors (SSRIs): Fluoxetine	BN	Approved and effective [59, 81, 82].
Lisdexamfetamine	BED	Approved and effective [59, 81, 82].
Combined and multimodal treatments		
Integrated multimodal	All eating disorders	Superior to psychotherapy alone [83, 84].
Emerging and novel therapies		
Self-help interventions	BN, BED	Effective and cost-efficient [63, 85].
Internet-based and adaptive treatments	Various eating disorders	Promising increasing accessibility [86–88].

Table 2.
The effectiveness of various treatments for eating disorders.

show promise throughout various stages of care. However, their effectiveness for AN is less clear [63–65]. Emerging therapies like Emotion-Focused Therapy (EFT) suggest post-treatment improvements in eating psychopathology and affective symptoms, but further research is needed to confirm its efficacy [66, 67]. Other therapies, such as Acceptance and Commitment Therapy [68, 69], Dialectical Behavior Therapy [70–72], and Mindfulness-Based Therapies, are showing some positive outcomes, though additional research is required [73, 74]. So, to understand the effectiveness of various treatments for eating disorders, it is essential to consider the evidence supporting different therapeutic approaches (see **Table 2**).

4. Understanding the causes: Risk factors and etiology of eating disorders

4.1 Biological risk factors

4.1.1 Genetic predisposition: Genetic factors play a crucial role in developing EDs

Twin studies have shown that individuals with a family history of EDs are at higher risk, suggesting a strong hereditary component. Specific genetic polymorphisms, such as those in the Fat Mass and Obesity-Associated (FTO) gene, have been linked to behaviors like binge eating and emotional eating [89–91]. However, genetics alone do not determine the onset of EDs; they interact with environmental factors, such as stress and cultural pressures, to increase vulnerability [92, 93].

4.1.2 Neurotransmitter dysregulation

Neurotransmitters such as serotonin and dopamine regulate mood and appetite, and their dysregulation has been linked to EDs. For instance, altered serotonin levels are associated with anxiety and avoidant temperamental characteristics in individuals with AN [94]; changes in neuropeptide secretion, which affect hunger and satiety signals, also contribute to the maintenance of ED symptoms [95].

4.1.3 Neuroimaging

Studies have revealed structural and functional abnormalities in the brains of individuals with EDs. These abnormalities may perpetuate the disorders by affecting cognitive processes related to body image and self-control [96]. Starvation and malnutrition, common in EDs, can lead to further neural circuit dysfunction, exacerbating the condition [95].

4.1.4 Gastrointestinal microbiota

Emerging evidence suggests that the gut microbiota may play a role in developing EDs. An imbalance in gut bacteria, known as dysbiosis, can affect how the body regulates hunger and fullness. This imbalance has been linked to symptoms of EDs, such as binge eating and restrictive eating patterns [97, 98].

4.1.5 Hormonal factors

Hormonal changes, particularly those related to ovarian hormones, have been implicated in the onset and course of EDs. These hormonal fluctuations can affect mood and appetite, contributing to the development of disordered eating behaviors [92].

4.2 Psychological risk factors

Understanding the psychological risk factors for EDs is essential for developing effective prevention and intervention strategies. Several key psychological factors have been identified.

4.2.1 Body dissatisfaction

Body dissatisfaction, particularly prevalent in adolescent girls, is an influential risk factor closely linked to the development of EDs [99, 100]. CBT addresses body dissatisfaction through cognitive restructuring, helping individuals challenge and modify maladaptive beliefs about their body image. By identifying and reframing distorted thoughts (e.g., "I must be thin to be valued"), CBT reduces the impact of body dissatisfaction on eating behaviors and improves overall body image satisfaction [101–104]. Research has shown that CBT significantly reduces body dissatisfaction and improves body image satisfaction in individuals with EDs [22, 105]; the therapy's focus on cognitive restructuring, body exposure, and addressing dysfunctional beliefs about weight and body image contributes to its success in treating these disorders [106, 107].

DOI: http://dx.doi.org/10.5772/intechopen.1009601

4.2.2 Low self-esteem

Low self-esteem is another significant psychological trait that increases vulnerability to these disorders [13, 108, 109]. CBT improves self-esteem by teaching individuals to identify and challenge negative self-talk (e.g., "I am not good enough") and replace it with more positive and realistic thoughts [31, 110, 111]. Through cognitive restructuring and conducting behavioral experiments, CBT helps build a healthier self-concept, which is crucial for recovery from EDs [112]. The effectiveness of CBT is well supported by various studies, highlighting its role in enhancing self-esteem and reducing ED symptoms [113, 114].

4.2.3 Negative emotionality and perfectionism

Negative emotionality and perfectionism are also critical factors, with these personality traits contributing to the internalization of societal ideals of thinness and influencing the selection of peer environments [115, 116]. Perfectionism, in particular, has been associated with increased dieting, carb restriction, and binge-eating tendencies [116]. CBT addresses perfectionism by helping individuals recognize the unrealistic standards they set for themselves and develop more flexible and self-compassionate thinking patterns [117–119]. Through cognitive restructuring, individuals learn to challenge perfectionistic beliefs (e.g., "I must be perfect to be accepted") and reduce the pressure they place on themselves, which can decrease disordered eating behaviors [120–122].

4.2.4 Mental health condition

Furthermore, EDs often co-occur with other mental health conditions, such as depression, anxiety, and posttraumatic stress disorder, which can worsen the severity of ED symptoms [123, 124]. Social anxiety and social appearance anxiety are also significant risk factors, with social appearance anxiety serving as a shared vulnerability for both social anxiety and ED symptoms [125]. Family dynamics, particularly maternal attitudes and behaviors, play a crucial role in developing EDs in children and adolescents [99]. In contrast, insecure attachment and negative family interactions can indirectly contribute to eating problems [109].

4.2.5 Emotional dysregulation

Emotional dysregulation, including emotional nonacceptance and a lack of emotional awareness, has been linked to higher risks of dieting, purging, and other disordered eating behaviors [116]. CBT helps individuals develop emotion regulation skills, such as identifying and labeling emotions, tolerating distress, and using healthy coping strategies (e.g., mindfulness, journaling) instead of disordered eating behaviors [126, 127]. By improving emotional awareness and regulation, CBT reduces the reliance on maladaptive coping mechanisms and supports long-term recovery [128, 129]. Stressful and traumatic life events also increase the likelihood of developing EDs, highlighting the importance of individual-specific risk factors [108]. Lastly, peer context and media influence are significant psychosocial risk factors, with peer-based interventions that challenge the internalization of the thin ideal serving as protective factors against eating pathology [115, 130].

4.3 Sociocultural influences

Sociocultural factors play a critical role in the development of EDs. In Western cultures, the media often promotes unrealistic beauty standards, such as extreme thinness, which can lead to body dissatisfaction and disordered eating behaviors. CBT addresses these sociocultural influences by helping individuals critically evaluate media messages and internalized ideals of thinness [131]. Through cognitive restructuring, individuals learn to challenge societal pressures and develop a more balanced and self-compassionate view of their bodies, reducing the impact of these influences on their eating behaviors [103, 132–134]. However, these influences are not limited to Western societies. In East Asia, for example, the rise of EDs has been linked to the adoption of Western beauty ideals through globalization. Similarly, in regions like South Asia, traditional cultural norms around body weight and appearance are being challenged by modern media, leading to increased rates of body dissatisfaction and EDs among young people [135–138]. CBT can be adapted by integrating local cultural values and beliefs into therapy. For example, in Southeast Asia, adaptations may include modifying core treatment components to incorporate local values during the CBT restructuring process [139].

In some cases, integrating traditional beliefs and practices, such as the concept of Yin-Yang balance in Chinese culture, can enhance the effectiveness of CBT in treating conditions like depression [140]. Culturally adapted CBT (CA-CBT) for Arab individuals includes integrating cultural characteristics into the therapy process. This can involve using culturally relevant examples and themes and adjusting the session structure to fit cultural norms [141]; for instance, in Saudi Arabia, the adaptation of CBT includes addressing the stigma associated with mental health and making therapy more accessible. This involves training mental health professionals and adapting therapy to be more culturally sensitive [142]. We can summarize that cultural adaptations of CBT are crucial for addressing the unique sociocultural pressures faced by individuals in East Asia and the Arab region. By incorporating local values, addressing specific cultural factors, and making therapy more accessible and acceptable, CBT can be made more effective for these populations.

4.4 Environmental contributors

Childhood adversity, such as abuse and trauma, has been strongly linked to the development of EDs. These adverse experiences can lead to psychological vulnerabilities that increase the risk of developing EDs later in life [97, 143, 144]; parental pressures towards thinness and negative family relations are significant risk factors. High parental expectations can create a stressful environment that fosters the development of EDs, particularly when combined with other psychological and social pressures [145]. Additionally, maladaptive paternal behavior, such as low communication and time spent with the child, increases the risk of EDs [146]. Stressful life events, including recent stressful experiences and childhood trauma, are associated with the onset of EDs. These events can lead to emotional dysregulation and depression, which are pathways to emotional eating and other disordered eating behaviors [108, 147, 148]. Ultimately, the etiology of EDs is multifaceted, involving an interplay of biological, psychological, and sociocultural factors. These disorders significantly impair QoL, necessitating comprehensive assessment and targeted interventions. Understanding these risk factors and their impact on QoL is crucial for developing effective prevention and treatment strategies [13, 89, 149, 150].

4.5 Quality of life

4.5.1 Physical and mental health impact

EDs significantly impair physical and mental health, reducing QoL [19, 151]. Medical complications, such as cardiovascular and endocrine issues, are common, particularly in AN [152]. Meta-analyses indicate that CBT leads to modest but significant improvements in subjective and health-related QoL from pre- to post-treatment and follow-up. These improvements are more pronounced when CBT is delivered individually by a therapist or according to specific models like CBT-BN or CBT-E [153]. Studies have shown that CBT can significantly reduce weight, body mass index (BMI), and abdominal perimeter, which is associated with better physical health outcomes. Additionally, improvements in physical health-related QoL have been observed, particularly in patients with BED [154, 155].

4.5.2 Psychosocial functioning

EDs disrupt social relationships and daily functioning, contributing to a lower QoL [156]. CBT has been effective in enhancing social functioning and self-esteem. Web-based CBT interventions have significantly improved social functioning and self-esteem, improving overall QoL [157, 158]. Patients undergoing CBT report significant reductions in ED psychopathology, anxiety, depression, and general functioning, leading to enhanced life satisfaction. These improvements are sustained over time, with effect sizes remaining stable at follow-up (**Table 3**) [159, 160].

Risk factor	Associated EDs	Evidence
Genetic predisposition	Anorexia Nervosa, Bulimia Nervosa	Strong genetic links, particularly in anorexia nervosa
Neurobiological factors	All EDs	Advances in neurobiology highlight their role
Puberty	All EDs	Hormonal changes during puberty increase risk
Personality traits	All EDs	Traits like perfectionism and low self-esteem
Body dissatisfaction	Bulimia nervosa, binge eating disorder	Common psychological risk factor
Dieting and thin-ideal internalization	All EDs	Significant predictors of EDs
Media influence	All EDs	Strong sociocultural risk factor
Family dynamics	All EDs	Dysfunctional family environments and high parental expectations
Stressful life events	Bulimia nervosa	Linked to early traumatic events
Critical developmental periods	All EDs	Adolescence to young adulthood

Table 3.
Summary of risk factors and etiology of eating disorders.

5. Treatment approaches

5.1 Non-pharmacological approach

5.1.1 Psychotherapy

Cognitive behavioral therapy (CBT): CBT is widely recognized as the most effective treatment for BN and BED, with substantial evidence supporting its use. In addition to reducing symptoms such as binge eating and purging, CBT has been shown to improve QoL significantly. **Figure 2** below outlines the key steps in CBT for EDs, from identifying triggers to developing healthier coping strategies, and has demonstrated significant success in reducing symptoms such as binge eating and purging [31, 165, 166]; enhanced CBT (CBT-E) has been developed to address more severe cases and comorbid conditions, showing promising results [29, 167].

Core components of CBT for eating disorders:

1. Behavioral analysis and symptom-oriented procedures

Behavioral analysis: This involves understanding the multifactorial causes and triggers and maintaining the conditions of the eating disorder through a detailed behavioral analysis [31].

Symptom-oriented procedures: These are standard procedures to address specific eating disorder symptoms, such as binge eating or purging behaviors [22, 168].

2. Cognitive techniques

Cognitive restructuring: This technique identifies and changes distorted beliefs about dieting, body shape, and weight [169].

Self-monitoring: Patients are encouraged to keep detailed records of their eating habits, thoughts, and feelings to identify patterns and triggers [167].

3. Emotion regulation and interpersonal skills

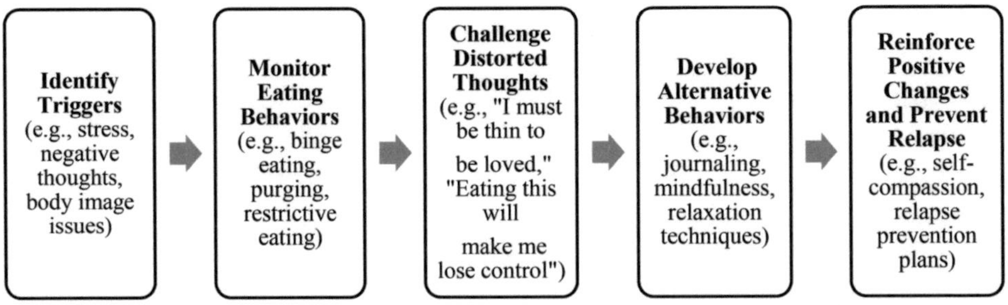

Figure 2.
CBT for EDs involves a structured process that begins with identifying triggers, such as stress or negative thoughts [161]. Patients are then encouraged to monitor their eating behaviors, including binge eating and purging, to gain insight into patterns and triggers [77]. The next step involves challenging distorted thoughts, such as the belief that one must be thin to be loved, through cognitive restructuring techniques [162]. Patients also learn to develop alternative behaviors, such as mindfulness and journaling, to replace disordered eating habits [163]. Finally, CBT focuses on reinforcing positive changes and preventing relapse through self-compassion and prevention plans [164].

Emotion regulation: Skills to manage and regulate emotions are taught to help patients cope with negative feelings that may trigger disordered eating behaviors [170].

Interpersonal competence: Improving interpersonal skills to handle social situations and relationships more effectively [170].

4. Body image disturbance

Body image interventions: Direct interventions to address dissatisfaction and distorted body image are crucial. Techniques may include body exposure therapy and cognitive restructuring focused on body image [103, 171, 172].

Enhanced CBT (CBT-E): This version includes specific components to address body image disturbances and is suitable for all eating disorders [101, 173].

5. Nutritional management

Normalization of eating patterns: Establishing regular eating habits and normalizing food intake are initial steps in the treatment process [174, 175].

Nutritional counseling: Providing education and guidance on healthy eating practices [176].

6. Addressing comorbidities

Modular-based treatment: This approach allows for the integration of interventions targeting comorbid conditions such as PTSD or personality disorders, which are often present in individuals with eating disorders [168, 177, 178].

7. Personal goals and individual needs

Goal setting: Working with patients to set personal goals considering their needs and preferences [31, 179].

8. Psychoeducation

Education on eating disorders: Providing information about the nature of eating disorders, their effects, and the importance of treatment adherence [180, 181].

9. Relapse prevention

Relapse prevention strategies: Techniques to help patients maintain progress and prevent relapse are particularly important in the treatment of anorexia nervosa [182, 183]. To improve relapse prevention, the following strategies are recommended:

Personalized relapse prevention plans: Developing individualized plans at the end of treatment and monitoring patients for at least 18 months post-discharge can significantly reduce relapse rates [184].

Family involvement: Involving family members in the treatment process, especially in younger patients, can support normalized eating and weight restoration [185, 186].

Continuous professional support: Maintaining contact with healthcare professionals during aftercare programs helps patients manage self-management strategies effectively [187].

Addressing comorbidities: Treating comorbid conditions such as depression and anxiety can improve overall treatment outcomes and reduce the risk of relapse [188, 189].

Bulimia nervosa (BN)	Binge eating disorder (BED)	Anorexia nervosa (AN)
Fluoxetine is FDA-approved and has shown efficacy in reducing binge-purge episodes [82].	Lisdexamfetamine is FDA-approved and effective in reducing binge eating episodes [191].	Olanzapine has shown some benefits in weight restoration for in-patient treatment, and fluoxetine may help prevent relapse in weight-restored patients [62].
Antidepressants (mainly SSRIs) have demonstrated moderate effectiveness in reducing symptoms [191].	Topiramate has shown promise in reducing binge episodes and promoting weight loss [192].	
	Antidepressants (SSRIs and SNRIs) have been effective in reducing binge eating frequency and associated psychopathology [193].	

Table 4.
Efficacy of pharmacotherapy for eating disorders.

10. Multidisciplinary approach

Team-based care: Involving a multidisciplinary team, including psychiatrists, nutritionists, and psychotherapists, to provide comprehensive care [190].

5.1.2 Pharmacotherapy

1. Antidepressants: Antidepressants, particularly selective serotonin reuptake inhibitors (SSRIs) like fluoxetine, are commonly used to treat BN and BED. These medications can help reduce binge eating episodes and improve mood, but they are less effective for AN. For AN, medications such as olanzapine, an antipsychotic, may be used to address anxiety and promote weight gain, but their efficacy is limited. Pharmacotherapy is often used in combination with psychological treatments, but it is not a standalone solution for eating disorders.

2. Other medications: Limited evidence for effectiveness in AN; some success with medications used for obesity and stimulants for BED (**Table 4**).

Pharmacotherapy plays a crucial role in the treatment of EDs, particularly for BN and BED, but its efficacy is often limited, and many patients do not achieve full recovery [59, 194]. There is a pressing need for more research to develop new medications and improve existing treatments, especially for AN [59]. Combining pharmacotherapy with psychotherapy and exploring innovative treatment targets may enhance outcomes for patients with EDs [195, 196].

6. Cognitive behavioral therapy (CBT) for bulimia nervosa (BN) and binge eating disorder (BED)

This therapy focuses on altering dysfunctional thoughts and behaviors related to eating, which significantly impact psychological factors such as body image and SE, ultimately improving the QoL for individuals with these EDs. Key Components of CBT for BN and BED:

1. Self-monitoring: Patients are encouraged to keep detailed records of their eating habits and related experiences, which helps identify patterns and triggers for binge eating and purging behaviors [197].

2. Psychoeducation: Educating patients about the nature of their disorder, including the cognitive-behavioral model of BN, helps them understand the vicious cycle of low self-esteem, extreme concerns about shape and weight, strict dieting, binge eating, and self-induced vomiting [198].

3. Cognitive restructuring: Involves challenging and changing distorted thoughts and beliefs about body image, food, and self-worth [199].

4. Behavioral interventions: Techniques such as exposure and response prevention reduce the frequency of binge eating and purging episodes [200].

6.1 Effectiveness and outcomes

1. Symptom reduction: CBT has been shown to significantly reduce the frequency of binge eating and purging behaviors in patients with BN and BED [201, 202].

2. Enhanced CBT (CBT-E) has been developed to address a broader range of eating disorder psychopathology and is effective for patients with severe comorbidities [167, 203].

3. Psychological improvements: Patients undergoing CBT often experience improvements in depression, self-esteem, and overall psychological functioning [165, 201].

4. Quality of life: Research has shown that individuals who undergo CBT experience significant improvements in QoL, including better physical health, stronger social relationships, and greater overall life satisfaction [30, 166, 198].

6.2 Case vignettes: Case study - Sarah - A 24-year-old woman with bulimia nervosa

Sarah, a 24-year-old woman, had been struggling with BN for several years. She experienced frequent episodes of binge eating, often triggered by stress at work and negative self-talk about her body [204–206]. After binge episodes, Sarah would purge through self-induced vomiting, which left her feeling ashamed and isolated. Her self-esteem was severely impacted, and she often avoided social situations out of fear of being judged for her appearance [207].

6.2.1 Initial assessment

Behavioral analysis in CBT for eating disorders: During Sarah's first cognitive behavioral therapy (CBT) session, her therapist conducted a detailed behavioral analysis to identify the triggers and maintaining factors of her eating disorder. This approach is consistent with evidence-based practices in CBT for eating disorders, which emphasize understanding the multifactorial nature of these conditions, including predisposing, triggering, and maintaining factors [31, 208].

Identifying triggers and maintaining factors: Sarah revealed that feelings of inadequacy at work and in social situations often preceded her binge episodes. This aligns with the cognitive-behavioral model, which identifies low self-esteem and interpersonal difficulties as significant maintaining factors for eating disorders [209, 210]. The model suggests that these feelings can trigger maladaptive behaviors, such as binge eating as a coping mechanism [211].

Beliefs about body image: She also strongly believed that she needed to be thin to be valued by others. This belief is a common cognitive distortion in individuals with eating disorders, where there is an over-evaluation of weight and shape [212]. Such beliefs are targeted in CBT to help patients develop healthier attitudes toward their bodies and reduce the importance placed on weight and shape [213].

6.2.2 CBT interventions

1. Self-monitoring: Sarah was asked to keep a daily food diary, recording what she ate and her thoughts and emotions before and after eating. This helped her and her therapist identify patterns, such as binge episodes occurring after stressful workdays or social interactions.

2. Cognitive restructuring: Sarah worked with her therapist to challenge her maladaptive beliefs, such as "I must be thin to be loved." Through guided questioning, Sarah began recognizing that her self-worth was not solely tied to her appearance. She replaced these thoughts with more balanced ones, such as "I am valued for who I am, not just how I look."

3. Behavioral experiments: Sarah participated in exposure exercises to reduce her fear of certain foods. For example, she gradually reintroduced "forbidden" foods into her diet in a controlled manner, learning that eating these foods did not lead to the catastrophic outcomes she feared.

4. Emotion regulation: Sarah learned mindfulness techniques to manage stress and negative emotions without binge eating. She practiced deep breathing and journaling as healthier coping mechanisms.

6.2.3 Outcomes

Over 12 weeks, Sarah's binge episodes decreased significantly, and she stopped purging altogether. She reported improved self-esteem and a more positive body image. Sarah also noted that her relationships with friends and family had improved, as she was no longer isolating herself due to shame about her eating behaviors [197].

Group therapy: Group CBT, which includes interpersonal elements, has shown effectiveness in treating BN, leading to significant improvements in bulimic behaviors and psychological functioning [201].

7. The importance of personalized and integrated approaches in treating eating disorders

Given the varied effectiveness of CBT across different EDs, personalized and integrated approaches have emerged as essential strategies to enhance treatment outcomes. By tailoring interventions to individual needs and involving a multidisciplinary team, these approaches address the complex and varied nature of EDs, ultimately improving treatment outcomes and patient well-being.

7.1 Personalized treatment approaches

Personalized interventions emphasize the importance of tailoring treatment plans to each patient's needs, preferences, and circumstances. This approach acknowledges that what works for one individual may not work for another. Key considerations in personalized interventions include:

Heterogeneity of symptoms: EDs present a high degree of symptom heterogeneity, making a one-size-fits-all approach ineffective for many individuals [214, 215]. Personalized treatments, such as Network-Informed Personalized Treatment (NIPT), have shown promise in improving treatment outcomes by tailoring interventions to individual symptom profiles [216].

Data-driven tools: Tools like the Awaken Digital Guide have been developed to assist clinicians in personalizing treatment plans. Both clinicians and patients have received these tools positively for their ability to enhance treatment efficiency and effectiveness [214]. Case studies, such as Sarah's experience with CBT for bulimia nervosa, demonstrate the effectiveness of personalized and integrated approaches in treating eating disorders. Sarah's treatment plan was tailored to her specific needs, incorporating cognitive restructuring, behavioral experiments, and family involvement, leading to significant improvements in her symptoms and QoL.

7.2 Integrated treatment approaches

Effective treatment of EDs often requires a multidisciplinary approach involving various healthcare professionals, including primary care physicians, dietitians, psychiatrists, and mental health professionals [217, 218]. This approach ensures that all aspects of the disorder, from medical to psychological, are addressed comprehensively. Dietitians play a crucial role in the treatment of EDs by developing individualized nutrition care plans, addressing nutritional deficiencies, and providing education to correct misconceptions about food and eating [176]. Incorporating occupational therapy into the treatment plan can help patients engage in meaningful daily activities, which supports their overall recovery journey [217].

CBT-E and Integrated Enhanced CBT (I-CBTE) have effectively treated severe and complex cases of EDs. These approaches combine psychological treatment with nutritional rehabilitation and have succeeded in long-term recovery [219].

For patients with co-occurring conditions like PTSD, integrated treatment approaches that address both ED and PTSD simultaneously have been developed. These approaches utilize interventions from both Cognitive Processing Therapy (CPT) for PTSD and CBT for ED to promote complete recovery from both disorders [220].

7.3 Recent research on EMDR for eating disorders

Recent research has explored the application of Eye Movement Desensitization and Reprocessing (EMDR) therapy in treating EDs; EMDR has been integrated with CBT in treating EDs. For instance, a case study involving a participant with BN who received 20 sessions of CBT followed by five sessions of EMDR showed significant improvements in symptoms, body satisfaction, and social relations.

This suggests that EMDR can enhance the effectiveness of CBT in treating EDs [221]. Another study involving two young girls with ED symptoms due to traumatic experiences found that combining EMDR with CBT effectively reduced their symptoms [222]. EMDR is particularly beneficial in addressing the trauma-related aspects of EDs. It helps in processing painful experiences and reducing the anxiety and shame associated with these disorders. This trauma-informed approach is crucial as many EDs are seen as dissociative coping strategies developed to handle intolerable experiences [223]. Several case studies have reported positive outcomes using EMDR for EDs. For example, a single case study on emotional eating (EE) showed that EMDR could positively change eating behavior and improve weight management over time [224]. Despite the positive preliminary findings, there is a consensus that more methodologically rigorous studies are required to establish the efficacy of EMDR for EDs. Current evidence is based on case studies and small-scale trials, which limits the generalizability of the results [225, 226]. The exact mechanisms through which EMDR exerts its effects on EDs are not fully understood. It is hypothesized that EMDR facilitates the reprocessing of maladaptive memories, which are central to the pathology of EDs [227, 228]. EMDR shows promise as a complementary treatment for EDs, particularly when integrated with other therapeutic approaches like CBT. It appears effective in addressing trauma-related aspects of EDs and improving body image and emotional regulation. However, further research with larger sample sizes and controlled designs must confirm these findings and better understand the underlying mechanisms.

We can conclude that personalized and integrated approaches are essential in the effective treatment of eating disorders. By tailoring interventions to individual needs and involving a multidisciplinary team, these approaches address the complex and varied nature of EDs, ultimately improving treatment outcomes and patient well-being.

8. Challenges and future directions

8.1 Underutilization of CBT

Despite its effectiveness, CBT is underutilized in clinical practice, partly due to a lack of trained clinicians [166, 199]. To address this issue, several strategies can be implemented to increase the availability of CBT-trained therapists (**Table 5**).

8.2 Self-help and technology

Self-help manuals and digital interventions, such as smartphone apps, are being developed to increase accessibility and support real-time interventions [237, 238].

8.3 Integration with other therapies

Combining CBT with other therapeutic approaches, such as motivational interviewing and dialectical behavior therapy, may enhance its effectiveness (**Table 6**) [199].

Future research should focus on further refining personalized and integrated approaches to treatment, enhancing accessibility, and ensuring that interventions are culturally sensitive and adaptable to diverse populations. Specific research questions could include: How can digital interventions be tailored to address the unique needs

Strategy	Description	Benefits
Online training programs	Web-based, flexible, scalable training	Increased accessibility, cost-efficiency, and remote supervision [229].
Supervision and consultation	Continuous supervision post-training	Improved competency and adherence [230, 231].
Government initiatives	National programs with training and support	Enhanced provider self-efficacy leads to better patient outcomes [232].
Train-the-Trainer models	Training clinicians to train others	Effective in school settings, ongoing support [233].
Self-practice/ self-reflection	Clinicians practice CBT on themselves	Increased competency and flexibility [234].
Educational campaigns	Addressing myths and misconceptions	Improved acceptance and implementation [235].
Computerized CBT (cCBT)	Use of automated programs for CBT delivery	Bridging therapist availability gap, positive clinician attitude [236].

Table 5.
Summary of CBT-trained therapists.

Component	Description
Self-monitoring	Tracking eating patterns, thoughts, and feelings.
Psychoeducation	Educating about the disorder and CBT principles.
Cognitive restructuring	Challenging and modifying dysfunctional thoughts.
Behavioral experiments	Testing beliefs through real-life experiments.
Group therapy	Incorporating interpersonal elements to enhance treatment.
Digital interventions	Using apps for real-time support and intervention.

Table 6.
Key components of CBT for BN and BED.

of diverse populations? What are the long-term outcomes of integrating EMDR with CBT for trauma-related eating disorders? How can we identify biomarkers that predict treatment response in different EDs?

9. The strengths and weaknesses of cognitive behavioral therapy (CBT): Effectiveness of eating disorder and the role of body image, self-esteem, and quality of life

9.1 Strengths

9.1.1 Effectiveness in reducing eating disorder symptoms

CBT is effective in treating BN and BED by focusing on symptom-oriented procedures, such as emotion regulation and cognitive techniques [31, 239]. Web-based CBT interventions have also demonstrated significant improvements in eating disorder psychopathology and related health outcomes [157, 158].

9.1.2 Improvement in body image

CBT, particularly cognitive-behavioral body image therapy, has been effective in reducing body image dysphoria and improving body satisfaction [102, 240].

Exposure-based CBT has been shown to reduce body checking and avoidance behaviors, which are crucial for improving body image [241].

9.1.3 Enhancement of self-esteem and quality of life

CBT interventions have improved self-esteem and QoL among patients with eating disorders [157, 158]. Addressing low self-esteem and body dissatisfaction is a key component of CBT for eating disorders [31].

9.1.4 Reduction of dysfunctional cognitions

CBT has effectively reduced dysfunctional cognitions related to body and self-esteem, dietary restraint, and eating control. Changes in these cognitions are linked to reductions in ED psychopathology [22].

9.2 Weaknesses

9.2.1 Limited effectiveness for Anorexia Nervosa (AN)

While CBT has shown promise in treating AN, its effectiveness is not as well-established as it is for BN and BED. One major challenge is patient attrition, as individuals with AN often struggle with motivation and may drop out of treatment prematurely. Additionally, CBT may not fully address the complex psychological and biological factors that maintain AN, such as severe body image distortion and fear of weight gain. As a result, alternative or adjunctive therapies, such as Family-Based Treatment (FBT), are often recommended for adolescents with AN [239]. FBT is considered the leading treatment for adolescents with AN, showing high efficacy and cost-effectiveness [242, 243]. Alternative and emerging therapies like CBT-E, ACT, and DBT show promise in addressing the limitations of existing treatments and providing additional options for patients and families. CBT-E has been identified as a potential alternative to FBT, particularly for adults with eating disorders. It has shown substantial improvements in weight and eating disorder psychopathology in adolescents [242]. ACT, a third-wave behavioral therapy, has shown promise in treating AN by focusing on psychological flexibility and acceptance. Preliminary studies indicate that ACT-based treatments can lead to significant reductions in eating disorder symptoms and improvements in psychological acceptance [244, 245]. DBT, known for its effectiveness in treating emotion regulation issues, is being explored for AN. It aims to improve emotion regulation skills, which are often impaired in individuals with AN [246]. There is a lack of specific treatment recommendations for AN due to scarce empirical evidence [22].

9.2.2 Challenges in usual care settings

Most evidence for CBT's effectiveness comes from controlled studies, and its efficacy in usual care settings remains less examined [102].

9.2.3 Therapeutic alliance

The strength of the therapeutic alliance in CBT for eating disorders can be influenced by initial emotional and interpersonal features, which may affect treatment outcomes [247]. Clinicians may overestimate the role of the therapeutic alliance, potentially impacting their approach to encouraging changes in eating patterns [248].

9.2.4 Personality factors

Personality disorders, particularly borderline personality disorder, can moderate the effectiveness of CBT, suggesting that additional modules focusing on effects and interpersonal relationships may be necessary [249].

10. Conclusion

In conclusion, EDs are complex conditions influenced by biological, psychological, and sociocultural factors that require comprehensive and individualized treatment strategies. Personalized and integrated approaches, which tailor interventions to the unique needs of each patient and involve multidisciplinary teams, are essential for improving outcomes and enhancing quality of life. CBT is the most effective treatment for BN and BED, but its effectiveness for anorexia nervosa is limited. FBT shows promise for adolescents with AN, while emerging therapies like DBT and ACT offer additional options. Future research should focus on improving access to treatment, addressing cultural influences, and developing more effective therapies for AN. As our understanding of EDs evolves, ongoing research is crucial to refine these therapies, enhance accessibility, and improve patient outcomes. The integration of technology and novel therapeutic approaches offers promising avenues for the future of eating disorder treatment, focusing on altering dysfunctional thoughts and behaviors related to eating. Future research should focus on several key areas: improving access to treatment in underserved regions, developing culturally sensitive interventions, and exploring the role of technology in delivering CBT and other therapies. Additionally, more studies are needed to understand the different treatments' long-term outcomes and identify biomarkers that could predict treatment response. By addressing these gaps, we can improve the lives of individuals affected by eating disorders worldwide.

Acknowledgements

I want to express my deepest gratitude to my mom, whose unwavering support, encouragement, and love have guided me throughout this journey. Your belief in me has been my greatest strength, and this chapter is as much yours as it is mine. Thank you for always being my inspiration and my rock.

Conflict of interest statement

The author declares that there is no conflict of interest regarding the publication of this chapter.

Abbreviation

ACT	acceptance and commitment therapy
AN	anorexia nervosa
ASRs	age-standardized rates
BN	bulimia nervosa
BED	binge eating disorder
CBT	cognitive behavioral therapy
CBT-E	enhanced cognitive behavioral therapy
CBT-ED	cognitive behavioral therapy for eating disorders
DBT	dialectical behavior therapy
DALYs	disability-adjusted life years
EFT	emotion-focused therapy
Eds	eating disorders
EMDR	eye movement desensitization and reprocessing
FBT	family-based therapy
FTO	fat mass and obesity-associated gene
IPT	interpersonal psychotherapy
MBI	mindfulness-based interventions
NIPT	network-informed personalized treatment
QoL	quality of life
SSRIs	selective serotonin reuptake inhibitors

Appendix

Key terms and definitions:

1. **CBT:** A type of psychotherapy that focuses on identifying and changing negative thought patterns and behaviors. It is widely used to treat eating disorders by addressing dysfunctional beliefs about body image, food, and self-worth.

2. **AN:** An eating disorder characterized by extreme food restriction, an intense fear of gaining weight, and a distorted body image. It often leads to severe physical complications and has a high mortality rate.

3. **BN:** An eating disorder marked by recurrent episodes of binge eating followed by compensatory behaviors such as vomiting, excessive exercise, or laxative use. It is associated with psychological distress and physical health issues.

4. **BED:** An eating disorder involving recurrent episodes of consuming large amounts of food without compensatory behaviors. It is often accompanied by feelings of shame, guilt, and distress.

5. **Body image:** A person's perception, thoughts, and feelings about their physical appearance. Negative body image is a common risk factor for eating disorders.

6. **Self-esteem:** A person's overall sense of self-worth or personal value. Low self-esteem is often linked to eating disorders and can be improved through therapies like CBT.

7. **QoL:** A measure of an individual's overall well-being, including physical health, psychological state, social relationships, and environment. Eating disorders often significantly impair QoL.

8. **FBT:** A treatment approach for eating disorders, particularly effective for adolescents with anorexia nervosa. It involves parents in the treatment process to help restore healthy eating behaviors and weight.

9. **IPT:** A therapy that focuses on improving interpersonal relationships and social functioning. It is often used to treat bulimia nervosa and binge eating disorder.

10. **DBT:** A form of therapy that combines cognitive-behavioral techniques with mindfulness practices. It is used to treat emotional dysregulation, which is common in eating disorders.

11. **MBI:** Therapeutic approaches that incorporate mindfulness practices to help individuals become more aware of their thoughts, emotions, and behaviors without judgment.

12. **SSRIs:** A class of antidepressant medications commonly used to treat bulimia nervosa and binge eating disorder. They work by increasing serotonin levels in the brain.

13. **EFT:** A therapeutic approach that focuses on helping individuals identify, understand, and manage their emotions. It is sometimes used to treat eating disorders.

14. **Exposure therapy:** A technique used in CBT to help individuals confront and reduce their fears or anxieties. In eating disorders, it may involve exposure to feared foods or body-related situations.

15. **ACT:** A form of therapy that combines cognitive-behavioral techniques with mindfulness practices. It focuses on helping individuals accept their thoughts and feelings rather than fighting or feeling overwhelmed by them, and it encourages commitment to positive behavior change.

16. **CBT-E:** An advanced form of CBT specifically designed to treat eating disorders. It includes additional components to address body image disturbances and is suitable for all types of eating disorders.

17. **CBT-ED:** A specific adaptation of CBT tailored for treating eating disorders, focusing on the unique cognitive and behavioral aspects of these conditions.

18. **EMDR:** A therapeutic technique used to help individuals process traumatic memories and reduce the anxiety and shame associated with them. It has shown promise in treating trauma-related aspects of eating disorders.

19. **FTO:** A gene associated with obesity and eating behaviors. Variations in this gene have been linked to binge eating and emotional eating.

20. **NIPT:** A personalized treatment approach that uses network analysis to tailor interventions to individual symptom profiles, enhancing treatment outcomes.

Author details

Fatema Ahmed[1,2*†], Chen Wu[1*†], Li Li[1†], Qingyuan Ye[1†], Waleed Ksebe[2†] and Kefang Wang[1*]

1 School of Nursing and Rehabilitation, Shandong University, Shandong, China

2 Faculty of Nursing, Tishreen University, Latakia, Syria

*Address all correspondence to: fatema92w@gmail.com; wuchen@sdu.edu.cn and wangkf@email.sdu.edu.cn

† These authors contributed equally.

References

[1] Pike KM, Hoek HW, Dunne PE. Cultural trends and eating disorders. Current Opinion in Psychiatry. 2014;**27**(6):436-442

[2] Sugermeyer J. Eating Disorders (ED), a Global Epidemic, De-Stigmatizing ED to Save Lives, in Innovations in Global Mental Health: Volume 1-2. Springer International Publishing; 2021. pp. 191-201

[3] Bogár N, Pászthy B, Túry F. The current sociocultural background of eating disorders. Trends in Molecular Medicine. 2024;**30**(4):311-313

[4] Pilecki MW. Psychogenic determinants of bulimia nervosa. Przegląd Lekarski. 2009;**66**(1-2):106-109

[5] Nasser M. Eating disorders across cultures. Psychiatry. 2006;**5**(11):392-395

[6] Nasser M, Katzman M. Eating disorders: Transcultural perspectives inform prevention. In: Preventing Eating Disorders: A Handbook of Interventions and Special Challenges. Taylor and Francis; 2013. pp. 26-43

[7] Strand M et al. Migration background, eating disorder symptoms and healthcare service utilisation: Findings from the Stockholm public health cohort. BJPsych Open. 2023;**9**(6):6

[8] AlHadi AN et al. The prevalence and correlates of bulimia nervosa, binge-eating disorder, and anorexia nervosa: The Saudi National Mental Health Survey. International Journal of Eating Disorders. 2022;**55**(11):1541-1552

[9] Hay P et al. Burden and health-related quality of life of eating disorders, including avoidant/restrictive food intake disorder (ARFID), in the Australian population. Journal of Eating Disorders. 2017;**5**:1-10

[10] Pohjolainen V et al. Long-term health-related quality of life in eating disorders. Quality of Life Research. 2016;**25**:2341-2346

[11] Keski-Rahkonen A, Mustelin L. Epidemiology of eating disorders in Europe: Prevalence, incidence, comorbidity, course, consequences, and risk factors. Current Opinion in Psychiatry. 2016;**29**(6):340-345

[12] Smink FR, Van Hoeken D, Hoek HW. Epidemiology of eating disorders: Incidence, prevalence and mortality rates. Current Psychiatry Reports. 2012;**14**(4):406-414

[13] Hewlings SJ. Eating disorders and dietary supplements: A review of the science. Nutrients. 2023;**15**(9):9

[14] Costa MB, Melnik T. Effectiveness of psychosocial interventions in eating disorders: An overview of Cochrane systematic reviews. Einstein (Sao Paulo, Brazil). 2016;**14**(2):235-277

[15] Shepherd CB et al. Weight restoration and symptom remission for longstanding, untreated anorexia nervosa in a remote eating disorder treatment program: A case study. Clinical Case Studies. 2024;**23**(3):230-249

[16] Klein DA, Walsh BT. Eating disorders: Clinical features and pathophysiology. Physiology and Behavior. 2004;**81**(2):359-374

[17] Pizano D et al. Eating disorders, feeding, and elimination disorders. In: Atlas of Psychiatry.

Springer International Publishing; 2023. pp. 671-708

[18] Tsuboi K. Eating disorders in adolescence and their implications. Japan Medical Association Journal. 2005;**48**(3):123-129

[19] Barney J, Wolinsky A, Juarascio AS. Eating disorders. In: The Wiley Encyclopedia of Personality and Individual Differences: Volume IV: Clinical, Applied, and Cross-Cultural Research. Wiley; 2020. pp. 139-144

[20] Voderholzer U, Cuntz U, Schlegl S. Eating disorders. State of the art research and future challenges. Nervenarzt. 2012;**83**(11):1458-1467

[21] Walsh BT, First MB. Eating disorders. In: Psychiatry. 3rd ed. John Wiley & Sons, Ltd; 2008. pp. 1609-1625

[22] Tuschen-Caffier B, Svaldi J. Evidence-based diagnostics and psychotherapy of eating disorders. Psychotherapeut. 2014;**59**(3):253-265

[23] Feng B et al. Current discoveries and future implications of eating disorders. International Journal of Environmental Research and Public Health. 2023;**20**(14):14

[24] Legenbauer T. Cognitive behavioral therapy. In: Handbook of Eating Disorders and Obesity. Berlin Heidelberg: Springer; 2024. pp. 317-326

[25] Wu J et al. Trends in the prevalence and disability-adjusted life years of eating disorders from 1990 to 2017: Results from the global burden of disease study 2017. Epidemiology and Psychiatric Sciences. 7 Dec 2020;**29**:e191. DOI: 10.1017/S2045796020001055

[26] Silén Y, Keski-Rahkonen A. Worldwide prevalence of DSM-5 eating disorders among young people. Current Opinion in Psychiatry. 2022;**35**(6):362-371

[27] Hudson JI et al. The prevalence and correlates of eating disorders in the National Comorbidity Survey Replication. Biological Psychiatry. 2007;**61**(3):348-358

[28] Pike KM, Dunne PE, Addai E. Expanding the boundaries: Reconfiguring the demographics of the "typical" eating disordered patient. Current Psychiatry Reports. 2013;**15**(11):11

[29] Agras WS. Cognitive behavior therapy for the eating disorders. Psychiatric Clinics of North America. 2019;**42**(2):169-179

[30] Agras WS, Bohon C. Cognitive behavioral therapy for the eating disorders. Annual Review of Clinical Psychology. 2021;**17**:417-438

[31] Terpitz C. Cognitive behavioral therapy for bulimia nervosa. Acta Academiae Medicinae Sinicae. 2019;**108**(14):917-921

[32] Yokoyama H et al. Factors associated with the improvement of body image dissatisfaction of female patients with overweight and obesity during cognitive behavioral therapy. Frontiers in Psychiatry. 2022;**13**:13

[33] Rossi E et al. The role of embodiment in the treatment of patients with anorexia and bulimia nervosa: A 2-year follow-up study proposing an integration between enhanced cognitive behavioural therapy and a phenomenological model of eating disorders. Eating and Weight Disorders. 2021;**26**(8):2513-2522

[34] Hambleton AL et al. Group-delivered enhanced cognitive behavior therapy: A focus on a young adult woman with

bulimia nervosa. Clinical Case Studies. 2020;**19**(1):62-77

[35] Qian J et al. Prevalence of eating disorders in the general population: A systematic review. Shanghai Archives of Psychiatry. 2013;**25**(4):212-223

[36] Qian J et al. An update on the prevalence of eating disorders in the general population: A systematic review and meta-analysis. Eating and Weight Disorders. 2022;**27**(2):415-428

[37] Brytek-Matera A. Prevalence of anorexia nervosa and bulimia nervosa in Eastern Europe. Psychiatria i Psychologia Kliniczna. 2023;**23**(4):332-337

[38] Santomauro DF et al. The hidden burden of eating disorders: An extension of estimates from the global burden of disease study 2019. The Lancet Psychiatry. 2021;**8**(4):320-328

[39] Ruhl U, Jacobi C. Cognitive-behavioral psychotherapy for adolescents with eating disorders. Praxis der Kinderpsychologie und Kinderpsychiatrie. 2005;**54**(4):286-302

[40] Sperling J, Boger K, Potter M. Associations between parental distress and pediatric anxiety and obsessive-compulsive disorder treatment outcomes. Clinical Child Psychology and Psychiatry. 2021;**26**(4):1102-1110

[41] Waller G, Beard J. Recent advances in cognitive-Behavioural therapy for eating disorders (CBT-ED). Current Psychiatry Reports. 2024;**26**(7):351-358

[42] de Jong M, van der Starre J. Recent developments within cognitive behavior therapy-enhanced. Gedragstherapie: Tijdschrift voor Gedragstherapie en Cognitieve Therapie. 2024;**57**(3):254-271

[43] Dalle Grave R et al. Cognitive behavioral therapy for anorexia nervosa: An update. Current Psychiatry Reports. 2016;**18**(1):1-8

[44] Gorrell S, Reilly E, Le Grange D. Family-based treatment for eating disorders. In: Encyclopedia of Mental Health, Third Edition: Volume 1-3. Elsevier; 2023. pp. V2-V19

[45] Lock J. Evaluation of family treatment models for eating disorders. Current Opinion in Psychiatry. 2011;**24**(4):274-279

[46] Lock J. Updates on treatments for adolescent anorexia nervosa. Child and Adolescent Psychiatric Clinics of North America. 2019;**28**(4):523-535

[47] Lock J, Fitzpatrick KK. Evidenced-based approaches to family-based treatment for anorexia nervosa and bulimia nervosa. In: Evidence Based Treatments for Eating Disorders: Children, Adolescents and Adults. 2nd ed. Nova Science Publishers, Inc; 2014. pp. 397-412

[48] Rienecke RD. Parental marital satisfaction in a family-based partial hospitalization program. Eating Disorders. 2018;**26**(2):143-148

[49] Lock J, Nicholls D. Toward a greater understanding of the ways family-based treatment addresses the full range of psychopathology of adolescent anorexia nervosa. Frontiers in Psychiatry. 2020;**10**:27

[50] Conti J et al. "I'm still here, but no one hears you": A qualitative study of young women's experiences of persistent distress post family-based treatment for adolescent anorexia nervosa. Journal of Eating Disorders. 2021;**9**(1):27

[51] Van Huysse JL et al. Weight gain and parental self-efficacy in a family-based

partial hospitalization program. Journal of Eating Disorders. 2022;**10**(1):27

[52] Robinson AL et al. 'I know i can help you': Parental self-efficacy predicts adolescent outcomes in family-based therapy for eating disorders. European Eating Disorders Review. 2013;**21**(2):108-114

[53] Johnson M et al. Empirically supported cognitive-behavioral interventions for adolescent anorexia and bulimia nervosa. In: Handbook of Lifespan Cognitive Behavioral Therapy: Childhood, Adolescence, Pregnancy, Adulthood, and Aging. Elsevier; 2023. pp. 219-236

[54] Karam AM et al. Interpersonal psychotherapy and the treatment of eating disorders. Psychiatric Clinics of North America. 2019;**42**(2):205-218

[55] Burke NL et al. Interpersonal psychotherapy for the treatment of eating disorders. In: The Oxford Handbook of Eating Disorders. Oxford University Press; 2017. pp. 287-318

[56] Tanofsky-Kraff M, Wilfley DE. Interpersonal psychotherapy for the treatment of eating disorders. In: The Oxford Handbook of Eating Disorders. Oxford University Press; 2012

[57] Hilbert A, Brhler E. Interpersonal psychotherapy for eating disorders: A systematic and practical review. Verhaltenstherapie. 2012;**22**(3):149-157

[58] McIntosh VVW et al. Three psychotherapies for anorexia nervosa: A randomized, controlled trial. American Journal of Psychiatry. 2005;**162**(4):741-747

[59] Grilo CM. Treatment of eating disorders: Current status, challenges, and future directions. Annual Review of Clinical Psychology. 2024;**20**(1):97-123

[60] Reas DL, Grilo CM. Psychotherapy and medications for eating disorders: Better together? Clinical Therapeutics. 2021;**43**(1):17-39

[61] Van den Eynde F, Schmidt U. Treatment of bulimia nervosa and binge eating disorder. Psychiatry. 2008;7(4):161-166

[62] Flament MF, Bissada H, Spettigue W. Evidence-based pharmacotherapy of eating disorders. International Journal of Neuropsychopharmacology. 2012;**15**(2):189-207

[63] Yim SH, Schmidt U. Self-help treatment of eating disorders. Psychiatric Clinics of North America. 2019;**42**(2):231-241

[64] Wilson GT, Zandberg LJ. Cognitive-behavioral guided self-help for eating disorders: Effectiveness and scalability. Clinical Psychology Review. 2012;**32**(4):343-357

[65] Bartosiewicz A, Strzelecki D. "Third wave"cognitive-behavioural therapy for eating disorders. Psychiatria i Psychologia Kliniczna. 2019;**19**(2):204-209

[66] Compare A et al. Emotionally focused group therapy and dietary counseling in binge eating disorder: Effect on eating disorder psychopathology and quality of life. Appetite. 2013;**71**:361-368

[67] Brennan MA, Emmerling ME, Whelton WJ. Emotion-focused group therapy: Addressing self-criticism in the treatment of eating disorders. Counselling and Psychotherapy Research. 2015;**15**(1):67-75

[68] Afari N et al. Acceptance and commitment therapy as an adjunct to the MOVE! programme: A randomized controlled trial. Obesity Science and Practice. 2019;**5**(5):397-407

[69] Ong CW et al. A randomized controlled trial of acceptance and commitment therapy for clinical perfectionism. Journal of Obsessive-Compulsive and Related Disorders. 2019;**22**:28

[70] de Souza LAS et al. Problematic and adaptive eating in people with obesity after a DBT-based skills training intervention: 3- and 8-month follow-up and mediation analysis. Psicologia: Reflexao e Critica. 2019;**32**(1):28

[71] Klein AS, Skinner JB, Hawley KM. Targeting binge eating through components of dialectical behavior therapy: Preliminary outcomes for individually supported diary card self-monitoring versus group-based DBT. Psychotherapy. 2013;**50**(4):543-552

[72] Bankoff SM et al. A systematic review of dialectical behavior therapy for the treatment of eating disorders. Eating Disorders. 2012;**20**(3):196-215

[73] Masuda A, Hill ML. Mindfulness as therapy for disordered eating: A systematic review. Neuropsychiatry. 2013;**3**(4):433-447

[74] Godfrey KM, Gallo LC, Afari N. Mindfulness-based interventions for binge eating: A systematic review and meta-analysis. Journal of Behavioral Medicine. 2015;**38**(2):348-362

[75] Cohen RS, Simpson KL, Bride BE. Treating anorexia nervosa and bulimia nervosa. Journal of Evidence-Based Social Work. 2004;**1**(1):27-39

[76] Russell H et al. Psychotherapies for eating disorders: Findings from a rapid review. Journal of Eating Disorders. 2023;**11**(1):28

[77] Wilson GT, Grilo CM, Vitousek KM. Psychological treatment of eating disorders. American Psychologist. 2007;**62**(3):199-216

[78] Monteleone AM, Abbate-Daga G. Effectiveness and predictors of psychotherapy in eating disorders: State-of-the-art and future directions. Current Opinion in Psychiatry. 2024;**37**(6):417-423

[79] Varchol L, Cooper H. Psychotherapy approaches for adolescents with eating disorders. Current Opinion in Pediatrics. 2009;**21**(4):457-464

[80] Linardon J et al. The empirical status of the third-wave behaviour therapies for the treatment of eating disorders: A systematic review. Clinical Psychology Review. 2017;**58**:125-140

[81] Hay PJ. Assessment and management of eating disorders: An update. Australian Prescriber. 2013;**36**(5):154-157

[82] Bello NT, Yeomans BL. Safety of pharmacotherapy options for bulimia nervosa and binge eating disorder. Expert Opinion on Drug Safety. 2018;**17**(1):17-23

[83] Ricanati EHW, Rome ES. Eating disorders: Recognize early to prevent complications. Cleveland Clinic Journal of Medicine. 2005;**72**(10):895-906

[84] Weipert D, Blasczyk-Schiep S, Große L. Multimodal concept for outpatient treatment of eating disorders: "Integrated care" in comparison to routine psychotherapy. Psychotherapeut. 2020;**65**(1):41-52

[85] Dalton B et al. Virtually delivered guided self-help for binge eating disorder and bulimia nervosa: Findings

from a service evaluation. Behavioural and Cognitive Psychotherapy. 2024;**52**(3):211-225

[86] Aardoom JJ, Dingemans AE, Van Furth EF. E-health interventions for eating disorders: Emerging findings, issues, and opportunities. Current Psychiatry Reports. 2016;**18**(4):29

[87] Hilbert A, Opitz L, De Zwann M. Internet-based interventions for eating disorders. In: The Oxford Handbook of Eating Disorders. Oxford University Press; 2017. pp. 505-519

[88] De Zwaan M. Should we use new media in the treatment of eating disorders? PPmP Psychotherapie Psychosomatik Medizinische Psychologie. 2015;**65**(1):30-32

[89] Rikani AA et al. A critique of the literature on etiology of eating disorders. Annals of Neurosciences. 2013;**20**(4):157-161

[90] Treasure J. Eating disorders. Medicine (United Kingdom). 2012;**40**(11):607-612

[91] Castellini G et al. Fat mass and obesity-associated gene (FTO) is associated to eating disorders susceptibility and moderates the expression of psychopathological traits. PLoS One. 2017;**12**(3):12

[92] Culbert KM, Racine SE, Klump KL. Research review: What we have learned about the causes of eating disorders - a synthesis of sociocultural, psychological, and biological research. Journal of Child Psychology and Psychiatry and Allied Disciplines. 2015;**56**(11):1141-1164

[93] Gáti A, Abrahám I. The role of gene-environment interaction in the development of eating disorders. Psychiatria Hungarica: A Magyar Pszichiátriai Társaság tudományos folyóirata. 2009;**24**(4):255-263

[94] Paulinyová M, Šuba J, Hradečná Z. Disorders in food intake from the child psychiatrist point of view. Cesko-Slovenska Pediatrie. 2011;**66**(3):169-176

[95] Herpertz-dahlmann B, Holtkamp K, Konrad K. Eating disorders: Anorexia and bulimia nervosa. In: Handbook of Clinical Neurology. Elsevier B.V; 2012. pp. 447-462

[96] Fleitlich-Bilyk B, Lock J. Eating disorders. Advances in Biological Psychiatry. 2008;**24**:138-152

[97] Barakat S et al. Risk factors for eating disorders: Findings from a rapid review. Journal of Eating Disorders. 2023;**11**(1):29

[98] Górski M et al. Specific eating disorders - selected aspects of pathogenesis and risk factors. Psychiatria i Psychologia Kliniczna. 2022;**22**(1):45-54

[99] Franko DL, Striegel-Moore RH. Psychosocial risk for eating disorders: What's new? In: Annual Review of Eating Disorders: Part 1-2007. Taylor and Francis; 2018. pp. 51-62

[100] Ruiz Lázaro PM, Imaz Roncero C, Pérez Hornero J. Self-esteem, self-image, and school bullying in eating disorders. Nutricion Hospitalaria. 2022;**39**(Ext2):41-48

[101] Devaraj S, Lewis V. Enhancing positive body image in women: An evaluation of a group intervention program. Journal of Applied Biobehavioral Research. 2010;**15**(2):103-116

[102] Nye S, Cash TF. Outcomes of manualized cognitive-behavioral body image therapy with eating

disordered women treated in a private clinical practice. Eating Disorders. 2006;**14**(1):31-40

[103] Vocks S, Bauer A. Treatment of body image disorders. In: Handbook of Eating Disorders and Obesity. Berlin Heidelberg: Springer; 2024. pp. 341-347

[104] Margolis SE, Orsillo SM. Acceptance and body dissatisfaction: Examining the efficacy of a brief acceptance based intervention for body dissatisfaction in college women. Behavioural and Cognitive Psychotherapy. 2016;**44**(4):482-492

[105] Aboody D, Siev J, Doron G. Building resilience to body image triggers using brief cognitive training on a mobile application: A randomized controlled trial. Behaviour Research and Therapy. 2020;**134**:30

[106] Pullmer R, Potter S, Laliberte M. Enhancing eating disorder recovery: Weight control beliefs predict body dissatisfaction in group cognitive behavioural therapy for body image. Eating Behaviors. 2023;**50**:30

[107] Laliberte MM, Lucibello KM. Weight control beliefs in the treatment of binge-eating disorder: Why might they matter? International Journal of Eating Disorders. 2022;**55**(6):820-825

[108] Keski-Rahkonen A. Eating disorders: Etiology, risk factors, and suggestions for prevention. Current Opinion in Psychiatry. 2024;**37**(6):381-387

[109] Mayer B et al. Brief report: Direct and indirect relations of risk factors with eating behavior problems in late adolescent females. Journal of Adolescence. 2009;**32**(3):741-745

[110] de Jong M et al. Effectiveness of enhanced cognitive behavior therapy for eating disorders: A randomized controlled trial. International Journal of Eating Disorders. 2020;**53**(5):447-457

[111] Abdelatif A et al. Cognitive behavioral group therapy on a sample of obese female patients with binge-eating disorder: Egyptian study. Middle East Current Psychiatry. 2017;**24**(4):187-190

[112] Korrelboom K et al. Competitive memory training (COMET) for treating low self-esteem in patients with eating disorders: A randomized clinical trial. Journal of Consulting and Clinical Psychology. 2009;**77**(5):974-980

[113] Okamoto Y et al. A 10-year follow-up study of completers versus dropouts following treatment with an integrated cognitive-behavioral group therapy for eating disorders. Journal of Eating Disorders. 2017;**5**(1):30

[114] Zhong J et al. The efficacy of internet-based cognitive behavioral therapy for adult binge spectrum eating disorders: A meta-analysis. Journal of Affective Disorders. 2024;**361**:684-692

[115] Keel PK, Forney KJ. Psychosocial risk factors for eating disorders. International Journal of Eating Disorders. 2013;**46**(5):433-439

[116] Bazo, Perez M, Frazier LD. Risk and resilience in eating disorders: Differentiating pathways among psychosocial predictors. Journal of Eating Disorders. 2024;**12**(1):30

[117] Hoiles KJ et al. A pilot randomised controlled trial of guided self-help cognitive behaviour therapy for perfectionism: Impact on diagnostic status and comorbidity. Journal of Behavior Therapy and Experimental Psychiatry. 2022;**76**:31

[118] Handley AK et al. A randomised controlled trial of group cognitive

behavioural therapy for perfectionism. Behaviour Research and Therapy. 2015;**68**:37-47

[119] Egan SJ, Hine P. Cognitive behavioural treatment of perfectionism: A single case experimental design series. Behaviour Change. 2008;**25**(4):245-258

[120] Robinson K et al. A randomised controlled evaluation of an online perfectionism intervention for people with disordered eating–how perfect does it need to be? Cognitive Behaviour Therapy. 2024;**53**(3):286-301

[121] Shafran R, Lee M, Fairburn CG. Clinical perfectionism: A case report. Behavioural and Cognitive Psychotherapy. 2004;**32**(3):353-357

[122] Kothari R et al. A randomised controlled trial of guided internet-based cognitive behavioural therapy for perfectionism: Effects on psychopathology and transdiagnostic processes. Journal of Behavior Therapy and Experimental Psychiatry. 2019;**64**:113-122

[123] Schweiger U. Psychological comorbidity and personality disorders. In: Handbook of Eating Disorders and Obesity. Berlin Heidelberg: Springer; 2024. pp. 181-187

[124] Torstveit MK, Sundgot-Borgen J. Disordered eating and eating disorders in female athletes. In: Handbook of Sports Medicine and Science: The Female Athlete. Wiley Blackwell; 2014. pp. 42-55

[125] Levinson CA et al. Social appearance anxiety, perfectionism, and fear of negative evaluation: Distinct or shared risk factors for social anxiety and eating disorders? Appetite. 2013;**67**:125-133

[126] Hardy KV. Cognitive behavioral therapy (CBT). In: Encyclopedia of the Neurological Sciences. Elsevier Inc.; 2014. pp. 822-823

[127] Otis JD, Pincus DB, Murawski ME. Cognitive behavioral therapy in pain management. In: Behavioral and Psychopharmacologic Pain Management. Cambridge University Press; 2010. pp. 184-200

[128] Huppert JD. The building blocks of treatment in cognitive-behavioral therapy. Israel Journal of Psychiatry and Related Sciences. 2009;**46**(4):245-250

[129] Cogodi E et al. Emotional dysregulation in anorexia nervosa: Evidence mapping review psychological treatments. Rivista Italiana di Medicina dell'Adolescenza. 2024;**22**(1):7-12

[130] Argyrides M, Anastasiades E, Alexiou E. Risk and protective factors of disordered eating in adolescents based on gender and body mass index. International Journal of Environmental Research and Public Health. 2020;**17**(24):1-11

[131] Rousseau A, Valls M, La Roque S. Media sociocultural influence and body dissatisfaction among French university students. Journal de Therapie Comportementale et Cognitive. 2012;**22**(2):53-59

[132] McLean SA, Paxton SJ, Wertheim EH. A body image and disordered eating intervention for women in midlife: A randomized controlled trial. Journal of Consulting and Clinical Psychology. 2011;**79**(6):751-758

[133] Fang A et al. Mechanisms of change in cognitive behavioral therapy for body dysmorphic disorder. Cognitive Therapy and Research. 2020;**44**(3):596-610

[134] Watson R, Vaughn LM. Limiting the effects of the media on body image:

Does the length of a media literacy intervention make a difference? Eating Disorders. 2006;**14**(5):385-400

[135] Treasure J. Eating disorders. Medicine (United Kingdom). 2016;**44**(11):672-678

[136] Demeter A, Túry F, Czeglédi E. A potential risk factor for eating disorders: Appearance-related parental expectations. Mentalhigiene es Pszichoszomatika. 2015;**16**(3):231-251

[137] Caqueo-Urízar A et al. Associations between sociocultural pressures to be thin, body distress, and eating disorder symptomatology among Chilean adolescent girls. Body Image. 2011;**8**(1):78-81

[138] Stanić S, Žuro D. Sociocultural pressures in the development of eating disorders – A sociological perspective. Jahr: Europski časopis za bioetiku. 2023;**14**(2):291-313

[139] Praptomojati A et al. A systematic review of culturally adapted cognitive behavioral therapy (CA-CBT) for anxiety disorders in Southeast Asia. Asian Journal of Psychiatry. 2024;**92**:32

[140] Ng P et al. Cognitive behavioral intervention in the Chinese cultural context: A case report. Asia-Pacific Psychiatry. 2013;**5**(3):205-211

[141] Hinton DE, La Roche M. Culturally appropriate CBT for the anxiety disorders. In: CBT for Anxiety Disorders: A Practitioner Book. John Wiley and Sons; 2013. pp. 191-224

[142] AlHadi AN. Cognitive behavioral therapy in Saudi Arabia: A scoping review on training, practice, and research. International Journal of Cognitive Therapy. 2024;**17**(3):335-346

[143] Mousa TY. Risk factors of eating disorders in females. In: Eating Disorders: Causes, Diagnosis and Treatments. Inc: Nova Science Publishers; 2012. pp. 141-153

[144] Bray B et al. Binge eating disorder is a social justice issue: A cross-sectional mixed-methods study of binge eating disorder experts' opinions. International Journal of Environmental Research and Public Health. 2022;**19**(10):32

[145] Gonçalves JA et al. Eating disorders in childhood and adolescence. Revista Paulista de Pediatria. 2013;**31**(1):96-103

[146] Wade T. Eating disorders. In: Psychopathology and the Family. Elsevier; 2005. pp. 147-165

[147] Ng ISF, Cheung KCK, Chou KL. Correlates of eating disorder in middle-aged and older adults: Evidence from 2007 British national psychiatric morbidity survey. Journal of Aging and Health. 2013;**25**(7):1106-1120

[148] Michopoulos V et al. The mediating role of emotion dysregulation and depression on the relationship between childhood trauma exposure and emotional eating. Appetite. 2015;**91**:129-136

[149] Milic J, Stankic D, Stefanovic D. Health-related quality of life questionnaires: Applications to eating disorders. In: Eating Disorders: Volume 1,2. Springer International Publishing; 2023. pp. 1517-1528

[150] Gao YM, Chen J. Advances on risk factor for eating disorders. Journal of Shanghai Jiaotong University (Medical Science). 2019;**39**(4):432-435

[151] Van Hoeken D, Hoek HW. Review of the burden of eating disorders: Mortality, disability, costs, quality of life,

and family burden. Current Opinion in Psychiatry. 2020;**33**(6):521-527

[152] Kim YR. Eating disorders and adolescent health. Pediatric Gastroenterology, Hepatology and Nutrition. 2012;**15**:1-6

[153] Linardon J, Brennan L. The effects of cognitive-behavioral therapy for eating disorders on quality of life: A meta-analysis. International Journal of Eating Disorders. 2017;**50**(7):715-730

[154] Pimenta F et al. Brief cognitive-behavioral therapy for weight loss in midlife women: A controlled study with follow-up. International Journal of Women's Health. 2012;**4**(1):559-567

[155] Vancampfort D et al. Changes in physical activity, physical fitness, self-perception and quality of life following a 6-month physical activity counseling and cognitive behavioral therapy program in outpatients with binge eating disorder. Psychiatry Research. 2014;**219**(2):361-366

[156] de Vos JA et al. Having an eating disorder and still being able to flourish? Examination of pathological symptoms and well-being as two continua of mental health in a clinical sample. Frontiers in Psychology. 2018;**9**:2145

[157] Ter Huurne ED et al. Web-based cognitive behavioral therapy for female patients with eating disorders: Randomized controlled trial. Journal of Medical Internet Research. 2015;**17**(6):e152

[158] ter Huurne ED et al. Long-term effectiveness of web-based cognitive behavioral therapy for patients with eating disorders. Eating and Weight Disorders. 2021;**26**(3):911-919

[159] Turner H et al. Cognitive-behavioural therapy for outpatients with eating disorders: Effectiveness for a transdiagnostic group in a routine clinical setting. Behaviour Research and Therapy. 2015;**68**:70-75

[160] Schnicker K, Legenbauer T, Hiller W. Longer-term outcome of CBT for eating disorders in a naturalistic setting. PPmP Psychotherapie Psychosomatik Medizinische Psychologie. 2012;**62**(3-4):120-128

[161] Fairburn C. Cognitive Behavior Therapy and Eating Disorders. Guilford Press; 2008

[162] Beck JS. Cognitive Behavior Therapy: Basics and beyond. Guilford Press; 2012

[163] Linehan M. DBT? Skills Training Manual. Guilford Publications; 2014

[164] Marlatt GA, Donovan DM. Relapse Prevention: Maintenance Strategies in the Treatment of Addictive Behaviors. Guilford Press; 2005

[165] Bowers WA, Andersen AE. Cognitive-behavior therapy with eating disorders: The role of medications in treatment. Journal of Cognitive Psychotherapy. 2007;**21**(1):16-27

[166] Wilson GT. Cognitive behavioral therapy for eating disorders. In: The Oxford Handbook of Eating Disorders. Oxford University Press; 2012

[167] Murphy R et al. Cognitive behavioral therapy for eating disorders. Psychiatric Clinics of North America. 2010;**33**(3):611-627

[168] Hail L et al. Cognitive behavior therapy for co-occurring of eating and substance use disorders. In: Eating Disorders, Addictions and Substance Use Disorders: Research, Clinical and Treatment Perspectives.

Berlin Heidelberg: Springer-Verlag; 2013. pp. 533-546

[169] Cooper Z, Fairburn CG. Eating disorders. In: Cognitive-Behavioral Therapy with Adults: A Guide to Empirically-Informed Assessment and Intervention. Cambridge University Press; 2010. pp. 121-134

[170] Trompeter N et al. Emotion dysregulation within the CBT-E model of eating disorders: A narrative review. Cognitive Therapy and Research. 2021;**45**(6):1021-1036

[171] Baur J et al. Efficacy and mechanisms of change in exposure-based and cognitive stand-alone body image interventions in women with overweight and obesity. Behaviour Research and Therapy. 2022;**159**:34

[172] Cassone S, Lewis V, Crisp DA. Enhancing positive body image: An evaluation of a cognitive behavioral therapy intervention and an exploration of the role of body shame. Eating Disorders. 2016;**24**(5):469-474

[173] Grave RD. Enhanced cognitive behavior therapy for eating disorders. In: Eating Disorders: Volume 1,2. Springer International Publishing; 2023. pp. 3-23

[174] Södersten P et al. Cognitive behavior therapy for eating disorders versus normalization of eating behavior. Physiology and Behavior. 2017;**174**:178-190

[175] Anderson LK et al. The integration of family-based treatment and dialectical behavior therapy for adolescent bulimia nervosa: Philosophical and practical considerations. Eating Disorders. 2015;**23**(4):325-335

[176] Stidwill S, Cook-Müller I. The role of nutritional counselling in the treatment of anorexia nervosa and bulimia nervosa. Acta Academiae Medicinae Sinicae. 2019;**108**(14):931-936

[177] Trottier K et al. Initial findings from Project Recover: Overcoming Co-occurring eating disorders and posttraumatic stress disorder through integrated treatment. Journal of Traumatic Stress. 2017;**30**(2):173-177

[178] Szalai TD. Attachment interventions in the treatment of a case of binge eating disorder. Psychiatria Hungarica: A Magyar Pszichiatriai Tarsasag tudomanyos folyoirata. 2020;**35**(3):307-321

[179] Bamford BH, Mountford VA. Cognitive behavioural therapy for individuals with longstanding anorexia nervosa: Adaptations, clinician survival and system issues. European Eating Disorders Review. 2012;**20**(1):49-59

[180] Halmi KA. Salient components of a comprehensive service for eating disorders. World Psychiatry. 2009;**8**(3):150-155

[181] Pisetsky EM et al. Emerging psychological treatments in eating disorders. Psychiatric Clinics of North America. 2019;**42**(2):219-229

[182] Steinglass JE et al. Confronting fear using exposure and response prevention for anorexia nervosa: A randomized controlled pilot study. International Journal of Eating Disorders. 2014;**47**(2):174-180

[183] Steinglass JE et al. Rationale for the application of exposure and response prevention to the treatment of anorexia nervosa. International Journal of Eating Disorders. 2011;**44**(2):134-141

[184] Berends T et al. Rate, timing and predictors of relapse in patients with

anorexia nervosa following a relapse prevention program: A cohort study. BMC Psychiatry. 2016;**16**(1):35

[185] Essayli JH, Vitousek KM. Cognitive behavioral therapy with eating disordered youth. In: Neuromethods. Humana Press Inc.; 2020. pp. 163-187

[186] Stefano EC et al. Eating. In: Child and Adolescent Psychotherapy: Components of Evidence-Based Treatments for Youth and their Parents. Cambridge University Press; 2018. pp. 224-245

[187] Giel KE et al. Specialized post-inpatient psychotherapy for sustained recovery in anorexia nervosa via videoconference – Study protocol of the randomized controlled SUSTAIN trial. Journal of Eating Disorders. 2021;**9**(1):35

[188] Mischoulon D et al. Depression and eating disorders: Treatment and course. Journal of Affective Disorders. 2011;**130**(3):470-477

[189] Convertino AD, Mendoza RR. Posttraumatic stress disorder, traumatic events, and longitudinal eating disorder treatment outcomes: A systematic review. International Journal of Eating Disorders. 2023;**56**(6):1055-1074

[190] Palos GR et al. A multidisciplinary team approach to improving psychosocial care in patients with cancer. Clinical Journal of Oncology Nursing. 2013;**17**(5):556-558

[191] Rodan SC et al. Pharmacotherapy, alternative and adjunctive therapies for eating disorders: Findings from a rapid review. Journal of Eating Disorders. 2023;**11**(1):35

[192] Mitchell JE, Roerig J, Steffen K. Biological therapies for eating disorders. International Journal of Eating Disorders. 2013;**46**(5):470-477

[193] Sioziou AL et al. Antidepressants compared to placebo for people with binge eating disorder: A systematic review and meta-analysis. European Neuropsychopharmacology. 2024;**84**:5-15

[194] Mendolicchio L, Apicella E, Ventura E. Eating disorders and psychofarmachology: Rethink the treatment of eating disorders. In: Psychiatria Danubina. Medicinska Naklada Zagreb; 2021

[195] Micioni Di Bonaventura MV et al. N/OFQ-NOP system in food intake. In: Handbook of Experimental Pharmacology. New York LLC: Springer; 2019. pp. 279-295

[196] Smith KE, Goldschmidt AB. Treatment of binge-eating disorder across the lifespan: An updated review of the literature and considerations for future research. Current Obesity Reports. 2024;**13**(2):195-202

[197] Glasofer DR, Devlin MJ. Cognitive behavioral therapy for bulimia nervosa. Psychotherapy. 2013;**50**(4):537-542

[198] Braun DL. Cognitive behavioral therapy for bulimia nervosa. In: Evidence Based Treatments for Eating Disorders: Children, Adolescents and Adults. 2nd ed. Nova Science Publishers Inc.; 2014. pp. 263-288

[199] Dudzińska M. Cognitive-behavioral psychotherapy of psychological bulimia: Theory, method, empirical status and future directions of development. Psychoterapia. 2018;**187**(4):19-30

[200] Hay PPJ et al. Psychological treatments for bulimia nervosa and binging. Cochrane Database of Systematic Reviews. 2009;**4**:36

[201] Openshaw C, Waller G, Sperlinger D. Group cognitive-behavior therapy for bulimia nervosa: Statistical versus clinical significance of changes in symptoms across treatment. International Journal of Eating Disorders. 2004;**36**(4):363-375

[202] Linardon J et al. The efficacy of cognitive-behavioral therapy for eating disorders: A systematic review and meta-analysis. Journal of Consulting and Clinical Psychology. 2017;**85**(11):1080-1094

[203] Dalle Grave R. Intensive cognitive behavioural therapy for eating disorders. European Psychiatric Review. 2011;**4**(1):59-64

[204] le Grange D. The cognitive model of bulimia nervosa. In: Cognitive Therapy across the Lifespan. Cambridge University Press; 2013. pp. 293-314

[205] Zeeck A et al. Bulimia nervosa. Therapeutische Umschau. 2006;**63**(8):535-538

[206] Mitchell JE et al. Bulimia Nervosa, in Encyclopedia of Human Behavior. 2nd ed. Elsevier Inc.; 2012. pp. 413-416

[207] Trunko ME et al. Management of bulimia nervosa. Women's Health. 2007;**3**(2):255-265

[208] Resmark G. Cognitive behavioral therapy models. In: Handbook of Eating Disorders and Obesity. Berlin Heidelberg: Springer; 2024. pp. 123-127

[209] Lampard AM et al. An evaluation of the transdiagnostic cognitive-behavioural model of eating disorders. European Eating Disorders Review. 2013;**21**(2):99-107

[210] Dakanalis A et al. Comprehensive examination of the trans-diagnostic cognitive behavioral model of eating disorders in males. Eating Behaviors. 2014;**15**(1):63-67

[211] Burton AL, Abbott MJ. Conceptualising binge eating: A review of the theoretical and empirical literature. Behaviour Change. 2017;**34**(3):168-198

[212] Linardon J. Meta-analysis of the effects of cognitive-behavioral therapy on the core eating disorder maintaining mechanisms: Implications for mechanisms of therapeutic change. Cognitive Behaviour Therapy. 2018;**47**(2):107-125

[213] Butler RM et al. Fear of weight gain during cognitive behavioral therapy for binge-spectrum eating disorders. Eating and Weight Disorders. 2023;**28**(1):36

[214] Ralph-Nearman C, Rae J, Levinson CA. Using clinician and patient input to assess utility, accuracy, efficiency, and therapeutic implementation of a new data-driven digital therapeutic for personalized clinical eating disorder treatment: Awaken digital guide. Psychotherapy Research. 2024;**2024**:1-14

[215] Burger J, Ralph-Nearman C, Levinson CA. Integrating clinician and patient case conceptualization with momentary assessment data to construct idiographic networks: Moving toward personalized treatment for eating disorders. Behaviour Research and Therapy. 2022;**159**:36

[216] Butler RM et al. A pilot randomized controlled trial of transdiagnostic network-informed personalized treatment for eating disorders versus enhanced cognitive behavioral therapy. International Journal of Eating Disorders. 2023;**56**(8):1674-1680

[217] Mack RA, Stanton CE, Carney MR. The importance of including occupational therapists as part of the multidisciplinary team in the management of eating disorders: A narrative review incorporating lived experience. Journal of Eating Disorders. 2023;**11**(1):37

[218] McMaster CM et al. The role of the dietitian: Treatment of anorexia nervosa, bulimia nervosa, and binge eating disorder. In: Eating Disorders: Volume 1,2. Springer International Publishing; 2023. pp. 385-410

[219] Viljoen D et al. Applying integrated enhanced cognitive behaviour therapy (I-CBTE) to severe and longstanding eating disorders (SEED) paper 2: An in-depth case study for clinicians. Journal of Eating Disorders. 2024;**12**(1):37

[220] Trottier K, Monson CM. Integrating cognitive processing therapy for posttraumatic stress disorder with cognitive behavioral therapy for eating disorders in PROJECT RECOVER. Eating Disorders. 2021;**29**(3):307-325

[221] Ergüney-Okumuş FE. Integrating EMDR with enhanced cognitive behavioral therapy in the treatment of bulimia nervosa: A single case study. Journal of EMDR Practice and Research. 2021;**15**(4):231-243

[222] Yaşar AB et al. Two cases with avoidant/restrictive food intake disorder (ARFID): Effectiveness of EMDR and CBT combination on eating disorders (ED). Klinik Psikiyatri Dergisi. 2019;**22**(4):493-500

[223] Seubert A. Becoming known: A relational model utilizing gestalt and ego state-assisted EMDR in treating eating disorders. Journal of EMDR Practice and Research. 2018;**12**(2):71-86

[224] Halvgaard K. Single case study: Does EMDR psychotherapy work on emotional eating? Journal of EMDR Practice and Research. 2015;**9**(4):188-197

[225] Balbo M et al. Eye movement desensitization and reprocessing (EMDR) and eating disorders: A systematic review. Clinical Neuropsychiatry. 2017;**14**(5):321-329

[226] McCabe S. EMDR: Implications of the use of reprocessing therapy in nursing practice. Perspectives in Psychiatric Care. 2004;**40**(3):104-113

[227] Scelles C, Bulnes LC. EMDR as treatment option for conditions other than PTSD: A systematic review. Frontiers in Psychology. 2021;**12**:37

[228] Szigeti FJ. Eye movement desensitization and reprocessing (EMDR) therapy in trauma: Effect, effectiveness and mechanisms of action. Mentalhigiene es Pszichoszomatika. 2018;**19**(4):335-356

[229] Khanna MS, Kendall PC. Bringing technology to training: Web-based therapist training to promote the development of competent cognitive-behavioral therapists. Cognitive and Behavioral Practice. 2015;**22**(3):291-301

[230] Waltman SH. Model-consistent cognitive behavioral therapy supervision: A case study of a psychotherapy-based approach. Journal of Cognitive Psychotherapy. 2016;**30**(2):120-130

[231] Henrich D, Glombiewski JA, Scholten S. Systematic review of training in cognitive-behavioral therapy: Summarizing effects, costs and techniques. Clinical Psychology Review. 2023;**101**:38

[232] Goldsmith ES et al. Evaluation of implementation strategies for

cognitive behavioral therapy (CBT), acceptance and commitment therapy (ACT), and mindfulness-based stress reduction (MBSR): A systematic review. Journal of General Internal Medicine. 2023;**38**(12):2782-2791

[233] Lawson GM et al. Therapist and supervisor perspectives about two train-the-trainer implementation strategies in schools: A qualitative study. Implementation Research and Practice. 2023;**4**:38

[234] Thwaites R et al. Developing metacompetence in low intensity cognitive-behavioural therapy (CBT) interventions: Evaluating a self-practice/self-reflection programme for experienced low intensity CBT practitioners. Australian Psychologist. 2015;**50**(5):311-321

[235] Ertekin E, Ergun BM, Sungur MZ. Misconceptions and myhts about cognitive-behavioral therapy among psychiatrists and psychiatry residents. Anadolu Psikiyatri Dergisi. 2014;**16**(1):60-64

[236] AlHadi AN et al. Perception of mental health care professionals in Saudi Arabia on computerized cognitive behavioral therapy: Observational cross-sectional study. JMIR Formative Research. 2021;**5**(5):38

[237] Sysko R, Walsh BT. A critical evaluation of the efficacy of self-help interventions for the treatment of bulimia nervosa and binge-eating disorder. International Journal of Eating Disorders. 2008;**41**(2):97-112

[238] Juarascio AS et al. Just-in-time adaptive interventions: A novel approach for enhancing skill utilization and acquisition in cognitive behavioral therapy for eating disorders. International Journal of Eating Disorders. 2018;**51**(8):826-830

[239] Pike KM et al. Cognitive behavioral therapy for anorexia nervosa. In: Evidence Based Treatments for Eating Disorders: Children, Adolescents and Adults. 2nd ed. Nova Science Publishers Inc.; 2014. pp. 239-262

[240] Vocks S et al. Body image therapy in eating disorders: Influencing of perceptive, cognitive-affective, and behavioral components of the body image. Zeitschrift fur Klinische Psychologie und Psychotherapie. 2006;**35**(4):286-295

[241] Farrell NR et al. Exploring mechanisms of action in exposure-based cognitive behavioral therapy for eating disorders: The role of eating-related fears and body-related safety behaviors. Behavior Therapy. 2019;**50**(6):1125-1135

[242] Dalle Grave R et al. Enhanced cognitive behaviour therapy for adolescents with anorexia nervosa: An alternative to family therapy? Behaviour Research and Therapy. 2013;**51**(1):R9-R12

[243] Murray SB, Labuschagne Z, Le Grange D. Family and couples therapy for eating disorders, substance use disorders, and addictions. In: Eating Disorders, Addictions and Substance Use Disorders: Research, Clinical and Treatment Perspectives. Berlin Heidelberg: Springer-Verlag; 2014. pp. 563-586

[244] Timko CA et al. An open trial of acceptance-based separated family treatment (ASFT) for adolescents with anorexia nervosa. Behaviour Research and Therapy. 2015;**69**:63-74

[245] Coyne LW, McHugh L, Martinez ER. Acceptance and commitment therapy (ACT): Advances and applications with children,

adolescents, and families. Child and Adolescent Psychiatric Clinics of North America. 2011;**20**(2):379-399

[246] Cunningham ML et al. Muscle dysmorphia: An overview of clinical features and treatment options. Journal of Cognitive Psychotherapy. 2017;**31**(4):255-271

[247] Waller G, Evans J, Stringer H. The therapeutic alliance in the early part of cognitive-behavioral therapy for the eating disorders. International Journal of Eating Disorders. 2012;**45**(1):63-69

[248] D'Souza Walsh K et al. Alliance, technique, both, or more? Clinicians' views on what works in cognitive-behavioral therapy for eating disorders. International Journal of Eating Disorders. 2019;**52**(3):278-282

[249] Fumagalli G, Margola D. Is personality the key in cognitive-behavioural therapy for eating disorders? A review. Clinical Psychology and Psychotherapy. 2022;**29**(1):164-177

Chapter 12

Developing and Testing Tele-Support Psychotherapy through Mobile Phones for Youth (15–30 Years) with Depression in Uganda

Etheldreda Nakimuli-Mpungu, Jeremiah Mutinye Kwesiga, John Mark Bwanika, Davis Musinguzi, Carol Nakanyike, Jane Iya, Benedict Akimana, Charlotte Hawkins, Patricia Cavazos, Jean B. Nachega, Ed Mills, Sabrina Bakeera Kitaka and Musisi Seggane

Abstract

In response to the rise in mental health problems among youth during the COVID-19 pandemic, we conducted a qualitative study in March 2022, using a user-centered design approach guided by ecological theories, to adapt group support psychotherapy into tele-support psychotherapy (TSP) via mobile phones. The development of a call platform, informed by the unified theory of acceptance and use of technology, was integrated into the Medical Concierge Group's (TMCG) telehealth services under Rocket Health Africa. This platform included a dedicated toll-free line for psychotherapy, connecting users with lay counselors. An open-label randomized controlled trial (PACTR202201684613316) was conducted to assess the feasibility, acceptability, and effectiveness of TSP in combination with standard mental health services (n = 154) compared with standard mental health services alone (n = 146) among youth with mild to moderate major depression in Kampala. Participants commonly equated mental health with mental illness and reported significant challenges, including financial stress, substance abuse, and family dysfunction. Although digital interventions were largely accepted, some participants preferred in-person services. The adapted TSP maintained gender sensitivity and used folk tales, stories, riddles, and creative visualizations to facilitate emotional expression, acquisition of coping strategies, and income-generating skills, addressing both emotional and socio-economic needs.

Keywords: tele-support psychotherapy, youth, depression, mobile phone, Uganda

1. Introduction

The COVID-19 pandemic has amplified pre-existing mental health challenges among adolescents and young adults, leading to a marked increase in mental health issues within this population [1]. These demographics face distinct stressors, including financial hardship, academic pressures, and social isolation, all exacerbated by disrupted access to mental health services [2]. With traditional care options strained, there is a pressing need for innovative and accessible mental health interventions tailored to young people.

Digital mental health solutions, such as mobile apps, online therapy platforms, and virtual reality (VR) applications, offer promising avenues for addressing the growing demand for mental health support among young people. Systematic reviews indicate these platforms can effectively deliver interventions for depression and anxiety [3]. By providing real-time support and reminders, these digital interventions enhance patient engagement and adherence, which are crucial for maintaining therapeutic progress [4].

A review of 15 studies comparing telephone-based and face-to-face psychological therapy found little difference in crucial areas like therapeutic alliance, disclosure, empathy, attentiveness, and participation [5]. However, telephone sessions were notably shorter than those conducted in person. These interventions have the potential to significantly improve access to mental health care, particularly in rural and underserved areas, offering a scalable and cost-effective solution. Despite these advantages, challenges such as ensuring data privacy, resolving technical issues, and bridging the digital divide continue to pose barriers to widespread adoption [6].

Further, maintaining user engagement, lack of personalization [7], technical issues [8], and varying levels of user motivation can affect the effectiveness of these tools [9]. Addressing these challenges requires designing interventions that are user-friendly, adaptable, and capable of catering to individual needs. Furthermore, concerns regarding data privacy and security are paramount [9]. Robust measures must be implemented to protect user information and ensure the ethical use of digital platforms, fostering trust and encouraging broader adoption.

Cultural and contextual relevance is also crucial for the success of digital mental health interventions [10]. Despite these challenges, the potential for mobile phone-based psychotherapy to provide accessible, real-time, and cost-effective mental health support makes it a promising avenue for expanding mental health services, especially in low-resource settings [11]. Further research is needed to explore the long-term efficacy of these interventions and to develop strategies to overcome barriers to their use.

In Uganda, we aimed to adapt the successful in-person group support psychotherapy (GSP) [12] into tele-support psychotherapy (TSP) using mobile phones to address youth depression. The adaptation retained the core theoretical frameworks of GSP, including Bandura's social cognitive theory, which emphasizes observational learning and modeling [13]. Additionally, cognitive behavioral therapy (CBT) techniques, grounded in the theory that the way we think determines the way we behave, were integrated into TSP through verbal thought record exercises, providing real-time feedback to participants [14]. The sustainable livelihood framework also informed TSP by offering verbal guidance on income generation, problem-solving, stress management, and fostering community support through voice calls [15].

To ensure the adapted tele-psychotherapy was culturally and contextually relevant to the youth in Kampala, we applied the ecological validity and cultural sensitivity framework [16]. This helped tailor the intervention to their unique environmental and social challenges. Furthermore, the unified theory of acceptance and use of technology (UTAUT) model [17] was employed to assess factors influencing the acceptance and usage of technology among youth. We hypothesized that combining TSP via mobile phones with standard mental health services would be more effective in reducing depression symptoms among youth than standard services alone in the Kampala district.

2. Materials and methods

2.1 Study design and settings

The study was conducted in three key areas of Kampala: Naguru Go-down, Kamwokya, and Makerere University. Kampala, home to 62 slums, faces significant public health challenges due to its high population density. Kamwokya, with approximately 6380 residents, struggles with inadequate infrastructure and severe health risks. Naguru Go-down, centrally located, comprises about 2080 households with a population of 10,400. Makerere University, Uganda's largest public institution, has around 35,000 students, mostly aged 18–30. These diverse and densely populated areas are particularly vulnerable to public health issues such as poverty, unemployment, financial and academic stress, substance abuse, and overcrowding, contributing to widespread health challenges [18].

2.2 The adaptation process

In the study's initial phase, nine focus group discussions (FGDs) were held across Naguru, Kamwokya, and Makerere, engaging youth, community health workers, and political representatives. Additionally, 10 key informant interviews (KIs) were conducted with stakeholders, including psychologists, health officials, and community and religious leaders, to explore views on tele-psychotherapy for addressing youth mental health challenges. Co-principal investigator JMB facilitated introductions to key local stakeholders, leveraging strong connections with officials and health centers in the Kampala district.

Purposive sampling was used to select participants for the qualitative interviews, which were conducted in the local language. The interviews were audio-recorded, transcribed, and, when required, translated verbatim. Informed consent was obtained from all participants before conducting the KIs and FGDs. Alongside these interviews, a community advisory board (CAB) was formed, comprising various community members, including a youth leader, faith healer, local council and student leaders, a community health worker, and a representative from key populations. The CAB was established to foster ongoing trust and ensure community engagement throughout the research process.

Community advisory board (CAB) members participated in key informant interviews, providing valuable feedback on the TSP model and study protocol, particularly regarding mental health and psychosocial issues. Their insights helped adjust GSP content for mobile delivery. Ten professional counselors were trained in TSP delivery, with workshops reviewing theoretical frameworks and adapting psychotherapeutic skills. These professionals trained and supervised 40 lay counselors who, using a virtual platform, provided tele-psychotherapy via mobile phones to youth with mild to moderate depression. Training materials and guides were also refined.

2.3 Developing the tele-psychotherapy call center

TMCG/Rocket Health, a digital health company leveraging technology to provide healthcare services, has gained extensive experience through telephone-based doctor consultations conducted in its medical call center staffed by medical personnel and customer support agents. This experience made TMCG/Rocket Health uniquely suited to develop the TSP call platform. The existing system was updated to improve client interactions and enhance service delivery.

2.4 Gathering user and technical requirements

The platform's design followed a structured, multi-step process, beginning with the identification of key stakeholders such as doctors, mental health providers, patients, caregivers, lay counselors, and key populations. A protocol training session was conducted to align stakeholders and gather requirements for the tele-support psychotherapy call center. Workshops, focus groups, and interviews with study staff, Rocket Health personnel, and mental health experts provided key insights on confidentiality, service availability, phone access challenges, virtual trust, gender-specific concerns, and continuity of care. Based on these insights, the existing Rocket Health call center platform was modified to incorporate mental health services delivered by lay counselors.

2.5 Prototype development

After gathering specific user requirements from stakeholders, the technical team used these insights and schematic diagrams to modify the TMCG/Rocket Health call center. This modification enabled community members to access mental health services through a toll-free line, with calls routed to lay counselors. When a client called, the system directed the call to an available counselor for real-time support. Following the setup of Version 1, orientation and training sessions were held for counselors and study participants to ensure familiarity with the platform. The system was then handed over for user testing to address technical and user needs before broader implementation.

2.6 Piloting and user feedback phase

During the pilot testing phase, stakeholders from the earlier workshops, focus groups, and interviewers were invited to test the platform and provide feedback on its functionality. Over 2 weeks, users evaluated the system's accuracy, completeness, and ability to meet their needs. As testing progressed, several issues were identified, including delayed or missed calls, an insufficient number of available counselors, sudden call drops, privacy concerns, and counselors being overwhelmed with too many calls. System conflicts and other challenges were also reported. This valuable feedback was relayed to the development team for further refinements to enhance platform performance and user experience.

3. Design and development of version 2 following user feedback

Upon receiving user feedback, the development team implemented several key improvements. Lay counselors were categorized by gender and key populations, with further division by language (e.g., Male-English and Female-Luganda), allowing clients to choose counselors based on gender and language preferences. The call response time for counselors was increased from 10 to 15 seconds, and a round-robin system was introduced to ensure equal distribution of calls among counselors. If one was unavailable, the call automatically moved to the next. All interactions were recorded with unique IDs and timestamps for future reference, data analysis, and quality control, ensuring efficient call handling and research tracking.

The final version, *Version 2* of the platform, was designed with enhanced user convenience and attention to detail:

Step 1: Client initiation: When a client feels the need to speak to a counselor, they dial the toll-free line. The system starts with an Interactive Voice Response (IVR) to guide the client through the process.

Step 2: First-time users: For first-time users, the system prompts the client to select a preferred language (English or Luganda) and then choose a category of counselors (male, female, or key population). Once a category is chosen, the call is forwarded to available lay counselors in that category, one at a time, until a counselor answers. Each call is recorded and stored in the database for future review, ensuring quality control during professional counselor evaluations.

Step 3: Returning users: For clients who have called previously, the IVR guides them, and the system automatically forwards their call to the counselor they spoke to during their last session, ensuring continuity in the counseling process. These interactions are also recorded and saved in the database for future reference.

Following the successful development of Version 2, another training session was conducted, allowing users to familiarize themselves with the updated features and improvements. After the training, the system was officially handed over to the users for continued testing and operation.

3.1 System updates and enhancements

A key update requested by the project team was enabling clients to reconnect with previously selected counselors for continuity of care. This required a major redesign of the IVR system to integrate with a database tracking past client-counselor interactions, fostering longer-term therapeutic relationships. Additionally, the call distribution logic was refined to ensure fairness among counselors.

The original system, based on availability, often resulted in uneven workloads. The updated system introduced an algorithm that evenly distributed calls, preventing counselor fatigue and ensuring a balanced workflow. These improvements enhanced both the client experience and counselor efficiency. The algorithm also took client preferences into account, such as language and gender, ensuring that each client was matched with the most appropriate counselor.

These updates required a redesign of the Asterisk-based setup, which used a Private Branch Exchange (PBX) system for internal call management and voice over IP (VOIP) for internet-based services. A more advanced IVR system is now needed to manage more complex decision trees, interact with a database, and handle dynamic call routing. A PHP framework utilizing the Model-View-Controller (MVC) architecture was implemented for the new system, with MySQL serving as the database technology to manage data. Nginx, a high-performance web server, was selected for its ability to handle high concurrency with low memory usage.

3.2 Calls review system (quality assurance)

In addition to these updates, a robust Calls Review System was implemented to monitor and ensure quality service delivery (**Figure 1**). TSP supervisors required the ability to securely access, monitor, and analyze recorded phone calls to ensure that clients received high-quality tele-psychotherapy services. Therefore, all client-counselor encounters were recorded and made available in a system for easy access and review. Specific updates to the QA system included the ability to automatically filter out and display TSP-specific call recordings and further filter recordings by phone number for detailed review. To accommodate secure remote access, the QA system was configured to be accessible outside TMCG premises via a Virtual Private Network (VPN).

This Calls Review System, built on the PHP framework and MySQL, became an essential tool for supervisors, allowing them to maintain high standards of service. Supervisors could securely access recorded sessions, analyze interactions, and ensure that counselors adhered to therapeutic guidelines. This continuous monitoring ensured that both client satisfaction and counselor performance were maintained at optimal levels, while also ensuring compliance with privacy and security standards.

In summary, Version 2 of the tele-psychotherapy platform not only enhanced client convenience and care continuity but also provided essential tools for quality assurance and counselor performance evaluation. These updates ensure that the system is client-focused, equitable, and capable of scaling to meet increasing demands for tele-psychotherapy services. This process is illustrated in the accompanying flow chart (**Figure 2**).

Figure 1.
Call review page.

DOI: http://dx.doi.org/10.5772/intechopen.1008155

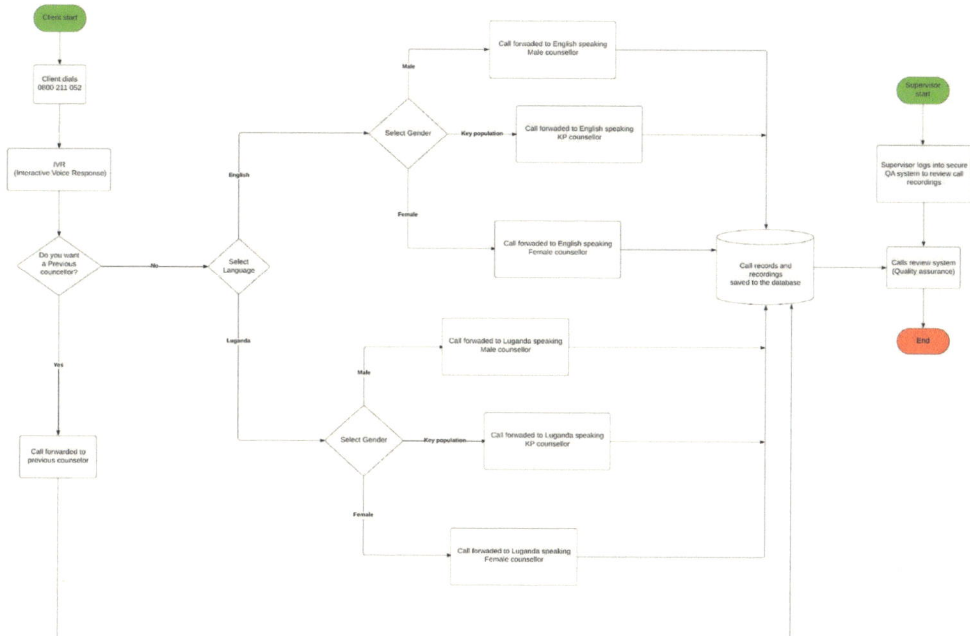

Figure 2.
Telephone system flow diagram.

3.3 The trial phase

In the trial phase, we conducted a pilot single-blinded randomized controlled trial to assess the feasibility, acceptability, and preliminary effectiveness of TSP in combination with standard mental health services compared with standard mental health services alone among youth with mild to moderate major depression in Kampala. We randomized 300 youth (1:1) to either both TSP and standard mental health services (SMHS) (N = 154) or SMHS only (N = 146). A process evaluation of the delivery of TSP using mobile phones and SMHS, utilizing mixed methods, ran alongside the trial to assess acceptability, feasibility, fidelity, and challenges encountered in the development process.

3.4 Participant eligibility criteria

To be eligible for the study, individuals had to be aged 15–30 years, have a diagnosis of mild to moderate depression, reside in the Kamwokya, Naguru, or Makerere areas in Kampala district, have a mobile phone, provide written informed consent, and be able to speak Luganda or English. Individuals aged 15–17 years needed to be either a mature minor or an emancipated minor, as mature and emancipated minors were permitted to independently provide informed consent to participate in research. Individuals who were mentally or physically disabled, as evidenced by a score below 50% on the Karnofsky performance scale, were excluded from the study.

3.5 Recruitment

To recruit participants, research assistants collaborated with TMCG staff to launch both online and offline mental health awareness campaigns. The online campaign utilized SMS messaging and TMCG's social media channels, notably their Facebook page with over 58,000 followers, to reach university students and young people. The project was explained in simple terms, inviting interested individuals to contact the study team.

Offline, the team worked with local leaders and health workers in Kamwokya and Naguru Go-down to conduct six to eight community sensitization meetings. These meetings aimed to raise awareness about mental health issues and available treatments, including the new tele-psychotherapy service. Young people aged 15–30 from these areas and the Makerere community were invited to participate and assessed for eligibility. Those who were excluded were linked to mental health services by a team member.

3.6 Randomization and masking

Participants were randomly assigned to intervention or control groups by a biostatistician using specialized software to ensure impartiality, as the biostatistician had no direct contact with participants. Randomized blocks of varying sizes were used to maintain balance between study arms and reduce predictability. Each participant was given a unique study code, identified only by their phone number and code for anonymity. Randomization was applied across three communities—Naguru, Kamwokya, and Makerere—with 100 participants from each. While participants knew their group, outcome assessors and data analysts were blinded to the interventions to prevent bias and ensure objective evaluation.

3.7 Study interventions

The results section outlines the developed TSP model. Study participants had access to standard mental health services at Makerere University, Naguru, and Mulago hospitals, where psychiatric clinical officers, nurses, and counselors primarily addressed mild to moderate mental health conditions. Upon seeking care, patients underwent thorough physical and mental health assessments. The primary services offered included informal counseling and medication management for various mental health disorders. For cases requiring more specialized care beyond the clinic's capabilities, a referral system was in place to direct patients to the Butabika National Referral Mental Hospital for advanced treatment.

3.8 Outcome measures

For this chapter, we focus on process evaluation outcomes and one trial outcome-depression symptoms. Feasibility was assessed by determining the proportion of eligible participants who engaged in either intervention (reach), the proportion who completed all eight sessions (dose delivered), and the rate of participant loss (attrition), using data from attendance registers. Acceptability was evaluated by examining participant satisfaction, TSP counselor knowledge and attitudes, and the perceived effectiveness of the intervention in reducing depression, as measured by a 9-item questionnaire [19].

Fidelity was assessed through a semi-structured questionnaire completed by supervisors after listening to recorded psychotherapy sessions via the in-built call review system to determine if the interventions were delivered as planned. Challenges were identified through a semi-structured questionnaire completed by TSP counselors and exit interviews. Depression symptoms were measured using the self-reporting questionnaire (SRQ-20), with SRQ scores treated as a continuous variable [20]. The reliability of the SRQ was confirmed with a Cronbach's alpha coefficient of 0.80.

3.9 Data analysis

Qualitative data, derived from focus group discussions and key informant interviews, were anonymized, transcribed, and analyzed using MAXQDA (v22.5.0) with a grounded inductive approach to identify recurring themes. Three research team members collaboratively conducted thematic analysis to ensure credibility. Coded data were displayed in matrices to compare responses across treatment groups, and inter-coder reliability was assessed.

Quantitative data were analyzed using bivariate analyzes, including χ^2 tests and independent t-tests, to compare baseline demographic and psychosocial variables between study groups. Differences in depression symptom scores 6 months after randomization were analyzed using intention-to-treat methods and generalized structural equation modeling. All analyzes were performed using STATA 18, with missing data handled through multiple imputations.

3.10 Ethical considerations

The study obtained approval from the Makerere College of Health Sciences Research Ethics Committee and the Uganda National Council of Science and Technology (UNCST). Full consent was secured from hospital and community leadership before the study commenced. All participants provided informed consent, and their identifying information was fully anonymized in the reporting.

4. Results

4.1 Post pandemic challenges of youth living in Kampala

At the individual level, personal characteristics, knowledge, attitudes, and behaviors directly influence the mental health of youth in Kampala. One significant challenge is the limited personal awareness and widespread misconceptions about mental health. Many youths have a vague understanding of mental health, often equating it solely with severe mental illness or madness due to inadequate information dissemination. As a female respondent from Naguru explained:

> *"Most people think that mental health has to do with madness. They don't think that these other forms are there. Even some people who are depressed, some people think it is stubbornness. Others think it is just bad manners. Here, for some people to recognize or to accept that this person has a problem, it's the one who has run mad—that violent one who undresses himself. But if you are there depressed, you have anxiety, you are misunderstood." (Respondent 6, Naguru Females)*

Substance use is another critical issue affecting individual mental health. Youth may engage in substance abuse as a coping mechanism due to stress or peer influence, which can lead to or exacerbate mental health problems. This is often a result of inadequate support systems and negative peer influences. As described in the narrative:

> *"Such kind of treatment leaves the children at the mercy of peer groups that influence them to get involved in substance abuse, which predisposes them to mental health challenges and illnesses." (Respondent 4 Naguru Females)*

Identity crises, particularly among key populations like LGBTQ+ youth, contribute significantly to mental health challenges. Personal struggles with understanding one's sexuality or identity, coupled with societal pressures, can lead to feelings of depression and anxiety. A respondent from the key population highlighted this struggle:

> *"Understanding my sexuality, understanding my family, understanding everything around me. So, that is basically the issue that deals with mental health that most of us, if not most trans people within the community, are dealing with depression." (Respondent 2, Key Population)*

Economic stress also plays a substantial role in affecting individual mental health. Personal financial difficulties contribute to stress, impacting daily functioning and overall well-being. A male participant from Naguru shared his experience:

> *"If your job is stressful and you also have issues at home, you could face mental health issues. It can also lead to suicide. When I had mental health issues, I was taken to Butabika for counselling." (Naguru Male)*

Furthermore, the influence of social media exacerbates mental health challenges among youth. The desire to fit in and prove oneself among peers, amplified by social media platforms, can lead to feelings of inadequacy, anxiety, or depression. A female student from Makerere University observed:

> *"I agree with the social media; I think it ties into the peer pressure thing. It doesn't stop in high school, but it gets bigger on campus. There is a desire to fit in and prove yourself among your mates. People indulge in so much." (Respondent 3, Makerere University Females)*

At the interpersonal level, relationships with family, friends, and peers significantly impact the mental health of youth in Kampala. One of the primary challenges identified is family dysfunction and a lack of parental support. Conflicts within the family, inattentiveness from parents, and strained parent-child relationships contribute to the mental health struggles of young people. As expressed by female respondents from Naguru:

> *"We ask you, mother and father, to get time to talk to your family. A child has gone to school—you don't know what happened there. When a child tries to tell you, 'Mummy, at school...' you scold, 'Stupid, I don't want to be disturbed when I'm tired.' The child wants to narrate what he went through but you, the mom or the caregiver, you've not given her or him the time to tell you what has happened." (Naguru Females)*

Another respondent highlighted how parental absence due to work commitments leads to inadequate supervision and guidance:

> *"I have gone to work; the father also doesn't care, and I have also gone to work and have left the children at home. We came back at night. You end up realizing the child is in a bad group. In that group, there is no one who can counsel him." (Naguru Females)*

These narratives illustrate how the lack of parental engagement leaves children vulnerable to negative peer influences and harmful behaviors.

At the community level in Kampala, social networks and cultural norms profoundly affect youth mental health by shaping individual behaviors and access to resources. A primary challenge is the pervasive stigma and misconceptions surrounding mental health, where it is often solely associated with madness. This misunderstanding leads to the stigmatization of individuals experiencing mental health issues, impeding their willingness to seek help and exacerbating their conditions.

> *"Most people think that mental health has to do with madness. They don't think that these other forms exist. Even people who are depressed—some think it's stubbornness; others think it's just bad manners." (Respondent 6, Naguru Females)*

This stigma is exacerbated by inadequate dissemination of mental health information. Minimal education and awareness campaigns result in a lack of understanding and the perpetuation of myths within the community. The same respondent highlighted this issue: *"The education about mental health is minimal. Very few people know about these other forms." (Respondent 6, Naguru Females).*

Due to these misconceptions and the lack of proper information, there is a reliance on non-professional sources of help. Communities often turn to spiritual places like churches, mosques, or traditional healers instead of professional mental health services. This preference was noted by the respondent: *"Most people, their first choice is a witch doctor." Respondent 6, Naguru Females).*

Furthermore, cultural expectations and social norms in Kampala inhibit open dialog about mental health, creating substantial barriers to help-seeking among youth.

At the organizational level, institutions such as schools, workplaces, and healthcare facilities significantly influence the mental health of youth in Kampala by either providing support or presenting hindrances. A primary challenge is the limited availability and utilization of mental health services within educational institutions. While universities like Makerere have established some mental health resources—for instance, *"a counselling centre just opposite Mary Stuart Hall" (Respondent 6, Makerere University Males)*—awareness and utilization of these services may be low among students. This gap is evident as another student acknowledged,

> *"The truth is that the general population of Makerere University sometimes perhaps does not understand the entire concept of mental health..." (Respondent 8, Makerere University Males).*

In other communities, schools often lack dedicated mental health facilities altogether, leaving students without accessible support within their educational environments. Additionally, insufficient healthcare services in the broader community contribute to the challenges faced by youth. In many cases, there is a lack of accessible local mental health services, leading individuals to seek help only when conditions become severe enough to warrant intervention at national psychiatric facilities. A male respondent from the Kamwokya community illustrated this issue:

> *"When someone is mentally ill, they call the police and take them to Butabika" (Respondent 5, Kamwokya Male Community).*

This reliance on distant, centralized facilities underscores the absence of adequate community-level mental health support. Moreover, due to inadequate organizational support, youth often turn to non-professional sources for assistance, such as social media or untrained individuals. This overreliance on informal support networks may not provide the necessary help for those struggling with mental health issues. A female student from Makerere University observed,

> *"People run to the places they feel safe, and one of those safe places is social media. They go to social media to post memes so that they can get someone to say hello to them" (Respondent 2, Makerere University Females).*

This tendency highlights the gap left by formal institutions in providing accessible and trusted mental health resources.

Policy and societal factors in Kampala exert a critical influence on youth mental health through cultural beliefs, societal norms, and legal frameworks. A pervasive challenge is the societal stigma associated with mental health issues, often linked to shame or perceived as a sign of weakness, which discourages individuals from seeking help. As one female participant observed:

> *"Even some people who are depressed, some people think it is stubbornness. Others think it is just bad manners." (Respondent 6, Naguru Females).*

This perception minimizes the seriousness of mental health conditions and fosters an environment where they are inadequately addressed.

Moreover, there is a tendency to view mental health struggles as mere circumstances to be endured rather than medical conditions requiring professional intervention. A participant from a key population expressed:

> *"You find there are certain circumstances, and me, I don't think it's a disease just like how people are describing it. It is just circumstances that we are living in that we just need to learn; how do you live with them." (Respondent 2, Key Population).*

This attitude reflects a broader reluctance to acknowledge mental health as a legitimate health concern, hindering efforts to promote mental well-being.

Stigma and discrimination against marginalized groups, such as the LGBTQ+ community, further exacerbate mental health challenges. The lack of legal protections and societal acceptance imposes additional psychological burdens on these individuals. One respondent highlighted:

> *"Another issue is about stigma and discrimination, which also leads to mental health issues. Because this stigma and discrimination come from the families, the communities, and everywhere—places where they seek services, the health service providers, the legal institutions. So, the whole community, the whole thing is a mess for them." (Respondent 2, Key Population).*

This pervasive discrimination not only impacts mental health but also restricts access to appropriate support and services. Insufficient national mental health policies lead to limited funding and resources, impeding the development and implementation of effective interventions for youth mental health. These systemic barriers highlight the urgent need for comprehensive policy reforms, public education campaigns to shift cultural perceptions, and legal protections for marginalized communities. As one participant from the key population remarked,

"The whole community, the whole thing is a mess for them" (Respondent 2, Key Population). Addressing these policy gaps is crucial to fostering an environment conducive to mental well-being among the youth in Kampala.

4.2 Relevance of maintaining the GSP structure in the TSP model

Study participants deemed the structure of GSP to be relevant in addressing the highlighted youth mental health challenges. The data support maintaining this structure for the TSP model. Each session is thoughtfully designed to tackle specific issues—from establishing trust and managing emotions to addressing stigma and improving socio-economic conditions—aligning with the expressed needs and concerns of the youth.

The first sessions focus on building a safe and confidential environment, which is essential for participants who may experience anxiety and distrust. Establishing ground rules and setting expectations promotes a sense of security, encouraging youths to share their experiences openly. Education about emotions provides participants with tools to understand and cope with intense feelings in session 2, such as anger, shame, guilt, and sadness, empowering them to process their experiences constructively.

Sessions 3 and 4 provide a platform for therapeutic sharing, reducing feelings of loneliness, and building social connections and a supportive network that many youths lack in their personal lives. These sessions address isolation and lack of social support, often stemming from family dysfunction and community stigma. Introducing positive coping strategies in sessions 5 and 6 helps youths replace negative behaviors—such as substance use and succumbing to peer pressure—with healthier alternatives, thus addressing the root causes of maladaptive behaviors.

Coping skills for stigma and discrimination, particularly toward marginalized groups like the LGBTQ+ community helps affected youth build positive self-image and develop strategies to navigate societal prejudices, providing critical support for youths grappling with external judgment and internalized stigma. The final sessions offer livelihood skills training to improve socio-economic status and reduce associated stressors. By enhancing employability and financial stability, GSP addresses the practical needs underpinning psychological well-being. This comprehensive approach suggests that the TSP model could play a pivotal role in improving mental health outcomes within this population.

Table 1 provides supporting statements from the qualitative study which indicate the relevance of the GSP structure in addressing youth mental health challenges.

4.3 Adaptations to tele-support psychotherapy

By integrating both the ecological validity and culturally sensitive framework [16] and the unified theory of acceptance and use of technology (UTAUT) model [17], the adaptation of tele-support psychotherapy delivered through mobile phones was optimized to enhance acceptance and engagement among youth. This combined approach not only addressed technological barriers but also aligned with the psychological,

GSP session	Youth problems addressed	Relevance to youth	Supporting quote from data
Session 1: Introductions and establishing trust	Anxiety and fear of sharing, trust issues, confidentiality concerns	Establishes a safe environment that promotes trust and confidentiality, which is crucial for managing anxiety and encouraging participants to share their experiences	*"For me, I would expect confidentiality and the service to be readily available as and when it is needed. Whenever a patient gets a problem, can they easily access the person who is giving them the help?" Respondent 6, Naguru Females*
Session 2: Education about emotions	Difficulty managing intense emotions (anger, shame, guilt, sadness)	Assists youth in understanding and managing intense feelings through education about emotions	*"They are not respected at all. They are not taken as humans by society. They are neglected and considered useless."—Respondent 3, Kamwokya Female*
Sessions 3 and 4: Sharing painful experiences	Continued feelings of loneliness, need for deeper connections	Reduces isolation by increasing social support and connections through therapeutic sharing of painful experiences	*"We ask you, mother and father, to get time to talk to your family... but you, the mom or the caregiver, you have not given her or him the time to tell you what has happened."—Naguru Females*
Session 5: Learning positive coping skills	Substance use, negative coping mechanisms, peer pressure	Encourages peer support and teaches positive coping skills to replace negative behaviors and manage stress	*"Such kind of treatment leaves the children at the mercy of peer groups that influence them to get involved in substance abuse, which predisposes them to mental health challenges and illnesses."— Naguru Male*
Session 6: Coping with stigma and discrimination	Stigma and discrimination, low self-image, relationship challenges	Promotes positive self-image and self-awareness; helps develop strategies for managing relationship challenges, including stigma and discrimination	*"Another issue is about stigma and discrimination, which also leads to mental health issues... So, the whole community, the whole thing is a mess for them."—Respondent 2, Key Population*
Sessions 7 and 8: Livelihood skills training	Economic stress, unemployment, financial difficulties	Equips youth with tools to improve their socio-economic status, addressing economic stressors that contribute to mental health issues	*"If your job is stressful and you also have issues at home, you could face mental health issues."—Naguru Male*

Table 1.
Relevance of maintaining the GSP structure in the TSP model.

social, and cultural factors influencing Ugandan youth, thereby increasing the likelihood of successful outcomes in treating depression.

4.4 Culturally appropriate language

In adapting TSP for youth in Kampala, using culturally appropriate language was vital for comprehension and engagement. Sessions were conducted in English and Luganda, reflecting community preferences: "*About three languages are enough for us. English and Luganda are a must" (Respondent 6 Kamwokya Female, Pos. 78)*. The language was simplified, avoiding clinical jargon and made relatable with analogies, such as comparing drug abuse to overeating junk food—pleasant initially but harmful over time. Lay counselors were trained in local languages and encouraged to use respectful, culturally relevant terms, fostering open communication and making therapy more accessible and effective.

4.5 Trusted persons

Integrating trained lay counselors supervised by professional counselors into Tele-Support Psychotherapy (TSP) proved effective and culturally appropriate. This approach addressed the shortage of mental health professionals by providing a scalable, cost-effective solution to expand access to mental health services. Lay counselors, embedded in their communities, built trust through their understanding of local culture and social dynamics. As one participant noted, *"The person you are going to put at the other end of the line should be calm, patient, a good listener, and free of judgment" (Respondent 4 KCTP Kamwokya Female, Pos. 81).* The involvement of respected community leaders further boosted TSP's acceptance: *"The ghetto people were very crucial in involving their leaders... they listened to them and would come once called upon" (Respondent 1 Makerere Local Community Males, Pos. 248–249).* Gender-specific sessions allowed participants to discuss gender-specific issues with counselors of the same gender, promoting openness. This model leveraged local resources, ensuring culturally sensitive care and viability in underserved areas.

4.6 Use of relevant metaphors

The scarcity of effective and comprehensive mental health support in the community has left many feeling helpless. Counseling remained the primary source of assistance, though it was often not specialized for mental health needs, as noted by a respondent: *"If there are no friends, then they opted for counselors of which some counselors had no mental health knowledge. They had experience in HIV counseling" (Respondent 1 Key Population, Pos. 75).* To address this gap, both professional and lay counselors in the tele-support psychotherapy program were trained to employ metaphors rooted in the local culture, enhancing the relatability and impact of therapy sessions.

Counselors used culturally relevant metaphors to enhance understanding in therapy sessions. For example, they likened substance misuse to "putting fuel on a fire"—offering temporary relief but causing lasting harm. To reinforce self-worth amidst stigma, they compared individuals to a Muvule tree, symbolizing strength and resilience: "Despite the changing seasons, it stands steadfast." These relatable metaphors, drawn from everyday life and local wisdom, helped youth connect more deeply with therapeutic concepts and apply them meaningfully.

4.7 Adjustments in content

Tele-support psychotherapy (TSP) sessions were expanded to address multifaceted challenges such as self-awareness, sexual health, financial literacy, and personal development based on community feedback. This broadened focus aimed to reflect the realities of economic hardship, unemployment, academic pressures, and rural-urban migration. For instance, one participant noted the transformative impact of these sessions, stating, *"In one of the sessions, the doctor told me that these words he's telling me are meant to change my life... That is why I am driving that boda right now" (Naguru Male Group One Male 4).*

Key population communities, particularly transgender individuals, highlighted that their mental health challenges were deeply intertwined with stigma, discrimination, and identity crises. As one respondent articulated, *"One, understanding my sexuality, understanding my family, understanding everything around me. So, that is basically the issue that deals with mental health that most of us, if not most trans people probably within the community, are dealing with depression. Another issue is about stigma and discrimination also leads to mental health issues. Because this stigma and discrimination comes from families, the communities, and everywhere. Places where they seek services, the health service providers, the legal institutions so the whole community, the whole thing is a mess for them" (Respondent 2 KP position 59)*. To enhance cultural relevance and acceptance, TSP integrated traditional healing concepts and utilized storytelling and folk tales, making the intervention more relatable.

4.8 Concepts and goals

Community feedback emphasized the need for more comprehensive services that cater to a broader range of health and welfare aspects. As one respondent put it, *"I was going to need something beyond mental health counseling to actually come to your facility. I wanted to make sure that I was attached to one facility for everything..." (Respondent 3 Key Population, Pos. 105).*

This sentiment was echoed by another community member who articulated the interconnectedness of mental health with other life aspects: *"When you talk about mental health, you're talking about everything. It's not just your mind, it's your life, your ability to work, to love, to live. We needed support that understood that" (Respondent 5, KCTP Makerere Community – Female).* TSP sessions included topics such as financial literacy and social skills, acknowledging the complexity of mental health as intertwined with overall well-being and daily living challenges, thereby highlighting the shift toward a more inclusive and supportive mental health care framework.

4.9 Contextual relevance

The adoption of TSP in Uganda addresses significant gaps in mental health service delivery, especially in areas with limited or no access to traditional in-person interventions. TSP leverages technology to provide accessible mental health support in underserved communities. The lack of mental health services was highlighted during community assessments, where all respondents from Makerere Local Community Males agreed, *"No, there are not,"* when asked about available services. This underscores the need for innovative digital solutions like TSP to fill this gap.

Tele-support psychotherapy (TSP) not only addresses the service shortage but also improves the quality of care. The digital platform allows for consistent, frequent contact between counselors and clients. One participant shared, *"The sessions have really helped. Before, we had to travel to town for any sort of mental health support, which many of us couldn't afford or manage. Now, help is just a phone call away" (Naguru Male Group One, Male 3)*. TSP reduces barriers related to distance, cost, and stigma, demonstrating its potential to transform mental health care in Uganda.

4.10 Methods

Tele-support psychotherapy (TSP) was designed to address concerns about access, confidentiality, and ease of use. Toll-free numbers made the service accessible

DOI: http://dx.doi.org/10.5772/intechopen.1008155

and affordable, as emphasized by one respondent: *"we would expect them to be free. Toll-free. Then professionalism on the other side" (Respondent 6 Key Population, Pos. 123).* Given the widespread use of basic mobile phones, TSP relied on voice calls as the primary communication method. Each session followed a structured format, with counselors using descriptive language, storytelling, and culturally relevant metaphors to simplify complex concepts. Interactive questioning engaged clients, helping them articulate their thoughts. SMS follow-ups reinforced key takeaways and scheduled reminders, enhancing retention and maintaining client participation.

Empathy and active listening were essential skills used by counselors to build rapport and trust, compensating for the lack of non-verbal cues in phone-based interactions. Regular feedback was solicited from clients to ensure that the therapeutic process remained responsive to their needs and preferences. In cases where clients could not reach the call platform or disengaged from the service, counselors exchanged contacts after the initial assessment to follow-up, ensuring that no client was left

TSP session goal	Summary activities
Session 1: Introductions, ground rules, expectations, understanding how tele therapy works	The counselor and client begin by getting to know each other. Tele-support psychotherapy (TSP) is explained using everyday metaphors, such as a trusted guide who listens and offers support. Trust is built through active listening, exploring the client's expectations, validating their feelings, and normalizing therapy. The session concludes with a culturally relevant self-awareness exercise.
Session 2: Education about emotions	The session begins with a warm check-in and recap of the previous session. Provide simple explanations of depression, anxiety, and anger using culturally familiar analogies. Explore the client's experience with these emotions, validate their feelings, and offer culturally relevant education on managing them. Conclude with a self-awareness exercise and a calming breathing technique.
Sessions 3 and 4: Sharing painful experiences	The session begins with a warm check-in and recap. Introduce sharing painful experiences, building trust for sensitive discussions, and encourage the client to share at their own pace. Validate their pain, explore its impact, and guide self-awareness of linked emotions. Introduce storytelling as a coping strategy, followed by a relaxation exercise. Conclude with encouragement.
Session 5: Learning positive coping skills	Session 5 teaches youth clients emotion-focused and problem-focused coping skills through culturally relevant activities. Clients learn techniques like deep breathing, gratitude practice, and problem-solving using relatable metaphors. They explore their current coping strategies, identify challenges, and plan small steps for improvement, promoting emotional regulation and practical problem-solving.
Session 6: Coping with stigma and discrimination	Session 6 focuses on helping youth clients cope with stigma and discrimination. Clients share personal experiences, receive validation, and learn culturally relevant coping strategies, such as seeking support from trusted individuals. Practical homework could include identifying trusted support (e.g., family, friends, and community leaders), practicing reframing negative thoughts into positive ones, and engaging in a community activity that fosters support and belonging.
Sessions 7 and 8: Livelihood skills training	Sessions 7 and 8 focus on teaching livelihood skills through culturally relevant activities. Clients are guided in identifying their strengths, creating simple budgets, exploring small business ideas, and overcoming barriers to employment. Practical financial literacy and networking tips are provided, along with encouragement to stay resilient and patient in building livelihoods. The session concludes with an income-generating project.

Table 2.
The adapted tele-support psychotherapy model.

without support. As one respondent expressed, *"Do follow-ups to ensure the people that have reached out are getting better" (Respondent 8 KCTP Kamwokya Female, Pos. 109).*

Tele-support psychotherapy (TSP) addressed practical and socio-economic challenges by using simple voice calls and SMS to bypass data limitations, ensuring accessibility for non-tech-savvy youth. Counselors, supervisors, and technicians communicated through a WhatsApp group for mentorship and technical support. Local expressions and culturally relevant metaphors made sessions relatable, while flexible scheduling accommodated participants' work, school, and family responsibilities. This approach ensured that TSP was accessible, practical, and sensitive to the socio-economic realities of the target community. **Table 2** illustrates summary activities in the adapted TSP model.

5. Trial results

5.1 Trial participants

The average age of participants is 21.57 years (SD = 4.21), ranging from 15 to 30 years. Most are female (64.33%), with males at 27.67%, and 8% preferring not to disclose. Participants come from Naguru (31.33%), Kamwokya (38.33%), and Makerere (30.33%). Education levels include certificates (42.33%), diplomas (2.67%), bachelor's degrees (2.67%), and others (52.33%). Economically, 67.67% lack income-generating activities, with an average income of 56,926.67 UGX (SD = 117,288.8). Employment status shows 25.67% are employed, while 74.33 are unemployed. These variables were comparable between cases and controls (**Table 3**).

5.2 Indicators of feasibility

The feasibility of delivering TSP to depressed youth in Kampala, as evaluated at 6 and 12 months after randomization, demonstrates a promising capacity for engagement and participation. At 6 months, 71 participants (46.10%) in the TSP arm had received therapy, compared to just 12 participants (8.21%) in the control arm who sought treatment at health centers. 23 (31.94%) attended 1–2 sessions, 19 (26.38%) had attended 3–5 sessions while 30 (41.66%) had attended 6–8 sessions.

At 12 months, 95 participants (61.69%) attended therapy sessions, compared to just 15 participants (10.27%) in the control arm who sought treatment at health centers, reflecting a strong engagement with remote therapy. While some participants attended only 1 or 2 sessions (22.15% attended up to two sessions), a significant proportion (32.63%) attended the full eight sessions. The data clearly demonstrate that engagement with TSP was significantly higher than with SMHS over time. However, 39 (25.23%) and 33 (21.4%) participants at 6 and 12 months, respectively, did not attend any therapy sessions.

5.3 Indicators of acceptability

Participants were asked to indicate whether or not they strongly agreed with the statements shown in **Figure 3**. At the 6-month follow-up, 31.88% of participants strongly agreed that TSP motivated them to make positive changes in their lives, while 27.54% felt it helped them talk to others about their problems. Additionally, 26% believed the intervention reduced their depression. Regarding counselor

Socio-demographic variable	Total sample N=300 N (%)	TSP (N=154) N (%)	SMHS (N=146) N (%)	X^2	P-value
Current residence					
Naguru	94 (31.33)	48 (31.17)	46 (31.51)	0.0064	0.997
Kamwokya	115 (38.33)	59 (38.31)	56 (38.36)		
Makerere	91 (30.33)	47 (30.52)	44 (30.14)		
Gender					
Female	193 (64.33)	108 (70.13)	85 (58.22)	5.2422	0.073
Male	83 (27.67)	34 (22.08)	49 (33.56)		
Prefer not to say	24 (8.00)	12 (7.79)	12 (8.22)		
Age category					
15-17	56 (18.67)	25 (16.23)	31 (21.23)	1.2406	0.538
18-25	184 (61.33)	97 (62.99)	87 (59.59)		
>25	60 (20.00)	32 (20.78)	28 (18.18)		
Marital status					
Married	60 (20.00)	39 (25.32)	21 (14.38)	7.2019	0.027
Separated	14 (4.67)	9 (5.84)	5 (3.42)		
Single	226 (75.33)	106 (68.83)	120 (82.19)		
Education level					
Secondary Education	157 (52.33)	83 (53.90)	74 (50.68)	2.9405	0.230
Certificate	127 (42.33)	60 (38.96)	67 (45.89)		
Diploma/Degree	16 (5.33)	11 (7.14)	5 (3.42)		
Income generating activity					
No	203 (67.67)	100 (64.94)	103 (70.55)	1.0792	0.299
Yes	97 (32.33)	54 (35.06)	43 (29.45)		
Employment status					
Unemployed	223 (74.33)	112 (72.73)	111 (76.03)	0.4278	0.513
Employed	77 (25.67)	42 (27.27)	35 (23.97)		
Saving group involvement					
Not involved	284 (82.67)	125 (81.18)	123 (84.25)	0.4655	0.482
Involved	52 (17.33)	29 (18.83)	23 (15.75)		

Table 3.
Baseline Socio-demographic outcomes by intervention arm.

relationships, 39% strongly agreed that their counselor was respectful, 33.33% felt supported, and 37.68% rated their counselor as knowledgeable. Furthermore, 31.88% would recommend TSP to others, and 28.99% agreed they had learned a lot from the intervention.

By the 12-month follow-up, positive responses significantly increased, with 58% agreeing that TSP motivated positive life changes, 54% communicating more about their problems, and 55% reporting reduced depression. Counselor satisfaction rose, with over 63% praising respectfulness and support. Additionally, 53.21% would recommend TSP, and 50.46% felt they learned a lot. The increasing percentage of participants expressing strong agreement with these key aspects of TSP from 6 to 12 months suggests growing acceptability and satisfaction with the intervention over time.

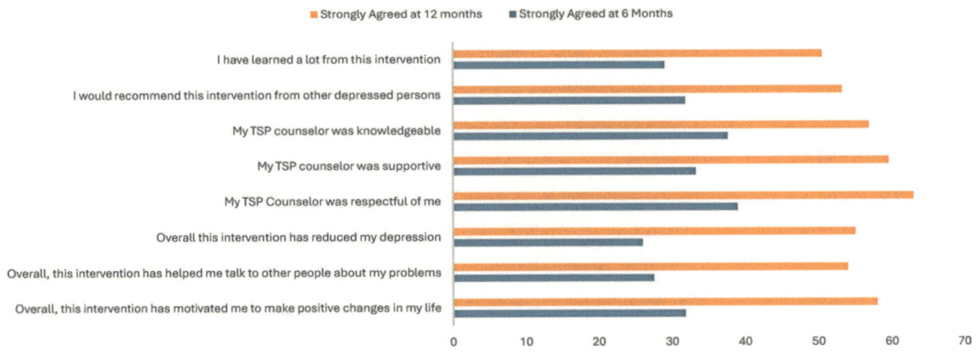

Figure 3.
Youth evaluation of tele support psychotherapy.

5.4 Depression outcomes

Depression symptoms, as measured by SRQ scores, showed a more significant reduction in the TSP group, with a mean score of 4.03 compared to 9.17 in the SMHS group ($p < 0.0001$), demonstrating that TSP was more effective than SMHS in reducing depression over time (**Figure 4**).

5.5 Performance of the call platform and technology challenges faced

The tele-support psychotherapy (TSP) call platform was active between June 2023 and May 2024, facilitating a total of 2752 calls made by 306 unique clients, with therapy sessions delivered by 25 lay counselors. In terms of call success rates, 65.9% of calls were classified as unsuccessful, while 34.1% were successful. Successful calls were defined as those lasting 3 minutes or more, totaling 939 calls, or 34% of all calls made during the 12-month period. Among the successful calls, the majority (43.3%)

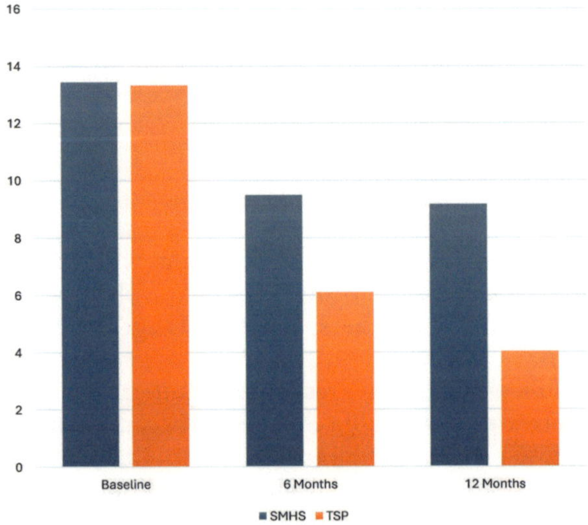

Figure 4.
Effect of TSP on youth with depression symptoms.

DOI: http://dx.doi.org/10.5772/intechopen.1008155

were brief, lasting between 3 and 10 minutes. Additionally, 24.4% lasted 10–30 minutes, 18.4% lasted 31–60 minutes, and 13.8% exceeded 1 hour.

Language data was not captured for 62.6% of the calls, indicating a need for improved data collection. Of the sessions where language was recorded, 27.6% were conducted in Luganda and 9.8% in English. Call volume peaked in October, accounting for 25.5% of all calls, followed by November (19.1%) and June (17.4%). In contrast, fewer calls were recorded in May (0.5%), March (0.7%), and April (1.0%). Engagement levels varied, with June 2023 seeing the highest number of new participants (52), while October had the greatest overall participation (87), including 68 new and 19 returning participants. November had the most returning participants (41), despite fewer new participants (18), suggesting increased client and counselor availability. Participant demographics revealed that most (83.6%) identified as "Others," while females represented 11.4% and males made up 5.0%, highlighting a need for more precise gender data collection to better understand participant engagement.

6. Discussion

This study successfully adapted group support psychotherapy (GSP) into a culturally sensitive tele-support psychotherapy (TSP) model, delivered via mobile phones, to address mild to moderate depression among youth aged 15–30 in Kampala District. The findings strongly align with Bernal and Sáez-Santiago's framework for culturally centered psychosocial interventions, emphasizing the importance of culturally tailored approaches in mental health care [21]. By incorporating local languages, engaging lay counselors from the participants' own communities, and using culturally relevant metaphors and storytelling, TSP not only enhanced participant engagement but also significantly improved mental health outcomes.

The mental health challenges identified among Ugandan youth, such as depression, anxiety, substance use, negative coping mechanisms, stigma, discrimination, low self-esteem, unemployment, and financial stress, are similar to those reported in other sub-Saharan African contexts [22–24]. These issues are often exacerbated by socio-economic hardships and cultural factors that stigmatize mental health conditions, creating barriers to seeking care. Studies have shown that such challenges are prevalent across the region, with young people particularly vulnerable due to limited access to mental health services, financial instability, and societal pressures [25].

In this study, we used mobile phones to deliver therapy to youth, demonstrating how digital interventions can overcome geographic and resource barriers. In sub-Saharan Africa, various strategies, such as task-shifting approaches [26–28], have been employed to address youth mental health challenges. While mobile-based interventions are still emerging, they offer promising, accessible, and scalable solutions [29]. However, research on digital mental health interventions remains limited.

A recent review of 6953 articles on digital mental health interventions for adolescents in sub-Saharan Africa found only six studies that met the inclusion criteria. These studies employed diverse approaches, including text messaging (SMS), phone call reminders, and smartphone apps like WhatsApp or game-based platforms [30], highlighting the experimental nature of mobile mental health interventions and the lack of a standardized approach.

In contrast, our tele-psychotherapy provided direct therapeutic support through voice calls using basic mobile phones, addressing both mental health symptoms and socio-economic factors affecting well-being. The intervention was culturally adapted, incorporating local languages and metaphors, and utilized lay counselors from the community to build trust and relevance. The focus on accessibility and cultural sensitivity allowed TSP to overcome barriers related to smartphone access and internet connectivity, particularly for underserved or remote populations. The flexibility of scheduling and technological adaptability further differentiated TSP from other interventions.

This approach aligns with the World Health Organization's recommendations for task-shifting and integrating mental health into primary care using technology [31]. Mobile platforms offer an effective way to provide continuous support, confidentiality, and flexibility, essential in settings where stigma and resource limitations often impede access to mental health services. Several studies have demonstrated the effectiveness of mobile phones in delivering health services [32, 33]. The widespread ownership of mobile phones in Africa [34], combined with their ability to overcome geographical barriers, makes mobile platforms a particularly relevant and scalable model for expanding mental health services. By integrating local languages, culturally relevant practices, and accessible technology, these platforms can enhance engagement, increase access to care, and deliver tailored mental health support to underserved populations, making them an effective and scalable approach to addressing mental health challenges in resource-constrained environments.

Technological challenges significantly impacted the performance of the call platform in the TSP study, reflecting similar findings from other studies [35]. Issues such as poor system navigation, language selection difficulties, and frequent network disruptions hindered smooth operation, resulting in 69.4% of calls lasting less than 2 minutes, indicating difficulties in participants reaching counselors or navigating the system. Additionally, incomplete data collection on participants' gender and engagement details limited the accuracy of monitoring and evaluating the platform's effectiveness. To mitigate these challenges, counselors and clients exchanged mobile numbers and conducted sessions directly when the platform failed, with session recordings sent to supervisors. However, this workaround compromised data security, confidentiality, and objective tracking, raising concerns about the integrity of data.

Improving the platform's user-friendliness, ensuring easier language selection, and addressing network stability will be crucial for future iterations of the program. Furthermore, enhancements to system design, such as more reliable connectivity and better language integration, will be necessary to ensure consistent engagement and secure interactions. Despite these limitations, the study demonstrated the feasibility and acceptability of mobile phone-based psychotherapy, confirming its potential as a scalable solution to bridge the mental health treatment gap in Africa.

Future evaluations of our TSP study will focus on its long-term effectiveness and cost-effectiveness in both reducing primary outcomes (depression and anxiety) and improving secondary outcomes (stigma, income generation, social functioning). Further investigation into the causal mechanisms behind the intervention's impact will help identify the most effective components. Additionally, understanding barriers and facilitators to implementation, such as technological literacy, network reliability, and cultural factors, will improve program fidelity. Detailed monitoring and evaluation of the call platform's performance over an extended period will provide insights into user engagement patterns and opportunities for technological enhancements.

In conclusion, the adaptation of tele-support psychotherapy for Ugandan youth demonstrated highly promising outcomes in addressing mild to moderate depression. By incorporating culturally sensitive approaches, utilizing accessible technology, local languages, and addressing the socio-economic realities of the target population, the

DOI: http://dx.doi.org/10.5772/intechopen.1008155

intervention significantly improved engagement and delivered positive clinical results. Despite existing technological challenges, the platform's feasibility, cultural relevance, and acceptability highlight its potential as a scalable, sustainable solution for expanding mental health services in low-resource settings. As digital interventions continue to evolve, such culturally adapted models can play a vital role in bridging the mental health treatment gap and improving access to care for underserved populations.

Acknowledgements

This study and report were made possible by the support of the American people through the United States Agency for International Development's Development Innovation Ventures program USAID(DIV), Grant ID Number: 7200AA21FA00017.

The contents are the sole responsibility of Makerere University and do not necessarily reflect the views of USAID or the United States Government.

Conflict of interest

EN-M holds the copyright for the group support psychotherapy manual. All other authors declare no competing interests.

Notes/thanks/other declarations

The authors gratefully acknowledge the valuable contributions of our research assistants, including Happy Banonya, Sowed Mutumba, and Brenda Kabakaari, for their support in conducting this study. We are also deeply appreciative of the dedication shown by the professional and lay counselors, as well as the clients who participated, without whom this research would not have been possible.

Author details

Etheldreda Nakimuli-Mpungu[1,2]*, Jeremiah Mutinye Kwesiga[1], John Mark Bwanika[3], Davis Musinguzi[3], Carol Nakanyike[4], Jane Iya[4], Benedict Akimana[5], Charlotte Hawkins[6], Patricia Cavazos[7], Jean B. Nachega[8], Ed Mills[9], Sabrina Bakeera Kitaka[2] and Musisi Seggane[2]

1 Medical Research Council, Uganda Virus Research Institute, London School of Hygiene and Tropical Medicine, Entebbe, Uganda

2 Makerere University College of Health Sciences, Kampala, Uganda

3 The Medical Concierge Group/Rocket Health, Kampala, Uganda

4 SEEK Group Support Psychotherapy Initiative, Kampala, Uganda

5 Butabika National Referral Mental Hospital, Kampala, Uganda

6 University College London, United Kingdom

7 School of Medicine in St Louis, Washington University, USA

8 Stellenbosch University, Cape Town, South Africa

9 McMaster University, Hamilton, ON, Canada

*Address all correspondence to: etheldreda.nakimuli@lshtm.ac.uk

References

[1] Kim AW, Nyengerai T, Mendenhall E. Evaluating the mental health impacts of the COVID-19 pandemic: Perceived risk of COVID-19 infection and childhood trauma predict adult depressive symptoms in urban South Africa. Psychological Medicine. 2022;**52**(8):1587-1599

[2] Addae EA. COVID-19 pandemic and adolescent health and well-being in sub-Saharan Africa: Who cares? The International Journal of Health Planning and Management. 2021;**36**(1):219

[3] Garrido S, Millington C, Cheers D, Boydell K, Schubert E, Meade T, et al. What works and what doesn't work? A systematic review of digital mental health interventions for depression and anxiety in young people. Frontiers in Psychiatry. 2019;**10**:759

[4] Lehtimaki S, Martic J, Wahl B, Foster KT, Schwalbe N. Evidence on digital mental health interventions for adolescents and young people: Systematic overview. JMIR Mental Health. 2021;**8**(4):e25847

[5] Irvine A, Drew P, Bower P, Brooks H, Gellatly J, Armitage CJ, et al. Are there interactional differences between telephone and face-to-face psychological therapy? A systematic review of comparative studies. Journal of Affective Disorders. 2020;**265**:120-131

[6] Boschen MJ. Mobile telephones and psychotherapy: I. Capability and applicability. The Behavior Therapist. 2009;**32**(8):168-175

[7] Borghouts J, Eikey E, Mark G, De Leon C, Schueller SM, Schneider M, et al. Barriers to and facilitators of user engagement with digital mental health interventions: Systematic review. Journal of Medical Internet Research. 2021;**23**(3):e24387

[8] Lipschitz JM, Pike CK, Hogan TP, Murphy SA, Burdick KE. The engagement problem: A review of engagement with digital mental health interventions and recommendations for a path forward. Current Treatment Options in Psychiatry. 2023;**10**(3):119-135

[9] Schueller SM. Grand challenges in human factors and digital health. Frontiers in Digital Health. 2021;**3**:635112

[10] Schneider ML, Cha BS, Borghouts J, Eikey EV, Schueller SM, Stadnick NA, et al. Individual and organizational outcomes of engaging peers in the cocreation of digital mental health interventions. Psychological Services. Advance online publication. 2024. DOI: 10.1037/ser0000889

[11] Baños RM, Herrero R, Vara MD. What is the current and future status of digital mental health interventions? The Spanish Journal of Psychology. 2022;**25**:e5

[12] Nakimuli-Mpungu E, Smith CM, Wamala K, Okello J, Birungi J, Etukoit M, et al. Long-term effect of group support psychotherapy on depression and HIV treatment outcomes: Secondary analysis of a cluster randomized trial in Uganda. Psychosomatic Medicine. 2022;**84**(8):914-923

[13] Beck JS. Cognitive Behavior Therapy: Basics and Beyond. 2nd ed. New York, NY: Guilford Press; 2011

[14] Bandura A. Human agency in social cognitive theory. The American Psychologist. 1989;**44**:1175-1184

[15] Carney D. Sustainable Livelihoods Approaches: Progress and Possibilities for Change. London: Department for International Development; 2003

[16] Bernal G, Bonilla J, Bellido C. Ecological validity and cultural sensitivity for outcome research: Issues for the cultural adaptation and development of psychosocial treatments with hispanics. Journal of Abnormal Child Psychology. 1995;**23**(1):67-82

[17] Venkatesh V, Thong JYL, Xu X. Consumer acceptance and use of information technology: Extending the unified theory of acceptance and use of technology. MIS Quarterly. 2012;**36**(1):157-178

[18] Ssemugabo C, Nalinya S, Lubega GB, Ndejjo R, Musoke D. Health risks in our environment: Urban slum youth' perspectives using photovoice in Kampala, Uganda. Sustainability. 2021;**13**:248. DOI: 10.3390/su13010248

[19] Purcell DW, Garfein RS, Latka MH, Thiede H, Hudson S, Bonner S, et al. Development, description, and acceptability of a small-group, behavioral intervention to prevent HIV and hepatitis C virus infections among young adult injection drug users. Drug and Alcohol Dependence. 2007;**91**:S73-S80

[20] Beusenberg M, Orley J, World Health Organization. A User's Guide to the Self-Reporting Questionnaire (SRQ). Geneva: World Health Organization; 1994

[21] Bernal G, Sáez-Santiago E. Culturally centered psychosocial interventions. Journal of Community Psychology. 2006;**34**:121-132. DOI: 10.1002/jcop.20096

[22] Juma K, Wekesah FM, Kabiru CW, Izugbara CO. Burden, drivers, and impacts of poor mental health in young people of west and Central Africa: Implications for research and programming. In: West African Youth Challenges and Opportunity Pathways. Cham, Switzerland: Palgrave Macmillan; 2020. pp. 233-265

[23] Jörns-Presentati A, Napp AK, Dessauvagie AS, Stein DJ, Jonker D, Breet E, et al. The prevalence of mental health problems in sub-Saharan adolescents: A systematic review. PLoS One. 2021;**16**(5):e0251689

[24] Bantjes J, Kessler M, Lochner C, Breet E, Bawa A, Roos J, et al. The mental health of university students in South Africa: Results of the national student survey. Journal of Affective Disorders. 2023;**321**:217-226

[25] Patel V, Flisher AJ, Hetrick S, McGorry P. Mental health of young people: A global public-health challenge. The Lancet. 2007;**369**(9569):1302-1313

[26] Nyamayaro P, Bere T, Magidson JF, Simms V, O'Cleirigh C, Chibanda D, et al. A task-shifting problem-solving therapy intervention for depression and barriers to antiretroviral therapy adherence for people living with HIV in Zimbabwe: Case series. Cognitive and Behavioral Practice. 2020;**27**(1):84-92

[27] Lange KW. Task sharing in psychotherapy as a viable global mental health approach in resource-poor countries and also in high-resource settings. Global Health Journal. 2021;**5**(3):120-127

[28] Mabrouk A, Mbithi G, Chongwo E, Too E, Sarki A, Namuguzi M, et al. Mental health interventions for adolescents in sub-Saharan Africa: A scoping review. Frontiers in Psychiatry. 2022;**13**:937723

[29] Naslund JA, Aschbrenner KA. Digital technology for health promotion:

Opportunities to address excess mortality in persons living with severe mental disorders. BMJ Mental Health. 2019;**22**(1):17-22

[30] Madonsela S, Ware LJ, Scott M, Watermeyer J. The development and use of adolescent mobile mental health (m-mhealth) interventions in low-and middle-income countries: A scoping review. South Africa Journal of Psychology. 2023;**53**(4):471-483

[31] World Health Organization. WHO Releases First Guideline on Digital Health Interventions. 2019. Available from: https://www.who.int/news/item/17-04-2019-who-releases-first-guideline-on-digital-health-interventions

[32] Källander K, Tibenderana JK, Akpogheneta OJ, Strachan DL, Hill Z, Ten Asbroek AH, et al. Mobile health (mHealth) approaches and lessons for increased performance and retention of community health workers in low-and middle-income countries: A review. Journal of Medical Internet Research. 2013;**15**(1):1-3

[33] Lund S, Rasch V, Hemed M, Boas IM, Said A, Said K, et al. Mobile phone intervention reduces perinatal mortality in zanzibar: Secondary outcomes of a cluster randomized controlled trial. JMIR mHealth and uHealth. 2014;**2**(1):e2941

[34] Krönke M. Africa's Digital Divide and the Promise of E-Learning. Afrobarometer Policy Paper No. 66. 2020. Available from: https://www.afrobarometer.org/publications/pp66-africas-digital-divide-and-promise-e-learning

[35] Naslund JA, Aschbrenner KA, Araya R, et al. Digital technology for treating and preventing mental disorders in low-income and middle-income countries: A narrative review of the literature. The Lancet Psychiatry. 2017;**4**(6):486-500

Chapter 13

Developing and Testing Group Support Psychotherapy for Children and Adolescents Living with HIV in Uganda

Etheldreda Nakimuli-Mpungu, Kizito Wamala, Carol Nakanyike, Jane Iya, Zubair Lukyamuzi, Justine Diana Namuli, Joyce Sserunjoji Nalugya, Benedict Akimana, Sabrina Bakeera Kitaka, Jean B. Nachega, Ed Mills and Musisi Seggane

Abstract

After successfully developing and evaluating group support psychotherapy (GSP) as a first-line treatment for mild-to-moderate depression in adults, we aimed to adapt and assess this approach for children and adolescents (CA) (ages 10–18) living with HIV. In June 2021, 30 young people and 30 caregivers participated in separate GSP sessions. Data on psychosocial issues and GSP effectiveness were collected through focus groups and interviews. Insights were guided by the ecological validity and culturally sensitive framework. An open-label randomized controlled trial in Kitgum, with 120 participants, registered with PACTR, number 202006601935462, compared GSP plus intensive adherence counseling (IAC) to IAC alone, assessing feasibility, acceptability, depression, anxiety, and HIV treatment outcomes. We found that CA with HIV struggled with self-esteem issues, suicidal thoughts, medication adherence, and food insecurity, alongside stigma, discrimination, and limited mental health programs. The adult GSP model was adapted for CA by creating gender- and age-specific groups, simplifying language, and incorporating play and expressive art activities. Caregivers were concurrently engaged with the adult GSP model. GSP participants showed a significantly greater reduction in depression symptoms compared to IAC participants.

Keywords: group support psychotherapy, children, adolescents, depression, anxiety, HIV/AIDS, viral suppression, Uganda

IntechOpen

1. Introduction

Human immunodeficiency virus (HIV) infection remains a significant public health crisis. The Joint United Nations Programme on HIV/AIDS (UNAIDS) reports that by the end of 2021, 1.15 million children under the age of 15 had HIV, and 97,500 children had died from HIV-related causes. Despite a decline in overall infections since 2010, the morbidity and mortality among children have risen, highlighting the critical need for focused interventions [1].

In Uganda, 98,000 children under the age of 15 live with HIV [2], with half experiencing significant psychological distress. This highlights the need for comprehensive care strategies to address both the physical and mental health impacts of HIV on this vulnerable group [3–6]. Research shows that unrecognized and untreated depression in adolescents with HIV is associated with cognitive impairment [7], poor academic performance [8], substance abuse [9], and risky sexual behavior [10], which heighten HIV transmission risks [11] and worsen health outcomes [12]. Despite the growing recognition of mental health issues among children and adolescents in Africa, there remains a significant scarcity of psychotherapeutic interventions tailored to this demographic. Limited resources, both financial and human, hinder the development and implementation of specialized mental health services [13].

Group support psychotherapy (GSP) has proven to be a cost-effective and enduring solution for alleviating mild-to-moderate depression among HIV-positive adults in Uganda, with benefits extending to enhanced viral suppression [14]. However, its applicability and effectiveness for young people living with HIV is yet to be explored, underscoring a crucial need to adapt and tailor GSP to meet the unique mental health and developmental needs of children and adolescents.

The adaptation of an adult GSP model into a child and adolescent (CA) model can be significantly informed by integrating the ecological validity and culturally sensitive framework [15] with key child development theories. Piaget's cognitive development theory emphasizes the need for concrete and simple language, alongside hands-on activities and visual aids, to match the cognitive stages of children [16].

Erikson's stages of psychosocial development stress the importance of fostering trust, autonomy, and initiative in children by creating supportive environments that encourage exploration and self-expression [17]. Bronfenbrenner's Ecological Systems Theory provides a comprehensive framework that considers the multiple environmental systems influencing a child's development, including family, school, and broader societal contexts, emphasizing the need for interventions that are contextually and culturally relevant [18].

Gardner's theory of multiple intelligences advocates for a diverse range of activities catering to different intelligences, such as musical, spatial, and interpersonal, ensuring that all children can engage meaningfully in the therapy process [19]. Lave and Wenger's [20] situated learning theory underscores the importance of learning in social contexts and through participation in communities of practice, which can be facilitated through group therapy sessions that mimic real-life social interactions. Bowlby and Ainsworth's attachment theory emphasizes the creation of secure attachments within therapeutic settings, ensuring that children feel safe and supported to explore their emotions and experiences [21].

By integrating these theories within the ecological validity and culturally sensitive framework, the adapted GSP model can address the social, emotional, developmental, economic, and cultural challenges faced by young people. This comprehensive approach ensures that the therapy is not only developmentally appropriate but also culturally resonant, enhancing its effectiveness and relevance. Tailoring the language, activities, and support structures to the specific needs and contexts of children and adolescents helps create an inclusive, engaging, and supportive therapeutic environment, ultimately promoting better mental health outcomes.

In this chapter, we detail the participatory process used to adapt the adult group support psychotherapy (GSP) model into the child and adolescent (CA) model and present the depression treatment outcomes from a pilot randomized trial of the adapted model among children and adolescents living with HIV.

2. Materials and methods

2.1 Study design and settings

The study was conducted at Kitgum District General Hospital's HIV clinic, serving 3000 PLHIV, including 250 adolescents (ages 10–18). Initially, 30 dyads of adolescents living with HIV and their caregivers participated in adult GSP sessions, followed by focus group discussions. The hospital serves a population of 232,000, primarily small-scale farmers and herders. The district endured a two-decade civil war (1987–2007), leading to the collapse of healthcare systems and infrastructure.

2.2 The adult GSP model

The adult GSP model treats depression by enhancing emotional and social support and improving the ability to practice positive coping and income-generating (livelihood) skills. The intervention consists of eight weekly sessions, and each session lasts for 2–3 hours. In formulating GSP, an initial qualitative study [22] was conducted to understand local perspectives on depression and existing treatment methods within the population in question. This research revealed common coping strategies in line with those reported in other African contexts, such as reliance on faith, social engagement, participation in community life, diversionary activities, acceptance, and the psychological process of reinterpreting or finding meaning in adverse experiences [23]. The GSP sessions were structured with opening and closing rituals, including songs, dances, or prayers selected by the group, to foster cultural connection and personal investment. The program also included homework that aimed to encourage involvement in community events and building social networks.

The first GSP session concentrated on establishing the group's functioning, outlining expectations, setting rules, and emphasizing commitment. Participants were partnered and tasked with connecting outside the sessions, then reporting back on their interactions. The second meeting focused on identifying depression's precipitators, symptoms, and treatment modalities, as well as the interplay between depression and HIV. This was followed by an exercise where participants communicated their insights with others in their community. This step addressed local attributions of depression to supernatural causes, such as ancestral spirits and witchcraft, emphasizing the importance of psychoeducation to bolster engagement and reduce dropout rates from treatment programs [24].

During the third and fourth sessions, individuals shared their most distressing personal stories and were then encouraged to discuss other concerns with a respected community or family elder. Such emotional release has been observed to reduce stress, clarify thoughts, and enhance emotional stability and overall well-being [25]. In sessions five and six, the discussion centered on personal methods of coping with depression, with the facilitator distinguishing between constructive and detrimental strategies.

The final sessions were devoted to teaching skills for generating income, responding to the identified necessity for an approach that simultaneously addresses depression symptoms and provides vocational training to better the economic standing of participants. The interconnection between mental health issues and poverty is well documented, prompting calls for interventions aimed at disrupting this detrimental feedback loop [26].

2.3 The adaptation process

We used a participatory adaptation process within a community partnership formed over the past decade during the development and evaluation of the adult group support psychotherapy (GSP) model. Over the past 10 years, through research, community engagement, and consultation with local cultural experts, the principal investigator (ENM) developed working relationships with community leaders, the local district officials, and the leadership of the community HIV clinics in northern Uganda. Consequently, we gained a deep understanding of the community's core values, beliefs, and traditions. We used this knowledge to guide the adaptation of therapy activities to ensure they resonate with children and adolescents living with HIV.

First, we supported the creation of a community advisory board that included a community leader, child probation officer, faith healer, community psychologist, and community member. The formation of this board was guided by the principle of maintaining both participants and community trust as embedded in the community-based participatory research theory [27]. The major roles of the board were to provide the research team with feedback about the research plan and provide input in the development of the theoretical framework for understanding adolescent mental health and psychosocial challenges.

Second, we delivered the available adult GSP to adolescents and their caregivers, followed by conducting focus group discussions (FGDs) to obtain information on the suitability of the intervention for the young people. This was supplemented with conducting key informant interviews (KII) with child and adolescent psychologists, psychiatrists and caregivers to obtain their perspectives on how the GSP training and counseling manuals could be enhanced with content that was culturally and developmentally suited to address the problems faced by young people living with HIV. Details of this qualitative research are described below.

Third, we conducted an expert consultation workshop in Kampala with child psychiatrists and child counseling psychologists who had previously worked with children living with HIV and other vulnerable children (victims of sexual trafficking). The aim of the workshop was to review findings from the literature review and qualitative study to inform adaptations in intervention content and training materials using the ecological validity and culturally sensitive framework [15].

2.4 Study population and sampling procedures

In the qualitative phase of the study, we identified HIV-positive CA (aged 10–18) with unsuppressed viral load 6 months after initiating anti-retroviral therapy (ART) and their caregivers in Kitgum district and surrounding areas. Thirty participants (30 adolescents and 28 caregivers) were randomly selected from the daily attendance of

Kitgum Hospital HIV clinic and consented to enroll in the study. Participants were divided into gender-specific groups of 10–12 participants and administered the adult version of GSP. Group facilitators were purposively selected HIV care providers with a minimum qualification of a diploma and were of the same gender as the facilitated participants. Purposively selected stakeholders, including psychologists, pediatricians, and child and adolescent psychiatrists were also involved in the study. The selection criteria for study participation aimed at increasing trust and ownership of the intervention in the target population.

2.5 Data collection and procedures

Participants were identified and recruited from Kitgum General Hospital HIV clinic, grouped into three groups and each group was administered 8 weekly sessions of the existing adult version of GSP. After completion of all the sessions, participants were gathered in FGD. Focus group discussions (FGDs) were conducted at community health centers. Six FGDs were conducted with—the adolescents (N = 2), their caregivers (N = 2), and their HIV care providers (N = 2). The standard method of conducting FGD was used [20].

All participants completed a demographic questionnaire before participating in the FGDs. Each FGD was conducted in the local language and lasted for approximately 90 minutes. Refreshments and meals were provided during the discussions, and transportation reimbursement and time compensation were provided. Community leaders, HIV care providers, psychologists, pediatricians, community leaders, health workers, and child and adolescent counseling psychologists were purposely selected for key informant interviews (KIIs), which lasted for about 90 minutes. During interviews, the key informants were asked to evaluate the structure of GSP using the eight elements of the ecological validity and culturally sensitive framework [15].

During the focus group discussions and key informant interviews, the responses were documented on flip charts to effectively showcase the participants' perspectives, opinions, and feedback. Meanwhile, the co-facilitator compiled a summary of the responses in a separate notebook. At the conclusion of the session, these summaries were reviewed to confirm the most common themes that emerged from the engagement.

During the trial phase, a pilot single-blinded randomized controlled trial was carried out to evaluate the feasibility, acceptability, and initial impact of GSP on mental health outcomes. We allocated 120 youth/caregiver pairs evenly between two groups: one receiving both GSP and IAC, and the other receiving only IAC. Assessments were made at the start of the trial, as well as 3 and 6 months after completing the treatment. Alongside the main trial, a longitudinal process evaluation involving both qualitative and quantitative methods was performed to monitor the delivery of the GSP-IAC by trained lay health workers, examining the intervention's fidelity and participants' reactions to different aspects of the program.

The research protocol was recorded in the Pan African Clinical Trials Registry and underwent review and approval by the Research Ethics Committee of the Makerere University School of Health Sciences as well as the Uganda National Council of Science and Technology. Each participant gave their written informed consent before taking part and was compensated for travel expenses. The reporting of the trial was consistent with the SPIRIT (Standard Protocol Items: Recommendations for Interventional Trials) guidelines for intervention trials [28] and adhered to the CONSORT guidelines for pilot randomized trials [29].

2.6 Participant eligibility criteria, recruitment, and masking

For inclusion in the study, each participant pair had to include a young HIV-positive individual (aged 10–18) with a viral load of 1000 copies/ml or higher 6 months following the start of their initial antiretroviral therapy (ART), accompanied by a caregiver aged 19 or older. Dyads were not eligible if they had sensory impairments like vision or hearing loss, active major mental illnesses that were not being treated (such as psychosis, mania, or severe depression with high suicide risk), or serious health issues (like active tuberculosis or pneumonia) that could hinder their involvement in the study activities.

All study participants were recruited from community-based HIV clinics located in the Kitgum district. The participants were identified by their HIV care providers as non-responders to their existing antiretroviral (ARV) treatment, defined by local clinic standards as having a viral load over 1000 copies/ml. Research assistants (RAs) and other study staff worked with clinic personnel to identify these individuals during their routine medication refill visits. The RAs, who were proficient in Luo and experienced in both GSP research and HIV clinical care, underwent thorough training on the study protocol and received weekly supervision from the project coordinator, who is a social worker. Screening for psychosis and mania was conducted using brief screening questions for psychotic and manic symptoms, along with the SAD PERSONS scale for high suicide risk. Those showing psychotic or manic symptoms or considered high risk for suicide were excluded from the study.

All eligible young people (ages 10–18) and their caregivers were approached by research assistants who explained the study procedures, determined eligibility, and obtained informed assent/consent. Upon obtaining consent, each pair of participants underwent an initial assessment conducted by an interviewer that included demographic and psychosocial evaluations. Subsequently, they were randomly allocated to either receive both group support psychotherapy (GSP) and individualized antiretroviral counseling (IAC) or only the IAC intervention.

Randomization was conducted using urn randomization, where each participant picked from opaque envelopes containing pieces of paper. Young males and females were separated into two groups, each presented with envelopes containing papers marked X or Y. Participants who selected papers labeled X received both GSP and IAC, whereas those who chose papers labeled Y were given only IAC. This method of assignment was also applied to caregivers. Although participants were aware of their intervention group, the identity of the groups was concealed from independent evaluators and data analysts who measured outcomes.

2.7 Outcome measures

Feasibility was evaluated by measuring the uptake of the intervention among eligible participants (Reach), tracking the number who attended all eight sessions (Dose delivered), and noting the number who did not complete the study (Attrition), as documented in the attendance logs. Acceptability was assessed using a 9-item survey [30] that evaluated participants' satisfaction, the knowledge and attitudes of the group facilitators, and the participants' perceptions of the intervention's effectiveness in alleviating depression.

Anxiety and depression symptoms were measured using the 25-item revised child and adolescent anxiety and depression scale (RCADS-25). While this tool has not undergone validation in Ugandan populations, its content is considered to have face validity. The RCADS-25 has been extensively utilized across Europe, North, and South America, demonstrating internal reliability scores between 0.87 and 0.90 [31, 32], along with a sensitivity of 90% and a specificity of 75% [33]. The scores from the RCADS were treated as a continuous variable in our analysis.

2.8 Data analysis

Data from focus group discussions (FGD) and key informant interviews (KII) were audiotaped and transcribed verbatim. A grounded theory approach [34] was employed to identify themes within the transcripts. To explore the challenges related to the lived experiences of children and adolescents living with HIV, an inductive thematic analysis [35] was conducted using the ecological framework [36].

Researchers independently reviewed the transcripts, conducting open coding to identify emerging themes and concerns. They then met to harmonize provisional synthetic codes. This was followed by focused coding, with researchers reconvening to discuss and revise the coding of both new and existing transcripts as needed. The qualitative data analysis software ATLAS.ti 8 (ATLAS.ti Scientific Software Development GmbH, Berlin, Germany) [37] was used for analysis, facilitating coding, data retrieval, theory building, and analysis. Guided by the ecological validity and culturally sensitive framework [15], the findings from this project were used to inform specific modifications to the adult group support psychotherapy (GSP) model.

Quantitative data analysis involved conducting bivariate analyses to compare baseline demographic and psychosocial variables between the study groups. We used cluster-adjusted chi-square tests for categorical variables and independent two-sample t-tests for continuous variables. Even though participants were randomized individually to either GSP & IAC or IAC alone, the interventions were administered in group settings (clusters). Given the likelihood of correlation among participants within each cluster, we employed cluster-level analyses to adjust for intra-cluster correlation.

2.9 Ethical considerations

The study protocol was presented to the relevant institutional review boards. The consent and assent forms for study participation were translated into the local language (Luo) and read aloud to all participants for easy comprehension. Separate consent/assent for audiotaping the FGDs was also obtained from all participants.

All participants received a transportation reimbursement calculated according to the distance traveled by the participant who came from the furthest location.

Additionally, refreshments were provided following each focus group discussion and group support session. Health workers who led these sessions were compensated with a financial incentive of $3 USD per session. Given that group support psychotherapy was integrated as an ongoing service at Kitgum General Hospital, every participant in the study had the opportunity to access GSP, particularly if it demonstrated significant benefits in enhancing adherence to antiretroviral therapy and viral load suppression. This trial was registered with the Pan African Clinical Trials Registry Number PACTR202006601935462.

2.10 Qualitative results

A total of 30 participants: 30 adolescents and 28 caregivers received the adult version of GSP, and all of them participated in the FGDs. Adolescents had a mean age 12 ± 1.6 and the majority was female, 54.5%. The mean age of caregivers was 38 ± 3.6 years. The mean age of health workers was 35 ± 4.6 years. Stakeholders included psychologists, pediatricians, and psychiatrists (**Table 1**).

2.11 Challenges of children and adolescents living with HIV

Challenges faced by children and adolescents (CA) living with HIV were categorized using the ecological framework as follows. At the individual level, adherence to medication was a significant challenge, with many young people struggling to remember or refusing to take their medication. Additionally, food insecurity

Characteristics	Young people N = 30	Caregivers N = 28	Stakeholders N = 20
Sex			
Males	14	10	8
Females	16	18	12
Age			
11–20	30	0	
21–30	0	4	8
31–40	0	12	6
41–50	0	10	4
51–60	0	2	2
Highest level of education			
Primary education	20		
Secondary education	0	8	22
Certificate	0	0	20
Diploma	0	0	10
University degree	10	0	8
Profession			
Peasant farmer	—	28	—
HIV care providers	8		
Counseling psychologists	—	—	4
Psychiatrist	—	—	2
Social worker	—	—	2
Pediatrician	—	—	1
Teacher	—	—	2
Hospital administrator	—	—	1

Table 1.
Characteristics of key informants and focus group discussion participants.

exacerbated these difficulties, as a lack of proper nutrition affected medication intake. Behavioral problems, including low self-esteem, social withdrawal, lack of interest in daily activities, and absenteeism from school, further complicate their lives. Suicidal thoughts and attempts also emerge from feelings of hopelessness and the perception that having HIV is a death sentence. Additionally, there are negative perceptions of the future, leading to a lack of motivation and hope, with many believing those with HIV will never become successful.

At the interpersonal level, children and adolescents reported experiencing significant social isolation due to stigma from family, community members, and schools. This stigma often results in them being shunned and left to feel alone. In addition to social isolation, there is a pervasive lack of parental support. Many youths face inadequate care and negative attitudes from their parents, who sometimes view them as outcasts. Such attitudes from family members are detrimental, as they reinforce feelings of worthlessness and hopelessness.

Fear of disclosing their HIV status is another significant issue for these CA. They often fear revealing their status to others due to the potential for increased stigma and rejection. This fear is particularly pronounced in school settings, where the risk of being ostracized by peers is high. This fear of disclosure perpetuates a cycle of secrecy and isolation, preventing them from seeking the support and understanding they need from others.

At the community level, one of the significant challenges faced by CAs living with HIV is the long distance to health facilities for medication. Many CA are required to travel great distances, often up to 15 km or more, to reach the nearest health center. This poses a substantial barrier to consistent medication adherence, as traveling such distances can be exhausting, time-consuming, and costly. Additionally, poverty and the lack of basic needs further exacerbate these challenges. Kitgum, like many other areas, experiences high poverty rates, which have a profound impact on the ability of families to meet their basic needs. Many families live in conditions where they struggle to afford food, shelter, and other essentials, often living "hand to mouth." This economic hardship means that priorities such as healthcare and medication may fall by the wayside, leading to missed medication refills and inconsistent treatment.

At the societal level, one of the key challenges faced by young people living with HIV is the inadequacy of government programs specifically targeting their needs. Despite the growing recognition of HIV/AIDS as a public health issue, there remains a significant gap in services and support systems designed to address the unique mental health challenges faced by children and adolescents with HIV. Many governmental initiatives fail to provide tailored interventions for this vulnerable group. As a result, their specific emotional and developmental needs are often overlooked. Additionally, the absence of professional training and awareness among healthcare providers further exacerbates the issue, as it limits the ability to offer compassionate and effective care. **Table 2** provides the supporting statements from key informants (KI) and focus group discussions (FGDs).

2.12 Relevance of GSP to challenges of children and adolescents living with HIV

Study participants deemed GSP to be relevant in addressing the highlighted CA challenges. The first session, which focuses on introductions, ground rules, expectations, and understanding how therapy works, can help establish a safe environment that promotes trust and confidentiality, crucial for managing anxiety and encouraging participants to share their experiences. In the second session, education about

Ecological level	CA challenge	Supporting statement
Individual	Adherence to medication	*"The biggest problem they have is how to take their medicine. Like when someone is supposed to take their medicine at 7 am, you find that by 8 am, they have not yet taken their medicine." -ART clinic Nurse*
	Food insecurity	*"Some of them tell you I take mangoes, then I take my ARVs, some of them take on an empty stomach…I better die of hunger than these ARVs." -ART clinic Nurse* *I was following up 40 CA aged around 10 who had malnutrition at the same time, and within three months 12 of them died. So, the consequence of not attending to their problems will cause many to die, particularly due to rampant extreme levels of poverty" -Hospital Administrator*
	Behavioral problems	*"They fear interacting with colleagues because they fear that at one time, they may reveal what is going on with them." -Science teacher*
	Suicidal thoughts and attempts	*"Some of them may have suicidal ideas…they perceive having HIV as a death sentence." -ART clinic Nurse*
	Negative perceptions of future	*"People always believe that…those ones with HIV will have no future, they will never become successful." -Adolescent living with HIV*
Interpersonal	Stigma and discrimination	*"There is a problem of social stigma from other children. Some of their colleagues abuse them because they are HIV positive." -Science teacher* *"People refuse to sit with me, and now I sit alone because even if I go to sit with them, they get away from me and leave me alone. (she breaks down in tears)." -Adolescent living with HIV*
	Lack of parental support	*"These youths' parents are not responsible…some of them consider these children outcasts and they use offensive language…'you are already a moving corpse.'" -Probation Officer*
	Fear of disclosing HIV status	*"It depends on the circumstances they find themselves in, for example, if they are at school you find them isolated…they fear that at one time they may reveal what is going on with them."*
Community	Distance to healthcare facilities	*"Some of them travel 15 km, 10 km coming to the facility that's the major challenge." -Village health worker*
	Poverty and lack of basic needs	*"The level of poverty in Kitgum is very high…so most of these people live hand to mouth…they keep on missing their refills." -hospital administrator*
Societal	Lack of targeted programs	*"There is not much attention to these categories of children and youth living with HIV/AIDS…it requires a professional to handle because…life is difficult." -Probation officer*

Table 2.
Challenges faced by children and adolescents (CA) living with HIV.

emotions will assist CA in managing intense feelings like anger, shame, guilt, and sadness. Sessions three and four focus on sharing painful experiences, which reduces isolation by increasing social support and connections through therapeutic sharing.

The fifth and sixth sessions involve learning positive coping skills, which encourage peer support and experience sharing. This approach helps participants develop strategies for managing relationship challenges, including stigma and discrimination. Sessions seven and eight provide livelihood skills training, equipping caregivers with tools to improve their socioeconomic status, thereby addressing household economic hardships that impact mental health. Empowering CA with practical skills also allows them to support their caregivers and appreciate their efforts.

The GSP sessions also tackle young people's challenges, underscoring the program's relevance. For instance, fear of visiting health centers can be mitigated by incorporating peer leaders, creating a friendly environment where adolescents feel comfortable discussing their issues.

To address gender-specific challenges, the program maintains separate groups for girls and boys and different age groups, facilitating open discussions about these issues. Transportation barriers are addressed by localizing sessions in villages or local health facilities and training health workers to deliver them locally. This approach makes regular attendance easier for young people, as noted by village health workers who highlighted the challenges of traveling long distances to facilities.

Finally, providing caregivers with their own GSP sessions alleviates their stress and equips them with knowledge and skills to support the CA effectively, enhancing the overall support system for young people. **Table 3**, which provides supporting statements from key informants (KI) and focus group discussions (FGDs), illustrates the relevance of group support psychotherapy in addressing these challenges for children and adolescents.

2.13 Adaptations to GSP using the ecological validity and culturally sensitive framework

2.13.1 Culturally appropriate language

We ensured that the therapist communicated in the local language of the group members to foster better understanding and connection. When explaining complex psychological terms to children or adolescents, we used language that matched their

Problem	GSP sessions	Relevance to children and adolescents (CA)	Supporting statements from FGDs and KIs
Stigma and discrimination	*Session 1*: Introductions, ground rules, expectations, understanding how therapy works	GSP establishes a safe environment, promotes trust, confidentiality, and clear expectations, helping CA manage anxiety, and share experiences.	*"I have a sister who keeps telling other friends in the village that I have HIV and I am going to spread it to them" -Adolescent living with HIV* *We have a boy who refused school up to date because he was being abused at school by calling him HIV. Fellow students used to discriminate him and could not share anything with him including a seat. -HIV Care Provider*
Intense emotions	*Session 2*: Education about emotions and how they are affected by living with a chronic illness	GSP aids CA in managing intense emotions like anger and sadness, promoting healthy expression, and addressing stigma and fear of disclosure.	*"People at home and friends always believe that those with HIV have no future, and they will never become successful. Such thinking and sayings drive the anger in me." -Adolescent living with HIV*

Problem	**GSP sessions**	**Relevance to children and adolescents (CA)**	**Supporting statements from FGDs and KIs**
Isolation and traumatic experiences	*Sessions 3 and 4:* Sharing painful experiences	Therapeutic sharing in GSP reduces isolation by encouraging participants to share their stories, fostering community support.	*Sharing problems and advice among ourselves has made me feel so much better. -Adolescent living with HIV* *Meeting like this has brought some positive changes to some people... After attending the group... they found out that the problem of one person was bigger than their own problem. -ART Clinic Nurse*
Sexual health and relationship challenges Stigma and discrimination	*Sessions 5 and 6*: Learning positive coping skills	GSP encourages peer support and sharing of experiences, allowing participants to learn from one another and develop strategies for managing relationship challenges.	*We have a boy who refused school up to date because he was being abused at school by calling him HIV. Fellow students used to discriminate him and could not share anything with him including a seat. -HIV Care Provider*
Economic hardships	*Sessions 7 and 8*: Learning livelihood skills	Livelihood skills training in GSP equips caregivers with tools to enhance their socioeconomic status, to alleviate household economic hardships that contribute to mental health challenges. Empowering children and adolescents with practical skills enables them to support their caregivers and appreciate their efforts.	*The level of poverty in Kitgum is very high... so most of these people live hand to mouth... they keep on missing their refills. -HIV care provider*
Young people's challenges that indicate the relevance of the GSP structure			
Fear of going to health centers	Incorporate peer leaders	Training peer leaders to work with health workers, fostering a friendly therapy environment where adolescents feel comfortable discussing their issues.	*"These adolescents fear to come to the clinic. Some come and stop at the gate..." -ART Clinic Nurse*
Gender-specific challenges	Maintaining gender-specific and age-specific groups	Forming separate groups for girls and boys, and for different age groups, to facilitate open discussions about gender-specific and age-specific challenges.	*"For me the way the intervention has helped me make friends, meeting others, and sharing thoughts and ideas. This has caused all my negative thoughts to disappear" -Adolescent living with HIV*

Problem	GSP sessions	Relevance to children and adolescents (CA)	Supporting statements from FGDs and KIs
Transportation barriers	Localizing sessions	Conducting GSP sessions in villages or local health facilities, and training health workers to deliver them locally, addresses transportation challenges and makes regular attendance easier for young people.	*"Some of them travel 15 km, 10 km coming to the facility that's the major challenge". -Village health worker "Traveling long distances for the sessions will also stop them due to lack of transport" -Village health worker*
Lack of support from caregivers	Involving caregivers in GSP sessions	Including caregivers in separate GSP sessions alleviates their stress, equips them to care for children and adolescents effectively, and enhances the support system for young people.	*"The parents can give guidance and counseling to the children so that children can have the courage take their medicine". -Village health worker "My sisters used to insult me, and I used to feel like nobody loved me. But ever since my family and siblings were talked to in this project, such problems no longer exist" -Adolescent living with HIV*

Table 3.
The relevance of GSP model in addressing challenges for children and adolescents.

level of understanding. For example, instead of describing depression as a clinical condition, it was explained as "feeling really sad or like there's a heavy cloud always above you, and not wanting to do things you normally enjoy, like playing with friends or helping with family chores." This approach helped children relate the concept to their daily experiences and surroundings. Using metaphors involving familiar environmental elements, like a heavy cloud, made the concept more tangible and relatable. Tailoring explanations to the cultural and everyday experiences of the child ensured that the message was both understandable and meaningful.

Drug abuse was described as "using medicine, alcohol, or other substances in a way that isn't safe." It might feel good at first, like eating too many sweets or chewing sugarcane all the time because they taste good, but it can harm your body and mind, making you very sick or unable to do things you love. We used locally familiar items such as sweets and sugarcane, which are common in many African settings, to draw a parallel with overindulgence. This approach helped children better relate to the concept of immediate pleasure leading to long-term harm, making the message more impactful and understandable.

Guilt was described as "feeling sorry or bad because you thought you did something wrong, even if you didn't mean to, like when you accidentally broke your friend's toy and felt really bad inside." Anger was likened to "feeling really mad or upset about something, like a big storm inside you, such as when someone took your favorite toy without asking, and it made you want to shout or cry." Instead of "anxiety disorder," we used phrases like "feeling worried a lot" or "having a lot of nervous feelings." These explanations helped children and adolescents grasp these complex emotions in a way that made sense to them.

All therapy manuals and materials were also translated into the local language, allowing participants to fully engage with the content and apply it to their everyday lives. When addressing sensitive issues like stigma, using respectful and culturally relevant terms can help clients feel valued and understood, making them more likely to open up about their experiences. As one child expressed, *"People refuse to sit with me, and now I sit alone because even if I go to sit with them, they get away from me and leave me alone. (she breaks down in tears)." Child living with HIV.*

Another adolescent girl expressed "I have a sister who keeps going to other friends in the village, saying "my sister has HIV, and she is going to spread the virus to other people"." Adolescent living with HIV. This highlights the harmful impact of stigma and the importance of fostering a supportive environment.

2.13.2 Person

Facility-based health workers were recruited and trained to serve as trainers and supervisors for community-based lay health workers, who were responsible for delivering therapy in community settings. This approach aimed to enhance accessibility and ensure therapy was grounded in the community context by leveraging existing health infrastructure and personnel. Additionally, study participants recommended that the sessions be led by adolescent peers, with girls leading sessions for other girls and boys doing the same for boys. As one adolescent boy noted, "*Having someone my age who understands what I'm going through makes it easier to open up and really talk about things.*"

Health workers emphasized the need for age and sex categorization in the intervention, noting that adolescents often become emotional during the first session but grow stronger and more engaged in subsequent sessions. They also observed that positive peer interactions emerge, with those who adhere well to ART encouraging their peers to do the same. As one health worker shared, *"It's powerful to see how, over time, the tears dry up and peers start lifting each other up and promoting healthy habits."*

2.13.3 Metaphors

To address issues like negative self-image, persistent sadness, anger, and low self-esteem, incorporating metaphors such as prayers, songs, dances, and riddles were found to be highly effective. As one HIV care provider shared during a focus group discussion, "*People struggling with these feelings often need prayers first; they might turn to the church for support. If that doesn't help, then seeking guidance from counselors at the hospital could be the next step.*"

Through the use of prayer as an opening and closing ritual, group members were able to express gratitude, release their worries, and gain hope and confidence as they surrendered their burdens to a "higher power." This practice allowed them to reflect on their blessings, seek solace, and find strength in their faith. By placing their concerns in the hands of a higher power, they often felt a sense of relief and renewed hope, which helped them cope with negative emotions and fostered a sense of inner peace and resilience.

Incorporating cultural symbols and shared cultural metaphors helped explain these concepts in a way that resonated with children and adolescents. These culturally familiar and meaningful tools allowed young people to express and understand their emotions more naturally, facilitating better communication and emotional processing. For instance, the cycle of the sun can be a powerful symbol: *"Emotions can be like the sun. Some days are bright and sunny, and other days might be a bit cloudy or even stormy."* This metaphor helped them understand that emotions could change and that it was normal to experience a range of feelings. By using these culturally relevant tools, therapy became more accessible and meaningful, helping participants navigate their emotions and improve their mental well-being.

Coping with negative emotions was effectively illustrated through riddles. For example, consider the riddle: *"I'm a balloon filled with air. The more you push, the bigger I get, but if you let me go, I'll fly away. What am I?"* The answer is "*anger.*" This metaphor helped explain how anger could build up inside, growing more intense if left unchecked, much like a balloon inflating with air. However, just as a balloon could be released to deflate or fly away, anger too could be managed and released through healthy coping strategies such as talking it out, practicing deep breathing, or taking a break. This riddle served as a creative way to understand and manage the buildup and release of anger, promoting emotional awareness and control.

2.13.4 Content

To address mental health issues like depression using the CA GSP model, we employed a range of culturally relevant approaches. We used traditional folktales that depicted characters overcoming challenges or seeking wisdom from elders. For instance, a story about a village hero who faced a dark time but found hope and strength through community support helped participants relate to their own struggles and see the importance of seeking help.

Role-playing activities were integrated, where participants acted out scenarios involving emotional struggles and solutions. For example, adolescents might role-play a situation where they help a friend who feels isolated, allowing them to practice empathy and problem-solving in a supportive environment.

We included traditional practices such as group gatherings for sharing experiences, which provided a sense of community and support. For instance, organizing communal drumming sessions or group dances allowed participants to express their emotions in a culturally familiar and therapeutic way.

Art therapy was used where participants created visual representations of their feelings. For example, drawings helped them articulate emotions that were difficult to express verbally. These artworks were then discussed in group settings to facilitate understanding and emotional processing.

Music therapy involved using traditional songs and rhythms to explore and express emotions. For example, participants performed songs that reflect themes of struggle and resilience, which helped them connect with their feelings and find comfort through familiar cultural expressions.

Traditional beliefs were acknowledged, for example emotional disturbances were explained in a way that respects both scientific and cultural perspectives. For example, while some may attribute mental health problems to ancestral spirits or witchcraft, it is important to recognize these beliefs and discuss how they intersect with modern understandings of mental illness. As one participant in a focus group discussion from Kitgum district noted, *"Spirits of the dead can get on somebody and cause mental illness."* By acknowledging these perspectives, therapy can be more inclusive and respectful, bridging the gap between tradition and contemporary mental health practices.

2.13.5 Concepts

We incorporated cultural concepts like Ubuntu, spiritual forces, and collective well-being to enhance healing. This approach aligns with cultural beliefs that emphasize communal support and holistic healing. Ubuntu emphasizes the interconnectedness of individuals within a community, highlighting the importance of collective well-being and mutual support. The homework activity after session two requires that group members share their learning with other children in the community to foster a sense of community and mutual support. In sessions 7 and 8, group members work together to acquire livelihood skills. These activities emphasized the interconnectedness of individuals and the importance of collective well-being, reinforcing the Ubuntu philosophy of "I am because we are."

We acknowledge the role of spiritual beliefs in understanding and addressing mental health challenges. By starting and ending each therapy session with prayers, the CA GSP model aligned with their spiritual beliefs, helping them find comfort and resilience. This activity acknowledged the role of spiritual forces in addressing mental health challenges and provided a sense of peace and support. Practicing faith can serve as a positive coping skill, providing comfort and resilience in times of stress.

The belief that counseling is crucial for healing underscores the need for health care to combine psychological and medical treatments. Our therapy respects cultural concepts of care by addressing both emotional and physical aspects of health. As expressed by mental health workers in Kitgum district, *"In my experience, medication alone cannot help. Counseling to heal the stress is the most important."* By acknowledging and integrating these cultural concepts, the CA models retained cultural sensitivity, resonating with the beliefs and values of the community.

2.13.6 Context

In a post-conflict setting characterized by poverty, stigma, discrimination, and a challenging political climate, therapy must address the multifaceted issues affecting individuals and communities. Acknowledge the impact of past conflicts on mental health, focusing on healing and rebuilding trust within communities.

Therapy includes discussing financial stressors and providing income-generating skills to alleviate economic hardships and empower individuals.

Address the stigma and discrimination faced by individuals, promoting acceptance and inclusivity within the community. Recognize how political dynamics influence access to resources and support systems, advocating for policies that support mental health initiatives.

Integrating discussions about financial stressors into therapy sessions helps participants learn skills that can improve their economic situation. As noted by a male participant from Namukora, Kitgum district, "It helps to reduce poverty through other group activities. You learn new skills in handling different situations." By providing income-generating skills, therapy not only addresses mental health but also empowers individuals to improve their socioeconomic status, creating a more resilient and self-sufficient community.

2.13.7 Goals

The treatment goals for the CA GSP Model for children and adolescents were designed to address their unique needs and challenges. In Session 1, the focus is on fostering friendships and building trust within the group, creating a supportive and welcoming environment. Session 2 aims to help participants explore and manage their emotions effectively, providing them with tools to understand and express their feelings. Sessions 3 and 4 are dedicated to creating a secure environment where participants can share their experiences and support each other's challenges, promoting empathy and solidarity. In Session 5, the group learns healthy ways to cope with various challenges, equipping them with strategies to handle difficult situations. Session 6 focuses on handling stigma and discrimination, teaching participants how to navigate these issues in a constructive manner. Finally, Sessions 7 and 8 involve creating age-appropriate projects that promote skill development, such as a garden project, which can be used to generate future income. These sessions aim to empower children and adolescents by providing them with practical skills and fostering a sense of purpose and self-efficacy.

3. Methods

Practical demonstrations using locally available materials served as powerful therapeutic tools to convey important messages and facilitate understanding. For example, blowing up balloons until they burst vividly demonstrated the dangerous effects of unchecked anger. Similarly, using flour and stones to represent positive and negative thoughts illustrated that while a meal could be made with flour, it could not be made with stones. When flour was mixed with stones, it became impossible to make food, symbolizing that our minds could not effectively hold both positive and negative thoughts simultaneously. These hands-on activities provided concrete examples that made abstract psychological concepts more relatable and easier to grasp. **Table 4** illustrates summary activities of the adapted CA GSP Model.

3.1 Trial results

3.1.1 Trial participants

The sample consisted of slightly more females (73/121, 60.30%) than males (48/121, 39.6%). The age of participants ranged from 10 to 19 years, with a mean age of 13.79 (SD 2.98) years. The majority had primary level education (105/121, 86.80%), had female caregivers (93/121, 76.80%), without an income-generating activity (86/121, 71.00%), and without food security (106/121, 87.6%). **Table 5** shows the comparison of baseline characteristics between GSP and IAC treatment groups.

3.1.2 Indicators of feasibility

All young people who were invited to participate in the study turned up to attend the intervention they were assigned. Of 58 participants assigned to GSP and 63 assigned to intensive adherence counseling (IAC), 56 (96%) and 58 (96%) participated in group sessions, respectively, suggesting that the reach of the intervention, dose delivered and received were favorable. Reasons for missing sessions included poor physical health and migration to another district. Attrition was similar in the two groups, with 1 (1.66%) GSP and 1 (1.66%) IAC. The reason for attrition was hospitalization for medical complications.

GSP session goal	Summary activities
Session 1: Introductions, ground rules, expectations, understanding how group therapy works.	Participants share their names through ball games and icebreaker games to build rapport and ease into the group setting. The group collaboratively creates ground rules and expresses expectations through engaging activities. Simple visual aids and relatable stories are used to explain the therapy process.
Session 2: Education about emotions and how they are affected by living with a chronic illness	Complex psychological terms were simplified to match the child's or adolescent's level of understanding. For instance, depression was described as "feeling really sad or empty for a long time, like the sun wasn't shining inside you, and you did not feel like doing anything, even things you used to enjoy." Guilt was described as "feeling sorry or bad because you thought you did something wrong, even if you did not mean to, like when you accidentally broke your friend's toy and felt really bad inside."
Session 3 and 4: Create a secure environment for sharing painful experiences	Assure confidentiality. Use metaphors and relatable language to help children and adolescents express and communicate their painful experiences in a way that feels understandable and manageable. A child might say, "Sometimes, I feel like I'm just a small piece of paper that keeps getting crumpled up. It's hard to feel like I'm worth anything when I feel so crumpled and ignored. Allow them to write or draw their painful experiences.
Session 5: Learning positive coping skills	Coping with negative emotions was effectively illustrated through riddles. For example, consider the riddle: "I'm a balloon filled with air. The more you push, the bigger I get, but if you let me go, I'll fly away. What am I?" The answer is "anger." This metaphor helped explain how anger could build up inside, growing more intense if left unchecked, much like a balloon inflating with air. However, just as a balloon could be released to deflate or fly away, anger too could be managed and released through healthy coping strategies such as talking it out, practicing deep breathing, or taking a break. *Garden metaphor*: "Imagine your mind is a garden. A gardener must remove weeds for his crops to grow. Likewise, we must identify bad thoughts and remove them in order for our brains to do their work well. We need to water our brains with positive experiences in order for the brain to generate positive emotions to give us positive energy.
Session 6: Learning how to cope with stigma and discrimination	Share stigma experiences. Use metaphors and relatable language help convey the concept of self-awareness in a way that makes it easier for CA to understand how it can aid in coping with stigma. *Shield metaphor*: "Think of self-awareness as a strong shield made of the best materials in our culture. Just like a warrior needs a shield to protect them from arrows in battle, knowing and accepting yourself helps protect you from negative thoughts and comments from others. It allows you to stay true to yourself and face challenges with confidence."
Sessions 7: Learning basic livelihood skills	Skills to promote self-reliance, personal development, and practical knowledge, helping children and adolescents build a foundation for their future well-being and independence. Simple activities might include creating a budget for a small allowance or setting savings goals. Making daily or weekly planners to help them balance school, chores, and leisure. Hands-on activities could include planting seeds and caring for a small garden.
Session 8: Choosing an income-generating activity or starting a new skill development project.	Children and adolescents can engage in various skill development projects to enhance their abilities and potentially generate income. They can explore crafting, gardening, learning musical instruments, making jewelry, growing plants, or offering services like tutoring, sewing or beading. These activities can enhance abilities and provide opportunities for future income generation.

Table 4.
The adapted child and adolescent group support psychotherapy model.

Variable	GSP (n = 58)	IAC (n = 63)	*X2* *t-test*	*p-value*
Age mean (SD)	13.36 (2.69)	13.96 (2.82)	−1.20	0.230
Sex				
Female	30 (51.72%)	43 (68.25%)	3.45	0.063
Male	28 (48.28%)	20 (31.75%)		
Education				
No formal education	3 (5.17%)	3 (4.76%)	2.17	0.338
Primary education	48 (82.76%)	57 (90.48%)		
Secondary education	7 (12.07%)	3 (4.76%)		
ART Adherence (>95%)				
Yes	40 (72.73%)	41 (66.13%)	0.59	0.440
No	15 (27.27%)	21 (33.87%)		
Viral suppression (<1000 copies)				
Yes	1 `(1.72%)	0 (0%)	1.09	0.476
No	57 (98. 28%)	63 (100%)		
Depression scores mean (SD)	13.18 (8.72)	13.62 (8.44)	−0.28	0.696

Table 5.
Comparison of baseline characteristics between GSP and IAC treatment groups.

3.1.3 Indicators of acceptability

The young people's evaluation of both interventions indicates that GSP participants were more satisfied with their intervention than IAC participants. However, the differences are not significant, as shown in **Figure 1**. Participants were asked to indicate whether or not they strongly agreed with the statements shown.

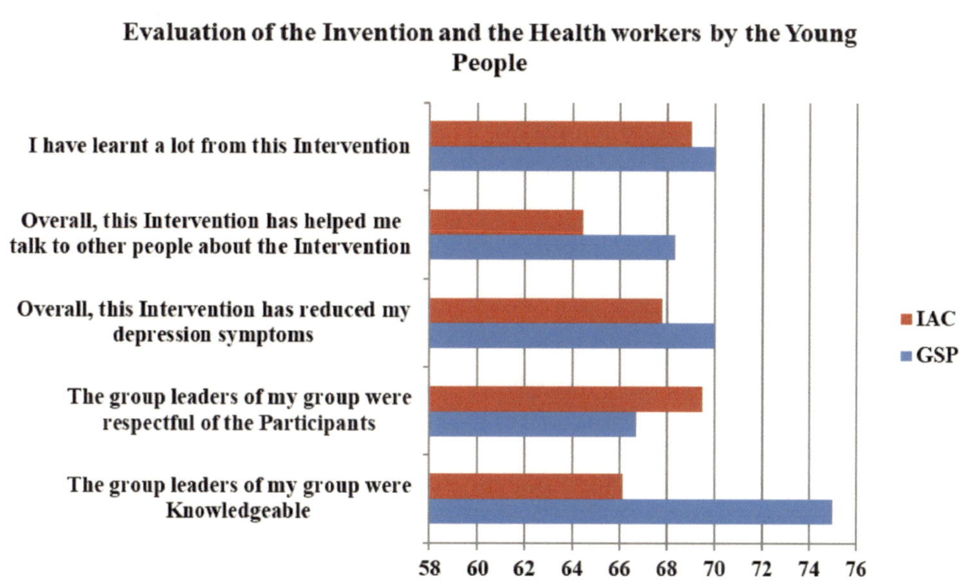

Figure 1.
Evaluation of GSP by the children and adolescent living with HIV.

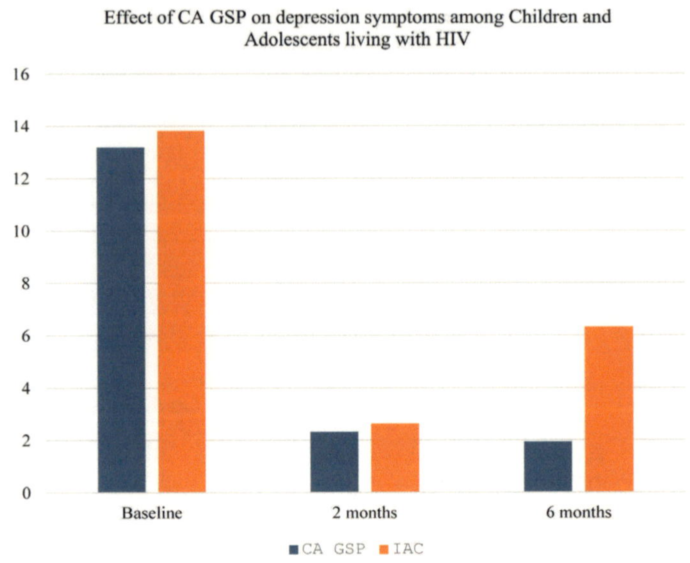

Figure 2.
Effect of GSP on depression symptoms among children and adolescents living with HIV.

3.1.4 Depression outcomes

At baseline, mean depression symptom scores between GSP and IAC groups were comparable (Mean (SD) 13.18 (1.72) versus Mean (SD) 13.82 (1.77); Mean difference (MD) = −0.62, 95%CI = −6.07 to 4.82; p-value = 0.801). Throughout the treatment phase, participants from both intervention groups experienced comparable decreases in depression symptoms, leading to no notable difference in the average depression scores measured right after the interventions concluded. (Mean (SD) 2.32 (0.24) versus Mean (SD) 2.63 (0.23); MD = −0.31, 95%CI = −1.05 to 0.44; p-value = 0.385).

However, at 6 months after intervention, participants in the GSP group had greater reduction in depression symptoms, which resulted in lower mean depression scores in participants in the GSP group than in those in the IAC group. (Mean (SD) 1.93 (1.01) versus Mean (SD) 6.32 (1.01); MD = −4.38, 95%CI = −7.52 to −1.26; p-value = 0.010) (**Figure 2**).

4. Discussion

We successfully adapted the group support psychotherapy model to address the cognitive, emotional, and social development stages of children and adolescents. To ensure comprehension and engagement, activities and discussions are simplified and made relatable. For example, role-playing and interactive games are used to convey complex concepts such as anger, stigma, and coping strategies in an accessible and engaging manner for younger participants. Stories, riddles, and practical demonstrations help adolescents articulate their feelings and learn essential social skills like cooperation, listening, empathy, and peer support. The group setting further alleviates feelings of isolation by demonstrating that others share similar experiences and emotions.

Adolescence is a crucial period for identity development [38]. GSP sessions facilitated this process by providing a supportive environment for exploring personal and social identities. Additionally, the adaptability of GSP to the local cultural and social context ensured that the content was both relevant and respectful of the participants' backgrounds. This relevance was essential for engaging children and adolescents, making the therapy a meaningful and relatable experience.

This GSP model effectively addressed several challenges faced by children and adolescents living with HIV, described based on the ecological framework. However, for purposes of this book chapter, we focused on the effect of the CA GSP model on depression symptoms. During the treatment period, both interventions led to a similar reduction in depression symptoms, which suggests that both approaches were effective in the short term. The observed lack of difference in reducing depression symptoms during therapy sessions can be explained by the occurrence of common therapeutic factors in all group interventions given that IAC was also delivered in a group format.

Additionally, there was the possibility that participants exchanged information between groups, which might have resulted in IAC participants acquiring some cognitive behavioral techniques. Moreover, the facilitators for the IAC sessions had prior training in conducting GSP from their involvement in the adult GSP trial, potentially leading to the inadvertent transmission of GSP skills to the IAC participants.

However, at the 6-month follow-up, the GSP group showed a significantly greater reduction in depression symptoms compared to the IAC group. This suggests that while both interventions were effective in the short term, the effects of GSP were more sustained over time. These effects are similar to the adult GSP effects on depression we observed in prior studies [39, 40]. The long-term benefit of GSP may be attributed to the group dynamics, peer support, and the continuous engagement with caregivers and health workers, which likely reinforced the therapeutic effects and contributed to the lasting improvement in mental health outcomes. Future studies will investigate the causal mechanisms of the CA model.

Despite this achievement, several challenges were encountered during the delivery of the group sessions. Geographic barriers posed a significant challenge, with some participants having to travel long distances to attend sessions, and others relocating to distant regions, leading to dropouts. Time management was another issue, with poor punctuality affecting the sessions, and weather disruptions, particularly rain, interfering with session continuity. Additionally, non-disclosure of HIV status by some caregivers complicated the counseling process, and the clash of session schedules with communal activities such as burials and clan meetings led to missed sessions. Health-related issues, like hospitalization of caregivers, also affected attendance. Communication barriers between parents and grandparents, who often took care of the children, further complicated the delivery of the sessions.

Despite these limitations, the study had several strengths. First, one of the most notable successes was the high attendance rate, indicating strong engagement and commitment from the children. This engagement extended beyond the sessions, as children took the initiative to interact with health workers independently, leading to the establishment of a special clinic day specifically for them. This suggests that the intervention helped demystify the health facility for the children, many of whom were previously unfamiliar with it due to their caregivers typically handling health-related visits. The integration of caregivers into the process was crucial, as it not only enhanced the children's participation in these activities but also encouraged a closer relationship between caregivers and children.

This project was conducted during the COVID pandemic, so the study participants were out of school. The income-generating activities were a vital component of the GSP, directly involving the children in tasks like piggery, farming, and goat rearing. The involvement of caregivers in setting up these projects was crucial, as it provided support and ensured the sustainability of these activities. The children's participation in these tasks likely contributed to their sense of responsibility and empowerment, and the integration of these activities into their daily lives outside of school provided them with practical skills and a means of contributing to their households.

Prior research has identified a significant scarcity of mental health interventions specifically designed for children and adolescents [41, 42]. Among the few available interventions, there is a notable emphasis on integrating family involvement and economic strengthening strategies to address mental health needs [43–45]. These approaches are crucial, but there remains a gap in understanding their mechanisms of action and effectiveness.

Our forthcoming studies aim to address this gap by evaluating the effectiveness and cost-effectiveness of the CA GSP model in promoting viral suppression among children and adolescents. We will investigate the specific mechanisms through which this model improves both depression treatment and HIV treatment outcomes. To achieve more robust and conclusive results, we propose conducting a definitive trial, preferably a cluster-randomized trial. Such a study design would provide a more concrete assessment of the CA GSP model's effectiveness, offering deeper insights into its impact and potential for broader application in enhancing overall health outcomes for this vulnerable population.

5. Conclusion

The challenges faced by children and adolescents living with HIV are complex and multifaceted, spanning individual, interpersonal, community, and societal levels. The relevance of group support psychotherapy (GSP) in addressing these challenges is well-supported by the literature, particularly when adapted using culturally sensitive and ecologically valid approaches. By integrating cultural concepts, metaphors, and community-based delivery methods, GSP can effectively address the unique needs of this population, improving not only the mental health outcomes but also enhancing social dynamics and family relationships in a meaningful and sustainable way. While there were challenges in delivery, the positive impacts observed, particularly in the long-term reduction of depression symptoms, highlight the value of this intervention. Addressing the logistical and communicative challenges encountered could further enhance the effectiveness and reach of GSP, making it a viable model for broader implementation in similar settings.

Acknowledgements

This study was funded by several small grants from the CRI Foundation through FIDELITY Charitable International Grants; Grant ID Numbers: 13624790, 12977146, 14789811, 15884099, 16583402.

Conflict of interest

EN-M holds the copyright for the group support psychotherapy manual. All other authors declare no competing interests.

Notes/thanks/other declarations

The authors would like to acknowledge the support of the management of the Kitgum local government administration and the general hospital HIV clinics where the project activities were conducted. We are deeply appreciative of the children and adolescents who participated in the study, as well as their caregivers, for their time and trust. We are also extremely grateful for the hard work and dedication of all the research assistants.

Author details

Etheldreda Nakimuli-Mpungu[1*], Kizito Wamala[1], Carol Nakanyike[2], Jane Iya[2], Zubair Lukyamuzi[3], Justine Diana Namuli[1], Joyce Sserunjoji Nalugya[4], Benedict Akimana[5], Sabrina Bakeera Kitaka[1], Jean B. Nachega[6], Ed Mills[7] and Musisi Seggane[1]

1 Makerere University College of Health Sciences, Kampala, Uganda

2 SEEK Group Support Psychotherapy Initiative, Kampala, Uganda

3 MU-JHU Research Collaboration, Kampala, Uganda

4 Mulago National Referral Hospital, Kampala, Uganda

5 Butabika National Referral Mental Hospital, Kampala, Uganda

6 Stellenbosch University, Cape Town, South Africa

7 McMaster University, Hamilton, ON, Canada

*Address all correspondence to: etheldreda.nakimuli@mak.ac.ug; ethelmpungu@yahoo.com

References

[1] UNAIDS. In Danger: UNAIDS Global AIDS Update 2022. Geneva: Joint United Nations Programme on HIV/AIDS. Licence: CC BY-NC-SA 3.0 IGO; 2022

[2] SECRETARIAT UAC. Factsheet - Facts on HIV and AIDS in Uganda 2021 (Based on Data Ending 31st December 2020). 2021. Available from: https://uac.go.ug/media/attachments/2021/09/13/final-2021-hiv-aids-factsheet.pdf

[3] Boyes ME, Cluver LD, Meinck F, Casale M, Newnham E. Mental health in South African adolescents living with HIV: Correlates of internalising and externalising symptoms. AIDS Care. 2019;**31**(1):95-104

[4] Okonji EF, Mukumbang FC, Orth Z, Vickerman-Delport SA, Van Wyk B. Psychosocial support interventions for improved adherence and retention in ART care for young people living with HIV (10-24 years): A scoping review. BMC Public Health. 2020;**20**(1):1-11

[5] Vreeman RC, McCoy BM, Lee S. Mental health challenges among adolescents living with HIV. Journal of the International AIDS Society. 2017;**20**:21497

[6] Bolbolizade P, Seyed-Kolbadi F, Davari-Dolatabadi N, Zamani F, Mirshahi F. HIV-associated neurocognitive disorder (HAND): A review study. Life Research. 2023;**6**(1):2

[7] Molinaro M, Adams HR, Mwanza-Kabaghe S, Mbewe EG, Kabundula PP, Mweemba M, et al. Evaluating the relationship between depression and cognitive function among children and adolescents with HIV in Zambia. AIDS and Behavior. 2021;**25**(9):2669-2679

[8] Bankole KO, Bakare MO, Edet BE, Igwe MN, Ewa AU, Bankole IA, et al. Psychological complications associated with HIV/AIDS infection among children in South-South Nigeria, sub-Saharan Africa. Cogent Medicine. 2017;**4**(1):1372869

[9] Starks TJ, MacDonell KK, Pennar AL, Dinaj-Koci V, Millar BM, Naar S. Drug use among adolescents and young adults with unsuppressed HIV who use alcohol: Identifying patterns of comorbid drug use and associations with mental health. AIDS and Behavior. 2020;**24**(10):2975-2983

[10] Luseno WK, Field SH, Iritani BJ, Odongo FS, Kwaro D, Amek NO, et al. Pathways to depression and poor quality of life among adolescents in Western Kenya: Role of anticipated HIV stigma, HIV risk perception, and sexual behaviors. AIDS and Behavior. 2021;**25**:1423-1437

[11] Shanaube K, Gachie T, Hoddinott G, Schaap A, Floyd S, Mainga T, et al. Depressive symptoms and HIV risk behaviours among adolescents enrolled in the HPTN071 (PopART) trial in Zambia and South Africa. PLoS One. 2022;**17**(12):e0278291

[12] Amankwah-Poku M, Klutsey DA, Asante KO. Disclosure and health-related outcomes among children living with HIV and their caregivers. AIDS Research and Therapy. 2021;**18**:1-8

[13] Bhana A, Kreniske P, Pather A, Abas MA, Mellins CA. Interventions to address the mental health of adolescents and young adults living with or affected by HIV: State of the evidence. Journal of the International AIDS Society. 2021;**24**:e25713

[14] Nakimuli-Mpungu E, Smith CM, Wamala K, Okello J, Birungi J, Etukoit M, et al. Long-term effect of group support psychotherapy on depression and HIV treatment outcomes: Secondary analysis of a cluster randomized trial in Uganda. Psychosomatic Medicine. 2022;**84**(8):914-923

[15] Bernal G, Bonilla J, Bellido C. Ecological validity and cultural sensitivity for outcome research: Issues for the cultural adaptation and development of psychosocial treatments with Hispanics. Journal of Abnormal Child Psychology. 1995;**23**(1):67-82

[16] Pulaski MAS. Understanding Piaget: An Introduction to Children's Cognitive Development. New York: Harper & Row; 1971

[17] Erikson EH. Childhood and Society. New York: Norton; 1963

[18] Bronfenbrenner U. Contexts of child rearing: Problems and prospects. American Psychologist. 1979;**34**(10):844

[19] Gardner H. Artistic intelligences. Art Education. 1983;**36**(2):47-49

[20] Lave J, Wenger E. Situated Learning: Legitimate Peripheral Participation. Cambridge, England: Cambridge University Press; 1991

[21] Ainsworth MD. The bowlby-Ainsworth attachment theory. Behavioral and Brain Sciences. 1978;**1**(3):436-438

[22] Nakimuli-Mpungu E, Wamala K, Okello J, Alderman S, Odokonyero R, Musisi S, et al. Developing a culturally sensitive group support intervention for depression among HIV infected and non-infected Ugandan adults: A qualitative study. Journal of Affective Disorders. 2014;**163**:10-17

[23] Gladden J. The coping skills of east African refugees: A literature review. Refugee Survey Quarterly. 2012;**31**:177-196

[24] Delgadillo J, Groom M. Using psychoeducation and role induction to improve completion rates in cognitive behavioural therapy. Behavioural and Cognitive Psychotherapy. 2017;**45**:170-184

[25] Vinogradov S, Yalom ID. Concise Guide to Group Psychotherapy. Washington, DC: American Psychiatric Pub; 1989

[26] Lund C, De Silva M, Plagerson S, Cooper S, Chisholm D, Das J, et al. Poverty andmental disorders: Breaking the cycle in low-income and middle-income countries. Lancet. 2011;**378**:1502-1514

[27] Israel B, Schulz A, Parker E, Becker A. Community-based participatory research: Policy recommendations for promoting a partnership approach in health research. Education for Health. 2001;**14**(2):182-197

[28] Chan A, Tetzlaff J, Altman D, Laupacis A, Gøtzsche PC, Krleža-Jerić K, et al. SPIRIT 2013 statement: Defining standard protocol items for clinical trials. Annals of Internal Medicine. 2013;**158**(3):200-207. DOI: 10.7326/0003-4819-158-3-201302050-00583

[29] Eldridge SM, Lancaster GA, Campbell MJ, Thabane L, Hopewell S, Coleman CL, et al. Defining feasibility and pilot studies in preparation for randomised controlled trials: Development of a conceptual framework. PLoS One. 2016;**11**:e0150205. DOI: 10.1371/journal.pone.0150205

[30] Purcell DW, Garfein RS, Latka MH, Thiede H, Hudson S, Bonner S, et al.

Development, description, and acceptability of a small-group, behavioral intervention to prevent HIV and hepatitis C virus infections among young adult injection drug users. Drug and Alcohol Dependence. 2007;**91**(Suppl 1):S73-S80. DOI: 10.1016/j.drugalcdep.2007.03.004

[31] Ebesutani C, Reise SP, Chorpita BF, Ale C, Regan J, Young J, et al. The revised child anxiety and depression scale—Short version: Scale reduction via exploratory bifactor modeling of the broad anxiety factor. Psychological Assessment. 2012;**24**:833-845. DOI: 10.1037/a0027283

[32] Piqueras JA, Martín-Vivar M, Sandin B, San Luis C, Pineda D. The revised child anxiety and depression scale: A systematic review and reliability generalization meta-analysis. Journal of Affective Disorders. 2017;**218**:153-169. DOI: 10.1016/j.jad.2017.04.022

[33] Park AL, Ebesutani CK, Bose D, Chorpita BF. Psychometric properties of a Spanish translation of the revised child anxiety and depression scale–parent version. Journal of Psychopathology and Behavioral Assessment. 2016;**38**:307-319. DOI: 10.1007/s10862-015-9517-7

[34] Martin VB, Gynnild A. Grounded Theory: The Philosophy, Method, and Work of Barney Glaser. Boca Raton, FL: Universal-Publishers; 2011

[35] Alhojailan MI. Thematic analysis: A critical review of its process and evaluation. West East Journal of Social Sciences. 2012;**1**(1):39-47

[36] Bronfenbrenner U. The Ecology of Human Development: Experiments by Nature and Design. Cambridge, MA: Harvard University Press; 1979

[37] Friese S, Soratto J, Pires D. Carrying Out a Computer-Aided Thematic Content Analysis with ATLAS.ti. MMG Working Paper 18-02. Max Planck Institute for the Study of Religious and Ethnic Diversity; 2018

[38] Branje S, de Moor EL, Spitzer J, Becht AI. Dynamics of identity development in adolescence: A decade in review. Journal of Research on Adolescence. 2021;**31**(4):908-927. DOI: 10.1111/jora.12678

[39] Nakimuli-Mpungu E, Wamala K, Okello J, Alderman S, Odokonyero R, Mojtabai R, et al. Group support psychotherapy for depression treatment in people with HIV/AIDS in northern Uganda: A single-centre randomised controlled trial. The Lancet HIV. 2015;**2**(5):e190-e199

[40] Nakimuli-Mpungu E, Musisi S, Wamala K, Okello J, Ndyanabangi S, Birungi J, et al. Effectiveness and cost-effectiveness of group support psychotherapy delivered by trained lay health workers for depression treatment among people with HIV in Uganda: A cluster-randomised trial. The Lancet Global Health. 2020;**8**(3):e387-ee98

[41] Sequeira M, Singh S, Fernandes L, Gaikwad L, Gupta D, Chibanda D, et al. Adolescent health series: The status of adolescent mental health research, practice and policy in sub-Saharan Africa: A narrative review. Tropical Medicine & International Health. 2022;**27**(9):758-766

[42] Bhana A, Abas MA, Kelly J, Van Pinxteren M, Mudekunye LA, Pantelic M. Mental health interventions for adolescents living with HIV or affected by HIV in low-and middle-income countries: Systematic review. BJPsych Open. 2020;**6**(5):e104

[43] Filiatreau LM, Tutlam N, Brathwaite R, Byansi W, Namuwonge F, Mwebembezi A, et al. Effects of a combination economic empowerment and family strengthening intervention on psychosocial well-being among Ugandan adolescent girls and young women: Analysis of a cluster randomized controlled trial (Suubi4Her). Journal of Adolescent Health. 2023;**72**(5):S33-S40

[44] Bhana A, Mellins CA, Petersen I, Alicea S, Myeza N, Holst H, et al. The VUKA family program: Piloting a family-based psychosocial intervention to promote health and mental health among HIV infected early adolescents in South Africa. AIDS Care. 2014;**26**(1):1-11. DOI: 10.1080/09540121.2013.806770

[45] Ssewamala FM, Dvalishvili D, Mellins CA, Geng EH, Makumbi F, Neilands TB, et al. The long-term effects of a family based economic empowerment intervention (Suubi+ adherence) on suppression of HIV viral loads among adolescents living with HIV in southern Uganda: Findings from 5-year cluster randomized trial. PLoS One. 2020;**15**(2):e0228370

Chapter 14

Alleviating Mathematics Anxiety and Enhancing Achievement through Systematic Desensitization: A Cognitive-Behavioural Approach for Secondary School Learners

Felix Egara and Moeketsi Mosia

Abstract

Mathematics anxiety is a critical barrier to academic success for many secondary school learners, often leading to reduced performance and negative attitudes towards mathematics. This chapter explores the application of systematic desensitization, a cognitive-behavioural therapy technique, as an effective intervention for mitigating mathematics anxiety and boosting mathematics achievement. By gradually exposing students to anxiety-inducing mathematical tasks in a structured and supportive manner, systematic desensitization aims to reduce fear responses and build confidence. The chapter will review existing literature on the prevalence and consequences of mathematics anxiety, outline the methodology of systematic desensitization, and present empirical evidence supporting its effectiveness. Additionally, practical recommendations for educators and therapists on implementing this intervention in school settings will be provided. This chapter highlights the integration of psychological strategies within educational frameworks to address emotional barriers to learning and improve academic outcomes.

Keywords: systematic desensitization, mathematics anxiety, mathematics achievement, secondary school learners, cognitive-behavioural therapy, educational interventions

1. Introduction

Mathematics anxiety is a pervasive issue affecting a substantial number of students worldwide. Mathematics anxiety is characterized by tension, apprehension, and fear that interfere with the ability to perform mathematical tasks [1]. This anxiety can manifest at various stages of education and can have long-lasting effects on students' academic trajectories and career choices [2]. The significance of addressing mathematics anxiety lies in improving academic performance and fostering positive attitudes towards mathematics, which is essential for personal and professional development in a world increasingly driven by quantitative and analytical skills [3]. Mathematics anxiety is a complex construct defined as discomfort associated with performing mathematics tasks. According to [4], it involves cognitive and emotional components, where individuals experience intrusive thoughts and physiological symptoms such as increased heart rate and sweating when engaging with mathematics. This anxiety can arise from various sources, including past negative experiences with mathematics, societal stereotypes, and inadequate teaching methods.

The impact of mathematics anxiety on academic performance is well-documented. Students with high levels of mathematics anxiety tend to avoid mathematics-related courses and activities, leading to gaps in knowledge and skills [5, 6]. This avoidance can result in lower achievement and decreased confidence, creating a cycle of anxiety and poor performance. Research has shown that mathematics anxiety can impair working memory, reduce problem-solving efficiency, and hinder conceptual understanding [3, 7]. Consequently, students with mathematics anxiety are at a disadvantage in an educational system that increasingly emphasizes STEM (Science, Technology, Engineering, and Mathematics) competencies.

Given the detrimental effects of mathematics anxiety, there is a pressing need for effective interventions that can alleviate this condition and enhance students' achievement. Traditional educational approaches often fail to address learning mathematics's emotional and psychological aspects. Therefore, integrating psychological interventions such as systematic desensitization can provide a more holistic approach to tackling mathematics anxiety [4, 8, 9]. Applying systematic desensitization to mathematics anxiety involves creating a hierarchy of mathematics-related tasks that induce anxiety, from least to most anxiety-provoking. Students are then guided through relaxation exercises and gradually exposed to these tasks in a controlled and supportive environment. This approach helps students build confidence and reduce their anxiety over time, ultimately improving their ability to perform mathematical tasks without experiencing overwhelming fear.

This chapter explores the application of systematic desensitization to reduce mathematics anxiety and enhance mathematics achievement among school learners. It will provide a comprehensive overview of the theoretical foundations of systematic desensitization, outline the methodology and techniques for implementing this approach in group therapy settings, and present case studies and practical examples to illustrate its effectiveness. By integrating this cognitive-behavioral technique into educational practices, this chapter offers practical insights and guidance for educators, therapists, and researchers interested in alleviating mathematics anxiety and improving student mathematics outcomes. The ultimate goal is to create a supportive learning environment where all students can achieve their full potential in mathematics.

2. Theoretical foundations

2.1 Cognitive-behavioural therapy (CBT) framework

Systematic desensitization fits within the CBT framework, which combines cognitive and behavioral techniques to address psychological problems. CBT focuses on identifying and modifying dysfunctional thoughts, beliefs, and behaviors [10]. Systematic desensitization specifically targets the behavioral aspect by addressing the avoidance behaviors and physiological arousal associated with anxiety. CBT employs several techniques to address psychological issues effectively. One such technique is cognitive restructuring, which involves identifying and challenging negative thought patterns and beliefs. This process helps individuals replace dysfunctional thoughts with more positive and realistic ones [13]. Another crucial aspect of CBT is behavioral interventions, which include exposure therapy, relaxation training, and systematic desensitization. These interventions focus on altering the behaviors and physiological responses associated with anxiety, helping individuals manage and reduce their anxiety over time [11].

The focus on systematic desensitization within this chapter is due to its proven efficacy in reducing anxiety through structured and replicable methods. Unlike other interventions, systematic desensitization provides a clear, step-by-step approach that combines both cognitive and behavioral elements, making it particularly suited for educational settings where structured interventions are beneficial. Furthermore, the growing body of research from 2015 to 2024 consistently supports its effectiveness, demonstrating significant reductions in mathematics anxiety and improvements in academic performance across diverse educational contexts. This robust evidence base underpins our decision to delve deeply into systematic desensitization as a central strategy for addressing mathematics anxiety.

2.2 The concept of systematic desensitization

Systematic desensitization is a therapeutic technique developed by Joseph Wolpe in 1958, grounded in the principles of classical conditioning. Systematic desensitization is a form of cognitive-behavioral therapy that aims to reduce anxiety through gradual exposure to anxiety-inducing stimuli while simultaneously engaging in relaxation techniques [4]. The underlying principle is reciprocal inhibition, where one response (relaxation) inhibits another (anxiety). Systematic desensitization effectively addresses mathematics anxiety through three key components. First, a *hierarchy of fears* is developed, ranking anxiety-provoking stimuli from least to most fearful [11]. Second, *relaxation training* involves techniques like deep breathing, progressive muscle relaxation, or guided imagery to induce calmness [12]. Third, *gradual exposure* systematically introduces individuals to anxiety-inducing stimuli, starting from the least fearful while maintaining relaxation techniques [11]. These components build confidence, reduce anxiety, and enhance the ability to perform mathematical tasks with less fear.

2.3 Classical conditioning and reciprocal inhibition

Systematic desensitization is rooted in classical conditioning, a learning process first described by Ivan Pavlov in 1903. In classical conditioning, a neutral stimulus becomes associated with an unconditioned stimulus to elicit a conditioned response. Wolpe expanded on this concept with reciprocal inhibition, positing that two incompatible responses (e.g., anxiety and relaxation) cannot occur simultaneously. By conditioning relaxation in the presence of anxiety-provoking stimuli, the anxiety response is gradually weakened [11]. Systematic desensitization is based on two key principles. The first principle is *classical conditioning*, which involves learning through association. In this context, a neutral stimulus, such as mathematics problems, is paired with an unconditioned stimulus, such as fear, leading to a conditioned anxiety response [13]. The second principle is *reciprocal inhibition*. This principle introduces a response that is incompatible with the anxiety response, such as relaxation, to inhibit and eventually eliminate the anxiety [11]. By consistently pairing relaxation with anxiety-provoking stimuli, the anxiety response is gradually diminished. These principles form the theoretical foundation of systematic desensitization, guiding the approach to reducing mathematics anxiety and improving student mathematics outcomes.

2.4 Application of systematic desensitization to mathematics anxiety

Applying systematic desensitization to mathematics anxiety involves creating a hierarchy of mathematics-related tasks that induce anxiety, from least to most anxiety-provoking. Students are taught relaxation techniques and gradually exposed to these tasks in a controlled and supportive environment. This approach helps students build confidence and reduce their anxiety over time [4].

The process of systematic desensitization for addressing mathematics anxiety involves several key steps. The first step is *assessment*, where the level and specific triggers of mathematics anxiety are evaluated by utilizing tools such as mathematics anxiety scales. This evaluation helps understand the individual's unique math anxiety profile and tailor the intervention accordingly. Next is *relaxation training*, where students are taught various relaxation techniques, such as deep breathing and progressive muscle relaxation, to manage physiological arousal and maintain calmness. Following relaxation training is the *hierarchy construction* phase. In this step, a graded list of mathematics tasks is developed based on the level of anxiety they provoke, starting from the least anxiety-inducing tasks to the most challenging ones. The final step is *gradual exposure*, where students are systematically exposed to the tasks in the hierarchy. This exposure is done incrementally, ensuring that students remain relaxed while facing each task, thereby reducing their anxiety response over time [11].

2.5 Integrating systematic desensitization into educational practices

Systematic desensitization can be integrated into educational settings to help students manage mathematics anxiety. This involves collaboration between educators, school counselors, and psychologists to create supportive environments where students can confront and reduce their anxiety.

The successful implementation of systematic desensitization for mathematics anxiety requires several strategic approaches. One crucial strategy is *teacher training*. This involves equipping teachers with the skills to recognize and address mathematics anxiety in their students, enabling them to provide appropriate support and interventions [4]. Another essential strategy is integrating *classroom activities* incorporating relaxation techniques and gradual exposure to mathematics tasks within the curriculum. By embedding these practices into regular classroom routines, students can continuously apply what they learn in a supportive environment [9]. Additionally, *support services* play a vital role. Offering group therapy sessions facilitated by trained counselors provides students with additional support. These sessions can help reinforce the techniques learned in the classroom and offer a space for students to share their experiences and progress in managing their anxiety [8].

Educators and therapists can effectively address this pervasive issue and improve students' mathematical achievement and overall well-being by comprehensively understanding the theoretical foundations of systematic desensitization and its application to mathematics anxiety.

3. Applications and settings

This section explores the practical applications of systematic desensitization for alleviating mathematics anxiety and enhancing achievement among secondary school learners. It discusses various settings where the technique can be implemented and provides detailed examples of adapting the approach to fit different educational and therapeutic environments.

3.1 Classroom settings

Systematic desensitization can be integrated into regular classroom activities, enabling teachers to address mathematics anxiety within daily instruction. Key strategies include: (i) Mathematics Anxiety Awareness Programs: Incorporating lessons on mathematics anxiety and coping strategies into the curriculum to normalize the experience and reduce stigma [14]. (ii) Relaxation Breaks: Scheduling short relaxation sessions during mathematics classes to teach and practice relaxation techniques, helping students manage anxiety in real time [9]. (iii) Gradual Exposure Activities: Designing classroom activities that progressively increase in difficulty, allowing students to build confidence and competence in a structured manner [15]. For example, starting with simple problems and gradually moving to more complex ones. (iv) Supportive Environment: Creating a classroom atmosphere encourages risk-taking and reduces fear of failure. This can include positive reinforcement, collaborative learning, and opportunities for students to share their experiences and strategies for managing anxiety [16].

3.2 Small group interventions

Small group interventions provide a more focused and supportive environment for implementing systematic desensitization. These settings can be particularly effective for students with moderate to severe mathematics anxiety. Key components include: (i) Group Formation: Organizing students into small groups based on similar levels of mathematics anxiety. Each group should ideally consist of 5–10 students to ensure individual attention while promoting peer support [17, 18]. (ii) Structured Sessions: Conduct regular, structured group sessions led by a trained facilitator (e.g., a school counselor or psychologist). These sessions can include relaxation training, hierarchy construction, and gradual exposure activities tailored to the group's needs [18]. (iii) Peer Support: Encouraging students to share their experiences, challenges, and successes. This peer support can help reduce feelings of isolation and increase motivation [19]. (iv) Role-Playing Exercises: Using role-playing to simulate anxiety-provoking situations and practice relaxation techniques in a controlled environment [20, 21].

3.3 Individual therapy

For students with severe mathematics anxiety or those who do not benefit from group settings, individual therapy may be necessary. In this setting, a therapist can provide personalized support and tailor the systematic desensitization process to the student's needs. Key elements include: (i) Personalized Hierarchy: Developing a detailed and individualized hierarchy of anxiety-provoking mathematics tasks based on the student's fears and experiences [22]. (ii) One-on-One Sessions: Conduct regular therapy sessions focused on relaxation training, gradual exposure, and cognitive restructuring [4, 11]. The therapist can provide immediate feedback and adjust the approach as needed. (iii) Homework Assignments: Assigning tasks for students to complete outside therapy sessions, helping them practice relaxation techniques and gradually face their fears in real-world situations [23].

3.4 Integration with school counselling programs

Systematic desensitization can be effectively integrated into existing school counseling programmes to provide comprehensive support for students with mathematics anxiety. Key components include: (i) Collaboration with Educators: Working closely with teachers to identify students who may benefit from systematic desensitization and to implement strategies within the classroom [17]. (ii) School-Wide Initiatives: Developing school-wide programmes that raise awareness about mathematics anxiety and promote relaxation techniques and gradual exposure [20]. (iii) Counseling Curriculum: Incorporating systematic desensitization into the counseling curriculum, offering regular workshops and sessions focused on reducing mathematics anxiety [9]. (iv) Parental Involvement: Engaging parents in the process by providing resources and training on supporting their children in managing mathematics anxiety at home [19].

By adapting systematic desensitization to various educational and therapeutic settings, we can provide targeted support to students with mathematics anxiety and help them achieve their full academic potential. This flexible approach ensures that all students, regardless of their circumstances, have access to effective interventions that can alleviate their anxiety and enhance their mathematical achievement.

4. Case studies and practical examples

This section provides illustrative case studies and practical examples to demonstrate the application of systematic desensitization for alleviating mathematics anxiety and improving mathematics achievement among school learners. These examples highlight different settings and approaches, showcasing the versatility and effectiveness of the technique. However, we tended to present a systematic review of only studies carried out to determine the effectiveness of systematic desensitization in reducing mathematics anxiety and enhancing mathematics achievement among school learners. **Table 1** summarizes reviewed studies conducted in mathematics education on the effectiveness of systematic desensitization techniques.

4.1 Research questions

The case studies and practical examples in this review are guided by the following research questions:

- What is the effectiveness of systematic desensitization in reducing mathematics anxiety and improving performance among students?
- How is systematic desensitization implemented in educational settings?
- What challenges are encountered in the implementation of systematic desensitization?
- What are the limitations of systematic desensitization, and what alternative methodologies exist to address mathematics anxiety?

S/N	References	Context/ Level/Grade	Focus of study/ Country	Methodology	Activities used in therapy sessions (Duration)	Findings	Challenges experienced (positive and negative)
1	[4]	Senior Secondary School/SSS 1	Effect of systematic desensitization on anxiety and achievement of secondary school students in mathematics in Enugu, Nigeria.	Design used: Quantitative (quasi-experimental study) Instruments used: Mathematics Anxiety Scale (MAS) and the Mathematics Achievement Test (MAT). Test statistics used: Analysis of Covariance (ANCOVA).	Participants were first introduced to the systematic desensitization treatment programme and its purpose. They then learned relaxation techniques to manage anxiety. Following this, they created a hierarchy of mathematics-related anxieties, which they later paired with relaxation techniques to reduce mathematics anxiety effectively. Students were attended to individually and in smaller groups. (6 weeks duration)	Systematic desensitization effectively reduced mathematics anxiety and improved mathematics achievement of secondary school students.	Some participants were initially resistant to systematic desensitization due to skepticism about its effectiveness or fear of confronting their anxieties. Again, some participants faced difficulties attending sessions regularly due to conflicts with their academic schedules or personal commitments. Participants' self-reported measures of anxiety and achievement may be influenced by social desirability or lack of self-awareness.
2	[18]	Senior Secondary School/SSS 2	Examined the effects of cognitive restructuring and systematic desensitization techniques on students' mathematics anxiety in senior secondary schools in Gombe State, Nigeria.	Design used: Quantitative (quasi-experimental study) Instrument used: Students' Mathematics Anxiety Questionnaire (SMAQ). Test statistics used: ANCOVA.	The study's group activities included teaching relaxation techniques like Progressive Muscle Relaxation and deep breathing, using visualization and gradual exposure to math tasks to build confidence, and addressing negative thoughts through cognitive restructuring. Role-playing and relaxation scripts provided practical coping strategies. Interactive math games and peer support groups promoted engagement and mutual support while self-monitoring and reflection encouraged students to track their anxiety levels and progress. (6 weeks duration)	Findings showed that the systematic desensitization significantly reduced mathematics anxiety inherent among secondary learners.	Limited resources, including time, materials, and support staff, impacted the quality and effectiveness of the systematic desensitization programme.

S/N	References	Context/ Level/Grade	Focus of study/ Country	Methodology	Activities used in therapy sessions (Duration)	Findings	Challenges experienced (positive and negative)
3	[8]	Junior Secondary School/JSS 2	Examined the effects of systematic desensitization on mathematics anxiety of junior secondary school students in Anambra state, Nigeria.	Design used: Quantitative (quasi-experimental study) Instrument used: Abbreviated Mathematics Anxiety Scale (AMAS). Test statistics used: ANCOVA.	The study involved three main activities: First, a smaller group of students were taught relaxation techniques, such as progressive muscle relaxation, and practised them daily for 10–15 minutes. Next, students and the therapist developed a fear hierarchy, listing 15–20 mathematics-related items ranked by increasing levels of anxiety. Finally, students imagined each item on the hierarchy, starting with the least fearful, while using relaxation techniques to manage their anxiety. (6 weeks duration)	Systematic desensitization was found effective in reducing junior secondary school students' mathematics anxiety.	Coordinating and scheduling sessions and providing individual support was time-consuming and often challenging to manage effectively. Some participants struggled with the gradual exposure tasks, finding it challenging to confront their fears incrementally.
4	[24]	Year-one College Students	Examined the effectiveness of systematic desensitization treatment on mathematics anxiety and performance among year-one college students in Malaysia.	Design used: Quantitative (quasi-experimental study) Instruments used: Fennama-Sherman Mathematics Attitude Scale (FSMAS), Neo-Five-Factory Personality Inventory (NEO-FFI) and Mathematics Performance Test (MPTs). Test statistics used: ANOVA.	The systematic desensitization programme activities include ten modules: initial selection, random assignment, deep muscle relaxation, creating a group desensitization hierarchy, and four sessions of group systematic desensitization. (6 weeks duration)	The study's findings revealed that systematic desensitization intervention significantly affects students' mathematics anxieties and mathematics performance.	Group desensitization is cost-effective and saves time, but it may not address each person's unique emotional and personal issues or individual therapy. Additionally, not all group members progress at the same pace during treatment.

DOI: http://dx.doi.org/10.5772/intechopen.1006745

S/N	References	Context/ Level/Grade	Focus of study/ Country	Methodology	Activities used in therapy sessions (Duration)	Findings	Challenges experienced (positive and negative)
5	[21]	Senior Secondary School/SSS 2	To examine the effect of cognitive restructuring and systematic desensitization in managing mathematics phobia among secondary school students in Rivers State, Nigeria.	Design used: Quantitative (quasi-experimental study) Instruments used: Mathematics Diagnostic Questionnaire (MDQ). Test statistics used: t-test.	The study included smaller groups of students' activities to reduce mathematics anxiety, such as Progressive Muscle Relaxation, deep breathing, visualization techniques, and gradually facing challenging math tasks. Cognitive restructuring replaced negative thoughts while role-playing and relaxation scripts provided coping strategies. Interactive math games and peer support groups enhanced engagement and support. Students also kept journals to monitor their anxiety and progress. (6 weeks duration)	The results indicated that cognitive restructuring and systematic desensitization effectively managed mathematics phobia among secondary school students, with systematic desensitization proving more effective.	Participants sometimes had a limited understanding of the desensitization process and its benefits, which impacted their commitment to the intervention.

Table 1.
Summary of reviewed studies on the effectiveness of systematic desensitization technique.

These questions aim to explore the efficacy, implementation process, and outcomes of systematic desensitization, providing a comprehensive understanding of its impact on mathematics anxiety and academic achievement.

4.2 Inclusion and exclusion criteria

To ensure the relevance and quality of the studies included in this review, specific inclusion and exclusion criteria were established. For inclusion, studies needed to provide empirical data on the effectiveness of systematic desensitization in reducing mathematics anxiety and improving mathematics achievement. The studies had to focus on educational settings ranging from K-12 to college. Only peer-reviewed publications in English were considered, and the studies needed to describe the implementation strategies and techniques used in systematic desensitization. Furthermore, to ensure contemporary relevance, only studies published between 2015 and 2024 were included.

On the other hand, studies that did not provide empirical data, such as opinion pieces, editorials, or theoretical papers, were excluded. Studies that were unrelated to mathematics or did not focus on systematic desensitization were also excluded. Additionally, studies conducted outside of educational settings or those that were not peer-reviewed were not considered for this review.

4.3 Search and selection process

A comprehensive search was conducted across three electronic databases: Web of Science, Scopus, and Education Research Complete. Web of Science and Scopus were chosen for their extensive coverage of peer-reviewed literature, including the social sciences, while Education Research Complete was selected for its focus on leading educational research. The aim was to understand the effectiveness of systematic desensitization on mathematics anxiety and achievement in learners.

Specific search terms and their combinations were used to identify relevant studies. The terms "systematic desensitization" or "desensitization therapy" were used in proximity to "mathematics," "math," "learn," "teach," or "subject" within three words of each other. These terms were combined with keywords representing various educational contexts, such as secondary, "high school," "middle school," K12, and "K-12." This approach included broad terms like "systematic desensitization in mathematics," "desensitization therapy for mathematics anxiety," and "desensitization techniques in education," as well as more specific phrases like "reducing mathematics anxiety through desensitization" and "impact of systematic desensitization on mathematics achievement."

The search yielded 36 journal articles published between 2015 and 2024. Following PRISMA guidelines, these articles were initially screened by titles and abstracts. Twenty-one articles were excluded for not meeting the criteria, often due to irrelevance or non-secondary school contexts. Fifteen full-text articles were then assessed, with ten more excluded for lacking clear details on the implementation of systematic desensitization. Ultimately, five articles were selected for review. Key data extracted from these studies included author(s), title, year, location, methodology, study focus, participants, duration, systematic desensitization technique, major findings, and challenges. The overall selection process for the review is illustrated in **Figure 1**.

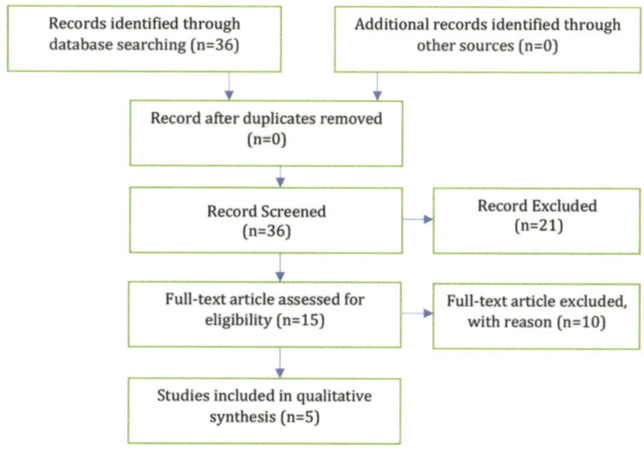

Figure 1.
Article selection process (Adapted from Moher et al. [25]).

4.4 General description of reviewed studies

The five reviewed studies investigate the impact of systematic desensitization on reducing mathematics anxiety and improving performance among students at different educational levels. Studies were conducted in Nigeria and Malaysia's senior secondary schools and colleges [4, 8, 9, 18]. These studies used quasi-experimental designs and ANCOVA to assess the effectiveness of systematic desensitization. The focus was primarily on reducing mathematics anxiety and enhancing achievement. Interventions included various activities such as relaxation techniques, cognitive restructuring, and peer support.

4.5 Systematic desensitization implementation of reviewed studies

The implementation of systematic desensitization in the reviewed studies involved several key activities. Generally, these included teaching relaxation techniques such as Progressive Muscle Relaxation (PMR) and deep breathing, as seen in the study by Aliyu et al. [18]. Participants were also guided in creating and addressing a hierarchy of mathematics-related anxieties, a common element in the studies by Egara and Mosimege [4]. Additional techniques such as visualization, cognitive restructuring, and gradual exposure to mathematics tasks were integrated into the interventions, as noted by Uzoekwe et al. [8]. Interactive mathematics games, role-playing scenarios, and peer support groups were employed to enhance engagement, particularly highlighted in the study by Ernest-Ehibudu and Wayii [21]. Most interventions spanned around 6 weeks, effectively combining these activities to address both anxiety and performance issues.

4.6 Challenges encountered with systematic desensitization

Implementing systematic desensitization presented several challenges. Common issues included participant resistance and difficulties with regular attendance, as reported by Aliyu et al. [18]. Limited resources, such as time and support staff, also impacted the effectiveness of the interventions, particularly in the study by Akeb-urai et al. [9]. Scheduling conflicts and academic pressures posed additional challenges, affecting the timing and effectiveness of the treatment, as noted by Uzoekwe et al. [8]. Furthermore, managing individual versus group therapy and ensuring consistent progress among participants were significant challenges, highlighted by Egara and Mosimege [4].

4.7 Effectiveness of systematic desensitization of reviewed studies

Systematic desensitization was found to be effective in reducing mathematics anxiety and improving performance. Studies by Refs. [4, 9, 18] demonstrated significant reductions in anxiety and improvements in performance among secondary and college students. Uzoekwe et al. [8] specifically found that systematic desensitization effectively reduced mathematics anxiety among junior secondary students. Despite these positive outcomes, the implementation challenges occasionally impacted the overall effectiveness of the interventions.

4.8 Limitations of systematic desensitization and alternative methodologies

While systematic desensitization has demonstrated effectiveness in reducing mathematics anxiety and improving academic achievement, it is essential to acknowledge its limitations. One significant challenge is the difficulty in implementation; the technique requires trained facilitators and can be time-consuming, making it less feasible in all educational settings. Additionally, some students may exhibit resistance to the process, either due to skepticism about its effectiveness or reluctance to confront their anxieties, which can impact the overall success of the intervention. Another concern is the long-term efficacy of systematic desensitization. There is limited evidence on the sustainability of the benefits over an extended period, and regular follow-up sessions might be necessary to maintain the improvements.

4.8.1 Alternative methodologies

Several other methodologies have been explored to address mathematics anxiety and improve achievement. One such approach is cognitive restructuring, which focuses on changing negative thought patterns related to mathematics. Studies have demonstrated that this method can be effective in reducing anxiety and improving performance [26, 27]. Another technique is exposure therapy, which involves gradual exposure to mathematics-related tasks. This approach helps students build confidence and reduce anxiety over time [28]. Additionally, behavioural interventions, including relaxation training, biofeedback, and systematic exposure to math tasks, have been employed with varying degrees of success [29].

4.9 Broader reflections and considerations

4.9.1 Earlier educational stages

While this review primarily focuses on secondary and higher education settings, the potential benefits of systematic desensitization for younger students should not be overlooked. Implementing these techniques in primary or elementary school could help build a strong foundation for positive attitudes towards mathematics from an early age. However, adaptations would be necessary to make the interventions age-appropriate and engaging for younger learners.

4.9.2 Pre-existing anxiety or psychiatric conditions

Students with pre-existing anxiety disorders or other psychiatric conditions might respond differently to systematic desensitization. It is crucial to tailor interventions to meet the specific needs of these students, possibly integrating additional support mechanisms such as counselling or cognitive-behavioural therapy.

4.9.3 Sustainability and duration of benefits

The long-term sustainability of the benefits from systematic desensitization remains an area for further research. It is possible that the initial gains in reducing mathematics anxiety and improving achievement might diminish over time without continued support. Regular booster sessions and ongoing monitoring could help sustain the positive outcomes.

4.10 Comparison with third-generation CBT approaches

Recent advancements in cognitive-behavioural therapies have introduced third-generation approaches such as Acceptance and Commitment Therapy (ACT), Rational Emotive Behavior Therapy and mindfulness-based interventions. These techniques focus on accepting negative thoughts and emotions rather than trying to change them, which can be particularly beneficial for students with high levels of anxiety [30–32].

Zettle [33] highlighted the potential of ACT in addressing various psychological issues. Applying ACT principles to mathematics anxiety involves helping students accept their anxiety and commit to engaging in mathematics tasks despite their fears. Mindfulness practices can also help students stay present and focused, reducing the impact of anxiety on their performance [32, 33]. Incorporating these third-generation CBT approaches could provide additional tools for educators and therapists, offering a broader range of strategies to support students in overcoming mathematics anxiety and achieving academic success [30, 33, 34].

4.11 Lessons learned and recommendations

The reviewed studies provide valuable insights into the effectiveness of systematic desensitization for managing mathematics anxiety and improving performance. Effective practices included combining various therapeutic techniques and maintaining participant engagement, as emphasized by Ernest-Ehibudu and Wayii [21]. To address challenges, the following recommendations are proffered to enhance the effectiveness of systematic desensitization programmes in educational settings: Firstly, it is essential to tailor systematic desensitization interventions to meet students' individual needs, considering their unique anxiety triggers and personal circumstances. This personalized approach can significantly increase engagement and effectiveness. Moreover, comprehensive training for educators and therapists in systematic desensitization techniques, including relaxation methods, cognitive restructuring, and gradual exposure strategies, is crucial. Proper training will enable them to deliver interventions more effectively. Adequate resource allocation is also necessary. This includes providing sufficient time, materials, and support staff to support the implementation of systematic desensitization programmes. Addressing resource limitations will enhance the quality and sustainability of the interventions.

Clear communication of the purpose, process, and benefits of systematic desensitization interventions to participants and their families is vital. Reducing skepticism and building trust will improve participant buy-in and commitment. Additionally, flexible scheduling options should be designed to accommodate students' academic and personal commitments. This flexibility will help ensure regular attendance and participation in systematic desensitization sessions. Continuous assessment and feedback mechanisms should be implemented to monitor student progress and adapt interventions as needed. Regular evaluations will help address any emerging issues and improve outcomes. Furthermore, it is recommended to foster peer support groups where students can share their experiences and coping strategies. Mutual encouragement and social support can enhance the effectiveness of systematic desensitization interventions.

5. Conclusion

This chapter discusses mathematics anxiety among school learners and presents systematic desensitization as an effective cognitive-behavioral technique to alleviate it and improve mathematics achievement. Through a detailed examination of theoretical foundations, methodologies, and practical applications, we have highlighted how systematic desensitization, incorporating relaxation techniques and gradual exposure to anxiety-provoking tasks, can effectively reduce mathematics anxiety and enhance academic performance. The systematic review of studies conducted between 2015 and 2024 provides robust evidence supporting the effectiveness of systematic desensitization in various educational settings. These studies consistently show that systematic desensitization significantly reduces mathematics anxiety and improves student achievement across different educational levels. Implementing systematic desensitization, however, comes with challenges such as participant resistance, scheduling conflicts, and resource limitations. Addressing these challenges through tailored interventions, comprehensive training for educators and therapists, adequate resource allocation, clear communication, flexible scheduling, continuous assessment, and fostering peer support can enhance the effectiveness and sustainability of systematic desensitization programmes. Overall, systematic desensitization is viable for addressing mathematics anxiety and boosting mathematics performance, provided that implementation challenges are carefully managed.

Acknowledgements

We sincerely thank the participants for their time and insights and the school administrators and staff for their cooperation. Special thanks to the educators and therapists for their dedicated implementation of the interventions. We also appreciate our institutions' financial and logistical support and invaluable feedback from our colleagues and mentors.

Conflict of interest

The authors declare no conflict of interest.

Author details

Felix Egara* and Moeketsi Mosia
University of the Free State, Bloemfontein, South Africa

*Address all correspondence to: felix.egara@unn.edu.ng

References

[1] Mosimege M, Egara FO, Nzeadibe AC, Chiedu E. Effect of group rational emotive behaviour therapy on mathematics anxiety on secondary school students. South African Journal of Psychology [Internet]. 2024;**54**(2):246-259. DOI: 10.1177/00812463241246865

[2] Nzeadibe AC, Egara FO, Eseadi C, Chukwuorji JC. Mindfulness-based cognitive therapy for mathematics anxiety among school adolescents: A randomized trial. Journal of Psychologists and Counsellors in Schools. 2023:1-12

[3] Wang C, Xu Q, Fei WQ. The effect of student-perceived teacher support on math anxiety: Chain mediation of teacher-student relationship and math self-efficacy. Frontiers in Psychology. 2024;**15**:1333012

[4] Egara FO, Mosimege M. Effect of systematic desensitization on anxiety and achievement of Nigerian secondary school students in mathematics. Counseling Outcome Research and Evaluation [Internet]. 2024;**15**(2):175-195. DOI: 10.1080/21501378.2024.2342586

[5] Terry J, Ross RM, Nagy T, Salgado M, Garrido-Vásquez P, Sarfo JO, et al. Data from an international multi-centre study of statistics and mathematics anxieties and related variables in university students (the SMARVUS dataset). Journal of Open Psychology Data. 2023;**11**(1):1-25

[6] Sarfo JO, Garcia-Santillan A, Adusei H, Molchanova VS, Drushlyak M, Semenikhina O, et al. Gender differences in mathematics anxiety across cultures: A univariate analysis of variance among samples from twelve countries. European Journal of Contemporary Education. 2020;**9**(4):878-885

[7] Kul Ü, Aksu Z, Satici SA. Adaptation of the modified abbreviated math anxiety scale: Its relationship with mathematics self-efficacy and academic buoyancy. Current Psychology. 2024;**43**:21586-21595

[8] Uzoekwe HE, Nnodum BI, Chima I, Nnadi GC, Mokwelu OB. Effects of systematic desensitization on mathematics anxiety among junior secondary school students. Global Journal of Arts Humanity and Social Sciences [Internet]. 2022;**2**(12):929-934. Available from: https://gsarpublishers.com/wp-content/uploads/2022/12/GJAHSS2592022-Gellary-script.pdf

[9] Akeb-urai N, Kadir NBYA, Nasir R. Mathematics anxiety and performance among college students: Effectiveness of systematic desensitization treatment. Intellectual Discourse. 2020;**28**(1):97-127

[10] Beck AT. Cognitive Therapy and the Emotional Disorders. New York (NY): International Universities Press; 1976

[11] Wolpe J. Psychotherapy by Reciprocal Inhibition. Stanford (CA): Stanford University Press; 1958

[12] Bernstein DA, Borkovec TD. Progressive Relaxation Training: A Manual for the Helping Professions. Champaign (IL): Research Press; 1973

[13] Pavlov IP. Conditioned Reflexes. Oxford: Oxford University Press; 1927

[14] Ashcraft MH, Moore AM. Mathematics anxiety and the affective drop in performance. Journal of Psychoeducational Assessment. 2009;**27**(3):197-205

[15] Karfe AS, Ntasin AA. Effects of systematic desensitization and study skills counselling therapies on test-anxiety in physics among senior secondary school students in Jalingo, Taraba state. Global Journal of Human-Social Science: A Arts & Humanities - Psychology. 2018;**18**(5):6-12

[16] Aihie ON, Igbineweka MN. Efficacy of solution focused brief therapy, systematic desensitization and rational emotive behavioural therapy in reducing the test anxiety status of undergraduates in a Nigerian university. Journal of Educational and Social Research. 2018;**8**(1):19-26

[17] Egara FO. Effects of systematic desensitization and rational emotive behaviour therapies on mathematics anxiety among senior secondary school students [Unpublished doctoral dissertation]. Nsukka: University of Nigeria; 2021

[18] Aliyu S, Idris A, Gurkuma AL, Saidu D, Amako TG. Effects of cognitive restructuring and systematic desensitization techniques on students' mathematics anxiety in senior secondary schools in Gombe Metropolis, Gombe State. Ilorin Journal of Education. 2023;**43**(2):1-13

[19] Ifeanyi A, Anyamene A, Nwokolo C. Effects of systematic desensitization technique on test anxiety among secondary school students. International Journal of Humanities Social Sciences and Education [Internet]. 2015;**2**(2):167-178. Available from: www.arcjournals.org

[20] Mohammad HA, Abdel-Rahman HA. Investigating the effectiveness of systematic desensitization in reducing anxiety among Jordanian EFL learners. Arab World English Journal [Internet]. 2015:54-70. Available from: www.awej.org

[21] Ernest-Ehibudu IR, Wayii AL. Effect of cognitive restructuring and systematic desensitization in the management of mathophobia among secondary school students in Khana LGA of Rivers state, Nigeria. American Journal of Educational Research. 2017;**5**(11):1131-1137

[22] Obi JSC, Oguzie AE. Effect of systematic desensitization technique on generalized anxiety among adolescents In Enugu east local government, Enugu state, Nigeria. iJournals: International Journal of Social Relevance & Concern [Internet]. 2019;**7**(5):1-9. Available from: www.ijournals.in

[23] Beck JS. Cognitive Behavior Therapy: Basics and beyond. 2nd ed. New York (NY): Guilford Press; 2011

[24] Akeb-Urai N, Kadir NBYA, Nasir R. Mathematics anxiety and performance among college students: Effectiveness of systematic desensitization treatment. Intellectual Discourse. 2020;**28**(1):99-127

[25] Moher D, Liberati A, Tetzlaff J, Altman DG. Preferred reporting items for systematic reviews and meta-analyses: The PRISMA statement. Research Methods & Reporting. 2009:1-8

[26] Ashcraft MH, Krause JA. Working memory, math performance, and math anxiety. Psychonomic Bulletin & Review. 2007;**14**(2):243-248. DOI: 10.3758/BF03194059

[27] Hembree R. The nature, effects, and relief of mathematics anxiety. Journal for Research in Mathematics Education. 1990;**21**(1):33-46. DOI: 10.2307/749455

[28] Beilock SL, Maloney EA. Math anxiety: A factor in math achievement not to be ignored. Policy Insights From the Behavioral and Brain Sciences.

2015;**2**(1):4-12. DOI: 10.1177/
2372732215601438

[29] Ramirez G, Shaw ST, Maloney EA. Math anxiety: Past research, promising interventions, and a new interpretation framework. Educational Psychologist. 2018;**53**(3):145-164. DOI: 10.1080/00461520.2018.1447384

[30] Hayes SC, Strosahl KD, Wilson KG. Acceptance and Commitment Therapy: An Experiential Approach to Behavior Change. New York: Guilford Press; 1999

[31] Mosimege M, Egara FO, Nzeadibe AC, Chiedu E. Effect of group rational emotive behaviour therapy on mathematics anxiety on secondary school students. South Africa Journal of Psychology. 2024;**54**(2):246-259. DOI: 10.1177/00812463241246865

[32] Nzeadibe AC, Egara FO, Eseadi C, Chukwuorji JC. Mindfulness-based cognitive therapy for mathematics anxiety among school adolescents: A randomised trial. Journal of Psychologists and Counsellors in Schools. 2023:1-12. DOI: 10.1177/20556365231207248

[33] Zettle RD. Acceptance and commitment therapy (ACT) vs. systematic desensitization in treatment of mathematics anxiety. Psychological Record. 2003;**53**:197-215

[34] Roemer L, Orsillo SM. Mindfulness- and Acceptance-Based Behavioral Therapies in Practice. New York: Guilford Press; 2009